Menus from History

MENUS FROM HISTORY

Historic Meals and Recipes for Every Day of the Year

Volume 1

Janet Clarkson

GREENWOOD PRESS

An Imprint of ABC-CLIO, LLC

A B C ☰ C L I O

Santa Barbara, California • Denver, Colorado • Oxford, England

Library of Congress Cataloging-in-Publication Data

Clarkson, Janet, 1947–
    Menus from history : historic meals and recipes for every day of the year /
    Janet Clarkson.
        p. cm.
    Includes bibliographical references and index.
    ISBN 978–0–313–34930–0 (hard copy : alk. paper) — ISBN 978–0–313–34931–7 (ebook)
1. Cookery—History. 2. Dinners and dining—History. 3. Food habits—History. 4. Menus. 5.
Cookery, International. I. Title.
TX645.C534   2009
641.3—dc22   2009011351

13 12 11 10 9   1 2 3 4 5

This book is also available on the World Wide Web as an eBook.
Visit www.abc-clio.com for details.

ABC-CLIO, LLC
130 Cremona Drive, P.O. Box 1911
Santa Barbara, California 93116-1911

This book is printed on acid-free paper ∞

Manufactured in the United States of America

The publisher has done its best to make sure the instructions and/or recipes in this book are
correct. However, users should apply judgment and experience when preparing recipes, especially
parents and teachers working with young people. The publisher accepts no responsibility for the
outcome of any recipe included in this volume.

Contents

Volume 1

Volume 2

Acknowledgments

I have learned many things while writing this book. Not the least of these is the sheer number of individuals aside from the author who are necessary to the completion of the process. I would now like to thank some of those people who have been of particular assistance to me during this project.

First, a big thank you to Ken Albala, food writer extraordinaire and Professor of History at the University of the Pacific, for remembering (for reasons no doubt not even clear to himself, at least two years after the original discussion) an idea for a book that I had mentioned to him in an email exchange—and for then contacting me, suggesting I submit the idea to Greenwood/ABC-CLIO, and supporting the subsequent proposal. I must also thank Wendi Schnaufer, my editor at Greenwood/ABC-CLIO, for her enthusiasm for the project, for her availability in the face of my frequent questions, and for her suggestions, reassurances, and support.

The production process for this book began at a particularly trying time for me personally, and my faded focus made the job of the production team much more difficult than it should have been. I would particularly like to thank Christine McGlumphy and Mark Thomas from BeaconPMG for their great patience and forbearance with me during this part of the project. They accommodated my frantic queries and very last minute changes with greater equanimity than I deserved, and the book is, of course, much better for their efforts.

A number of people helped with translations or language queries, for which I am grateful. Marleen Willebrands clarified the Dutch menu of January 10, the trio of Bob Felby, Jill Miller, Jacob Schwartz helped unravel the Esperanto menu of October 7, and Diana Romano translated the Spanish (Argentinian) menu of December 10 and added some local insights. Special thanks must go to my dear friend Marisa Raniolo Wilkins for her invaluable assistance with translating and understanding the Italian Renaissance menus (February 16, May 28, June 4).

Several people gave approval for their material to be used, and they are credited in the relevant pages but also deserve their mention here. They are Robin Carroll-Mann (February 9), Louis Sorkin (May 20), and Richard Seltzer (January 11).

Heaven, for any writer, researcher, or avid reader, is having the world's libraries at one's fingertips. I am enormously grateful to the thousands (millions?) of invisible people quietly working away behind the scenes, uploading free reading gifts to us all in the form of the many digitized library collections around the world, as well as the increasingly amazing Google Books and Internet Archive.

   And last, but by no means least, I want to thank my family and friends for their enthusiasm and support, and for their love and patience when I was distracted and absorbed in my research and writing, and under the dreaded deadline pressure!

Preface

This book had a long gestation period. The wonder is that it ever got conceived at all, given that I disliked history at school.

Make that "I hated history at school." I was not remotely interested in who was on the throne or the winning side at any point in time, and I do not have the sort of brain that can memorize lists or remember dates with any sort of enthusiasm or accuracy. In retrospect, this was perhaps a reflection of the way history was inflicted on me at school in the north of England in the 1950s and in Australia in the 1960s. I remember one teacher in particular whose idea of giving a history lesson was to sit and snooze at the front desk while we students took turns reading aloud from the textbook. I got as far away from history as I could and decided on medicine as a career.

Along the way I also developed an interest in cooking. This stood me in good stead when I married a man who liked eating and who gave me two children who liked inviting friends home for meals and weekends—and sometimes for considerably longer periods. There is something frighteningly challenging about facing a horde of growing adolescent boys in the kitchen at the end of a busy working week, knowing they will be there for the duration of the weekend and looking for food almost the whole time.

A general curiosity about food went hand in hand with the practicalities of cooking for family and friends, and it slowly dawned on me that I had shed my prejudices and had become fascinated by food and culinary history. It began innocently enough with a collection of food history and trivia related to every day of the year—a never-ending project that I grandly called my *Food History Almanac*. By the time I became serious about culinary history, and began writing about it, I had accumulated a huge database of information ripe for dipping and rich for mining.

A large subsection of my almanac was a menu collection. It is this menu collection that formed the nidus for this book. The collection is electronic (the best sort of collection—only byte-sized storage required, and no dust) and runs into many thousands. There are menus from many centuries and many countries, from all sorts of occasions, and from locations as diverse as battlefields and palaces.

Because my interest in food history developed out of my love of feeding people, my primary focus is at the "eating end" of the story rather than the big picture of such things as the agricultural revolution and the spice trade (although menus can tell us much about these grand processes too). I am intrigued by what we choose to eat when power and money are no object (such as at coronations), or how we respond when we have little or no choice of food (in war or in prison, for example), and how we prepare, serve, and share that food. I am equally fascinated by what food *means* to us, individually and culturally—for food has *meaning* to humans far and above its caloric and nutritional value.

I now, finally, appreciate and understand that the history of our food and food ways tells us at least as much about our history as human beings as does our military or political history—and it is surely of greater intrinsic interest to most of us, for we all must eat.

My hope is that you will find this book fun. If it is interesting, intriguing, and enlightening, so much the better. If you recreate any of the menus, I will be delighted, and hope you will let me know how they turn out. And if by dipping into this book one or two reluctant history students have their interest piqued, and the realization dawns upon them that history does not have to be dry and insipid but can indeed be rich and tasty, then I will consider the project a great success.

I would be most grateful if any errors or any other comments or queries could be communicated to me at jclarkso@bigpond.net.au.

Introduction

What we and how we eat tells us a great deal about ourselves, our attitudes, our beliefs, and our history. A menu can be far more revealing than a first glance at the list of dishes would appear. The big picture of human history —the great agricultural and industrial revolutions, the massive waves of migration of peoples around the world, and the recurring struggles for dominance—can all be evidenced at the dinner table.

Many of the great voyages of exploration of the fifteenth and sixteenth centuries were driven by the desire for a source for spices, and by the demand for vast quantities of fish, such as cod, that lent themselves to preserving by drying and salting (an important attribute at a time when the Church decreed a large number of "fasts," that is, meatless days a year, and when there were very few preserving methods available). A great deal of later colonial expansion—particularly into Africa—was driven by the greed for land to grow staple crops—and for cheap labor to grow them.

The most dramatic change in the food available on the European table came about after the opening up of the "New World" following the voyage of Christopher Columbus in 1492. Truly national cuisines only developed in Europe after this time. It is impossible today to think of a "tomato-less" Italian cuisine (or a "potato-less" British one), but the tomato and the potato came from the Americas.

Power can be demonstrated as clearly at a meal as it can be in the military sphere. What is social status after all but a hierarchical power system? Consider the strong message inherent in the seating arrangements of the medieval feasts described in these pages, and the dual bill of fare at the visit of the Spanish Infanta to New York on May 26, 1896.

The small picture, too, is unveiled in our daily meals—our very human foibles (July 30) and our great human strengths (such as the humor under duress shown in the menu of March 7). The dinner table is where we make our religious observances (there are numerous examples here), demonstrate our beliefs about ethical living, health, and nutrition (the "Uncooked Banquet" on June 18 is interesting), and where we express our familial love and patriotic sentiment.

Menus

There are 365 menus in this book—one for each day of the year, for an event that happened on that day. They appear in the book in calendar order, and they are also listed chronologically, by country, and by type of occasion in the front matter. Each menu is accompanied by a commentary on some aspect of the event or the food, and by one or more appropriate recipes from the era. Some stories are embellished with tempting tidbits of boxed material.

The provenance and exact dating of a very small handful of the menus has been difficult to authenticate unequivocally, but as they were among the most intrinsically interesting, a "best guess" was made.

The choice of menu (meal descriptions as well as formal bills of fare) for some days of the year was difficult, but the goal was to cover as great a variety of eras and occasions as possible.

Other than one from ancient Rome, the menus span 700 years of meals— from the fourteenth to the twentieth centuries. Forty countries are represented, as is outer space. Western countries predominate (and of these most are from the United States and England), but Asia and the Middle East are represented as well, and the selection is made truly global by the inclusion of menus from Antarctica and Tibet.

Many menus are written in French, even if the meals were held a long way geographically and culturally from France—such as those in Antarctica (June 22) and Turkey (July 1). French was the dominant culinary language throughout the nineteenth and the first half of the twentieth centuries, although as will be seen, it was not always used accurately or well. Not all menus are in English or French, however. There are examples in other European languages. A number of menus are written in medieval English, and as these represent a different sort of linguistic challenge, an interpretation follows the original. Their interpretation is fraught with difficulty, and many medieval dishes remain puzzles in spite of considerable attention from culinary historians.

The meals recorded here represent a huge range of situations. They include primarily dinners but also breakfasts, lunches, suppers, and teas, plus there are several *tiffins* (a light midday meal in colonial India and the East) and one *ambigu* (a meal in which all the dishes were presented at once). The individual locations vary from the sublime (a royal palace, for example) to the strange (one meal takes place in a harem) to the truly awful (such as the battlefield and poorhouse), and there are many meals on the move, aboard planes, trains, and ships.

There are meals almost exclusively of one ingredient—whale meat, horsemeat, insects, or soybeans. There are dinners with bizarre themes, such as the "Upside Down Dinner" of January 16 and the "Dinner on a Clock Face" of November 18. Further, there are several examples of obscenely conspicuous consumption to contrast with the punitively frugal.

The hosts and guests too come from many different walks of life. There are kings, queens, and presidents, soldiers and sailors, bishops, engineers, housewives, explorers, musicians, movie stars, sportsmen, prisoners, writers, vegetarians, teetotallers, and prohibitionists. Readers can share a meal with all sorts of celebrities here—including Thomas Jefferson, Elvis Presley, Jane Austen, Charles Dickens, and Buffalo Bill, as well as many of the unsung heroes of history such as war veterans and women suffragists.

The occasions range from national festivals (such as Thanksgiving), historic anniversaries (VJ Day, for example), occasions of great state and diplomatic importance (such as royal coronations and presidential inaugurations), personal celebrations (such as weddings), and ordinary meals recorded by ordinary folks in diaries and letters.

Recipes

A word is needed about the recipes. Good recipe-writing is a modern science. Recipes from previous times can be difficult to follow for a number of reasons. First and most obviously, language is a dynamic and constantly changing thing in itself, and this is compounded by the fact that consistency in spelling was not an issue for much of history. Second, to modern eyes there appear to be many gaps or leaps in method instructions, particularly in medieval texts. Medieval cookery manuscripts functioned more as *aides-memoires* for experienced cooks; they were not meant as detailed manuals for kitchen staff (most of whom were not literate). This changed slowly, but it was not until the seventeenth century that cookbooks for the nonprofessional became common. Another large frustration today is that old cookbooks often give few or no quantities for ingredients. Measuring tools were essentially nonexistent in kitchens until relatively recent times, so amounts of ingredients are not mentioned, or at best are in old units of measurement.

A cautionary note is needed about recreating old recipes. Many of the dishes that appear in this book would not be sensible, safe, ethical, or even legal to eat today. Many of the recipe instructions fall far short of modern safety requirements but are included for their historic interest. Should you wish to follow any or the recipes, or recreate any of the menus, you should forsake historical accuracy in the interests of food safety, and follow accepted rules of food preparation, hygiene, and so on. If in doubt, your local food safety authorities should be consulted.

Many dishes appear in various guises in many menus over long periods of time. Rather than repeat recipes, a cross-reference to another day's menu with a recipe for the dish is given. This sometimes simply shows how widely a recipe idea can be interpreted, but it also shows how a dish develops and changes over time. *Blancmange* is a good example of a dish that is radically different in its modern form compared with its medieval origins.

Selected Bibliography and Glossary

General background sources of reading on food history, and several sources of menus and historic recipe books are listed in a selected bibliography at the end of the book.

An exhaustive glossary of all ancient words in their various spellings, plus all of the foreign terms, would have taken almost another volume in itself. The glossary is therefore necessarily restricted to the most frequently appearing words and terms, and excludes those that are explained in the text. The bibliography also includes several online and freely available glossaries of historic culinary words for the reader's reference.

List of Menus Chronologically

August 22, 70 BCE	Italy	An Ancient Roman Dinner, Rome
May 28, 1368	Italy	Wedding Feast, Milan
September 23, 1387	England	Feast for King Richard II, Durham House, London
October 13, 1399	England	Coronation Feast of King Henry IV, Great Hall of Westminster, London
August 2, 1413	England	Harvest Meals in an English Medieval Manorial Household, Acton Hall, Acton, Suffolk
February 23, 1421	England	Coronation Feast of Queen Catherine, Westminster Hall, London
December 4, 1424	England	Funeral Feast of the Bishop of Bath and Wells, Bishop's Palace, Wells, Somerset
September 16, 1425	England	Induction Feast of the Bishop of Bath and Wells, The Bishop's Palace, Wells, Somerset
November 6, 1429	England	Coronation Feast of King Henry VI, Great Hall of Westminster, London
September 22, 1465	England	Installation Feast of the Archbishop of York, Cawood Castle, York
September 22, 1465	England	Installation Feast of the Archbishop of York, Cawood Castle, York
June 4, 1469	Italy	Medici Wedding Feast, Palazzo Medici, Florence
October 28, 1478	England	Dinner of the Worshipful Company of Wax Chandlers, Newcastle-upon-Tyne
July 6, 1483	England	Coronation Feast of King Richard III, Westminster Hall, London
March 9, 1504	England	Inthronization Feast of the Archbishop of Canterbury, The Archbishop's Palace, Canterbury
August 16, 1522	England	Dinner of the Wardens of the Drapers' Company, Home of the Master of the Company, London
June 19, 1549	France	Banquet for Queen Catherine, Bishop's Palace, Paris

June 23, 1908	United States	Yale Reunion Dinner, Bishop's Colonnade, Savin Rock, West Haven, Connecticut
June 27, 1908	Scotland	Breakfast at Central Station Hotel, Glasgow
July 27, 1908	SS *Colon*	Lunch En Route to the Canal Zone aboard the SS *Colon*
February 12, 1909	United States	Former Slave Attends a Republican Dinner, Lincoln Dinner, Waldorf-Astoria Hotel, New York
April 9, 1909	Germany	Emperor Wilhelm's Lunch, Royal Palace, Berlin
August 31, 1910	RMS *Saxonia*	Second Cabin Tea aboard RMS *Saxonia*
November 18, 1910	England	Dining on a Clock Face, Trades Hall, Leicester
May 19, 1911	United States	Prison Menu for a Week, Indiana State Prison
August 13, 1911	United States	Dinner for Admiral Togo Heihachiro, Knickerbocker Hotel, New York
August 25, 1911	Canada	Hotel Dinner, Grand Hotel, Yarmouth, Nova Scotia
October 7, 1911	United States	Esperanto Society Meeting Dinner, New England
December 21, 1911	England	"Pease and Pork Dinner," Livery House, Bristol
April 2, 1912	RMS *Titanic*	First Dinner, RMS *Titanic*
June 22, 1912	Antarctica	Midwinter Dinner, Winter Quarters, Commonwealth Bay, Adelie Land
August 19, 1912	England	Hotel Breakfast, Exchange Station Hotel, Liverpool
October 16, 1912	Canada	Tribute Dinner for a Cow, Red Deer, Alberta
April 24, 1913	United States	Opening Banquet Woolworth Building, Broadway, New York
April 30, 1913	United States	Harvard Club of Boston Dinner, Hotel Somerset, Boston, Massachusetts
July 15, 1913	USMS *Philadelphia*	Dinner aboard a U.S. Mail Ship, USMS *Philadelphia*
September 27, 1913	United States	Traffic Association Banquet, Café Nat Goodwin, Crystal Pier, Santa Monica, California
October 22, 1913	United States	Women Suffragists's Dinner, New York City
October 31, 1913	England	Dinner for the Palace Workmen, King's Hall Restaurant, Holborn, London

List of Menus by Country

On Train

List of Menus
by Occasion

Club/Society/Institute/Company Meal

October 28, 1478	England	Dinner of the Worshipful Company of Wax Chandlers, Newcastle-upon-Tyne
August 16, 1522	England	Dinner of the Wardens of the Drapers' Company, Home of the Master of the Company, London
March 11, 1687	England	Ironmongers' Company Dinner, Ironmongers Hall, Fenchurch Street, London
January 30, 1710	England	Calves Head Club Annual Feast, London
October 29, 1742	England	Dinner for the Worshipful Company of Barbers and Surgeons, The Barber-Surgeons Hall, Monkwell Square, London
September 30, 1847	England	Sheriff's Dinner, Hall of the Fishmongers' Company, London
July 28, 1848	England	First Annual Dinner of the First Vegetarian Society of England, Manchester
September 8, 1853	United States	Temperance Banquet, Metropolitan Hall, New York
October 1, 1854	United States	Dinner in Utopia, Red Bank, Monmouth County, New Jersey
July 5, 1856	United States	Firemen's Dinner, American Exchange Hotel, San Francisco, California
January 23, 1862	Germany	Dinner of Exotic Animals, Hamburg
December 1, 1869	England	Australian Meat Banquet, Lambeth Baths, London
December 16, 1870	United States	Chicago Press Club's First Annual Banquet, Briggs House, Chicago, Illinois
November 30, 1871	England	Patriotic Dinner, The Freemasons' Tavern, London
April 21, 1881	France	Banquet of the French Vegetarian Society, Rue St. Honoré, Paris
September 15, 1883	New Zealand	Masons' Banquet to Celebrate Their New Lodge, Criterion Hotel, Taranaki
August 30, 1885	Norway	Medical Conference Dinner, Bergen

April 14, 1886	France	Stanley Club Dinner in Honor of Louis Pasteur, Continental Hotel
January 10, 1888	United States	Holland Society Annual Dinner, Hotel Brunswick, New York
December 11, 1888	England	Encyclopædia Britannica Dinner, Hall of Christ's College, Cambridge
January 4, 1889	Canada	Second Annual Dinner of the Toronto Board of Trade, Horticultural Gardens, Toronto, Ontario
June 5, 1889	United States	Journalists' Dinner, Bohemian Club, San Francisco, California
September 7, 1889	Sweden	Dinner for the Congress of Orientalists, Stockholm
March 8, 1891	United States	Dinner Given by the "Chinese Delmonico," Lenox Lyceum, New York
May 13, 1891	England	Dinner for Nobody's Friends, Hôtel Metropole, London
September 10, 1891	United States	Fat Men's Club Clambake, Power's Hotel, Dorlon's Point, South Norwalk, Connecticut
October 24, 1891	Norway	Medical Dinner, Bergen
June 12, 1893	England	After-Concert Dinner, King's College, Cambridge University, Cambridge
September 20, 1894	United States	Library-Themed Dinner for the American Library Association, Annual Conference, Grand View House, Lake Placid, New York
October 5, 1894	United States	Druggists' Luncheon, Steamboat *Sandy Hook*, New York
January 17, 1895	United States	Benjamin Franklin Honored by *Typothetæ*, Hotel Brunswick, New York
February 5, 1895	United States	Debut Dinner at the New York Vegetarian Society's Vegetarian Restaurant No. 1, New York
October 4, 1896	Denmark	Insurance Company Dinner, Copenhagen
February 2, 1897	United States	First Annual Banquet of the Founders and Patriots of America, Hotel Manhattan, New York
February 22, 1897	England	George Washington's Birthday Celebration, Hotel Cecil, London
December 15, 1897	Italy	Piemontese Society Banquet, All Hotel Campidoglio
February 19, 1898	United States	Creole Dinner for the New Orleans Press Club, The Atheneum, New Orleans, Louisiana
March 1, 1898	United States	63rd Annual Dinner of the St. David's Society, Hotel Savoy, New York

December 2, 1898	Scotland	Scottish Mountaineering Club 10th Annual Dinner, Central Hotel, Edinburgh
July 13, 1900	United States	Dinner of the Thirteen Club, Central Restaurant, New York
May 22, 1901	United States	Seafood Feast, Squantum Club, East Providence, Rhode Island
June 18, 1903	United States	"Uncooked Banquet" Hotel Hygeia, New York
November 12, 1904	Scotland	20th Anniversary Banquet of the Scottish Geographical Society, North British Station Hotel, Edinburgh
March 31, 1906	Sri Lanka	Tiffin at the Cricket Club, Cinnamon Gardens, Colombo, Ceylon
April 3, 1907	United States	Spelling Reform Dinner, Waldorf-Astoria Hotel, New York
February 12, 1909	United States	Former Slave Attends a Republican Dinner, Lincoln Dinner, Waldorf-Astoria Hotel, New York
November 18, 1910	England	Dining on a Clock Face, Trades Hall, Leicester
October 7, 1911	United States	Esperanto Society Meeting Dinner, New England
April 30, 1913	United States	Harvard Club of Boston Dinner, Hotel Somerset, Boston, Massachusetts
September 27, 1913	United States	Traffic Association Banquet, Café Nat Goodwin, Crystal Pier, Santa Monica, California
October 22, 1913	United States	Women Suffragists's Dinner, New York City
January 16, 1914	England	"Upside-Down" Dinner, Royal Automobile Club, London
August 20, 1914	United States	Mining Company Dinner, Calaveras Hotel, Angel's Camp, California
April 17, 1916	United States	New York Society of Restaurateurs Dinner with "Diamond Jim" Brady, Terrace Garden, New York
June 14, 1916	United States	Telephone Banquet, Symphony Hall, Boston, Massachusetts
February 4, 1916	Australia	Dinner for Fox Films, Hotel Australia, Sydney
February 13, 1918	United States	YMCA Father and Son Dinner, Nyack, New York
September 19, 1918	United States	Patriotic "Hooverized" Dinner, Daniel's and Fisher's Tower, Denver
May 3, 1918	England	Dilettante Society Dinner, Grand Hotel, Trafalgar Square, London

December 20, 1919	United States	Heinz Company 50th Anniversary Dinner, Pittsburgh, Pennsylvania
June 8, 1923	Canada	Women's Institute Luncheon, Hotel Windsor, Alliston, Ontario
February 1, 1928	United States	Broadway Association Dinner to Celebrate the Dodge Brothers' Sign, Hotel Astor, New York
December 9, 1928	France	Firefighters Banquet, Hôtel de la Madeleine, Barberaz
May 16, 1929	United States	First Academy Awards Banquet, Blossom Room, Roosevelt Hotel, Hollywood, California
May 5, 1932	England	"May Dinner," Simpson's on the Strand, London
August 17, 1934	United States	Henry Ford's "All Soy" Dinner, Century of Progress International Exposition, Chicago, Illinois
November 22, 1934	United States	German Society 150th Anniversary Dinner, Hotel Astor, New York
January 15, 1935	England	Portuguese Luncheon, Café Royal, London
January 24, 1937	United States	Gourmet Society Eat "Eskimo Fare," Cavanagh's, New York
November 17, 1937	England	Humble Meal, Café Royal, London
February 21, 1947	France	Business Dinner, Hotel Lutetia, Boulevarde Rapail, Paris
April 10, 1948	United States	Dinner for President Harry S. Truman, The Gridiron Club, Hotel Statler, Washington, DC
January 31, 1952	England	Luncheon at the Variety Club, 35 Dover Street, London

Commemorative Event

August 22, 70 BCE	Rome	An Ancient Roman Dinner
September 16, 1425	England	Induction Feast of the Bishop of Bath and Wells, The Bishop's Palace, Wells, Somerset
September 22, 1465	England	Installation Feast of the Archbishop of York, Cawood Castle, York
September 13, 1619	England	Dinner Celebrating the Founding of Dulwich College, Camberwell, Surrey
December 22, 1769	America	First Celebration of Forefathers' Day Dinner, Old Colony Club of Plymouth, Massachusetts
September 17, 1830	United States	Centennial Dinner, Exchange Coffee House, Boston, Massachusetts
January 25, 1882	United States	Burns Night Supper, Sutherland's, New York

January 26, 1888	Australia	Centennial Banquet, Sydney, Australia, Town Hall
April 24, 1913	United States	Opening Banquet Woolworth Building, Broadway, New York
April 6, 1918	England	Anniversary Luncheon of the Entry of the United States into World War I, Mansion House, London
August 1, 1831	England	Banquet for the Official Opening of London Bridge, London
March 19, 1932	Australia	Luncheon to Celebrate Opening of Sydney Harbour Bridge RMS *Maloja*, Sydney Harbour
October 8, 1971	United States	Chicago Fire Centennial Anniversary Banquet, Conrad Hilton Hotel, Chicago, Illinois
October 14, 1971	Iran	Banquet to Celebrate the Persian Empire, Persepolis
October 2, 1998	United States	Banquet for the 75th Anniversary of the Biltmore Hotel, Los Angeles, California
September 1, 1999	China	''First State'' Banquet, Beijing Hotel, Beijing

Daily Meal

August 2, 1413	England	Harvest Meals in an English Medieval Manorial Household, Acton Hall, Acton, Suffolk
February 9, 1568	Spain	Archbishop's Meals, Valencia
November 20, 1576	England	Dining with Queen Elizabeth I
December 23, 1626	England	Noble Family's Dinner, Aldersgate Street, London
November 8, 1701	Scotland	Duchess of Buccleuch and Monmouth's Table, Dalkeith Castle
February 18, 1749	France	French Royal Supper, Château de la Muette, Paris
August 5, 1786	Germany	Frederick the Great's Dinner, *Sans Souci*, Potsdam
March 2, 1788	Germany	Prince Ernest's Dinner
July 24, 1788	France	Dining with Marie-Antoinette, Le Petit Trianon, Versailles
May 10, 1806	United States	Lewis and Clark Eat with the Nez Perce, Idaho
April 13, 1811	France	Dinner for the Bonapartes, Tuileries Palace, Paris
September 14, 1813	England	Jane Austen's Dinner, Henrietta Street, Covent Garden, London

Dinner Party

February 6, 1802	United States	Dinner with President Thomas Jefferson, The White House, Washington, DC
January 22, 1848	United States	Dinner for Six Gentlemen, Revere House, Bowdoin Square, Boston, Massachusetts
April 29, 1851	England	Dinner for Ottoman Visitors, Mayor's Residence, Winchester, England
August 27, 1855	Crimea	"Great Martial Banquet Alfresco," Scutari
January 19, 1864	France	Dinner for 36, Home of Alexandre Dumas, Paris
October 30, 1865	United States	Dinner with Sir Morton Peto, Delmonico's, New York
November 16, 1875	United State	Dining with James McNeill Whistler, Chelsea, London
June 22, 1912	Antarctica	Midwinter Dinner, Winter Quarters, Commonwealth Bay, Adelie Land
October 27, 1936	Tibet	Dinner with a Tibetan Monk, Gyantsé, Tibet
November 9, 1975	France	Quiet Dinner for Two in Paris, *Chez Denis*, Paris
December 31, 1995	France	Final Dinner Party Given by François Mitterand, Souston, Landes

Diplomatic/Political Meal

May 9, 1676	Syria	Dinner at the English Embassy, Aleppo
May 25, 1816	England	Parliamentary Dinner, Carlton House, London
July 19, 1821	England	Coronation Banquet of King George IV, Westminster Hall, London
July 3, 1846	England	Dinner for Ottoman Visitors, Reform Club, London
July 9, 1851	England	Midnight Supper with Queen Victoria, Guildhall, London
April 29, 1851	England	Dinner for Ottoman Visitors, Mayor's Residence, Winchester, England
August 21, 1863	Germany	Frankfurt Congress of Princes Banquet, Römer, Frankfurt
March 6, 1865	United States	Abraham Lincoln's Inauguration Ball, Patent Office, Washington, DC
June 7, 1867	France	Dinner of the Three Emperors, Café Anglais, Paris
July 1, 1868	Turkey	Ottoman Sultan Entertains the French Prince, Constantinople (Istanbul)
July 25, 1873	Italy	Dinner for the Shah of Persia, Royal Palace, Turin

September 4, 1874	Canada	Dinner for the Governor-General, The Arlington, Cobourg, Ontario
July 12, 1876	United States	Reform Democrats Hold a Crow Banquet, Detroit Opera House, Detroit, Michigan
August 14, 1878	England	Ministerial Fish Dinner, The Ship Tavern, Greenwich, London
June 24, 1879	Japan	Dinner for Ulysses S. Grant, Nagasaki
March 20, 1893	Denmark	American Maize Banquet, Hotel King of Denmark, Copenhagen
May 26, 1893	United States	Royal and Plebeian Supper, Madison Square Garden, New York
January 11, 1898	Ethiopia	Dining with the Ras, The Royal Palace, Andracha, Abyssinia
February 26, 1902	United States	German-American Press Honors Prince Henry of Prussia, Waldorf-Astoria Hotel, New York
December 5, 1903	France	British MPs' Dinner, Hotel Cosmopolitan, Nice
July 2, 1906	Peru	Peruvian Presidential Dinner, Lima
February 12, 1909	United States	Former Slave Attends a Republican Dinner, Lincoln Dinner, Waldorf-Astoria Hotel, New York
August 13, 1911	United States	Dinner for Admiral Togo Heihachiro, Knickerbocker Hotel, New York
April 22, 1914	France	State Dinner for King George V and Queen Mary, British Embassy, Paris
February 8, 1918	United States	Whale Meat Luncheon, American Museum of Natural History, New York City
January 20, 1919	France	Luncheon in Honor of U.S. President Woodrow Wilson, Luxembourg Palace, Paris
July 18, 1921	Mexico	Picnic for the Mexican President, San Luis Potosi, Mexico
January 8, 1936	United States	Jackson Day Dinner, Mayflower Hotel, Washington, DC
May 17, 1939	Canada	English Royals Dine in Canada, Chateau Frontenac, Quebec
October 20, 1944	England	Dinner with the British Secret Service, Claridge's Hotel, London
February 10, 1945	Russia	Tripartite Dinner Meeting, Vorontsov Villa, Yalta, Ukraine
June 25, 1950	United States	Dinner on the Eve of the Korean War, Blair House, Washington, DC
October 11, 1951	Canada	Dinner for Princess Elizabeth, Ottowa

Holiday/Feast Day Meal

Hotel and Restaurant Fare

In-Flight Meal

Military Meal

Outdoor Meal

August 26, 1825	Switzerland	Breakfast and Dinner on Mont Blanc
September 21, 1842	United States	Daily Diet of the "American Pedestrian," Cambridge Park Trotting Course, Boston
August 7, 1853	Canada	Dinner in a Wigwam, Burnt Church Point, Miramichi Bay, New Brunswick
August 27, 1855	Crimea	"Great Martial Banquet Alfresco," Scutari
July 17, 1859	Switzerland	Dinner on the Mountain, The Aletschhorn
November 26, 1868	United States	Thanksgiving on the Plains, Camp Supply, Oklahoma
September 26, 1871	United States	Dinner Out Hunting with Buffalo Bill, near Fort McPherson, Nebraska
June 11, 1939	United States	Picnic for the English Royals, "Springwood," Hyde Park, New York

Personal/Family Celebration

May 28, 1368	Italy	Wedding Feast, Milan
June 4, 1469	Italy	Medici Wedding Feast, Palazzo Medici, Florence
January 2, 1682	England	Christening Feast, Cockley Cley, Norfolk
June 6, 1699	England	Wedding Supper
May 21, 1753	England	A Wedding Feast, Bishopwearmouth, Durham
April 19, 1770	Wales	Coming-of-Age Party, Wynnstay Hall, Denbighshire
July 22, 1896	England	Royal Wedding Breakfast, Buckingham Palace, London
April 26, 1923	England	Royal Wedding Breakfast, Buckingham Palace, London
May 1, 1967	United States	Elvis Presley's Wedding, Aladdin Hotel, Las Vegas
July 29, 1981	England	Royal Wedding Breakfast for Prince Charles and Lady Diana, Buckingham Palace, London, England

President/Prime Minister Meal

February 6, 1802	United States	Dinner with President Thomas Jefferson, The White House, Washington, DC
March 6, 1865	United States	Abraham Lincoln's Inauguration Ball, Patent Office, Washington, DC
July 2, 1906	Peru	Peruvian Presidential Dinner, Lima
April 22, 1914	France	State Dinner for King George V and Queen Mary, British Embassy, Paris

Railway Meal

September 5, 1687	England	Ambigu for King James II, Bodley Library, Oxford University, Oxford
March 28, 1690	France	Dinner for the Duke of Orléans
January 28, 1698	England	Peter the Great Dines at The King's Arms, Godalming, Surrey
February 18, 1749	France	French Royal Supper, Château de la Muette, Paris
September 29, 1757	France	Supper with the King, *Château de Choisy*
August 5, 1786	Germany	Frederick the Great's Dinner, *Sans Souci*, Potsdam
October 23, 1787	France	"Thousand and One Nights" Dinner, Château de Bellevue
July 24, 1788	France	Dining with Marie-Antoinette, Le Petit Trianon, Versailles
March 2, 1788	Germany	Prince Ernest's Dinner
April 13, 1811	France	Dinner for the Bonapartes, Tuileries Palace, Paris
January 18, 1817	England	Prince Regent of England Entertains the Archduke of Russia, Royal Pavilion, Brighton
July 19, 1821	England	Coronation Banquet of King George IV, Westminster Hall, London
August 24, 1821	Scotland	King George IV's Visit to Scotland, Great Hall of Parliament House, Edinburgh
July 31, 1826	France	King's Dinner
June 30, 1841	England	Her Majesty's Dinner, Buckingham Palace, London
July 3, 1846	England	Dinner for Ottoman Visitors, Reform Club, London
July 9, 1851	England	Midnight Supper with Queen Victoria, Guildhall, London
November 27, 1866	France	Dinner at the Court of Napoleon III, Paris
June 7, 1867	France	Dinner of the Three Emperors, Café Anglais, Paris
July 1, 1868	Turkey	Ottoman Sultan Entertains the French Prince, Constantinople (Istanbul)
July 25, 1873	Italy	Dinner for the Shah of Persia, Royal Palace, Turin
June 13, 1885	Germany	King Ludwig's Dinner, Hunting Lodge, the Tirol
January 29, 1889	Austria	Last Meal of the Crown Prince of Austria, Royal Hunting Lodge, Mayerling

School/Hospital/Prison Meal

Shipboard Meal

October 5, 1894	United States	Druggists' Luncheon, Steamboat *Sandy Hook*, New York
November 3, 1896	RMS *Miowera*	"All-Red Route" Luncheon aboard the RMS *Miowera*
July 26, 1897	*Maha-Chakri*	Lunch aboard the Royal Yacht *Maha-Chakri*, Copenhagen
July 16, 1900	SS *Lahn*	Dinner at Sea, SS *Lahn*
March 26, 1901	HMS *Ophir*	Grand Dinner Given by the Duke and Duchess of Cornwall aboard HMS *Ophir*, Malta
August 28, 1905	SS *Königin Luise*	Lunch at Sea, SS *Königin Luise*
August 10, 1907	SS *Zeeland*	Dinner aboard an Immigrant Ship, SS *Zeeland*
September 9, 1907	RMS *Lusitania*	Maiden Voyage Dinner aboard the RMS *Lusitania*
July 27, 1908	SS *Colon*	Lunch En Route to the Canal Zone aboard the SS *Colon*
August 31, 1910	RMS *Saxonia*	Second Cabin Tea aboard RMS *Saxonia*
April 2, 1912	RMS *Titanic*	First Dinner, RMS *Titanic*
July 15, 1913	USMS *Philadelphia*	Dinner aboard a U.S. Mail Ship, USMS *Philadelphia*
August 11, 1916	SS *Megantic*	Luncheon aboard a World War I Troop Ship, SS *Megantic*, En Route from Alexandria, Egypt, to Marseilles
August 4, 1920	SS *Imperator*	Dinner aboard the Pride of the Fleet, RMS *Imperator*
April 28, 1921	RMS *Aquitania*	Lunch at Sea, RMS *Aquitania*
March 14, 1922	SS *Prince Rupert*	Dinner at Sea, SS *Prince Rupert*
June 29, 1924	RMS *Saxonia*	Cornell Students Dine aboard RMS *Saxonia*
November 25, 1928	SS *Port Victoria*"	Menu for the Indisposed aboard the SS *Fort Victoria*
March 10, 1928	SS *New york*	Dinner at Sea, SS *New York*
March 13, 1928	SS *Majestic*	Dinner at Sea, Tourist Class RMS *Majestic*
April 8, 1929	SS *Abangarez*	Dinner for Peace and Goodwill Mission, SS *Abangarez*, Puerto Barrios, Guatemala
September 28, 1929	SS *Majestic*	"Menu for Jews" aboard the SS *Majestic*
August 8, 1932	*Chojo Maru*	Breakfast aboard a Japanese Ship, MS *Chojo Maru*

Social Event

February 14, 1901	United States	Valentine's Day Dinner, Sherry's, New York
December 10, 1901	Sweden	First Nobel Prize Banquet, Hall of Mirrors, Grand Hotel, Stockholm
June 26, 1902	England	British Empire Breakfast, North Pole, Dartford, London
June 23, 1908	United States	Yale Reunion Dinner, Bishop's Colonnade, Savin Rock, West Haven, Connecticut
October 16, 1912	Canada	Tribute Dinner for a Cow, Red Deer, Alberta
October 31, 1913	England	Dinner for the Palace Workmen, King's Hall Restaurant, Holborn, London
July 14, 1916	France	Dinner for the American Ambulance, Lycée Pasteur, Neuilly-sur-Seine
June 20, 1919	England	Dinner for the Transatlantic Air-Race Winners, Savoy Hotel, London
December 21, 1911	England	"Pease and Pork Dinner," Livery House, Bristol
December 28, 1919	Canada	Queen Victoria Diamond Jubilee Ball, Toronto City Armouries, Toronto
October 19, 1927	United States	Testimonial Dinner for Charles Lindbergh, Hotel Chelsea, Atlantic City, New Jersey
May 24, 1933	England	Empire Day Luncheon, Junior Carlton Club, London
November 15, 1936	United States	Gilbert and Sullivan Dinner, Park Central Hotel, New York
July 30, 1938	United States	Banquet Honoring Howard Hughes, Rice Hotel, Houston, Texas
October 20, 1944	England	Dinner with the British Secret Service, Claridge's Hotel, London
March 27, 1957	France	Gay Rugby Dinner, Hotel Lutetia, Paris
May 20, 1992	United States	Banquet of Insects, Explorer's Club, New York
June 16, 1999	South Africa	A Banquet to Nelson Mandela, Pretoria

Vegetarian Meal

July 28, 1848	England	First Annual Dinner of the First Vegetarian Society of England, Manchester
September 8, 1853	United States	Temperance Banquet, Metropolitan Hall, New York
April 21, 1881	France	Banquet of the French Vegetarian Society, Rue St. Honoré, Paris

January

New Year's Day Meal
Kosseir, Egypt, 1828

When Englishman Charles Lushington's term of office as secretary to the government of Bengal ended in 1827, he and his wife Sarah decided to return to England via Egypt rather than face the monotonous and notoriously rough sea passage around the Cape of Good Hope. The largely overland trip was itself no insignificant undertaking in those days, especially for a refined and elegant woman, and "Mrs. Charles Lushington" later published an account of her adventure. The couple was joined in Bombay (Mumbai) by Mount-stuart Elphinstone, the Scots-born governor of Bombay, who was also returning "home." At the Red Sea port of Cosseir (Kosseir) the party was obliged to wait until sufficient camels and donkeys could be procured for their journey across the desert. It was New Year's Day, and Mrs. Lushington noted that "Anniversaries passed in strange countries, and at long distance from home, are generally celebrated by travelers with extraordinary zest and cordiality." She then described their own particular celebration of this day:

> ... behold our party, consisting of ten persons sitting in a comfortable tent lined with yellow baize, and cheerfully lighted up: a clean tablecloth, and the follow-ing bill of fare: roast turkey, ham, fowls, mutton in various shapes, curry, rice, and potatoes, damson tart, and a pudding; Madeira, claret, sherry, port, and Hodgson's beer. For the dessert, Lemann's biscuits, almonds and raisins, water-melons, pumplenose (or shaddock), and a plumcake as a finale.... What astonished me was the ease with which the whole arrangement of our meals was conducted: however, I believe this was principally to be attributed to the skilful superintendence of Mr. Elphinstone's head servant, Antonio.... The cook, dining-tent, and apparatus, were sent forward early in the morning, before we started ourselves; and at six in the evening, our dinner was ready.

Expatriates in strange and distant places have two alternatives: to em-brace the novelty of the food in their new land, or cling to the nostalgic food of "home." Often, by virtue of necessity, their meals end up a blend of both, and this bill of fare is no exception. The fresh meat (turkey, fowl, and mut-ton) and fruit must have been sourced locally, and although damsons would have been very familiar to the English, they originated in the Middle East. Damsons are a type of plum—the name comes from "plum of Damascus," which is were they are believed to have originated. The shaddock (an ancestor of the grapefruit) originated in Malaysia and the watermelon in South Africa, but they clearly adapted well to the climate in Egypt.

Some of the food was making a return trip to Britain. Lehmanns's biscuits were the first biscuits produced commercially on a wide scale in the late eighteenth century and were specifically advertised for "Travellers on the Continent." The beer is even more interesting. Hodgson's beer was "the beer in almost universal use" in India. It was a seasonal, October-brewed pale ale rather than a true beer, and it is said that the temperature changes and movement of the barrels on the voyage to India wreaked a particular change, ripening it to a far greater maturity than beer cool-cellared in England.

Recipes

~~~

The "curry" on this menu demonstrates that more than simple substitution of ingredients occurs when people move between cultures. "Curry" is a British rather than an Indian concept. The long period of British colonial rule in India resulted in a blended Anglo-Indian cuisine that is sufficiently distinctive to be worthy of consideration in its own right. In India there is an almost infinite variety of "curries," each individually spiced (and named), but most early non-Indian cookbooks simply specified generic "curry powder." The following recipe, from the same era as Mrs. Lushington's dinner, is an exception as the dish is not called "chicken curry" as it would be in a less authentic cook book, and the spices are listed separately rather than a pre-prepared curry powder mix being used.

Fried Fowl of Muhammed Shah

Take
Rice, 1/2 ser (1 lb. avoir.)
Meat gravy, 1 ser (2 lb.)
A fowl
Butter, 1/2 ser (1 lb.)
Cream, 1/4 ser (1/2 lb.)
Milk, 1/4 ser (1/2 lb.)
Boiled milk, 1/4 ser (1/2 lb.)
Almonds, 1/4 ser (1/2 lb.)
Aniseed (or wild onion), 2 masha
Salt, 1 chittank (2 oz.)
Cardamums, 4 masha, (1 1/2 drachms)
Cloves, 2 masha (1 1/4 drachms)
Cinnamon, 2 masha (1 1/4 ditto)
Raw ginger, 1 chittank (2 oz.)
Lime, 1 chittank (2 oz.)
Dry coriander, 4 masha (2 1/2 drachms.)

First clean the fowl, and pierce it with the point of the knife; then having ground half the weight of the ginger and salt together, rub it into the fowl; put the

---

butter into the pot, and place it on the fire; and having mixed the curdled milk with the fowl, throw it into the pot with the butter, and dress it with a slow fire. When it is well browned, throw in a quarter of a pound of water, and take it off the fire. The cream and the milk and the ground almonds, strain through a cloth, and put them into the pot: add lemon. Then having taken about two pounds of flesh, washed and cleaned, and put it into a pot of proper size, boil it. When four pounds of water are reduced to two, take it off, strain and boil the rice in the meat gravy and sprinkle it with salt: then take it off, and having strained it, throw the rice into the pot containing the fowl; and having put in aniseed, cinnamon, cloves, and cardamums, close the mouth of the pot with flour, and replace it on the trivet and cook it with a gentle fire. When the steam rises, having taken it down, put it on a charcoal fire and place some of the coals round it, and after twenty-four minutes, open the mouth of the pot and serve it up.

"Indian Cookery as Practiced By and Described By the Natives of the East," in *Miscellaneous Translations from Oriental Languages,* trans. Sandford Arnot (London: Oriental Translation Fund, 1831).

Mince Pie: see January 9.

A Conversion Chart: Indian and Imperial Measurements: A table of the relative value of the weights used, according to the best authorities, is subjoined.

		lb.	oz.	drs.	Drops	
A Ser	=	2	0	13	13.648	Avoirdupois
A Pā'o	=	0	8	3	7.888	do.
A Chattank	=	0	2	0	14.208	do.
A Māsha	=	0	0	0	10.5129	do.
A Dām	=	0	0	0	2.6282	do.
A Ratti	=	0	0	0	1.3141	do.

London Oriental Institution, June 13, 1831.

January 2

Christening Feast
Cockley Cley, Norfolk, England, 1682

There were two simultaneous feasts on the joyous occasion of the christening of Rector William Constable's child in the small village of Cockley Cley in Norfolk in 1682. His parishioners were treated to "rost an boil'd bief, geese, and turkeys" at another house in the village, while his personal guests sat down to an even more impressive feast at the rectory.

1. A whole hog's head, souc'd, with carrotts in the mouth and pendants in the ears, with guilded oranges thick sett.

2. 2 ox's cheekes stewed, with 6 marrow bones.
3. A leg of veal larded, with 6 pullets.
4. A leg of mutton, with 6 rabbits.
5. A chine of bief, chine of venison, chine of mutton, chine of veal, chine of pork, supported by 4 men.
6. A venison pasty.
7. A great minced pye, with 12 small ones about it.
8. A gelt fat turkey, with 6 capons.
9. A bustard, with 6 pluver.
10. A pheasant, with 6 woodcocks.
11. A great dish of tarts made all of sweetmeats.
12. A Westphalia hamm, with 6 tongues.
13. A jowle of sturgeon.
14. A great chargr of all sorts of sweetmeats, with wine and all sorts of liquors answerable.

This was without doubt a spectacular and extravagant celebration, particularly since it took place in the depths of winter in an era when almost all stock not required for breeding were slaughtered in November. It is not known how many sat down to this feast, but there was a great amount of food. Four men were required to carry the great roasts, presumably on some sort of huge board. Each individual joint of meat was massive—a chine consists of the whole of the spine of the animal, with the meat on each side (so it the same as a "saddle" or double sirloin), and a venison pasty at that time was a huge affair which might contain a whole haunch of the animal. No expense seems to have been spared: oranges were an imported luxury, and the sugar (required for the large amount of sweetmeats) was very costly at the time. It was expected that guests at family celebrations would take away many of the "sugar, biskets, compacts, and caraways, marmalet, and marchpane (marzipan), with all kind of sweet suckers and superfluous banquetting stuff, with a hundred other odd and needless trifles" that were supplied at the feast.

Life was much more fragile in the seventeenth century, and every successful milestone was worthy of celebration. A successful lying-in (confinement) meant relieved and grateful friends and family, and "groaning cake" and "groaning cheese" ("groaning" being the very apt term for childbirth) were offered to visitors of the mother and child. Survival of the infant for the week or so to baptism (infant mortality was 17–25 percent in seventeenth-century England) was another reason for thanksgiving, and a Christening feast, or at least a Christening Cake. After a varying interval, the mother was "churched" or officially accepted back into the Church in a ceremony that had its roots in the ancient purification rites (parturient women were considered spiritually "unclean"), and a Churching Feast might follow.

Tragically, the little girl child who was received into the family and the church with so much fanfare on this day on 1682 died soon afterwards, and the christening was quickly followed with a funeral of much more modest cost—expenses came to 6 pence.

Recipes

~~~

In the days before canning and refrigeration, the only ways of preserving food were by drying, salting, pickling, or enclosing in a very thick, hard airtight pastry case. As long as the pastry did not crack or get damp, the contents would keep well—some old recipes even state that such pies would keep "a twelvemonth."

How to Season and Bake a Pasty of Venison

When you have ordered your side or haunch of Venison by taking out the bones and sinews and the skin on the fat, season it with pepper and salt only, beat it with your rolling pin, and proportion it for your pasty, by taking away from one part, and adding to another; your paste being made with a peck of fine flower, and about four pound of butter, and a dozen eggs, work it up with cold water into as stiff a paste as you can; drive it forth for your pasty, let it be as thick as a man's thumb, roll it upon a rolling pin, and put under it a couple of sheets of Cap-paper well flowred; then your white [fat] already being minced and beaten with water, proportion it upon your pasty, to the length and breadth of your Venison; so lay on your Venison on your said white, wash it round with your feathers, and put on a border: season your Venison at the top, and turn over your other leaf of past, so close your pasty; then drive out another border for the garnishing the sides up to the top of the pasty; so close it up together with your rolling pin, by rolling it up and down the sides and ends: and when you have flourisht your garnishing, and edg'd your pasty, vent it at the top: and indore it with butter, set it into the oven, it will ask five or six hours baking, according it may be; when it is enough, draw it, and put it on your pasty plate.

William Rabisha, *The Whole Body of Cookery Dissected* (London, 1682).

January 3

Luxurious Dinner for the King's Officers
Boston, Massachusetts, 1774

Almost 50 years after the defining moment of the start of the American Revolutionary War—"the shot heard 'round the world" from Lexington, Massachusetts (April 19, 1775)—a correspondent to the *Boston Daily Advertiser* in 1823 suggested that "one of the direct causes that excitement ripened into open resistance of the mother country, in this colony, was the luxurious mode of life of some of the King's officers." He gave as support for his argument a memorandum which he found in "an old diary of a maiden lady" of a dinner given to the officers on January 3, 1774, in Boston, a mere few weeks after the infamous Boston Tea Party (December 16, 1773).

Boston Tea Party. Courtesy of the Library of Congress.

"The fish was excellent, it was caught in cold weather on the Grand Bank—the *beef* uncommonly fine, came from Vermont, and was dressed by a cook, who had learned his art in France. The *canvas back ducks* were sent by a Provincial Commissioner, who had gone to the South, and were done to a turn—the venison came from Canada, and never was there better, or better done—and the *beaver tail,* dressed according to directions from an Indian Princess, came from Lake Ontario—the liquors were all good, and among them Corsica and Madeira, and Champagne wines; but these were, at length, neglected for the *native Curracoa,* which some of the Commissioners excelled in brewing."

The writer thought that the disappearance of such luxury was "among the blessed fruits of the revolution," and that "the descendants of the Pilgrims in these days, though not ignorant of what are good things, delight to exhibit on their tables, among other plain good fare, the *beans* and *hominy* in which their forefathers delighted." His patriotic sentiment is to be applauded, although it clearly obscured the evidence of banquet menus of his own time, which were very luxurious indeed. The luxurious lifestyle enjoyed by some was still in evidence in 1779, judging from a letter written from Philadelphia by General Nathaniel Greene (1742–1786) to General James Varnum (1748–1789):

Luxury and dissipation is everywhere prevalent. When I was in Boston last Summer I thought luxury very predominant there: but they were no more to compare with than now prevailing in Philadelphia, than an Infant Babe to a full grown Man. I dine'd at one table where there was a hundred and Sixty dishes: and at several others not far behind.

Recipes
~~~

The beef at this dinner would most likely have been simply roasted. "Roasting" refers to meat cooked on a spit directly over (or in front of) the fire. The term "roasting" is used now for meat cooked in the oven, but technically this is "baked," not roasted. The following recipe for roasting beef comes from *American Cookery* by Amelia ("An American Orphan"). It was published in 1796 and was the first American cookbook by an American author (as distinct from an English cookbook republished in the colony).

To Roast Beef

The general rules are, to have a brisk hot fire, to be placed on a spit, to baste with salt and water, and one quarter of an hour to every pound of beef, tho' tender beef will require less, while old tough beef will require more roasting; pricking with a fork will determine you whether done or not; rare done is the healthiest, and the taste of this age.

In June 1795, George Turner (ca. 1750–1843), an English-born American Revolutionary War officer from South Carolina, jurist, and judge in the Northwest Territory, wrote to George Washington. He sent Washington a gift of a Buffalo robe and some beaver tails and included this recipe with the letter.

Canadian Recipe for Dressing Beaver's Tails

First boil the Tail till it becomes soft & then broil it upon a gridiron until the fat or oil of it exudes in every direction. After this spread over the whole a coat composed of fine crumbs of bread & parsley, chopped very fine. Again lay it upon the gridiron till it becomes brown and crisp. In this state serve it up with vinegar salt and pepper.

Canvas Back Duck: see December 17.

January 4

Second Annual Dinner of the Toronto Board of Trade
Horticultural Gardens, Toronto, Ontario, 1899

Although the Toronto Board of Trade was founded in 1845, it seems that it managed to avoid the annual dinner ritual for many decades. On the second occasion when the commercial and business leaders of the city did come together for a dinner, they sat down to a menu that would have held no surprises for guests used to formal dining.

This was a standard civic dinner menu for the time. It could easily be transposed several decades either way, or to any other country with a British

MENU

Oyster soup.

*

Mayonnaise of Salmon.   Bread and Butter rolled.

Roast Young Turkey.

Jellied Turkey.   Sugar cured Ham.

Jellied Tongue.

*

Roast Chicken.   Roast Duck.   Galantine of Jellied Veal.

Roast Lamb.

*

Spiced Beef.   Boar's Head, stuffed.

*

Lobster Salad.

Chicken Salad.   Salmon Salad.

*

Rolls.   Pickles.   Hot Potatoes.

Hot Tomatoes.

*

Madeira Jelly.   Champagne Jelly.   Chocolate Creams.

Italienne Creams.   Charlotte Russes.   Filled Meringues.

Spanish Pies.   Macaroons.   Fancy Cakes and Pastry.

*

Strawberry, Vanilla and Lemon Ice Creams and Ices.

*

Celery. Cheese. Biscuits.

Coffee. Lemonade.

*

Apples. Oranges. Grapes. Bananas. Pine apples.

*

Almonds. Raisins.

heritage, without anyone noticing. There are two surprises for us today: the first is that there is nothing obviously "Canadian" about the offerings. Even though the Dominion of Canada had been established in 1867, the cuisine remained firmly rooted in the British tradition (see March 19). The second is the presence of the boar's head—a dish that would never be expected today, no matter what the occasion. Even at the end of the nineteenth century, it was becoming something of an anachronism but was no doubt presented at this dinner as a concession to the official Christmas season.

The boar's head is a richly symbolic dish with a long lineage. In medieval times it was presented with great fanfare at important feasts—held high on a platter for all to see, an apple in its jaws. The roots of the tradition go back to very ancient times in a number of cultures which revered, or feared, or held sacred the wild and fierce ruler of the forest. There was always a political agenda to great medieval feasts, and the boar's head on a platter became a bit of theatrical propaganda, carrying a clear message to the guests that the feast-giver was the one with the power. Many Christmas traditions have pagan roots, partly because the early Church was pragmatic enough to see the value in absorbing and reassigning old traditions and making them its own. By the fourteenth century, the boar's head had become particularly associated with Christmas—the head now representing the head of Satan, and the dish therefore symbolizing the church's triumph over evil and paganism.

Recipes
~~~

Oyster Soup

One quart boiling water, one quart rich milk; stir in one teacupful rolled crackers, pepper and salt. When it comes to a boil, add one quart fresh oysters; stir all so as not to scorch; add a piece of sweet butter about the size of an egg; let it boil up once, and remove from the fire. Dish up and send to the table.

Chocolate Creams

Two teacups of white sugar, one-half teacup of skim milk, one half-teacupful of chocolate. Boil the milk and sugar three minutes, briskly, then beat till stiff enough to roll into small balls, and set away to harden. Dissolve the chocolate in a bowl over steam, then drop into it the sugar balls, until well covered, and set to cool. Flavor the milk and sugar to the taste.

Mixed Pickles

Little cucumbers about two inches long, green tomatoes, ears of sweet corn about the size of the cucumbers, a dozen small white onions, some pods of string beans, and the tender pods of the radish, four or five green peppers and some bits of horse radish root; all of these soak overnight in a weak brine; drain through a colander and pack in a two-quart can and fill the can with boiling hot spiced vinegar.

Gems of Fancy Cookery: A Collection of Reliable and Useful Household Recipes (Ontario, ca. 1890).

Charlotte Russe: see September 4.
Macaroons: see February 17, November 15.

January 5

Household of the Marquess of Tweeddale
Yester House, Gifford, East Lothian, Scotland, 1817

George, the eighth Marquess of Tweeddale (1787—1876), succeeded to his title at the age of 17. He continued to pursue his military career and did not return to live at the ancestral family home in the border country of southern Scotland until 1814. His settlement back into domestic life was complete in 1816 when he married Lady Susan Montagu, one of the daughters of the Duke of Manchester.

The household manual kept by his steward survives to give us a marvellous insight into life on a great estate at the time. The steward's job was to keep track of the household expenses, the supply and issuing of food, and the bills of fare served each day to the family, servants, visitors, and visitors' servants. The details of the meals served each day were recorded on the right hand pages of the manual. There are no nursery meals noted on this day, for Lady Sarah had not yet borne the first of their 13 children.

Family:	Breast of Veal
	Sur loine of Beef
	Mutton Cuttelettes
	1 phaisant
	1 hare
Servants:	Boiled mutton
	Roast Beef

Yester House was a fine mansion set beside a stream, adjacent to beautiful woodland, and surrounded by thriving farms—totalling over 43,000 acres of fertile and productive land. Two centuries later there is great interest in the idea of "eating local," but in the Marques' time, there was no other way of life. A few items such as spices, sugar, some dried fruits, and perhaps dried fish were obtained from faraway places, but almost everything else needed to supply a household—all the meat, grain, dairy produce, and vegetables—were produced locally. In the case of an aristocratic family that meant right on the family estate, by the farmer tenants and employees.

The steward was responsible for ensuring that no food was wasted (a more difficult responsibility before refrigeration) or stolen. The left hand page of the manual had two columns—an "Account of Meat Taken Out" (from farm or gamekeeper) and another of meat "Given to the Cook." Grain grown on the estate for baking and brewing was tracked in a separate book. Dairy produce does not seem to have been recorded—perhaps because daily milking and the inherent perishability of the product made it unnecessary. Neither was the supply of fruit and vegetables tracked—they were of less commercial value and therefore required a lower level of accountability.

The bill of fare states only what main dishes were prepared for the family and servants. Bread was a staple at every meal for every class, and certainly some vegetables would have been eaten—those that could be stored over winter such as cabbage and onions and perhaps potatoes. Naturally the family had finer fare than the servants, such as pheasant and hare (which was definitely more upper class than rabbit).

Recipes

~~~

It is highly unlikely in a household such as this that a dish of hare would be served without its traditional accompaniment of currant sauce or jelly. It would not have been thought necessary to record this—or other traditional accompaniments and preserves—in the daily record of meals.

To Roast a Hare

Take of bread-crumbs and shred suet equal quantities, some chopped parsley and thyme, salt, pepper and nutmeg, two eggs, two spoonsfull of port wine, and a little lemon-peel. Mix these ingredients well together, and sew them up in the hare's belly; place it before a slow fire, baste with milk till it becomes very thick, then make your fire brisk, and baste with butter. Serve with currant jelly. N.B. If not convenient the wine may be left out of the stuffing.

Red or White Currant Jelly

Strip off your fruit, and put it in a jug, stand the jug in a kettle of water, and let it boil one hour, then throw your currants into a fine sieve, and press out all the juice, to every pint of which add one pound of loaf sugar; put it in your preserving pan over a clear fire, and stir it till it becomes jelly, observing to scum it carefully; when done, pour it into glasses, and when cold, lay some brandy paper on top: then cover with white paper, pricked full of holes.

(To Carve) A Breast of Veal

Is composed of two parts, the ribs and brisket, the latter is thickest, and is composed of gristels, the division of which you may easily discern, at which part you must enter your knife, and cut through it, which will separate the two parts, then proceed to help your guests to whatever part they chance to prefer.

 E. Hammond, *Modern Domestic Cookery, and Useful Receipt Book* (London, 1819).

January 6

Twelfth Day Dinner and Supper in a Tudor Household
Ingatestone Hall, Essex, England, 1552

Sir William Petre was a wealthy diplomat who served four Tudor monarchs. He began the building of the family home of Ingatestone Hall—where his descendants still live—in 1540, continuing to add to it and improve it for the next two decades. In common with other medieval manorial estates, Ingatestone Hall was virtually self-sufficient (see August 2). It had its own bake-house, brew-house, buttery (general storeroom), and granary. All grain, meat, game, vegetables, fruit, freshwater fish, eggs, and dairy produce came from its farms. Virtually all that was purchased was wine, spices (including sugar), dried and salt fish, and some luxury foods such as dried fruit.

 Also in common with other similar households, the Petre family were expected to offer hospitality to all who claimed it, and it was an unusual day when there was only the family and its own servants and workers to feed. The intense organization required to keep track of the provisions, costs of goods that were purchased, and guests served is detailed in the account book kept by the steward of the household.

 Twelfth Day is the traditional end of the Christmas season, the anniversary according to the Christian calendar of the festival of the Epiphany, or the visit of the three kings to the infant Jesus, and a final day for celebrating. The dinner and supper bills of fare and guest list for Twelfth Day, 1552, were given as follows:

WENISDAY TWLEFFE DAY DYNNER

Boylde beiffe 9 peces, a pestell & legge of porke, 2 legges of veale, rosting beiffe 6 peces, 3 gesse, a loyne & brest of veale, a pygge, 10 pasteis of beiffe, 2 pasteis of motton, 6 conneis, 4 pasteis of venson, 2 capons, 2 partriches, a woodecoke, 2 teles, a dosen of larkes

Strangeres—Mr. Richarde Baker & his brother, Mr. Tyrell of Warley, Mr. Pownsett, with 12 messe in the hall, Harris, Drywoode, Mr. Clovell, Geffreis of Cowbridge [in Mountnessing].

SUPPER

A motton & 2 oiyntes, a shoulder of venson, a brest of porke, 6 conneis, a duke, 2 capons, 2 partriches, a pastie of venson, 2 teles.

Strangeres—Mr. Richarde Baker & his brother, Mr. Tyrell of Warley, Mr. Pownsett, with 8 messe of serving men and of Ingatston, besydes a grett number of boys.

A "mess" usually consisted of four people, so the house fed 56 visitors for dinner, and an uncertain number (27 plus the "grett number of boys") at supper on this day.

This was solid, traditional fare, with a heavy emphasis on meat, but vegetables were probably served as well. For the poor, vegetables were subsistence food, along with a grain porridge such as frumenty (see Feburary 23). For the wealthy they appeared in meat dishes, such as stews and pies, but rarely as side dishes in their own right. Raw vegetables and fruits were suspect throughout the medieval period, perhaps because water for irrigation and rinsing was frequently contaminated. The author of the early sixteenth-century *Boke of Kervynge* [Carving] wrote "Beware of green sallets & rawe fruytes for they wyll make your soverayne seke [sick]," and a century after this meal, the diarist Samuel Pepys attributed the death of a neighbor to eating "cowcumbers." As the early modern period progressed, the obstruction of the spice trade due to the expansion of the Ottoman empire switched the emphasis to herbs, and improvements in horticulture expanded the range and quality of vegetables available. The golden age of English vegetable gardening had begun.

As to the meat on this menu, much of it would be familiar today. The rather alarming "duke," is probably "duck" and a pestell (pestle) is a leg, so in this case perhaps a ham. Pigeons were a very useful source of meat, particularly over winter, and would have come from the estate's pigeon-cotes. The only thing here unlikely to be encountered today are the larks—a common delicacy of the time, which would have been served to the most honored persons present.

Recipes

~~~

Venyson Rost

To rost venison tak feletes of venyson bound and cutt away the skyne and parboile it and let it be throughe stiff then lard it with salt and put it on a smale broche and rost it and if it be ned leche it abrod in leskes and lay them in a dysshe and strow on pouder of guinger and salt, and ye may do with buttes of venyson in the same manner.

A "pestel" is the leg of the pig, and can refer to the "ham" (thigh) or the foreleg. "Endored" means "made golden," in the case of a large piece of meat, as in this example, this was achieved by brushing with egg yolks, but in other dishes saffron or other yellow spices might be used, and occasionally real gold leaf.

To Mak Pestelles of Pork Endored

To mak pestelles of pork, endored tak and broche pestellis of pork and put of the skyn and rost it then tak poudur and baist it and yolk of egge draw throughe a strener and when they be rosted dry it at the greuyng up and endor hem with yolks of eggs and serue them furthe.

A Noble Boke Off Cookry Ffor a Prynce Houssolde or Eny Other Estately Houssolde (ca. 1500).

Venison pasty: see January 2.

January 7

Dinner aboard Steamship
SS *New York,* 1866

The SS *New York* was en route from Aspinwall (Colón), Panama, to New York and probably in the Bahamas, when the cabin-class passengers sat down to the following bill of fare:

SOUP
Green Turtle

FISH
Salted Cod and Egg Sauce

BOILED
Fowls and Parsley Sauce
Mutton and Caper Sauce
Corn Beef

ENTREES
Calves Feet & Sauce Piquante
Pork Chops & Tomato Sauce
Harricot Mutton
Hashed Beef Heart

ROAST
Beef
Pork
Mutton
Turkey & Cranberry Sauce

VEGETABLES
Boiled & Mashed Potatoes, Squash
Turnips, Parsnips, Onions, Rice

PASTRY
Plum Pudding, Hard Sauce
Charlotte de Russe
Small Pastry
Pies Assorted
Blanch Monge

DESSERT
Nuts Assorted
Bananas
Oranges
Figs
Tea & Coffee

The dishes represent the sort of solid, reliable food that would have been very familiar to the passengers. Presumably the steerage passengers were not so well supplied, and the first-class passengers had rather more elegant fare.

The only dish that might be puzzling to a modern reader or eater is *Blanch Monge,* a spelling variation of *blancmange* (or *blamange* or *blomange*)—the chilled and moulded dessert beloved of Victorian-era dining tables and children's birthday parties. It is most unlikely that the passengers who selected the *Blanch Monge* would have realized that in that one dish is encapsulated at least 600 years' of culinary history.

Blancmange comes from the French words *blanc* (white) and *manger* (to eat) and literally means "white food." In early medieval times the white ingredients were chicken, rice, and almond milk, and it was an elegant dish for the tables of the very wealthy. It was sweetened, but at that time sugar was used sparingly, as an exotic imported spice—there was no clear divide between sweet and savory dishes as now. The transition to the very sweet, variously flavored, but essentially bland molded dessert made opaque with cornflour and set with gelatin took hundreds of years.

Recipes

~~~

The extreme transition of blancmange is illustrated well by the following recipes, taken from cookbooks written over 400 years apart.

Blank Maunger

Take Capouns and seeþ hem, þenne take hem up. take Almandes blaunched.
grynd hem and alay hem up with the same broth. cast the mylk in a pot.
waisshe rys and do þerto and lat it seeþ. þanne take brawn of Capouns teere it
small and do þerto. take white grece sugur and salt and cast þerinne. lat it

seeþ. þenne messe it forth and florissh it with aneys in confyt rede oþer whyt. and with Almaundes fryed in oyle. and serue it forth.

[Interpretation: Take capons and boil them, then take them out. Take blanched almonds, grind them, and mix them with the same broth. Put the almond milk in a pot. Add washed rice and let it simmer. Then take the meat of the capons, tear it into small pieces and add it. Take white grease (lard) and sugar and salt and add. Let it simmer. Then serve it garnished with red or white aniseed comfits and with almonds fried in oil.]

The Forme of Cury (ca. 1395).

Lemon Blancmange

1 quart of milk	the yolks of 4 eggs
3 oz. of ground rice	6 oz. of pounded sugar
1 1/2 oz. of fresh butter	the rind of 1 lemon
the juice of 2	1/2 oz. of gelatine

Make a custard with the yolks of the eggs and 1/2 pint of the milk, and, when done, put it into a basin: put half the remainder of the milk into a saucepan with the ground rice, fresh butter, lemon-rind, and 3 oz. of the sugar, and let these ingredients boil until the mixture is stiff, stirring them continually; when done, pour it into the bowl where the custard is, mixing both well together. Put the gelatine with the rest of the milk into a saucepan, and let it stand by the side of the fire to dissolve; boil for a minute or two, stir carefully into the basin, adding 3 oz. more of pounded sugar. When cold, stir in the lemon-juice, which should be carefully strained, and pour the mixture into a well-oiled mould, leaving out the lemon-peel, and set the mould in a pan of cold water until wanted for table. Use eggs that have rich-looking yolks; and, should the weather be very warm, rather a larger proportion of gelatine must be allowed.

Beeton's Book of Household Management (London, 1861).

Turtle Soup: see November 10.
Salt Cod, Egg Sauce: see March 11.
Harricot Mutton: see April 30.
Caper Sauce: see December 8.
Parsley Sauce: see May 29.
Charlotte Russe: see September 4.
Plum Pudding: see June 28.

January 8

Jackson Day Dinner
Mayflower Hotel, Washington, DC, 1936

In 1936, as the United States geared up for a presidential election, it was estimated that 250,000 Democrats attended Jackson Day dinners at 1,700 different locations. Andrew Jackson (1797–1845), the president of the United States from 1829–1837, was especially honored on the anniversary of the

Boston Jackson Day dinner with President Franklin D. Roosevelt (center) and Vice President John Nance Garner (left). (AP Photo)

Battle of New Orleans in 1815 because it was he who led the attack on the British in what was the final military engagement of the War of 1812. Jackson's nickname of "Old Hickory" arose out of his "tough as old hickory wood" approach to troop discipline.

Democrats all over the country gathered in many locations on Jackson Day in 1936 to hear the broadcast of the speech of President Franklin D. Roosevelt, who attended the dinner held in Washington. According to *The New York Times,* diners were "openly overcharged" for the dinners, raising in the process a total of over $200,000, "the excess going toward the $400,000 deficit in the national party treasury."

Washington Democrats paid $50 (equivalent in purchasing power to approximately $777 in 2008) for the following menu:

Tomato stuffed with Fresh Lobster, Crabflakes
and Shrimps, Rachel
Diamond Back Terrapin Soup, au Madere
Rastegais
Celery   Olives   Nuts
Breast of Capon with Irish Bacon, Southern Style
Broccoli Polonaise   Rice Croquette with Guava Jelly
Heart of Romaine with Hearts of Palm, Artichoke,
and Alligator Pear, Lorenzo Dressing

> Graham Bread and Cheese Sandwich
> Coupe of Fresh Strawberries
> with Nougat Ice Cream, Chantilly
> Gateau Jackson
> Demi Tasse

The Great Depression was in full swing and the purpose of the dinner was to raise funds, not eyebrows. Essentially, this menu was standard for the time, although it appears that there may have been one minor disappointment. *The New York Times* noted:

> Seeing Gateau Jackson on the menu, some of the diners expected a delicious cake containing, of course, hickory nuts, in honor of Old Hickory. They got the Mayflower Hotel's Gateau Diplomat, renamed for the occasion. It is a pastry containing cherries.

The only other possible surprise on the menu was the rather uncommon "Rastegais." *Rastegaïs* are warm *hors d'oeuvres* of Russian origin consisting of small "buns" of yeast dough with a savory filling (fish or meat). The name means "unbuttoned" because the dough is not completely closed over the filling, leaving it exposed in the center. They are often served as an accompaniment to soup.

Recipes

~~~

Perhaps the Democrats at this dinner would have been happier with this rather more authentic old Hickory Cake.

Hickory Nut or Walnut Cake

Two cups of fine white sugar creamed with half a cup of butter, three eggs, two-thirds of a cup of sweet milk, three cups of sifted flour, one heaping teaspoonful of baking powder sifted through the flour; a tablespoonful (level) of powdered mace, a coffeecup of hickory nut or walnut meats chopped a little. Fill the cake-pans with a layer of the cake, then a layer of the raisins upon that, then strew over these a handful of nuts, and so on until the pan is two-thirds full. Line the tins with well-buttered paper and bake in a steady, but not quick, oven. This is most excellent.

Mrs. F. L Gillett and H. Ziemann, *The White House Cookbook* (New York, 1913).

Lorenzo dressing is said to be named after the waiter at the famous "21 Club" in Manhattan who invented it. As with so many recipe "inventions," it is an adaptation of an existing idea, in this case a standard vinaigrette dressing. There are many recipes for Lorenzo dressing that claim to be the original. This is a basic version.

> ### Lorenzo Dressing
>
> 2 tablespoons red-wine vinegar
> 6–8 tablespoons olive oil
> 2 tablespoons chili sauce
> 2 tablespoons finely chopped watercress
> salt, pepper to taste.

Graham Bread: see February 5.
Terrapin Soup: see May 16.
Guava Jelly: see May 24.

January 9

Gentleman's Dinner
Ockenden House, Cuckfield, England, 1708/9

Timothy Burrell (1643–1717), barrister-at-law, was left with an infant daughter when his third wife died in 1696. The brief entries in his journal show him to be a good and kindly man devoted to his daughter, generous with gifts at Christmas, and quite sociable. In spite of his widowed state he entertained regularly, and on this day in 1708/9 he invited Mr. Middleton, Mr. Willy, Mr. Shore, and Mr. Carpenter to dinner. He served them the following bill of fare.

> Peas pottage
> 2 carps   2 tench
> Capon   Pullet
> Fried oysters
> Baked pudding
> Roast leg of mutton
> —
> Apple pudding
> Goos[e]
> Tarts   Minced pies

   Essentially each dish in this early eighteenth-century dinner is recognizable today, although there are a couple of minor mysteries in the composition of the overall meal. The baked "pudding," appearing with the fish and meat of the first course, would have been a plain suet pudding (see June 3) whose purpose was to act as a starchy "filler"—just as dumplings, Yorkshire puddings, or bread might serve at other meals. This meal was in the middle of winter, when stored apples and "mincemeat" (made as it had been since medieval times, with actual meat included) were staple ingredients in sweet dishes such as pies. Mincemeat pies are almost exclusively associated nowadays with Christmas or Thanksgiving, but they were regular items on seventeenth- and eighteenth-century tables in England (and America) throughout the year.

   Both capon and pullet were served at this meal. It was usual at the time to specify the type of "chicken" suitable for each dish or meal. Today it is rare for a cookbook to specify, or a supermarket to stock, anything other than simply "chicken." There are two factors that have led to this. In the West, the Humoral Theory (see February 23), which accepted that animals of different genders and life stages had different "temperaments" or qualities, and therefore different medicinal effects which had to be taken into account when planning a meal, is no longer subscribed to. The second is that modern, large-scale chicken-producing methods are geared towards the exact opposite —uniformity of product.

Recipes

~~~

Capon Boiled and Larded with Lemons

First scald your Capon, and take a little dust of Oatmeal to make it look white, then take three Ladlefuls of Mutton-broth, a faggot of Sweet-herbs, two or three Dates cut long in pieces, a few parboiled Currans, a little whole Pepper, a piece of whole Mace, and one Nutmeg, thicken it with Almonds, season it with Verjuice, Sugar, and a small quantity of Sweet-butter; then take up your Capon, and lard it with thick and preserv'd Lemon, and then lay your Capon in a deep Dish, for boiled Meats, and pour the Broth upon it; Garnish your Dish with Sippets and preserv'd Barberries.

Mince-Pyes

Take a large Neats Tongue [calf's tongue], parboil it, then cut away the Roof and peel it, then weigh it, and to three pound of Tongue take five pound of Beef-suet, cut the Tongue in thin slices, and shred it, but shred the Suet by it self; when they are both pretty fine, put in the Suet by degrees, keep shredding them both together until they are as fine almost as Flower, then put in three pound of Currans, being first clean washed, pick'd and dry'd, Cloves, Mace, Nutmeg, Cinamon, beat very fine, of all together three Quarters of an ounce, half a pound of White Sugar, a pound of Dates ston'd and shred small, three ounces of green Citron, three ounces of candied Orange, cut into small thin bits, the yellow Rind of two raw Limons, grated, three spoonfuls of Verjuice, a Gill of Malaga Sack, half a Gill of Rosewater; these being well mingled, fill your Pyes; have a care they do not stand too long in the Oven to dry after they are just enough.

Carp Stewed

Having bled him, save the Blood, scrape off the Scales, then take out the Intrals; then put him into your Stew-pan with Mace, Ginger, Cloves, Nutmeg, Sweet-herbs, and a large Onion quartered, with half a pound of Butter; mix some of the Blood with Claret; put it in, and being enough, garnish it with sliced Lemons, and green Spinage, and serve it up to the Table.

   William Salmons, *The Family-Dictionary: or, Houshold* [sic] *Companion*, third edition (1715).

To Make Capons

This operation belongs to the country housewife. ... To cut them, the cock must lie on its back, and held fast, while with a very sharp knife she cuts him only skin-deep about an inch in length, between the rump and the end of the breast-bone, where the flesh is thinnest; next she makes use of a large needle to raise the flesh, for her safer cutting through it to avoid the guts, and making a cut here big enough to put her finger in, which she thrusts under the guts, and with it rakes or tears out the stone that lies nearest to it. This done, she performs the very same operation on the other side of the cock's body, and there takes out the other stone; then she stitches up the wounds, and lets the fowl go about as at other times, till the capon is fatted in a coop, which is commonly done from Christmas to Candlemas, and after. Now if the stones are but big enough, as they lie to the back, they may be safely taken out with a greased fore-finger, without much danger of killing the creature, but when they are too small there is danger.

William Ellis, *The Country Housewife's Family Companion* (1750).

Pease Pottage: see March 7.
Apple Pudding: see November 5.

January 10

Holland Society Annual Dinner
Hotel Brunswick, New York, 1888

The Holland Society was incorporated in New York in 1885, although an informal club by that name had been in existence for about two decades. Those wishing to join had to prove their descent through the direct male line from Dutch settlers who lived in the fledgling colony before 1675. The Society's great goal was to collect and preserve material relating to the history of the Dutch in New York, but they also fostered social and business relationships amongst themselves in the manner of other fraternal organizations.

At their third annual dinner in 1888 the heritage of the members was acknowledged and celebrated in the menu, which was written in both Dutch and English. The food, however, was standard American-international banquet fare of the time—including the "Holland Pudding," which was Dutch in name only. Holland was famous from early in its history for the quality of its dairy produce, and dishes in the "Holland Style" are usually rich in butter or cream (see April 14, for Hollandaise Sauce).

Blue Point Oysters.
Sauternes 1874

POTAGE.
Clear Green Turtle Soup.
Topaz Sherry

HORS D'OEUVRE.
Herrings   Caviar   Olives   Celery   Radishes
Timbales Rothschild.
Topaz Sherry

RELEVÉS
Young Chicken Halibut à la Vierge
Boiled Parisienne Potatoes
Sauternes 1874
Tenderloin of Beef Balzac
Bénédictine Potatoes   String Beans à l'Anglaise
Pontet Canet.

ENTRÉES
Snipe en caisse, sauce Périgeux
French Beans au Beurre
—
Artichoke à la Dubarry
Pontet Canet
Lobster à la Newburg with mushrooms
Perrier Jouêt Special.   Duminy Extra Dry Cuvée 1884
Sorbet à l'Africaine.
Cigarettes.   Irroy Extra Dry Cuvée
Rôti
Canvas-back Duck with currant jelly
Burgundy
Pains St Hubert
Celery Salad mayonnaise
Duminy Extra Dry Cuvée. 1884. Louis Roederer Grand Vin Sec.

PIÈCES FROIDES.
Boned Turkey Renaissance.   York Ham historic
Tongue Montpelier
Irroy Extra Dry

ENTREMETS SUCRÉS
Holland Pudding
Fancy Ice Cream.   Curaçao Jelly.   Petits Fours.   Mottoes.
Perrier Jouêt Special   Louis Roederer Grand Vin Sec

PIÈCES MONTÉES
Fruit   Dessert
Café Moka
Liqueurs.   Cognac Robin, 30 years old.   Cigars.

SPIJSKAART

De Weleerwaarde Heer Theo. L. Cuyler, Th. D. zal bidden over tafel.
"Eet wat gaar is, Drinck wat klaar is, Spreeck wat waar is."

Blauwe Landtongsche Oesters.
      Sauterneswijn van 1874.

Soep.   Heldere Schildpadsoep.

Zijschoteltjes.
Topaasche [?]
      Haringen, Kaviaar, Olijven, Selderij, Radijs,
      Paukenvorm Rothschild

Gekruide Gerechten.
      Jong Kip Heilbot in Maagde Stijl.
      Gekookte Parijzer Aardappelen. *Roodewijn.*
      Ossehaas, Balzac Stijl. *Pontet Canet*
      Aardappelen Benedictinorum.
      Snijboonen, Engelsche Stijl. *Champagnewijn.*
      Bijzonder Perrier [?]
      Irroy, Buitengewoon droog.

Voorgerechten.
      Snippen en busjes, met Perigeux saus.   *Louis Roederer,*
      Doperwten met Boter.   *Grand vin Sec.*
      Artisjokken in Dubaket Stijl.
      Kreeft in Newburgsche Stijl met Paddenstoelen.
      Sorbet, Afrikaansche Stijl.

Gebraad
      [Kanefasrug?] Endvogels met Gelei van Aalbessen.
Broodjes, St. Hubert Stijl.
      Gekruide Selderij-sla.   *Bourgognewijn.*

Koude stukken.
      Kalkoen van beenderen ontdaan, Renaissance Stijl.   Versierde
Yorksche Ham.
      Ossetong, Montpellier Stijl.

Zoete gerechten.
      Hollandsche Podding.   IJs in Verschillende Figuren.   Gelei van
Curaçao.
      Koekjes.   Ulevellen.

Gemonteerde Stukken.
      Vruchten.   Nagerecht.   Mokka Koffie.
            Likeuren.
Goudsche Pijpen, en Amsterdamsche Tabak, "Het Wapen der Nederlanden,"
            gebracht van Holland door den Secretaris.
      Fransche brandewijn van Robin, dertig jaaren oud.

Recipes

~~~

Dishes styled "à la Dubarry" are named after the Comtesse du Barry (1743–1793). They always contain cauliflower, the traditional explanation being that the vegetable reminds one of the powdered wigs that were fashionable in the eighteenth century.

Cold Fonds D'Artichauts, Du Barry

Boil four fresh artichoke bottoms in salt water, to which has been added the juice of a lemon. Also boil a head of cauliflower. When both are cold fill the bottoms with some of the cauliflower, and cover with a well-seasoned thick mayonnaise sauce. Place each artichoke on a leaf of lettuce, and serve.
   Victor Hirtzler, *The Hotel St.Francis Cook Book* (1919).

Pouding Hollandaise
(Holland Pudding)

Warm a gill of milk, and add 1/2 lb. of butter; when melted stir in four well-beaten eggs. Work this into 1 lb. of flour which has been sifted with two teaspoonfuls of baking powder. Add 1/2 lb. of picked currents which have been dried in flour. Add 4 oz. of caster sugar. Butter a mould, and decorate with strips of angelica and candied peel, or cherries. Turn in the pudding, and bake in a quick oven. Make a sweet sauce of eggs, milk, and butter, flavoured with wine. Serve very hot with the sauce round.
   M. Jebb Scott, *Menus for Every Day in the Year* (1912).

Turtle Soup: see November 10.
Parisienne Potatoes: see June 23.
Petit Fours: see November 14.
Mottoes: see January 17.
Lobster Newburg: see April 16.

January 11

Dining with the Ras
The Royal Palace, Andracha, Abyssinia (Ethiopia), 1898

The "Scramble for Africa" had been settled to the satisfaction of the European powers at the Conference of Berlin in (1884–85), and it was assumed that no African nation would be able to mount any significant resistance to its decisions. Abyssinia (present-day Ethiopia) had been allocated to Italy, but King Menelik II (who claimed descendance from the biblical King Solomon and the Queen of Sheba) did indeed take up arms and shocked Europe with a decisive victory over the Italians at Adowa in 1896.
   Alexander Bulatovich (1870–1919), a Russian military officer and explorer, was sent on a diplomatic mission by the Russian Red Cross, to assist King

Menelik II in his ongoing fight with Italy. In the book of his exploits (*With the Armies of Menelik II* [1900]), he described a dinner with the Ras (a nobleman) on this day.

> In front of the Ras and in front of me were placed two large baskets, covered with red calico cloth. A file of cooks, dressed in shirts clasped at the waist, carried in a great number of earthenware pots of various sizes, with foods. The chief cook, a rather beautiful woman, dressed more neatly than the others, with silver ear-rings and a silver necklace on the neck, removed the cloth from our baskets. The Asalafi of the Ras (a special post which in translation means "he who serves the food") dropped down on his knees in front of the basket and, having tasted each dish brought to him by the cook, began to take them out on chunks of injera and place them before the Ras.
>
> For me, the Ras prepared a special dinner, which, in his opinion, should satisfy the taste of a European. Here is the menu: 1) fried chicken, 2) thin slices of meat fried in a pan, 3) beef ribs grilled on hot coals, 4) afilye—an Abyssinian national dish, 5) meat that was scraped and boiled in butter, and 6) soft-boiled eggs. . . . I was hungry and, to the great satisfaction of the Ras, I ate everything with great appetite . . . A line of wine servers adroitly gave the banqueters huge horn goblets of mead [tej] through the whole room. . . . They also served red wine—"Bordeaux"—as the Ras called it—and a local vodka distilled from mead.
>
> A. K. Bulatovich, Ethiopia Through Russian Eyes:
> Country in Transition 1896–1898, trans. Richard Seltzer (1993).

Alongside the delicacies specially provided for an honored guest, the meal given to Bulatovich included the staple food of Ethiopia—*injera,* and favorite beverage—*tej.* Injera is an unleavened sourdough flatbread made from an ancient grain called *teff* (*Eragrostis tef*) and is used as a base or wrap for cooked dishes. Tej is a fermented honey wine (mead).

Bulatovich makes no mention at this meal of Ethiopia's great gift to the world—coffee. Coffee originated in Ethiopia and spread to the Yemen perhaps as long as 3,000 years ago.

Recipes

~~~

Bulatovich included a recipe for "the national dish" in the book.

Afilye

Afilye is prepared in the following manner. The back leg of a ram is freed from the tibial and shin bone, the meat is cut in thin long strips which hanging on the end of the bone form a kind of flower cluster. Then the meat is dipped for several minutes in a boiling sauce made from butter, pea meal, red pepper and other spices—and the dish is ready.

A. K. Bulatovich, *Ethiopia Through Russian Eyes: Country in Transition 1896–1898*, trans. Richard Seltzer (1993).

The National Drink

Another military traveler of the time, Captain M. S. Wellby, published *An Account of a Year's Expedition from Zeila to Cairo Through Unknown Abyssinia,* and in it he describes the method of making tej. The "geichi" bush is a particular species of buckthorn whose bitter leaves are used to flavor and strengthen the drink in the same way that hops are used in making beer.

Adjoining the bakery were the "tej" brewers. To drink tej is the highest bliss of some Abyssinians ; it is one of the main objects of their existence. Without tej and without women life would be a blank to them. The process of making it is simple enough. Water and honey, in the proportion of 5 to 1, are mixed together, and to this is added an infusion of the leaves of the geichi bush, which gives the drink its intoxicating strength. The longer this mixture stands, the stronger it becomes, till finally the essence of tej known as araki is distilled from it.

January 12

Meals at Shugborough Hall
Staffordshire, England, 1920

The end of World War I, the "war to end all wars," brought a mood of great excitement and optimism in its wake. Change was inevitable and desirable, and the old social rules and restrictions crumbled progressively as the "roaring twenties" got under way. The English landed gentry on their grand country estates, however, seemed oblivious to the fact that their way of life was crumbling, and they carried on much as they had always done, until the outbreak of World War II changed everything. It was a lifestyle beautifully demonstrated in the Robert Altman movie *Gosford Park* (2001), a lifestyle that some historians say was the best of all possible lifestyles. Many of those "upstairs" had never done a day's honest toil in their lives, but for the brief period between the wars they partied on, buffered by their wealth from the looming Depression, their every whim attended to by an army of servants "downstairs."

The surviving household books of Shugborough Hall, the ancestral home of the Earls of Lichfield, give a clue to a very ordinary day's meals.

Lord Lichfield and his guests:
Potage Parmentier
Fish and Cutlets
Chocolate Eclairs
Sardines Diable

Children in the nursery:
Meat juice
Chicken Broth
Cutlet
Rice pudding and Plum Compôte

Servants' Hall:
Rabbit Pie
Rice Pudding

Thomas Edward Anson, the 4th Earl of Lichfield (1883–1960), was clearly not doing any flamboyant entertaining on January 12, 1920—these are very homely meals indeed. Nevertheless, the menus provide a lot of insight into the class and family structure of the time. Dinner dishes for the family in this most English of homes appear in French—the soup is a "potage," and even the profoundly English dish of deviled sardines are "sardines diable." The children and servants, however, get broth, pie, and pudding, and in spite of its name, the apparently French "compôte" also has an ancient English history (see February 23). Much of the food would have been sourced from the estate and whatever vegetables were in season were also probably served, but as in the household of the Marquis of Tweeddale a century earlier (January 5), it was likely not considered necessary that they be recorded.

The menu also shows the traditional English habit of a small savory dish to end the meal—in this case the great favorite of a "deviled" dish (usually containing cayenne, curry, mustard, or some other hot spice). Paradoxically perhaps, the other great love of the English of all classes is for bland "nursery" or "school" puddings made with milk and a starch such as rice, sago, or tapioca.

Feelings can run pretty high in the most surprising circles when puddings are discussed in England. In 1853, the Committee of Management of the Carlton Club in London received a complaint from the Duke of Birmingham about "the unfair way in which Members help themselves to rice pudding." Happily, it was resolved that the steward would henceforth indicate to any such member that their behavior was improper.

Recipes
~~~

Dishes styled "Parmentier" always contain potatoes. They are named after the eighteenth-century French scientist who worked vigorously to popularize the vegetable (see October 21).

Potage Parmentier

Chop onions, celery, carrots, and leeks, and fry them in butter. Pour in the boiling stock, and add some whole-peeled potatoes. Cook it for an hour, then pass it through a sieve and put it back on the fire; skim it while it simmers. Beat up the yolks of two eggs with a little cream and butter; mix this with a little of the hot soup and strain it into a tureen, then pour in the soup.

Mrs. C. F. Leyel and Miss Olga Hartley, *The Gentle Art of Cookery* (1926).

Rice Pudding, Baked

Wash six ounces of rice, and boil it gently in a little more milk that it will absorb. When it is tender without being broken, pour it out, and mix with it a pinch of salt, two tablespoonfuls of finely-shredded suet, or, if preferred, a slice of butter, and a little grated nutmeg, or any other flavouring. Let the rice cool, then stir into it one or two eggs, according to the richness required. It will be very good without any. Bake the pudding in a moderately-heated oven, and serve with sifted sugar.
   Cassell's New Dictionary of Cookery (London, 1910).

Devilled Sardines

6 Sardines.	Salt, Lemon Juice.
1/2 teaspoonful Curry Powder.	Buttered Toast.
1/2 teaspoonful Mustard.	Chopped Parsley

   Scrape off the skins from the sardines. Mix the curry powder, mustard, and a very small pinch of salt into a thin paste with some of the oil from the sardines, then brush the fish well with the paste. Lay them on a buttered baking dish in a hot oven for 5 minutes. Cut six fingers of buttered toast, lay the sardines on them, sprinkle with a few drops of lemon juice and a little finely chopped parsley. Serve very hot, laying them side by side on a paper d'oyley.
   Elizabeth Craig, *New Standard Cookery* (1933).

Chocolate Eclairs: see November 7.

January 13

Samuel Pepys Gives Dinner for Friends
London, England, 1663

The English naval administrator and diarist Samuel Pepys (1633–1703) lived through one of the most turbulent times in English history—the period encompassing the English Civil War, the subsequent rule of Oliver Cromwell, and the eventual restoration of Charles II (1630–1685) to the throne. His diary is a marvellous source of information on the political and diplomatic personalities and events of the time. It is also a fascinating, sometimes very amusing, insight into all sorts of details of everyday life. Pepys was an ambitious, if slightly snobby, man, and he recorded gossipy anecdotes about the aristocracy, his career manipulations, his trips to the theatre, his affairs —and often, his meals.

Pepys was also a sociable man, always very keen to be fashionable, to have all modern conveniences, and to impress with his entertaining. In 1663, he decided to give a dinner to friends and colleagues at his home on Seething Lane. The guests stayed on, as was common, until the evening, when he gave them a light supper before they left.

   13th. So my poor wife rose by five o'clock in the morning, before day, and went to market and bought fowls and many other things for dinner, with which I was highly pleased, and the chine of beef was down also before six o'clock, and my own jack, of which I was doubtfull, do carry it very well. Things being put in order, and the cook come, I went to the office, where we sat till noon and then broke up, and I home, whither by and by comes Dr. Clerke and his lady, his sister, and a she-cozen, and Mr. Pierce and his wife, which was all my guests. I had for them, after oysters, at first course, a hash of rabbits, a lamb, and a rare chine of beef [see January 2]. Next a great dish of roasted fowl, cost me about 30s., and a tart, and then fruit and cheese. My dinner was noble and enough. I had my house mighty clean and neat; my room below with a good fire in it; my dining-room above, and my chamber being made a withdrawing-chamber; and my wife's a good fire also. I find my new table very proper, and will hold nine or ten people well, but eight with great room. After dinner the women to cards in my wife's chamber, and the Dr. and Mr. Pierce in mine, because the dining-room smokes unless I keep a good charcoal fire, which I was not then provided with. At night to supper, had a good sack posset and cold meat, and sent my guests away about ten o'clock at night, both them and myself highly pleased with our management of this day; and indeed their company was very fine, and Mrs. Clerke a very witty, fine lady, though a little conceited and proud. So weary, so to bed. I believe this day's feast will cost me near L5.

Dinner at this time in history was in the middle of the day, hence the need for his wife to get to the market early. In keeping with his status as a man rising fairly rapidly through the ranks of the bureaucracy, he had several servants, but for an occasion such as this he hired a "man cook" for the day.

True roasting is done over (or in front of) the naked fire, not in an oven. The meat is placed on a spit which is turned regularly to ensure even cooking—sometimes for many hours. The job of turning the spit was a job so lowly and contemptible that the boy or man (or dog) who turned it was not even worthy of an individual name. He was the *turnbroche* or turnspit, or simply "Jack"—the old version of "John Doe." The name "jack" was then inherited by the various mechanical turning devices that were developed in the seventeenth century. Some, perhaps including Pepys's hanging jack, were turned by the streams of smoke rising up the chimney, others were based on clock technology with pulleys and levers and springs.

Recipes

~~~

A posset was a drink made from hot milk curdled with ale, wine, or other liquor, flavoured with sugar, herbs, and spices. It was essentially the same as a syllabub (see May 5) and was often drunk as a nightcap or for medicinal purposes. "Sack" was a general name for a class of white wines formerly imported from Spain and the Canaries, and is generally taken to refer to sherry.

To Make a Sack Posset the Best Way

Set a gallon of milk on the fire, put therin a grain of Musk, a whole Cinamon and large Mace, when it boils, stir in half a pound of Naple-Bisket grated, keeping of it stirring while it boyles; then beat eight eggs together, casting four of the whites away; beat them well with a ladleful of milk or two amongst them; take off the fire the aforesaid milk, and stir in your eggs; put it on the fire again (but keep it stirring for fear it curdles) having almost a pint of sack in your Bason (upon the coals, with a spoonful of Rose-water) your milk being seasoned with sugare, and taken off the fire pour into your said sack stirring of it apace; while it is so pouring forth, take out your grain of Musk, and throw thereon beaten Cinamon, and send it up.

William Rabisha, *The Whole Body of Cookery Dissected, Taught, and Fully Manifested* (1661).

January 14

Mallard Night Feast
All Souls' College, Oxford, England, 1901

The ceremony of "Hunting the Mallard" is a long-standing tradition on the night of January 14 (the beginning of the new term) at All Souls' College in Oxford. It was once held annually, and by the time of the first known reference to it in 1632 was already being reported as a rowdy drunken revel that disturbed the peace and resulted in damage to property. The ceremony fell into disrepute and was abandoned in the early eighteenth century, to be revived in 1801 (as part of the celebration of the new century), and again in 1901 and 2001, with the next event planned for 2101.

The 1901 event began with a grand dinner.

Potâge des Tourterelles du Siècle Nouveau.
Tourbot, Sauce du Warden.
Éperlans à la Custodes Jocalium.
Vol-au-Vent du Ris de Veau à la Sub-warden.
Filets de Boeuf de L'Estates Bursar.
Châpons Rotis à la Roi Edouard.
Jambon d'Yorck.
Selle du Mouton.
Mallard Swapping Sauce.
Pouding d'All Souls.
Gâteau de Chichele.
Sardines de Chichele.
Merluches Salade des Junior Fellows.
Dessert du Common Room.

A great deal of effort obviously went into planning the dishes (or at least their names) for this dinner. The menu references the *Siècle Nouveau* (new century), college office-bearers and students, the archbishop of Canterbury and founder of the college, Henry Chicele (1364–1443), and the *Custodes Jocalium* or custodian of the "jewels" (items of value)—a grand name for the librarian. The inclusion of "King Edward" is a mystery save to say he appears in the chorus of the "Song of the Mallard"—although there are no clues as to which King Edward the song refers. In spite of the college-themed menu, it is most likely that standard recipes were used with only their names being changed for this particular dinner.

The focus of the evening's festivities is a symbolic hunt around for the college totem—the mythical "swapping, swapping mallard" ("swapping" is an old English word meaning "whopping" or huge), to the accompaniment of the traditional mallard song. The roots of the tradition are very old; the most popular and enduring explanation is that it commemorates an event in 1437 when the digging of the foundations of the college caused the release of a giant mallard from the drains where it had been trapped for a long time.

Recipes
~~~

It is unclear which dish the Mallard Swapping Sauce was to accompany—presumably the Saddle of Mutton. At first sight it seems strange that there is no duck of any species on this menu, and although in many societies it is taboo to eat one's personal or tribal totem, it is unlikely that the staunch men of Oxford would have avoided it for this reason.

A traditional sauce to serve with mallard since medieval times was a *sauce noir,* or black sauce.

Sawce Noyre for Malard

Take brede and blode iboiled, and grynde it, and drawe it thurgh a cloth with vynegar. Do thereto powdor of gynger; and of peper, and the grece of the malard. Salt it, boile it wel, and serve it forth.

[Interpretation: Take bread and blood boiled together and grind them and add vinegar and strain them through a cloth. Add ginger, pepper, and mallard fat. Salt it and boil it well, and serve it forth.]

The Forme of Cury (1395).

What constituted the *Pouding d'All Souls* in this menu is unknown, but recipes for Oxford Pudding are common in cookbooks from the early eighteenth century. There are several completely different recipes—rice puddings, apricot tarts, and suet puddings all called by this name. The following recipe is a very early version; it is a fried dumpling.

An Oxford Pudding

A quarter of a pound of biscuit grated, a quarter of a pound of currants clean washed and picked, a quarter of a pound of suet shred small, half a large spoonful of powder-sugar, a very little salt, and some grated nutmeg; mix all well together, then take two yolks of eggs, and make it up in balls as big as a turkey's egg. Fry them in fresh butter of a light brown; for sauce have melted butter and brown sugar, with a little sack or white wine. You must mind to keep the pan shaking about, that they may be all of a light brown.

Hannah Glasse, *The Art of Cookery, Made Plain and Easy* (London, 1747).

Vol-au-Vent: see September 17.

How to Carve a Mallard

To unbrace a duck, or mallard.

Raise up the pinions and legs, but take them not off, and raise the merry-thought from the breast; then lace it down each side of the breast with your knife, wriggling your knife to-and-fro, that the furrows may lie in and out.

Charles Carter, *The London and Country Cook* (London, 1749).

Merry-thought: The forked bone between the neck and breast of a bird; the furcula, wishbone. Also: the portion of a cooked bird when carved that includes this bone.

Oxford English Dictionary.

January 15

Portuguese Luncheon
Café Royal, London, England, 1935

The Wine and Food Society was started in England in 1933 "to raise the standard of eating and drinking throughout the country," with the well-known wine expert and gourmet André Simon (1877–1970) as its president. For the first 12 months or so their regular demonstrations focused on English and French food, beginning with an "Alsation" luncheon on November 14, 1933. By January 1935, the Society ventured to hold a Portuguese luncheon and was confident enough to invite the Portuguese Ambassador Rey L. Ulrich as guest of honor. The luncheon was held at the Society's usual venue of the Café Royal and was "deliberately of a kind that might be found in a Portuguese middle-class household."

Caldo Verde.
Grilled Fresh Sardines, Salad of Pimentos.
Carne Guisado can Ervilhas e Chouriços.
Toucinho do ceu.
Queijo da Sarra.

The Times described the composition of each of these dishes for the benefit of its readers. *Caldo Verde* was "green soup," which it described as being in its country of origin as shredded cabbage boiled in water with a little oil. On this occasion it was confessed that potatoes had been added, and butter substituted for the oil—"culinary elaboration" that met with general approval. The sardines were almost the size of pilchards—quite large, apparently, "to those only familiar with the tinned variety" but nevertheless "quite good." The *Carne Guisado can Ervilhas e Chouriços* should have been, said the newspaper, a stew of peas "forming a vehicle to introduce the flavour of the *chouriço,* a form of sausage made of bacon and pimento, with a suspicion of garlic," but it appeared that the ratios of the ingredients were somewhat reversed, with meat predominating and the peas as a garnish.

The sweetmeat which followed was *Toucinho do ceu* (translated as "bacon from heaven"), which turned out to be the material familiar to the guests as "that which formed the upper layer to a Christmas cake"—in other words marzipan (almond paste). Marzipan was a favorite sweetmeat from medieval times (see September 9) and was often used to make elaborate "mock foods" such as the marzipan fruit we can still buy from confectionary specialists. There is a recipe in one medieval text for "mock bacon" made from pink and white marzipan formed into "rashers," but the Portuguese name is probably a more general reference to the fact that this delicious sweetmeat was the "bacon" allowed by the church (representing "heaven") on the many regulated fast days.

The final course was the *Queijo da Sarra,* a cheese made from the milk of sheep which had fed entirely on clover, and was acclaimed by the guests as a great success. To lubricate the meal, four wines were served: a dry Madeira, *Bucellas* (a dry white), *Collares* ("some resemblance to a fairly full Beaujolais"), and *Commendador* (tawny port).

The Ambassador's response to each course was not noted, so we do not know how he felt about the replacement of oil with butter or the mere suspicion of garlic, or the other liberties taken with traditional dishes from his country. He clearly chose his words carefully, however, giving an assurance "that his country could provide more sumptuous fare, but the dishes served were interesting and appetising, and the wines had been chosen to go with the food." He also graciously indicated that English people who visited Portugal would be received with friendship.

Recipes

~~~

The following recipes are taken from *365 Foreign Dishes,* an English publication by an unknown author in 1908. They give some idea of the English interpretation of Portuguese dishes.

Portugal Salad (with Pimentos)

Slice 2 cucumbers, 2 tomatoes, 1 onion and two green peppers. Then sprinkle with 1 chopped clove of garlic, salt and pepper and cover with some thin slices of bread. Pour over all a cup of vinegar and 1/4 cup of olive-oil and serve.

Portugal Soup

Boil 2 pounds of beef and 2 pig's feet in 4 quarts of water; season with salt and pepper. Let boil well. Add 1 head of lettuce, 1/2 head of cabbage, a few thin slices of pumpkin, 2 carrots and 1 clove of garlic, all cut fine, and 1 herb bouquet. Let all cook until tender; then add 1/2 can of peas. Remove the meat; cut into thin slices; season, and serve with the soup.

January 16

''Upside-Down'' Dinner
Royal Automobile Club, London, 1914

The early twentieth century was an exciting time for aviation. It seemed that every week a new record was broken or a death-defying stunt was attempted, and aviators were the superheroes of the age, fêted and banqueted wherever they went. The Royal Automobile Club gave a special dinner in 1914 to Bentfield C. Hucks (1884–1918) and Gustave Hamel (1889–1914), in honor of their "looping the loop" and "upside-down" flying. The menu was strictly in theme. The English traditionally end their meal with a small savory (see January 12), so the normal order of courses was turned "upside-down."

Fine champagne et Liqueurs variées
Café – Pégoud
Savoury – Canapés à la Chanteloup
Entremet – Soufflé Hucks
Légume – Asperges renversées, Sauce Gnome
Salade – Blériot
Rôti – Bécassines Hamel
Entrée – Vol au Vent à la Hendon
Grosse Pièce – Baron de Paulliac à l'Aviation
Poisson – Looping Lobsters à l'Aerodrome de Londres
Consommé – Essence de Volaille Graham-White
Hors d'Oevre – Caviare à la Morane

The hallmark of a fine dinner had for a very long time been a regular and predictable sequence of classical dishes reproduced faithfully and consistently. Toward the end of the nineteenth century, there began among sophisticated and rich diners (some said tasteless and obscenely wealthy diners) a new fashion for "freak dinners." Hosts and hostesses tried to outdo each other with increasingly outlandish ideas: dining on horseback, or aboard a bus, or in a mock desert for example. There was sometimes a fine line between a "theme" dinner and a "freak" dinner, as there was on this particular occasion.

A great deal of creativity had gone into the planning of this evening, and no opportunity was lost to apply the upside-down theme. The invitation cards and menu were printed so as to read from right to left. The table was arranged in the form of a loop, the center of which was designed to represent the Hendon Aerodrome as seen from 1000 feet in the air. The two guests of honor sat under large mirrors which reflected them upside-down at a table, the illusion being enhanced by extra table legs being screwed onto the table tops.

The dishes served were named in honor of famous aviators (Louis Blériot, Adolphe Pégoud, Pierre Chanteloup, Graham-White, Robert and Léon Moran) and places of aviation interest (Hendon, Pauillac), and even the Gnome rotary engine was acknowledged. When it came time for him to respond to the toast to his health, Hucks's reply began with "Lastly" and went on to "Thirdly," and finished with a "Firstly."

When the idea of an "upside-down" theme was first mooted, "M. Pruger, the manager of the club, was able by careful choosing of dishes to make it a novel and most enjoyable dinner." Not every guest was convinced. Nearly all said at the end of the meal that they still felt hungry. Some suggested the plan of following the upside-down dinner with one "right side up." One astute dinner reflected that "The dinner requires even more practice to enjoy than flying."

Recipes

~~~

It was, and still is, common for chefs to invent a new recipe to honor an important person or commemorate a historic event—or at least for them to modify an existing recipe. It is impossible to know what exactly went into "Souffle Hucks," but a souffle was no doubt deemed appropriate because of its light and airy nature.

Apricot Souffle

Twelve fresh or canned apricots
eight ounces of Vienna flour
four ounces of butter
four ounces of castor sugar
one pint of milk
six yolks of eggs
eight whites of eggs

Drain the apricots well, and pass them through a hair sieve. Melt the butter, stir in the flour, add the milk (some of the milk may be replaced by apricot syrup) and cook over the fire until the mixture no longer adheres to the sides of the stewpan. Let it cool slightly, then beat in the yolks of eggs, add the sugar, apricot pulp, and stir in as lightly as possible, the stiffly-whisked whites of eggs. Have ready a well-buttered souffle mold, turn in the mixture and steam slowly from forty to forty-five minutes. Unmold and serve with a suitable sauce. Send to table as quickly as possible.

Nicholas Soyer, *Soyer's Standard Cookery* (1912).

Vol-au-Vents: see September 17.

January 17

Benjamin Franklin Honored by *Typothetæ*
Hotel Brunswick, New York, 1895

When the master-printers of New York founded their professional organization, they called themselves the *Typothetæ*, after the Greek word for a typesetter. They held an annual dinner on January 17, the

MENU.

*

Blue Point Oysters.

Hors d'œuvres.

Celery.   Olives.   Radishes.
Caviar Canapes.

Potage.

Cream of Asparagus.

Hors d'œuvres (Chaud).

Cassolettes à la Napolitaine.

Poisson.

Escaloppes of Bass Renaissance.
Potatoes Surcouf.

ENTRÉES.

Filets Mignons Bayard.   Brussels
Sprouts Sauté.

Duchesse Potatoes.

Sweetbread Cotelettes Nesselrode
French Peas

Sorbet au Rhum.

Roti.

Quails on Toast with Cresses.   Salad.

Entremets Sucres.

Fancy Forms Ice Cream.   Muscovite
Jelly.

Friands.   Croquets Parisiens.
Petits Fours.

Dessert.

Roquefort.   Camembert.   Fruit.
Mendiants.   Mottoes.

Pièces Montées.   Café.

birthday of the most famous member of their profession, Benjamin Franklin (1706–1790).

This was a typical grand banquet of the time. The nineteenth century saw a huge change in the way that great dinners were served, and the meal on this occasion had features of both the old and the new. In medieval times great feasts consisted of several courses, with each containing a large number of both "sweet" and "savory" dishes (although there was no such distinction then), all placed simultaneously on the table. One course was then completely cleared away before the next course was set up in another display of great abundance—the guests being entertained in the meanwhile. This type of service did not change, essentially, until the early nineteenth century. The idea of single dishes served in strict sequence appeared in about the early nineteenth century in Europe, supposedly due to the influence of the Russian Prince Kourakin (1752–1818)—and became known as *service à la russe.* The civic and corporate world in particular was reluctant to let go of the almost obsolete *service à la française* in favor of the new style of service because it did not offer such an opportunity for grand spectacle.

Pièces montées (mounted pieces) were impressive decorative food "sculptures" reminiscent of medieval subtelties (see September 23). Their exact form in this particular menu is not detailed, but surely they were impressive, if descriptions of earlier efforts are any guide. In 1886 there was a "dainty sugar model of the old-fashioned Franklin band press," and in 1893 there were many special pieces in sugar illustrative of Franklin's life such as "The First Printer's Dinner" (Franklin snacking on a loaf of bread when he first arrived in Philadelphia). The dinner of 1892 must have been particularly amusing. As well as the superb sugar and nougat piece representing "Franklin at the case" there were on all tables "musical automatons, each set to start between the courses."

The *pièces montées* were marvelous examples of the patissier's and confectioner's skills, but they were not primarily meant to be eaten. There was no shortage of sweet treats at this dinner, however. It would have been unthinkable for an American dinner of the time to be without ice cream. There was also Muscovite jelly—a fruit or liqueur flavored jelly made in a decorative hinged "Muscovite" mold and served with the outside frosted. *Mendiants* comes from *mendicant,* French for beggar, supposedly because they are so delicious that everyone begs for a piece. Originally it referred to foods containing dried fruit and nuts. In the Christmas tradition of Provence in the south of France, the color of 4 of the 13 traditional dessert items represented the robes of the four mendicant monastic orders—raisins (Dominicans), hazelnuts (Augustins), dried figs (Franciscans), and almonds (Carmelites.) Now the term "Mendiant" usually applies to discs or broken slabs of chocolate containing these dried fruits and nuts. Finally, the "mottoes" were a popular form of candy containing a short saying or line of poetry, an idea that gave rise to the fortune cookie—a uniquely American invention.

Recipes

~~~

Candies for Mottoes

Have some small conical-shaped plaster molds, the bottoms being detruncated and rounded; they should be an inch in diameter at the bottom and one inch high. Fasten these molds on a ruler slightly apart from each other, then with this ruler imprint the molds into the starch. Put two pounds of sugar in a copper sugar basin and dissolve it; with a pint and a half of water; stand this on the fire to cook to "large ball," being careful to remove all the scum and keep the sides of the pan clean. When the sugar has reached the proper degree let it fall to "small ball" by adding a few spoonfuls of orange flower water, then remove the pan from the fire and with a wooden spoon rub the sugar against the sides to mass it. As soon as it begins to whiten stir it well and cast it into the starch impressions, using a spring funnel for this purpose; when the box is full bestrew the candies lightly with a handful of starch and put the box in a heater for two or three hours. After the candies are hard remove them from the starch and range them on grates or on a sieve to cool thoroughly, then brush over with a camel's hair or feather brush.

To wrap up these candies spread open some variegated colored motto papers, in the center of each lay a printed motto folded in four and on this one of the candies, then fold the paper all around toward the center and use a string attached to the table to enclose the candy (this is done by giving the string a turn around the motto and pulling on it, then the motto is released and will be found firmly twisted) and form a bouquet with the fringed ends of the paper.

Charles Ranhofer, *The Epicurean* (New York, 1894).

Duchesse potatoes: see July 11.
Brussels Sprouts saute: see February 11.

January 18

Prince Regent of England Entertains the Archduke of Russia
Royal Pavilion, Brighton, England, 1817

One of the most spectacular and spectacularly extravagant banquets ever held was created by the French chef Antonin Carême (1784–1833) for his employer the Prince Regent (1762–1830), the future King George IV. The occasion was the visit of the Archduke Nicholas of Russia (1796–1855), the future Tsar Nicholas I, and the venue was the Prince's seaside retreat, the Royal Pavilion at Brighton. Carême outdid himself on this, the third banquet of the Archduke's stay, masterminding the preparation of 127 dishes to create an event that was as much about theatre, propaganda, and the display of power and wealth as it was about food.

SOUPES
Les profitralles de volaille à la moderne
Le potage santè au consommé
Le potage de mouton à l'anglaise
Le potage de riz à la Crècy
Le potage de pigeons à la marinière
Le potage de karick à l'Indienne
Le potage à la d'Orléans
Le potage de celeri, consommé de volaille

8 RELEVÉS DE POISSON
Les perches à la Hollandaise
La truite saumonée à la Génoise
Le cabillaud à la crème
Le brocket à l'Espagnol garni de laitances
Les soles au gratin et aux truffes
Le turbot, sauce aux crevettes
Les merlans frits à l'Anglaise
Le hure d'esturgeon au vin de Champagne

15 ASSIETTES VOLANTS À SERVIR APRÉS LES POISSONS
De petits vol-au-vents à la Reine
De petit pâtès de mauviettes
De croquettes à la royale
De canetons à la Luxembourg
De filets de poissons à l'Orly

8 GROSSES PIÉCES
Le quartier de sanglier marine
Les poulardes à l'Anglaise
Les filets de boeuf à la Napolitaine
Les faisans truffés à la Perigueux
La dinde à la Godard moderne
La longe de veau à la Monglas
Les perdrix aux choux et racines glacés
Le rosbif de quartier de mounton

40 ENTRÉES
[arranged around the relevés de poissons as indicated]
La sante de poulardes à la d'Artois
Les ris de veau glacés à la chicorèe
La croustade de grives au gratin
Les poulets à la reine, à la Chevry
Les côtelettes de lapereaux en lorgnette
(Les perches à la Hollandaise)
Les quenelles de volaille en turban
Les cailles à la mirepoix, ragout à la fiancière
La magnonaise de perdreaux à la gelée
L'emince de langues à la Clermont
Les poulets dépèces l'Italienne
(La truite saumonée à la Génoise)
Les filets de volaille en demi-deuil
Les aiguillettes de canrds à la bigarade
La darne de saumon au beurre de Montpellier
Le pain de volaille à la royale
Les filets d'agneaux à la Toulouse
(Le cabillaud à la crème)
La caisse de lapereaux au laurier
La blanquette de poulardes aux champignons
La casserole au riz à la Monglas
Les petits canetons à la Nivernoise
Le sauté de faisans à la Perigord
Les sautés de perdreaux au suprême
La chevalier de poulets garni d'Orly
La timbale de nouilles à la Polonaise
Les escalopes de chevreuil à l'Espagnole
Les ballotines de poulardes à la tomate
(Les soles au gratin)
Les bécasses, entrée de broche à l'Espagnole
Les filtes de volaille à la belle vue
Les hâtelets d'aspic de filets de soles

Les cervelles de veaux à la Milanaise
Les escalopes de gelinottes, sauce salmis
(Le turbot, sauce aux crevettes)
Les filets de poulardes glacés aux concombres
Les boudins de faisins à la Richelieu
La salade de volaille à l'ancienne
La noix de jambon aux épinards
Les ailerons de poulardes à la Piémontaise
(Les merlans frits à l'Anglaise)
Les pigeons au beurre d'écrevisses
La poularde à la Maquignon
Le vol-au-vent à la Nesle, Allemande
Les cotelettes de moutons à la purée de pommes de terres
Les filets de poulardes à la Pompadour

8 PIÉCES MONTÉES
An Italian pavilion
A Swiss hermitage
Giant Parisian meringue
Croque-en-bouche aux pistache
A Welsh hermitage
A grand oriental pavilion (the Brighton Pavilion in pastry)
Un gros nougat à la française
Croque-en-bouche aux anis

8 ROASTS
Les bécasses bardées
Le dindonneau
Les faisans piqués
Les poulardes au cresson
Les sarcelles au citron
Les poulets à la reine
Les gelinottes
Les cailles bardées

32 ENTREMETS
(of which 16 are desserts, with indication of arrangement
around roasts and grosses pièces)
Les concombres farcies au velouté
La gelée de groseilles (conserve)
(Les bécasses bardées)
Les gaufres aux raisins de Corinthe
Les épinards à l'Anglaise
(Le Pavilion Italian)
Le buisson des homards
Les tartelettes d'abricots pralineés
(Les dindonneaux)
La geléé de marasquins fouettée
Les oeufs brouilles aux truffes
(La grosse meringue à la Parisienne)
Les navets à la Chartres

Le pouding de pommes au rhum
(Les faisans piques)
Les diadémes au gros sucré
Les choux-fleurs à la magnonaise
(L'Hermitage Suisse)
Les truffes à la serviette
Les fanchonettes aux avelines
(Les poulardes au cressons)
La gelée de citrons renversées
La croute aux champignons
Les cardes à l'Espagnol
La gelée de fraises (conserve)
(Les cailles bardées)
Les gateaux renversés, glacés au gros sucré
Le buisson de crevettes
(Le Pavilion Asiatique)
La salade de salsifis à l'Italienne
Les gateaux à la dauphine
(Les gelinottes)
Le fromage Bavarois aux abricots
Les laitues à l'essence de jambon
(Le gros nougat à la française)
Les champignons grilles demi-glacé
Les pannequets à la Chantilly
(Les poulets à la reine)
Les pains à la duchesse
Les truffes à la serviette
(L'Hermitage Gaulois)
Les pommes de terre à la Lyonnaise
Les gateaux d'amandes glaces à la rose
(Les sarcelles aux citrons)
La gelée de cuirassau de Hollande
Les céleris à l'Espagnol

12 ASSIETTES VOLANTES
4 soufflés de pomme
4 soufflés à la vanille

The gluttonous Francophile future King George IV of England had managed to retain the services of the man already styled the "Cook of Kings and the King of Cooks" at great expense, and with the lure of the most vast and modern kitchens imaginable. Carême was a man of many paradoxes. He was acknowledged as the greatest chef of his time, yet his first love and passion was architecture. He simplified and codified French cooking yet clung to the old style of serving that demanded that all food for one course was set on the table at one time. He had the salary and kitchen of his dreams yet he was unhappy and homesick and did not stay long in the prince's employ. Carême is considered to be the father of modern *haute cuisine* for his work in refining the classic dishes of the French repertoire. He defined four basic sauces (béchamel, velouté, espagnol, and allemande) that underlie all others and are the foundation of classic French cuisine.

Recipes

~~~

Carême's recipes are very complex and labor intensive. They require the prior preparation of multiple other stocks and flavoring mixtures, and even in professional kitchens they are rarely made today without some shortcuts. The following more accessible versions are taken from *The Book of Sauces,* by Charles Herman Senn (Chicago, 1915).

Béchamel Sauce (White Sauce)

Dissolve one ounce of butter in a small stewpan, add one ounce of flour; stir over the fire for a few minutes, just long enough to cook the flour, without allowing it to brown. Stir in a pint of boiling milk; add a small onion stuck with a clove, ten white peppercorns, half a bay-leaf , a sliced carrot, a pinch of salt, and a little grated nutmeg. Stir until it boils, and allow to simmer for fifteen minutes. Pass through a tammy cloth or napkin, return to the stewpan, and finish with a small piece of butter, and half a teaspoonful of lemon juice.

Velouté Sauce (Velvet Sauce)

1 oz. flour	2 oz. butter
1 pint of veal stock	1/4 gill mushroom liquor
1/2 gill of cream	1 small bouquet garni
6 peppercorns	salt
nutmeg	lemon juice

Cook the flour with an ounce of butter together without browning, stir in the stock and mushroom liquor, add the bouquet and crushed peppercorns, boil slowly for twenty minutes, stir frequently, and skim. Pass through a sieve or tammy. Keep on the side of the stove, put a few tiny pieces of butter on top to keep from forming a skin. Just before using it add the cream. Stir well and let it get thoroughly hot without boiling, season with salt if necessary, a pinch of nutmeg, and about a teaspoonful of lemon juice.

Espagnole Sauce (Spanish Sauce)

3 quarts of rich stock	4 oz. lean veal
1 bouquet garni	12 peppercorns
4 oz. butter	4 oz. flour (sifted)
4 oz. raw ham or lean bacon	1 carrot
1 onion	2 cloves
1/2 pint tomato pulp	1 gill claret
1 glass sherry	some mushrooms (fresh or preserved)

Wash and peel the carrot, turnip, and onion, cut up small and put in a stew-pan with the bouquet, peppercorns, cloves, and the veal and ham, both cut into pieces. Add an ounce of butter, and stir over the fire until of a nice light brown color; this forms a true mirepoix. Pour off the fat, moisten the mirepoix with the stock, claret, sherry, and tomato pulp, boil gently for about an hour. Skim occasionally.

Meanwhile, prepare a brown roux by melting 3 oz. of butter in a stewpan, stir in the flour, and cook very slowly over a moderate fire, stirring all the while with a wooden spoon until it acquires a chestnut-brown color; or place the stewpan in the oven and let it cook, stirring from time to time to prevent it from burning, and to blend the flour better. Allow the roux to cool a little, pour in gradually the prepared stock, etc., stir over the fire until it boils, let simmer slowly for another hour, skim well, and pass through a tammy cloth or fine sieve. If found too thick, add a little more stock. To prevent a thick crust forming on the top of the sauce, stir occasionally until quite cool.

Allemande Sauce

1 1/2 oz. butter	1 oz. flour
2 yolks of eggs	1 tablespoonful of cream
1 teaspoonful lemon juice	chicken stock
nutmeg	salt, pepper

Melt the butter in a stewpan, add the flour, stir a few minutes without allowing it to brown, dilute with rather more than a pint of chicken stock, and stir until it boils. Season with pepper and salt and grated nutmeg. Let it simmer for half an hour, skim, and finish with liaison made of the yolks of eggs, the cream, and l/2 oz. of fresh butter. Stir over the fire until the eggs begin to set, but do not let it boil; add the lemon uice, and pass through fine strainer or tammy cloth.

Souffle au Vanille: see May 18.

January 19

Dinner for 36
Home of Alexandre Dumas, Paris, 1864

Alexandre Dumas (1802–1870) is best known as the author of the great adventure novels *The Count of Monte Cristo, The Three Musketeers,* and *The Man in the Iron Mask.* He was also a great gourmet and wanted to be remembered for his great passion—his *Grand Dictionnaire de Cuisine.* He died, however, while Paris was under siege during the Franco-Prussian War, and the book was not published until 1873. The dictionary is an astounding work. It is an encyclopaedia with recipes and anecdotes (and plenty of name-dropping), intended "to be read by worldly people and used by professionals." Many of the dinners that Dumas attended or held for friends were recorded in detail by himself and others, including one at his home, on January 19, 1864.

POTAGES
Printanier à la royale
Viennoise

HORS-D'ŒUVRE
Petites bouchées à la
Cancale Caisses à la marquise

RELEVÉS
Turbots à l'amirale
Selles de venaison à l'anglaise

ENTRÉES
Poulardes à la Rozolio
Filets de bécasses à la Favorite
Quenelles de rouget au velouté
Chauds-froids d'alouettes

EXTRA
Punch à l'ananas

RÔTS
Faisans truffés sauce Périgueux
Chapons rôtis au cresson

ENTREMETS
Salade suédoise
Asperges en branches
Petits soufflés aux mandarines
Gâteau Marie-Louise

DESSERT

The serving of meals in nineteenth-century France had great symmetry. There was always an even number of dishes in each course, with the correct proportions being maintained across courses. The individual dishes at this dinner are classics from the French repertoire. It can be assumed that the "Petites bouchées à la Cancale" contained oysters, the name being in honor of Le *Rocher de Cancale,* one of Dumas's favorite Paris restaurants, which was famous for them (see November 28).

Recipes
~~~

Asparagus was an enormously popular vegetable in Europe in the eighteenth and nineteenth centuries. Recipes for "Asperges en branches" only vary in the sauce and garnish, the stems always being simply and briefly blanched in boiling water.

Asperges à la Pompadour

Choose three bunches of the most beautiful asparagus from large young Dutch plants, that is to say white ones with purple tips. Trim them, wash and cook them in the ordinary way, that is to say by plunging them in boiling water. Slice them afterwards by cutting them on the bias near the tip, into pieces the length of the little finger. Use only the best parts, setting aside the rest of the stems. Put the chosen pieces in a hot napkin so as to drain them and keep them hot while you prepare your sauce.

Empty a medium-size pot of butter from Vanvre or Prévalais and put the contents in spoonfuls in a silver dish. Add a few grains of salt, a good pinch of powdered mace and a generous spoonful of pure wheat flour; and in addition the yolks of two fresh eggs diluted with four spoonfuls of the juice of sour Muscat grapes. Cook this sauce in a double boiler; do not allow it to thicken excessively and thus become too heavy. Put your sliced pieces of asparagus in the sauce, and serve it all in a covered casserole as an extra, so that this excellent course does not languish on the table and can be appreciated at the height of its perfection.

From his *Grand Dictionnaire de Cuisine* (1873), as translated by Alan and Jane Davidson in *Dumas on Food.*

Dumas's Salad Recipe

Dumas held regular Wednesday evening suppers at his Paris home, and, unusually for the time, took some part in the actual preparation himself. He was particularly proud of his salad, which, he wrote "was not just like any other salad," but was "a salad of great imagination." It comprised five principal ingredients: slices of beet, half-moons of celery, minced truffles, rampion [bellflower *Campanula rapunculus*] with its leaves, and boiled potatoes.

> First I put the ingredients into the salad bowl, then overturn them onto a platter. Into the empty bowl I put one hard boiled egg yolk for each two persons—six for a dozen guests. These I mash with oil to form a paste, to which I add chervil, crushed tuna, macerated anchovies, Maille mustard, a large spoonful of soya, chopped gherkins, and the chopped white of the eggs. I thin this mixture by stirring in the finest vinegar obtainable. Finally I put the salad back in the bowl, and my servant tosses it [he is ordered to do this several times during the hour before it is to be served.] On the tossed salad I sprinkle a pinch of paprika, which is the Hungarian red pepper.

Louis Colman, ed., trans., *The Dictionary of Cuisine* (Paris: A. Lemerre, 1873).

Potage Printanier: see February 28.
Chaud-froids: see July 25.

January 20

Luncheon in Honor of U.S. President Woodrow Wilson
Luxembourg Palace, Paris, France, 1919

For six months in 1919, the leaders of over 30 countries met in Paris to consider how the security and peace of Europe might be maintained in the aftermath of World War I. Never had so many national leaders been in the same place at the same time, and the most powerful were "the big four"—President Woodrow Wilson (1856–1924) of the United States, the Prime Minister of Britain, David Lloyd George (1863–1945), the Prime Minister of France, Georges Clemenceau (1841–1929), and the Prime Minister of Italy, Vittorio Orlando (1860–1952). It was to be "the six months that changed the world," and if the Peace Conference was not ultimately judged a success it was because the task was nigh on impossible. Nevertheless, the conference opened on January 18 in an air of great optimism.

It was the first time a serving American president had traveled to Europe, and Wilson was received with great enthusiasm by the French. Two days into the conference he was fêted at a luncheon given in his honor by the French Senate, in the Luxembourg Palace.

MENU

Hors d'oeuvre
Bar Glacé Vénitienne
Selle De Paulliac Moissonneuse
Dindonneau A La Broche
Fonds D'artichauts Au Velouté
Mazarine De Fruits Au Kirsch
Petits Fours Variés
Plateaux De Fruits
Café—Fromage

VINS
Graves & Médoc En Carafes
Volnay—Sauternes
Th. Roederer Frappé
Liqueurs

The luncheon for 300 guests included some of the most important political and military figures of the day. It was held in the throne room of the Bourbon Kings, the very room where Napoleon had banqueted his victorious generals. After the luncheon, coffee was served and conversation enjoyed in the magnificent Salon Victor Hugo. President Wilson's portrait graced the cover of the very elegant menu card. It was without doubt one of the finest functions of the conference.

Europe was exhausted and devastated, and already fearful of events taking place in Russia. Food shortages were severe, and many ordinary people were hungry. Did they begrudge their leaders meals such as this? It was an elegant meal—a classic sequence of chilled fish, meat, artichokes in a velouté sauce, and a fruit and liqueur filled cake, with the classic "bookends" that are among France's enduring culinary (and linguistic) legacies to the world—hors d'œuvre and petits fours. "Hors d'œuvre" literally means "outside the (main) work." The term is now used almost exclusively for small savory items served before the main dishes, but at one time at large banquets there

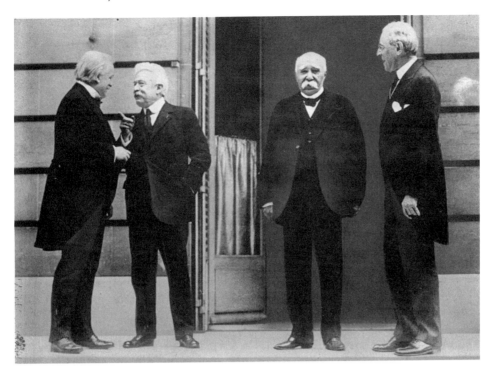

Lloyd George of Great Britain, Vittorio Orlando of Italy, Georges Clemenceau of France, and Woodrow Wilson. (AP Photo)

might be cold hors d'œuvre served at some point during the meal, and warm hors d'œuvre served at another.

Recipes

~~~

Many things go by the name of *mazarine*. The term originally meant a deep perforated platter that fit inside a serving dish, but it extended to refer to small tarts filled with sweetmeats and a variety of moulded sweet and savory dishes. Most dessert mazarines have a sponge cake base (a *Genoese*). The sponge may then be garnished with dried fruit and nuts, soaked in liqueur, reassembled and served warm. At banquets such as this it was more commonly scooped out, the hollow filled with chopped crystallized fruit, fruit puree, and a liqueur such as kirsch, and a disc of the cake was placed back to fill the base.

Genoese Cake

Beat the yolks of fourteen eggs for a good quarter of an hour, then stir in gradually a pound of loaf-sugar finely powdered and sifted and a dessert-spoonful of noyeau. Continue beating it for another fifteen minutes, and by degrees dredge in half a pound of very dry flour. Whisk the whites of the eggs to a snow and put them with the other ingredients. Butter the inside of your cake-mould, sift powdered sugar into it, shake out the loose sugar, put in your cake, strew sugar on the top, and bake it for an hour and a quarter in a moderately quick oven. Do not turn it out of the mould until half an hour after it has been taken from the oven.

Foreign Desserts for English Tables (1862).

Velouté Sauce: see January 18.
Petits Fours: see November 14.

January 21

Luncheon En Route from London to Bahrain during the Inaugural Flight of the Concorde, 1976

The world's first supersonic passenger air service was inaugurated at 11:30 A.M. on January 21, 1976 when the Concorde took off from London's Heathrow airport, bound for Bahrain. At a time when the average weekly wage for an Englishman was around 70, passengers aboard the Concorde had paid 45 more than the usual one-way first class fare for the excitement and privilege of flying at 1,350 mph and getting to their destination two hours earlier.

Concorde was planned to be "an ambassador abroad for good British design." The distinctive Concorde logo was on everything from the silver-plated cutlery to the fine-cut glass wine goblets, and everything was designed by British designers. The crew's polyester uniforms were created by the famous English fashion designer Hardy Amis in the corporate colors of blue and white, and the color theme was extended to the specially commissioned Royal Doulton bone china tableware.

Airline food has been the butt of jokes throughout its history, but Concorde passengers were presumably expecting something out of the ordinary to come out of the sophisticated galleys of the Concorde and onto those blue and white china plates.

Canapés

Smoked Salmon

Breast of Duck Bigarade
or
Fillet Steak, Café de Paris Butter

Strawberries with Double Cream

Cheese   Petits Fours

Coffee

Inaugural Concorde flight. (AP Photo)

For such a determinedly British ambassadorial flight, the caterers had clearly been unable to come up with English alternative words for *canapés* or *petits fours*. The *Oxford English Dictionary* describes a *canapé* as "a piece of bread or toast, etc., on which small savouries are served"—in other words they are a particular type of small hors d'œuvre (see January 20). There are in fact older English words for these little "appetizers"—at one time they were called "zests" or "whets" (because their function was to whet the appetite), although the words had not been in common use for a long time. *Petits fours* are essentially little cakes (see November 14), but there is no equivalent English phrase that gives quite the same impression of French elegance.

Recipes

~~~

The classic dish of duck bigarade has ancient roots. "Bigarade" refers to the bitter Seville orange, which was the only "orange" known in Europe until the sweet orange was introduced by the Portuguese (via their South-East Asian voyages) in the sixteenth century. Originally, therefore, the dish had a bitter citrus edge to it, a great contrast to the rich fatty duck flesh. By the mid-twentieth century, many if not most of the recipes for this dish used sweet oranges—some even suggesting marmalade and adding sugar, taking the dish to a cloyingly sweet realm far away from its original.

The following recipe from *The Times* of January 20, 1958, uses the sweet orange (which is much more easily available) but the Seville orange would give greater authenticity.

Duck with Sauce Bigarade

Parings of orange rind are inserted between the skin and flesh of a young duck which is stuffed with an orange cut into eight triangular pieces, a sprig of sage, a bay leaf, a finely chopped shalot, three or four cloves and the edible offal.

The duck is next put in a casserole along with the juice of an orange and a tablespoon of Marsala or Vermouth. Put the lid on the casserole and cook for about 10 minutes in a fierce oven. Remove from the oven, pour off and keep the liquid. Skim off any fat and baste the duck with a little of it, then return the bird to the oven, this time leaving it uncovered. After five minutes reduce the heat and then add some slices of orange. Total cooking time should be from 25 to 35 minutes according to the size of the duck and the degree of cooking liked.

Now put the duck and orange slices on a dish and keep hot. Remove any fat from the casserole and mix the remaining juice with the liquid saved from the first cooking. If necessary add a little more Marsala or Vermouth and heat over a fierce flame until the mixture is reduced to a thickish almost jelly-like sauce but taking care not to burn it. Serve duck and sauce separately, and with potatoes that have been finely sliced, piled into a dish, cooked gently in the oven with only a knob of butter and sprinkled with salt, and served in the dish in which they are cooked.

Petits fours: see November 14.

Airline Catering Timeline

September 13, 1919	A five-course lunch was served aboard Airship R33 during a 20-hour trip over Belgium and the Netherlands.
October 19, 1919	The first regular airline meals were served on a Handley-Page flight from London to Paris. They were prepacked lunch boxes containing sandwiches, fruit and chocolate, and cost passengers three shillings each.
May 1, 1927	Imperial Airways began its London-Paris "Silver Wing" service. A four-course luncheon was served during the two-and-a-half-hour flight.
May 21, 1927	Charles Lindberg was the first to fly solo across the Atlantic. The flight took 33 1/2 hours. He took five sandwiches and a quart of water, saying that it would be enough for him to get to Paris, and if he didn't get there, it would be enough anyway.
May 2, 1928	The new Croydon (London) Airport was opened. Food for Imperial Airways' "Silver Wing" service was sourced from local shops and markets in Croydon. The food was served on blue-and-white china on damask tablecloths.
1928	In the United States, Western Air Express stewards served sandwiches prepared by the Los Angeles restaurant *The Pig 'n Whistle* on the

	two-hour, fifty-minute flight between LA and San Francisco.
1933	Imperial Airways offered "Tea Flights" over London. Passengers took "tea" while they flew over the city and observed the sights.
1934	United Airlines hired a Cornell University food consultant Don Magarrell to develop the first airline flight kitchen in Oakland, California.
1936	American Airlines introduced airplane galleys in their DC-3. There was no electrical power available for heating (or chilling) foods or beverages; heat was maintained in insulated thermos-type containers. Canned food was carried for emergencies. Later, the Boeing 314 had a food-heating capability via a system which used glycol, heated by the plane's engines and circulated through pipes.
1954	The first frozen TV dinners went on sale in the United States. They had been inspired by airline food trays.
1957	TWA was the first airline to provide freshly brewed coffee in-flight.
June 30, 1971	The British entrepreneur Freddie Laker introduced his low-cost airline. He had reduced costs by cutting out some airline services, such as meals. If passengers wanted meals, they were charged extra.
1999	Delta Air Lines reduced its food service: sandwiches in its SkyDeli bags were replaced with crackers and cheese or carrots and dip, and in first class, snacks were replaced with beverages.
November 23, 1999	Captain Floyd Dean of Northwest Airlines left his cabin before takeoff on a flight from Las Vegas to Detroit, to go and get something acceptable to eat. There being nothing to his liking at the airport, he got a cab downtown and returned ninety minutes later. Passengers and his employers were not amused, and he was fired.

January 22

Dinner for Six Gentlemen
Revere House, Bowdoin Square, Boston, Massachusetts, 1848

The identities of the six gentlemen entertained at this dinner at this historic venue remain a mystery. To judge from the very beautiful and heavily gold-

embossed menu card, it was an exclusive, privately catered affair. Even without the benefit of seeing the menu card itself, it is clear from the list of dishes
served that it was a fine and expensive dinner served in the most elegant way.

The food is as elaborate as the menu card. There is a preponderance of
complex, time-consuming, labor-intensive dishes rarely cooked anywhere
else than in a professional kitchen—and a nineteenth-century professional
kitchen at that. The *chartreuse* (see November 9), for example, is a complicated, highly artistic moulded dish almost never cooked nowadays. The
omelette souffle seems like a simple dish, but the skill here is in the exact timing—it must be served immediately when it comes out of the oven as it begins
to collapse immediately. Other dishes at this dinner are boned, larded, or
jellied—techniques also requiring a great deal of skill.

Making "jelly" at this time was not a simple matter of emptying a pack of
powdered gelatin into the desired liquid and refrigerating it. It was a prolonged process beginning with boiling a pot full of calves' feet, and repeatedly
skimming, straining, concentrating, and clarifying the liquor (see July 5).
Eventually the collagen in the feet broke down to "gelatin," and the (now
clear) liquid would set on cooling and could then be flavored and used as
desired. "Larding" is also rarely carried out these days. The term means to
thread (with a special "larding needle") thin strips of bacon or other fat
through the flesh of the meat or fish to enrich and tenderize it.

BILL OF FARE

Oysters in Shell.

SOUP.

A la reine.

FISH

Baked Pickerel, Larded.

BOILED.

Capon, Celery Sauce.

COLD DISHES.

Boned Quail on a Form.

Pattie of Turkey Liver in Jelly.

Lobster Salad in Border of Jelly.

Boned Canvasback Duck sur socle.

SIDE DISHES.

Sweetbreads in cases, with

Green Peas.

Chartreuse of Partridge.

ROAST.

Filet of Beef, Larded.

GAME.

Grouse.

Red-head Duck.

Teal.

Canvas-back Ducks.

PASTRY.

Ornament of Cake.

Omelette Souffle.

Charlotte Russe.

Blanc Manger.

Calf's Feet Jelly.

DESSERT.

Roman Punch, Ice Cream, Fruit.

COFFEE AND LIQUEURS.

The presentation of the dishes, too, is professional to the highest degree. Several are served "on a form" or "in cases" or "sur socle." A *socle* is a wooden block or plinth, so to serve "sur socle" is an upmarket way of "planking" a dish.

Recipes

~~~

Fillet of Beef, Larded and Marinaded

Take the inside fillet of a sirloin of beef, pare off the sinews, and lard it with fat bacon; prepare a pickle with shalots, onions, carrots cut in slices, a little parsley, pepper, salt, vinegar, and sweet oil; let the beef remain in this marinade for twenty-four hours, occasionally basting it; then the fillet is to be braised the way you do a rump of beef; but it is to be observed that the braise is not to cover the larded part: when it is quite done serve with a ravigotte sauce.

To braise a rump of beef . . . place it in a large braising kettle, with any trimmings of meat you may have, half a dozen onions, celery, leeks, carrots, a bunch of sweet herbs, a little mace, cloves, and half an ounce of whole pepper; add broth sufficient, close the braising kettle, and when it boils, remove it to a small slow fire, and also put lighted charcoal on the top; try the beef in about four hours' time; it should braise very slowly, and must be perfectly tender: when done, take it out, carefully trim it and cut away the string, glaze it, and put it in the screen to dry, and before the beef is dished, glaze it again.

I. Roberts, *The Young Cook's Guide: With Practical Observations* (America 1841).

Omelette Soufflé

Mix the yolks of six eggs with four ounces of powdered sugar, and a spoonful of orange flower water. Whip, to a solid froth, the whites of eight or nine eggs, which mix with the yolks. Melt some butter in a spider [a long-handled,

three-legged frying pan], turn in the above mixture, and when it begins to turn yellow, put it on a dish kept hot, and place it in the oven. These *entremets* must be eaten as soon as cooked, as they soon fall.
    American Matron (1851).

Charlotte Russe: see September 4.
Blanc Manger: see January 7.
Punch à la Romaine (Roman Punch): see July 1.

January 23

Dinner of Exotic Animals
Hamburg, Germany, 1862

On January 23, 1862, the administrators of the Zoological Society of Hamburg sat down to a most unusual bill of fare, the likes of which would be impossible to repeat in modern times, for all sorts of reasons.

Donne en l'honneur di Conseil d'Administration
de la
Société zoologique
de HAMBOURG
par son Président
le 23. Janvier 1862

DEUX POTAGES.
Consommé de Boa Constrictor.   Purée de pommes au Beurre de Cocos.

DEUX HORS-D'OUVRES.
Buisson de sauterelles garni de hannetons.   Rognures de griffes de Lion au
naturel.

POISSON.
Requin au bleu garni de jeunes.   Alligators frits.

DEUX RELEVÉS.
Croupion de shameau garni de tetes de singe.   Filet de Rhinoceros à la
Leopard.

HUIT ENTRÉES.
Yeux de Gazelles en bellevue.
Herisson sur socle.
Timbale garni d'entrailles de tigre.
Pieds d'Elephants en papillote.
Rognons d'Hippopotame garni de feuilles de Lotus.
Gallantine de pattes d'ours a la siberienne.
Terrine de fore de cachalot.
Serpents a sonnette gratine de millepieds.

PONCHE DE LARMES DE CROCODILE GLACE

QUATRE RÔTS
Autruche garni de parroquets.
Quartier de Giraffe.
Colibris sur broche.

Roche forme d'enorme lezard,
de six marsouins et de quarante
queue de rats a la moelle de lion.

QUATRE ENTREMENTS
Pommes de pin a la *Renne*.
Salade de sensitive de huile de Castor.
Croquettes de fil de fer.
Toile d'araignee en beignets.

POUR EXTRA GORELLA EMPAILLE.
Lait d'Hyene au musc.

PÂTISSERIE.
Croquembouche de Coquilles de nacre et nois de Cocos.

DESSERT.

A menu such as this strikes horror into some modern hearts. Even if they could bring themselves to eat the animals entrusted to their care, zoologists and zoo curators would be forbidden to do so by local food safety laws as well as international conservation regulations. The nineteenth century was a time of great scientific interest, and acclimatisation societies were founded in many countries, their brief being to expand the understanding of the flora and fauna of other countries, and to experiment with producing them elsewhere. It was not rare for them to stage dinners in which some of this exotica was eaten—ostensibly to provoke interest, but it is hard to avoid the feeling that a lot of it was for its shock or exotica value.

The ethical dilemmas aside, there is a deep and abiding curiosity about eating such exotica. The first author to explore this topic was Peter Lund , in *The Curiosities of Food, or the Dainties and Delicacies of Different Nations Obtained from the Animal Kingdom,* first published in 1859. He acknowledged that "Amid all the multiplicity of special dainties, appreciated by different peoples, the prejudices of the stomach are, perhaps, more unconquerable than any other that tyranize over the human mind."

What do these strange meats actually taste like? As with the menu for February 15, to get some idea of the taste of these, the accounts of hunters, explorers, frontiersmen, and eccentrically adventurous eaters such as the English zoologist Frank Buckland (1826–1880) must be relied on. Buckland was infamous for his willingness to eat anything and everything that he could get his hands on, to the consternation sometimes of his guests. One day a boa constrictor that had been killed in an accident came into his possession and he said he "cooked a bit of him; it tasted very [much] like veal, the flesh being exceedingly white and firm. If I had nothing else and could have forgotten what I was eating, I could easily have made a dinner of it." His comments on horsemeat are also insightful (see December 19).

   quoted other authorities on various other items that appear in this menu. The flesh of a particular type of lizard "when cooked, is white, and by those whose stomachs rise above all prejudices is relished as very good" and "the flesh of the giraffe is said to be good eating. The Hottentots hunt the animal principally on account of its marrow, which, as a delicacy, they set high value on." The famous David Livingstone, who was often starving during his exploration of Africa, described his first taste of hippopotamus: "It is a coarse-grained meat, something between pork and beef—pretty good food when one is hungry and can get nothing better."

Recipes

~~~

Recipes for the dishes in this menu do not appear in conventional cookbooks. Travelers' tales often do tell how the "natives" prepare a dish, however. Gordon Cumming, the authority quoted by , wrote an account of his adventures in *Five Years of a Hunter's Life in the Far Interior of South Africa*, in 1851, and included this explanation of "the whole art and mystery" of the preparation and cooking of elephants' feet.

Baked Elephants' Paws

" ... A party, provided with sharp-pointed sticks, dig a hole in the ground for each foot and a portion of the trunk ... the excavated earth is banked around the margin of the holes ... they next collect an immense quantity of dry branches and trunks of trees, ... These they pile above the holes to the height of eight or nine feet, then set fire to the heap .... When these strong fires have burnt down ... take out the ashes with a pole about sixteen feet in length .... When all the ashes are thus raked out beyond the surrounding bank of earth, each elephant's foot and portion of the trunk is lifted by two athletic men, standing side by side, who place it on their shoulders, and, approaching the pit together, they heave it into it. ... shove in the heated bank of earth upon the foot, shoving and raking until it is completely covered with earth. The hot embers, of which there is always a great supply, are then raked to a heap above the foot and another bonfire is kindled over each and allowed to burn down and die a natural death; by which time the enormous food or trunk will be equally baked throughout its innermost parts. When the foot is supposed to be ready, it is taken out of the ground with pointed sticks, and is first well beaten, and then scraped with an assegai, whereby adhering particles of sand are got rid of. The outside is then pared off and is transfixed with a sharp stick for facility of carriage. The feet thus cooked are excellent, as is also the tongue, which very much resembles buffalo's tongue."

January 24

Gourmet Society Eat ''Eskimo Fare''
Cavanagh's, New York, 1937

The Gourmet Society "went Arctic" at their dinner on 258 West Twenty-Third Street in New York City on this night, the theme being mostly in evidence on account of the guest speakers rather than the menu. As *The New York Times* pointed out, the society members merely "trifled with Eskimo fare" by only going so far as to include reindeer loin in the dinner, with "blubber and vintage fish" appearing only in the speeches.

Lynnhaven Bay Oyster Cocktail
Hearts of Celery   Queen Olives
Bisque of Soft Clams
Broiled Loin of Alaska Reindeer
Currant Jelly   Fresh Mushrooms
New String Beans, Julienne
Candied Sweet Potatoes
Green Vegetable Salad
Cavanagh Dressing
Apple Pudding
Hard and Brandy Sauce
Café, Demi-Tasse
(Two Wines)

At the conclusion of the dinner, "amid wreaths of smoke," the epicures settled in to enjoy the program for the evening. The supposed Arctic theme notwithstanding, the president of the society, J. George Frederick, considered the meal an illustration of the superiority of American over French cooking traditions. The French, he said, have a philosophy of regarding food as "a plastic raw material from which to create new things. It is a standard of artificiality and recreation," but "through repasts like the one just finished, this country might rid itself of the American inferiority complex on cookery."

A lighter note was introduced by the poet and humorist Gelett Burgess (1866–1951) who declaimed ("by heart . . . with lapses") his poem *An Epic of Arctic Grub,* making it into an interactive exercise by enjoining the audience to fill in the missing words at the end of each stanza. The real star of the evening, however, was the famous polar explorer and ethnologist Vilhjalmur Stefansson (1879–1962) who seized the opportunity to discuss his favorite theme—the all-meat diet. No doubt the guests at the dinner were relieved that seal blubber was not on the menu in spite of Stefansson's enthusiasm for this "most delectable" form of raw fat. He likened it when fresh to "cow's cream with a very light grating of walnut on it" but admitted that the fermented "decayed" variety was an acquired taste, as was that for ripe cheese and well-hung grouse.

Stefansson had lived with the Inuit of the Canadian archipelago for prolonged periods of time and was very interested in their diet. In his record of
his experiences he described one meal which was in stark contrast to the
Gourmet Society event.

> My host was the seal-hunter whom we had first approached on the ice .... Our
> meal was of two courses: the first, meat (*seal meat*); the second, soup. The soup
> is made by pouring cold seal blood into the boiling broth immediately after the
> cooked meat has been taken out of the pot, and stirring briskly until the whole
> comes nearly (but never quite) to a boil. This makes a soup of thickness compa-
> rable to our English pea-soups, but if the pot be allowed to come to a boil, the
> blood will coagulate and settle to the bottom.

Stefansson became convinced that this virtually all-meat, essentially no-
carbohydrate diet conferred great health benefits, and to prove his he point
later took part in an experiment in which he and a colleague lived entirely
on meat for twelve months and were declared perfectly healthy at its conclusion. Medical opinion remained divided on the benefits of the diet—with one
expert pointing out that it was actually a high fat diet, with no more lean protein than an ordinary diet, making, he said, Stefansson's experiment of no
great significance.

Recipes

~~~

Oyster Cocktail

One dessertspoonful tomato sauce, one shake of tabasco, a sprinkle of horse radish, about half a dozen oysters, and the same on top. Serve in small tumblers on
a plate with pounded ice around them and with oyster biscuits.
  My Pet Recipes, Tried and True, Contributed by the Ladies and Friends of St.
Andrew's Church (Quebec, 1900).

Venison Steak

Take a steak about one inch thick. Heat 2 oz. butter in the chafing-dish, sprinkle
the steak with pepper and salt; cook about five minutes on each side, then add 1
wineglass port wine, 1/2 teaspoon extract of meat, and 1 teaspoon currant jelly.
Cook ten minutes and serve.
  Amy Richards, *Cookery* (Montréal, 1895).

Arctic Food

"The outside fat of your walrus sustains your little moss fire: its frozen slices
give you bread, its frozen blubber gives you butter, its scrag ends make the
soup."
  Elisha Kent Kane, *The Second Grinnel Expedition in Search of Sir John
Franklin* (Philadelphia, 1856).

"Many times . . . during my twenty-three years of Arctic exploration, I have thanked God for even a bite of raw dog."
Robert Edwin Peary (1856–1920), polar explorer.

"Speaking of native customs I may mention, that having within the last few days killed some ptarmigan, and having no means of cooking them, we followed the Indian practice of freezing them and eating them raw. I can assure those who have not tried the experiment that, though not equal to " perdrix rote," a frozen ptarmigan, after a hard day's march, is by no means an unwelcome addition to an Arctic traveller's bill of fare."
William Kennedy, *A Short Narrative of the Second Voyage of the Prince Albert, in Search of Sir John Franklin* (London, 1853).

Bisque of Soft Clams: see May 22.
Candied Sweet Potato: see February 1.
Currant Jelly: January 5.

January 25

Burns Night Supper
Sutherland's, New York, 1882

Robert Burns (1759–1796), the much-loved national poet of Scotland, has almost a cult following. All around the world there are clubs in his honor, made up of members who have Scots heritage, or wish they had. The most important function of these clubs is to hold an annual celebration on the annivesary of their hero's birth. Most clubs attempt a thoroughly Scottish menu on the night, as did the New York branch in 1882.

BILL OF FARE.

OYSTERS.

SOUP.
Cock-a-Leeekie.   Scotch Hare.
FISH.
Boiled cod's head and shouthers, Meg Dodd's style.
Fried smelts.

ENTREES.
Curried Rabbit.
Stewed Ox Tails, à la St.Ronan's Well.

JOINTS.
Roast.   Boiled.
Beef.   Gigot o'Mutton.
Saddle of Scotch Mutton.   Round of Beef, with Kail.
Singed Sheep's Head and Trotters.
Haggis.   Black and White Puddings

GAME.

Scotch Pheasants.   Bread Sauce.   Canvas-back Ducks.

PASTRY.

Plum Pudding.   Apple Pie.
Mince Pie.   Short Cake.

VEGETABLES.

Boiled Taties.
Baked Taties.
Neeps.
Rumble-ty-Thump.
Scotch Kail.
Carrots.
Oat Cake.   Cheese.
Celery.   Coffee.

DRY MONOPOLE CHAMPAGNE

There is another Scottish literary theme running through this particular menu. Sir Walter Scott (1771–1832) was a contemporary of Burns and was an enormously popular novelist. His novel *St. Ronan's Well* is referenced in this menu, as is one of its characters, Meg Dodds, the landlady of the Cleikum Inn. In 1826 a book called *The Cook and Housewife's Manual* attributed "Mrs. Margaret Dods" of the Cleikum Inn, St. Ronan's, was published in Edinburgh. So successful was it that it was commonly believed that she was a real person, and the inn a real inn. It was eventually shown to have been written by a novelist—Christian Isobel Johnstone (1781–1857)—and is a wonderfully witty work as well as being a marvelous source of nineteenth-century Scottish recipes (see haggis, below).

Important as the bill of fare might be, the focus (and fun) of the evening revolved around a time-honored program of speeches and toasts, the highlight of which is "piping in the haggis."

The program of the evening was as follows:
1. The welcome by the Chairman.
2. All present recite Burns's *Selkirk Grace*.

Some hae meat and cannae eat,
　　And some wad eat that want it.
　　But we hae meat and we can eat
　　And so the Lord be thankit

3. At the appropriate point in the meal, the company all stand, and perform a slow handclap during the piping in of the haggis. The procession consists of the piper, the chef bearing the haggis on a silver platter, the whiskey bearer, and the honored guest who will address the haggis.
4. The honored guest recites Burns's ode *To a Haggis* (which must be done with great gusto and feeling), and at the line "His knife see Rustic-labour

dight, An cut you up wi ready slight" he plunges his own knife into the haggis, spilling out its "gushing entrails."

Cod's head.

5. At the final line "Gie her a Haggis!" ("her" being Scotland), the company applaud, raise their whiskey glasses, and make a toast "To the Haggis."

6. After the meal, a short speech on some aspect of Burns's life is given by another specially chosen guest.

7. Various other toasts follow, including the *Toast to the Lasses* (women not being present early in the history of Burns suppers).

8. The evening ends with the traditional rendering by the company of "Auld Lang Syne."

Recipes

~~~

The Scotch Haggis

Clean a sheep's pluck thoroughly. Make incisions in the heart and liver to allow the blood to flow out, and parboil the whole, letting the wind-pipe lie over the side of the pot to permit the phlegm and blood to disgorge from the lungs; the water maybe changed after a few minutes' boiling for fresh water. A half-hour's boiling will be sufficient; but throw back the half of the liver to boil till it will grate easily; take the heart, the half of the liver, and part of the lights, trimming away all skins and black-looking parts, and mince them together. Mince also a pound of good beef-suet and four onions. Grate the other half of the liver. Have a dozen of small onions peeled and scalded in two waters to mix with this mince. Toast some oatmeal before the fire for hours, till it is of a light-brown colour and perfectly dry. Less than two tea-cupfuls of meal will do for this quantity of meat. Spread the mince on a board, and strew the meal lightly over it, with a high seasoning of pepper, salt, and a little cayenne, well mixed. Have a haggis-bag perfectly clean, and see that there be no thin part in it, else your whole labour will be lost by its bursting. Some cooks use two bags. Put in the meat with a half-pint of good beef-gravy, or as much strong broth, as will make it a thick stew. Be careful not to fill the bag too full, but allow the meat room to swell; add the juice of a lemon, or a little good vinegar; press out the air, and sew up the bag; prick it with a large needle when it first swells in the pot, to prevent bursting; let it boil slowly for three hours if large.

January 26

Centennial Banquet
Sydney, Australia, Town Hall, 1888

The anniversary of the first century of white settlement was celebrated around Australia in January 1888. The dumping ground for British convicts had by now become "a free and prosperous nation" of four million people and was on the brink of federation. A public holiday was declared in all capital cities except Adelaide—the colony of South Australia refusing to participate in the centenary celebrations on the grounds that it was built on free settlement and had no wish or need to be associated with the country's convict past.

The most spectacular celebrations took place in Sydney, and many of the rural folk of New South Wales were able to take advantage of the specially reduced train fares to enjoy the festivities. A statue of Queen Victoria was unveiled, several foundation stones laid, gifts of food were given to the poor, there were free band concerts, parades, fireworks, and a piece of former swampland was renamed Centennial Park and formally handed over for the permanent enjoyment of the people of Sydney. In the evening, for the politicians and civic leaders, there was, of course, "the inevitable banquet."

POTAGE.
Tortue.

POISSONS.
Saumon à la Royale.
Filet de Sole, Crème des Anchoies.   Schnapper à la Maréchal.

ENTREES.
Les Pâtes à la Reine.
Salmi des Perdrix.
Chaud Froid de Volaille.

RELEVES.
Dinde Rôti à la Perigord.   Dinde Boulli, Sauce aux Champignons.
Jambon de Yorc.   Langues de Bœuf.
Selle d'Agneau.   Haut de Bœuf.
Bœuf en Preserve.

GIBIER.
Faisans, Sauce au Pain.
Pâte de Foie Gras en Aspic.
Salade à la Russe.
Mayonnaise des Crevettes.

ENTREMETS.
Gelée à l'Australienne.
Gelée des Oranges.   Gelée au Ponche.
Charlotte aux Fraises.
Pouding à la Princesse.   Pouding aux Amandes.
Crème à la Vanille.   Crème au Fleur des Oranges.
Crème au Chocolat.
Nougat au Crème.
Fanchettes.
Bouchées des Dames.   Tartelettes au Crème.

Pouding Glacé à la Nesselrode.
Eau Glacé aux Oranges.

DESSERT.
Café.

WINES.
Sherry, Hock, Chablis, Australian Wine.
Champagnes: Ruinart, Irroy, Pommery and Greno.
Clarets: Mouton de Rothschild, Latour.
Port.
Liqueurs: Curacoa, Maraschino, Old Brandy.

The move toward Federation was already underway, but for most in Australia at this time—even for those born in the colony—England was "home." Loyalty was to the Empire, and the culture was resolutely British. There was nothing intrinsically "Australian" about this menu, apart from the small concession of the *Gelée à l'Australienne* and a few unspecified Australian wines. As it would have been at a comparable banquet in England, the menu was in French and the dishes were based in classic French cuisine.

The first Australian cookbook had been written in 1864, by a Tasmanian politician called Edward Abbott. It was called *The English and Australian Cookery Book: Cooking for the Many as Well as the Upper Ten Thousand,* and it was a resounding failure, never having a second printing. It was far too eccentric with its strange blend of English recipes and aggressively Australian ideas such as "Slippery Bob"—a delightful sounding dish of kangaroo brains. Most Australian settlers remained faithful to the cookbooks they had brought from "home," such as Mrs. Beeton's *Household Manual,* and the other Victorian classic *Warne's Everyday Cookery.*

Recipes

~~~

There was no major Australian cookbook after Abbott's until *The Art of Living in Australia* by Philip Muskett in 1893. As its title suggests, it was primarily a treatise on life in the colony, but it had an appendix "with three hundred Australian cookery recipes and accessory kitchen information by Mrs. H. Wicken, Lecturer on cookery to the Technical College, Sydney."

Fish A La Crème

4 Whiting or Schnapper.
1 gill Milk.
1 oz. Butter.
1/2 oz. Flour, and Lemon Juice.
Pepper and Salt.

Fillet the fish, wash the bones, and put them into half a pint of white stock, and boil them for half an hour. Strain out and mix with 1 gill of milk. Wash the fillets and roll them up, stand them in a stewpan and cook them in this liquor, covering them with a piece of buttered paper; they will take about 20 minutes.

Dish them carefully, strain the liquor, and make a sauce of it with the butter and flour by directions given. Season and flavour this and pour it over the fillets; garnish with chopped parsley and red bread crumbs, and serve hot.

Crevettes are freshwater crayfish, unless they are on a genuine French menu, in which case they are shrimps. Here is a recipe that will substitute for the *Mayonnaise des Crevettes* on this menu.

Prawn Salad

1 pint Prawns
6 Tomatoes
Mayonnaise or Salad Dressing.

Pick the prawns, leaving the skin on a few fine ones for a garnish. Peel and slice up the tomatoes and arrange them on a dish; put over them the prawns, and pour over all some mayonnaise or salad dressing. Place the other prawns round as a garnish with a few lettuce leaves broken up.

Turtle Soup: see November 10.

January 27

Diet Squad Experiment
New York, 1917

In January 1917, twelve police rookies from the New York Police Department took part in a widely publicized diet experiment. There was increasing protest about the dramatic rise in the price of staple foods due to the progress of World War I, and the experiment was designed to demonstrate to the ordinary housewife that good wholesome food could be prepared very cheaply. The Hygiene Life Extension Institute was to oversee the experiment, and for its duration the rookies lived at quarters prepared for them in Lafayette Street. They were under the supervision of Miss Mary S. Rose of the Teachers College at Columbia University, with Miss Eula McClary in charge of budgeting for provisions, and the meals were cooked by Hannibal V. Parsons, "the $1,800-a-year colored chef." With one day remaining, the volunteers' bill of fare for January 27 was as follows:

BREAKFAST.
Oatmeal and milk.
Rolls and butter.
Coffee, with milk.
Cost, 7 cents; 870 calories.

LUNCHEON.
Fried mush and syrup.
White bread and butter.
Steamed apricots.
Tea, with milk.
Cost, 7 cents; 1,100 calories.

DINNER.
Baked beans, with salt pork.
Whole wheat bread and butter.
Molasses cakes.
Tea, with milk.
Cost, 11 cents; 1,150 calories.

The experiment had been inspired by one a few months earlier in Chicago. It had been run by the Health Commissioner John Dill Robertson, the volunteers being six men and six women from his department, who lived for two weeks on a diet that cost 40 cents a day each, their health being monitored closely throughout the time. Volunteers were directed to eat slowly because "the faster you eat, the more you eat," and although in-between meal snacks were forbidden, an unlimited quantity was allowed at meals. Not surprisingly, the volunteers gained weight (an average of 3.8 pounds each), which was seen as part of the proof positive that the experiment was a success. To reduce the cost further, towards the end of the time "butterine" was substituted for the real butter, and the final cost came out at a very satisfying 30 cents per person per day.

Diet squad at table. Courtesy of Library of Congress.

The New York Police experiment was designed to do even better. The twelve rookies would stay on the diet for three weeks at an estimated cost of only 25 cents a day each. Additionally, half would receive meat twice a day, the other half only once a day. There was great interest in the experiment, with many organizations, schools, and hospitals as well as individuals requesting menus and recipes. The day after the experiment finished, Miss McClary headed for the White House to leave information for the First Lady, who had expressed an interest in making use of the menus.

Recipes

~~~

</div>

<div align="center">

Fried Mush

</div>

Place in a saucepan
Two cups of boiling water,
One teaspoon of salt,
Two-thirds cup of cornmeal.

Stir to prevent lumping then cook slowly for one half-hour. Now rinse a bread pan with cold water and turn in the mush. Let mould for twenty-four hours, then cut in one-half inch slices. Dip in flour and fry brown in hot fat.
   Mrs. Mary Elizabeth Lyles Wilson, *Mrs. Wilson's Cook Book* (1920).

<div align="center">

Molasses Cakes

</div>

1 cup molasses	1 teaspoon salt
1/2 cup sugar	1/2 teaspoon soda
1/2 cup melted shortening	2 teaspoons cinnamon
1/2 cup boiling water	1 teaspoon nutmeg
3 cups flour	1 teaspoon cloves
3 teaspoons Dr. Price's Baking Powder	1 cup stale breadcrumbs

Mix molasses, sugar, shortening and boiling water together; add flour, baking powder, salt, soda, and spices which have been sifted together; add breadcrumbs; mix well. Drop by spoonfuls on greased baking sheet and bake in moderate oven 10 to 20 minutes.
   Dr. Price, *The New Dr. Price Cook Book* (1921).

Baked Beans: see June 11.

<div align="center">

January 28

Peter the Great Dines at The King's Arms
Godalming, Surrey, England, 1698

</div>

The Tsar of Russia, Peter I (1672–1725), called "Peter the Great," embarked on a great European tour in 1697–98 to study technological developments, particularly in his great area of interest—shipbuilding. He spent four months in England, and on the return trip to London after visiting the docks at Portsmouth, he and his party stopped for the night of January 28 at a coaching inn in Godalming in Surrey.

There were 13 at the table for dinner that night, plus 8 servants who also had to be fed. Following is the bill of fare for dinner:

---

5 ribs of beef (weighing three stone)
1 sheep of 56 lbs
3/4 of a lamb
A shoulder roasted and a loin of veal boiled with bacon
8 pullets
4 couple of rabbits
3 dozen (bottles) of sack
1 dozen (bottles) of claret
bread and beer proportionable

For breakfast the next morning the company sat down to

1/2 sheep
1/4 of a lamb (19 pounds)
10 pullets
1 dozen of chickens
3 quarts of brandy
6 quarts of mulled wine
7 dozen eggs
salad in proportion

It is likely that the landlord had only very brief advance warning of his special guests, and likely that he feared immediately for the financial implications of their stay. In the tradition of Royal Progresses (royal tours around the country) of the time (see April 18) royal visitors usually assumed that the honor alone would be sufficient reward. True to form, the landlord was never paid for his hospitality. According to contemporary accounts of the visit, the party was very boisterous and significant damage was done to the premises.

Recipes

~~~

The mulled wine must have been welcome on a cold January night. It is a hot spiced wine drink, which in those times was often thickened with eggs and called a *posset* (see January 13).

The salad (or "sallat") that appears on seventeenth century menus such as this one was not necessarily a dish made from raw vegetables, served cold. The prevailing medical view of the time was that raw fruit and vegetables were potentially dangerous. This was often the case, as the water used to irrigate and wash them was likely to be polluted. "Salads" referred to any predominantly vegetable dish, including the cooked, as in these seventeenth-century examples taken from a famous cookbook of the time, *The Whole Body of Cookery Dissected,* by William Rabisha (London, 1682.)

A Sallet of Fennel

Take young Fennel, about a span long in the Spring, tye it up in bunches as you do Sparragrass; when your skillet boils, put in enough to make a dish; when it is boiled and drained, dish it up as you do Sparragras, pour on Butter and Vinegar, and send it up.

A Sallet of Green Pease

When your green Pease appear, about a handful and a half from the ground, cut off enough to boil for your Sallet, let your liquor boil before you put it in; when it is tender, pour it forth into your Cullender, let all the water be drained clean out of it into a dish, with some drawn butter; season it with salt, and hack it with your knife, and toss it together in the Butter, so dish it up. Thus you may do with Turnip or Raddish-tops, that are young.

January 29

Last Meal of the Crown Prince of Austria
Royal Hunting Lodge, Mayerling, Austria, 1889

The valet for Crown Prince Rudolph of Austria (1858–1889), Joseph Loschek, prepared a humble dinner for the prince and his mistress the Baroness Mary Vetsera (1871–1889) on the night of January 29, 1889. The simple meal was accompanied by two bottles of Tokay. The prince and his paramour then retired for the night, with the valet being instructed to allow no one into the room, "not even the Emperor."

Pheasant
Mushrooms   Leeks
Baked Potatoes

The next morning, the prince and the baroness were both dead. The exact circumstances have fuelled speculation ever since and the truth will probably never be teased out from the spectacular cover-up efforts that were immediately set in place. The official story was that the prince had died of "apoplexy of the heart," which was a masterpiece of spin-doctoring as most reports state clearly that he had a bullet wound to the head. Mary, who was officially never there, may have been poisoned, or beaten to death, or shot. The prince may have been depressed. The baroness may have been pregnant. The body buried in her grave may not actually be hers. It was a murder-suicide (the most popular view), or a double suicide, or a double murder.

There is an endless fascination with the idea of choice of one's last meal, and the topic is good fuel for dinner party conversation. Those most commonly associated with the idea (and the practice) in real life are the inhabitants of Death Row, who are more likely to come from the ranks of those who have had little choice in material matters during their lives. It is unlikely that someone such as a royal prince, accustomed to fine food all his life, would have felt it necessary to make any special meal requests for his last night. The supper was a modest meal, and the pheasant no doubt from the Vienna Woods themselves.

Recipes

~~~

The mushrooms are a small mystery. Mushroom season in Austria is between April and November, and by January the snow is usually thick in the woods. Royal families can afford the best horticultural methods, however, so the mushrooms at this dinner may have been grown in a dark, insulated cellar, or they may have been preserved by bottling or drying.

Mushrooms, Pickled

Take button mushrooms, as nearly as possible of the same size (small ones are best) and freshly gathered. Cut off the stalks, and rub away the outer skin with a piece of new flannel and some fine salt. Rinse them in salted spring water, drain quickly, and dry in a soft cloth until no water hangs about them. Boil together spice and vinegar in proportion to the mushrooms to be pickled, allowing nearly a quart of vinegar to a quart of the buttons, and with one quart of the best white wine vinegar put three small blades of mace, an ounce of crushed ginger, half the quantity of white peppercorns, and a small pinch of cayenne. When the pickle boils, put in the mushrooms, and continue the boiling until they are rather soft, which will be in from eight to ten minutes, according to their size. Fill jars, or large-mouthed bottles, and distribute the spice as evenly as possible in them. When cold, tie down securely with bladder, and remove to a dry place. Field mushrooms are much to be preferred to those artificially raised.

Cassell's Dictionary of Cookery (ca. 1870s).

Stewed Pheasant

Truss the pheasant for boiling, lard it with fine strips of bacon, sprinkle with salt, pepper, and mixed spice; be careful to lard even the legs, cover with slices of bacon, and place in a stew-pan lined with bacon; moisten with equal quantities of white wine, and stock, and simmer for two hours; when done, drain the pheasants, remove the slices of bacon, and dish up covered with game sauce.

366 Menus and 1200 Recipes of the Baron Brisse (1869; from the 1905 English translation).

January 30

Calves Head Club Annual Feast
London, England, 1710

A correspondent to *The Gentleman's Magazine* of 1820 contributed a "curious original Document" for the interest of its readers. He felt compelled to vouch for the authenticity of the document (a bill of fare for a feast) by noting that it appeared on the fly-leaf of a book previously owned by the Honorable Archibald Campbell (the bishop of Aberdeen), who followed it with the following handwritten declaration:

> That a sett of men were wicked enough to meet and feast according to the Bill of Fare in the year of our Lord 1710. And that this was truly the Bill of their eatables, besides drink, was attested to me by one of honour and reputation, and in a considerable publick post, who had the bill at first hand.
>
> This I do attest,
>
> A. Campbell, London, 1711.

This was a feast held at the Calves Head Club, a club whose origins, founder members, and club rituals were, even at the time, shrouded in secrecy and notoriety—such secrecy that its very existence as an actual club is debated.

A True Bill of Bare for the Calves Head Feast, 1710.

	£	s.	d.
For Bread, Beer, and Ale	3	10	0
For fifty Calves Heads	5	05	0
For Bacon	1	10	0
For 6 Chickens and 2 Capons	1	00	0
For Three Joints of Veal	0	18	0
For Butter and Flower	0	15	0
For Oranges, Lemons, Vinegar and Spices	1	00	0
For Anchovies, Capers, and Samphire	0	05	0
For Oysters and Sausages	0	15	0
For Sorril, Sage, Parsley, Sweet Herbs, and Onions	0	05	0
For the use of Pewter and Linnen	1	00	0
For Firing in the Kitchen	0	15	0
For Firing in the Parlour	0	3	0
For Boat Hire and Porterage	0	05	0
For Cook's wages	0	15	0
For Garnishing and Strewing	0	05	0
	£18	06	0

There was no doubt, however, as to the club's profoundly anti-Royalist sentiment. It was founded to celebrate the execution of King Charles I for treason on January 30, 1649. In a process as old as politics, the members of this club were denounced as "old Roundheads and New Commonwealth Men," independents, dissenters, Presbyterians, Anabaptists, and "Atheistic King-killing Miscreants."

Diagram of calf's head for carving.

They were accused of all manner of sacrilegious, lewd, and destructive practices—drinking toasts from calves' skulls, singing anti-Royalist "anthems," and burning copies of the *Eikon Basilike,* a book of prayers and meditations said to have been written by King Charles himself. First mention of the club appears several decades after the restoration of the monarchy in 1660, and it lingered until a night of wholesale drunken revelry and property destruction in 1735—by which time membership was presumably not primarily politically motivated.

The choice of the calf's head as a motif was not mysterious. It represented the head of Charles I and echoed the practice at ancient feasts of presenting a boar's head on a platter to symbolize the triumph over Satan (see January 4). Some descriptions of the Calves Head Feasts include other symbolic dishes too—a cod's head to represent the physical person of Charles (as distinct from his divinely entitled regal role), and a pike with smaller fish in its mouth to indicate tyranny.

Recipes

~~~

Calf's head was a common dish at a time when no good animal protein was wasted, and a carcass had to be used up quickly before it decomposed. Almost every cookbook of the time gave multiple ways of preparing it, such as this one, from the year of the Restoration.

To Boil a Calf's Head

Take the head, skin, and all unflayed, scald it, and soke it in fair water a whole night or twelve hours, then take out the brains and boil them with some sage, parsley, or mint; being boild chop them small together, butter them, and serve them in a dish with fine sippets about them: Then the head being finely cleansed, boil it in a clean cloth and close it together again in the cloth; being boild, lay it on one side by another with some fine slices of boild bacon, and lay some fine picked parsley upon it, with some borage or other flowers.

Robert May, *The Accomplisht Cook* (London, 1660).

Samphire is a plant with thick fleshy leaves that grows on rocks at the sea-shore and was very popular when pickled. Cookbooks often suggested that pickles be "greened" (a highly desirable color) by cooking in brass or copper pots. The action of the pickling vinegar on the metal produced bright green copper salts—which are known now to be highly toxic. If you wish to try the following recipe, use a stainless steel pan.

To Pickle Samphire

Samphire being gather'd in the Month of *May* (when 'tis in its Prime) let it be pick'd and laid in Salt and Water for two Days. Then taking it out, put it into a Brass-pot, and soak it very well in the best White-Wine Vinegar; it being extremely subject to Waste: afterwards having set it ove a gently Fire, let it continue close cover'd till 'tis become very green and crisp, but not soft or tender; at that Instand it must be disposed of in Pots, ty'd down close with Leather.

The Compleat Cook: Prescribing the Most Ready Ways for Dressing Flesh, and Fish, Ordering Sauces, Pickles, Jellies, &c. (London, 1710).

January 31

Luncheon at the Variety Club
35 Dover Street, London, 1952

The Variety Club began in 1927 in Pittsburgh, Pennsylvania, as a social club for those working in show business. Its slogan (and reputation) as "the heart of show business" began a year later when a baby girl was abandoned in the Sheridan Square Theatre, a note pinned to her clothing, signed by "a heartbroken mother" who gave her baby's name as Catherine. The mother pleaded with the good folk of show business to take care of her daughter as she could not do so herself as she had eight other children and her husband was out of work. Eleven members of the club committed to supporting baby Catherine, and the Variety Club's charitable work for children had begun.

The Variety Club of Great Britain, with its special name of "Tent 36" was formed in 1949, and in a little over a year had raised almost $10,000 for children's charities. It held regular "celebrity luncheons" and gave regular awards for services to the entertainment industry. On January 31, 1952, the luncheon menu was

---

Hors d'Œuvres Variés

—

Potage Longshamps

—

Truite de Rivière Meunière

—

Porc Roti a L'Anglaise
Pommes Chateau
Choux de Bruxelles

—

Coupe Jacques
Gaufrettes

—

Café

The menu shows the persistence of the use of French as the language of menus—a strangely resistant tradition given that few in England in the 1950s spoke it well, or at all. It is doubly strange in view of the long-standing friction, and sometimes outright war, between the two countries. French was, in fact, the language of the English aristocracy for several centuries after the Norman invasion of 1066, and many French words inevitably became absorbed into English. For the ordinary folk who tilled the fields and tended the cattle, however, English in all its dialects remained the day-to-day language. Our modern words for many food items reflects the ancient class-language division. English words for "meat" such as beef and pork have French origins (*boeuf* and *porc*), but the names of the animals from which those meats come—cow and pig—betray their old English origins. The nobility (for whom English was almost a second language) did not need to consider, or even speak of, the animals who provided their dinner, but the farmers, peasants, and butchers who did the dirty work in bringing them to the aristocratic tables (rarely being able to eat them themselves) never had any necessity to change their names.

The sweet dishes on this menu reflect history too, but in a different way. The ice cream (in the *Coupe Jacques*) is one of the most modern inventions, only being possible on any scale when refrigeration technology became widespread. The *gaufres* or *gaufrettes* (wafers), on the other hand, represent the oldest "dessert" in history. In medieval times, a feast consisted of several courses, each of which had similar dishes, with no distinction between savory and sweet, and ended with wafers, sweet wine, and spices to aid digestion. It is from these final dishes that the dessert course finally developed.

Recipes

~~~

Gaufres

Put in a bowl some flour, a little salt, a spoonful of brandy, eggs, powdered sugar; moisten by degrees with cream or good milk; heat your gaufre-iron, butter it, and pour in a large spoonful of the batter; let the two sides be done equally; when done, turn them out. Eat cold.

Frances Crawford, *French Cookery Adapted for English Families* (1853).

Coupe Jacques

Half-fill the glass goblets with fruit salad, flavoured with kirsch, cover this with a layer of vanilla ice cream, and then add a layer of strawberry ice. Decorate with a glacé cherry.

  Good Housekeeping (Home Encyclopaedia, 1951).

Pommes Chateau: see October 3.

February

Broadway Association Dinner to Celebrate the Dodge Brothers' Sign
Hotel Astor, New York, 1928

The opening of the Woolworth Building in 1913 may have "brought daylight to Broadway" (see April 24), but it got a whole lot brighter when the Dodge Brothers' sign on the roof of the Strand Theatre building was switched on at 7:30 P.M. on February 1, 1928. It was half a block long and five stories high and by far the largest and most brilliant electric sign on "the Great White Way." Twenty miles of wire carried 280,855 watts—the largest current consumption of any other electrical sign in the city—and modern technology allowed a moving message or "motograph" at its base for the Dodge Brothers' new "Victory Six"—a six-cylinder automobile built to honor the tenth anniversary of the end of World War I. The Broadway Association, formed in 1911 to develop and promote the cultural and economic activities of that region of New York, held a dinner to celebrate the historic moment.

The menu card was decorated with amusing little black and white drawings, which, with the names of the courses and dishes, paid homage to the automobile and electrical industries, to the advertising sign itself, and to and the Victory Six.

WATT'S WATT ON THE MENU

A DAZZLING VICTORY SERVED IN SIX CYLINDERS

FIRST CYLINDER
Orange Juice
Coupe Sedan

SECOND CYLINDER
Light Bouillon
Accessories
Salted Nuts   Celery   Olives

THIRD CYLINDER
Electric Fish

FOURTH CYLINDER
Chassis of Lamb

Fresh Artichoke Bases
Mushroom Rivets

FIFTH CYLINDER
Vermont Turkey
Sport Body
Chestnut Interior
Decoration
Glazed Surface Yams
Direct and Alternating Current Jelly
Lettuce Spring Leaves with
Improved Oiling System

SIXTH CYLINDER
Illuminated Ices
Petits Fours
(Fastest in America)

High Frequency Coffee
Differential Service

It is unlikely that there were any new dishes developed for this occasion. The theme was played out entirely in the renaming of regular dishes, which no doubt added to the fun of the evening and the great sense of pride in the automobile and the electrical grid—two great products of the modern industrial age.

As to the actual dishes in this menu, it is highly unlikely that the "electric fish" on this menu was truly one of the species that are *electrogenic*, that is, that can generate a weak electric current. The flesh of some species of electric eel is certainly edible, and it was eaten by the ancient Egyptians and Romans, perhaps for medicinal reasons (a "shock" from a live fish was also used for such things as headaches, gout, epilepsy, and labor pains). The electric fish that was served here was probably an ordinary variety renamed to suit the theme. The "chassis" of lamb was probably some sort of joint on the bone, served with artichokes and mushrooms, undoubtedly the turkey had a chestnut stuffing and a currant jelly relish on the side, and of course the lettuce salad had an oil dressing. Perhaps the names of the illuminated ices and petits fours (see November 14) indicate that they were

DINNER

TENDERED BY THE

BROADWAY ASSOCIATION

AT THE

HOTEL ASTOR

ON THE OCCASION
OF THE
INAUGURATION OF THE

DODGE BROTHERS

ELECTRIC SIGN ON BROADWAY

℘

WEDNESDAY
FEBRUARY THE FIRST
1928

Dodge Brothers dinner invitation. Courtesy of Library of Congress.

brilliantly colored like the Broadway sign, and the coffee that it was extra strong.

Recipes
~~~

Chestnut Stuffing

Shell one quart of large chestnuts. Pour on boiling water, and remove the inner brown skin. Boil in salted water or stock till soft. Mash fine. Take half for the stuffing, and mix with it one cup of fine cracker crumbs; season with one teaspoonful of salt, one saltspoonful of pepper, and one teaspoonful of chopped parsley. Moisten with one third of a cup of melted butter. Professional cooks sometimes mix a little apple sauce, flavored with wine, lemon, and sugar, with a chestnut stuffing.

Mary Johnson Bailey, *Mrs. Lincoln's Boston Cook Book: What To Do and What Not To Do in Cooking* (Boston: Lincoln, 1884).

"Yam" is the botanically incorrect name in the southern states of the United States for the sweet potato.

Petits Fours: see November 14.

Candied Sweet Potato: see December 20.

February 2

First Annual Banquet of the Founders and Patriots of America
Hotel Manhattan, New York, 1897

The Order of the Founders and Patriots of America was founded in 1896. Membership was, and is still, open to any male citizen of the United States over the age of 18 years, "of good moral character," who can prove his ancestry back to one of the first colonists (before May 13, 1657) and who has forefathers in the same male line who fought on the side of the patriots in the American Revolution.

More than 200 guests, members, and prominent men of the city gathered at the first annual banquet of the society to commemorate the 244th proclamation of "Burgher Government" for "Nieuw Amsterdam." There may be some question as to the culinary authenticity of that first bill of fare, but the enthusiasm of the organizers is impossible to fault. Almost every word on the menu card honors the early history and citizens of New York.

DISHES FOR YE FEASTE

Thus Ayre and Earthe, bothe sea and lande,
Yielde store of Nature's Daynties.

Sandwiches prepared for ye Palates of ye
Founders and Patriots with ye proper Moysture.

Oisters as Founde at ye James-towne.

Chicken Soupe as compounded by ye
Madam Alice Bradford.

Turtle Soupe by ye Recipe of ye Anneke Jans.

Celerie and raddishes growne on ye Director's bouwerie.

Almonds just received from ye West Indies.

Timbales of Crabbes and Oisters as Enjoyed
by ye Hendrick Hudson.

Manhaddoes Sole, with Cucumbers from ye
Midwout and Potatoes as Prepared by ye
Madam Schuyer at Beverwyck.

Salem Beefe, with Connecticut Love Apples.

Chicken, as suited to the taste of ye
Worshipful Governor Winthrop, with ye Beans.

Nieuw Netherland's Canvas Back Ducks,
and Salad from ye Paulus Hoeck.

Figge Puddinge as Comforted he Hearte of
ye Reverend Cotton Mather.

Pieter Stuyvesant Congealed Creame and Cakes
baked at Nieuw Amsterdam.

Standishe cheese.
Sweets just come in from ye East Indies
and Fruites from ye Islande of Jamaica.

Colonial Coffee.

There will be Served ye Suitable Beverages necessary Properly to digest
ye Dishes of ye Feaste from ye Cellar of ye late Director, William Kieft.

It is highly unlikely that "love apples" (tomatoes) and potatoes (unless they were sweet potatoes) served at this meal were enjoyed by the early colonists. Although both were products of the New World, and had been taken to England and Europe in the early sixteenth century by returning explorers, unlike maize and chocolate they were not taken up with enthusiasm. They were in fact viewed with great suspicion, perhaps because they were from the same family that includes the poisonous "deadly nightshade," a highly toxic plant, *Atropa belladonna*, ingestion of which can prove fatal with lesser doses causing hallucinations. They were both accused of having aphrodisiac properties (hence the early name of the

Key to the Menu

Jamestown:	the first English settlement, founded in Virginia in 1607.
Alice Bradford:	wife of Plymouth Governor William Bradford.
Anneke Jans (Bogardus):	the original owner of what is now Manhattan.
Hendrick Hudson:	the English seaman who, while seeking a North-West passage to the spice islands, explored what is now New York harbor and the Hudson River.
Midwout:	"Middle Woods," on western Long Island.
Manhadoes:	an early name for what is now New York City.
Madam Schuyler (Margareta van Slichtenhorst):	the wife of Colonel Philip Pieterse Schuyler of Albany, famous for her financial assistance to the defense of the colony.
Beverwyck:	now Albany, New York.
Salem Beef:	a reference to the 150 head of cattle from Salem which saved Washington's starving troops at Valley Forge in 1778.
Governor John Winthrop:	the English Puritan who became the first governor of the colony of Massachusetts.
Paulus Hoeck (Hook):	the site (in what is now Jersey City) of a battle in 1779, during the American Revolutionary Wars.
Cotton Mather:	New England Puritan minister; associated with the Salem witch trials.
Pieter Stuyvesant:	the last Dutch director-general of the colony of New Netherland.
Myles Standishe:	military advisor for Plymouth colony; arrived on the *Mayflower*.

tomato) and of causing various diseases such as leprosy (in the case of the potato). When the potato was introduced to the colony (or reintroduced to the New World), it became known as the Virginia potato to distinguish it from the sweet potato.

Recipes

~~~

Fig Pudding

One cupful of molasses
one of chopped suet
one of milk
three and a quarter of flour
two eggs

</div>

one teaspoonful of soda
one of cinnamon
half a teaspoonful of nutmeg
one pint of figs

Mix together the molasses, suet, spice, and the figs, cut fine. Dissolve the soda with a table-spoonful of hot water, and mix with the milk. Add to the other ingredients. Beat the eggs light, and stir into the mixture. Add the flour, and beat thoroughly. Butter two small or one large brown bread mould. Turn the mixture into the mould or moulds, and steam five hours. Serve with creamy or wine sauce.

Miss Parloa's New Cookbook: A Guide to Marketing and Cooking (New York, ca. 1880).

"Congealed" cream is the same as clotted, or clouted cream, an essential part of an authentic "Devonshire tea" in England. It is very thick (about 60 percent butterfat) and a golden-yellow color.

Clouted Cream

Take four quarts of milk from the cow, in the evening, put it into a broad earthen pan, and let it stand until the next day, then put the dish over a very slow fire, and another dish over it to keep out the dust; make it nearly hot, to set the cream; put it away to get cold, then take the cream off into a bowl, and beat it well with a spoon. It is accounted very fine in the West of England for tea and coffee, or to put over fruit pies and tarts.

Richard Briggs, *The English Art of Cookery* (1801).

Love-Apple Sauce

Boil ten very ripe tomatoes or love-apples in some stock for half an hour; add pepper and salt, and strain to a *purée*. Should your sauce not be thick enough, boil it again. Put a little meat gravy into three or four spoonfuls of the purée, and, when about to serve, add two ounces of butter, letting it melt in the sauce.

French Domestic Cookery, by an English physician (1825).

February 3

Postrevolutionary Meal
Havre de Grace, France, 1796

Theobald Wolfe Tone (1763–1798) is often referred to as "the father of Irish republicanism and separatism." He eventually died for his principles by his own hand, before the sentence of death handed down to him for his part in the Irish Rebellion could be carried out. Most of his last couple of years were spent traveling. In June 1795 he fled to America to escape arrest, and in early 1976 he left there for France. The French revolutionary process that culminated in the storming of the Bastille in 1789 was a source of great interest and inspiration to Irish revolutionaries of the time, and Tone went there to raise support for the rebellion in his homeland.

Tone arrived in the French port of Le Havre on February 1, 1796, after a rough winter passage of 31 days from New York. He found the town ugly and dirty. He booked into "the Hotel de Paix, formerly the Hotel of the Intendant, but reduced to its present state by the Revolution." Tone's journal of his travel experiences is witty and engaging and provides an interesting perspective on post-revolutionary conditions. The country was reputed to be starving, and as always in times of social and economic chaos, individuals made do and made money when and how they could. Tone's opinion of the privations and the quality of the food take up most of his journal entry on February 3.

Rose early; difficult to get breakfast; got it at last; excellent coffee, and very coarse brown bread, but, as it happens, I like brown bread. Walked out to see the lions; none to see. Mass celebrating in the church; many people present, especially women;

. . . went into divers coffee-houses; plenty of coffee, but no papers. *No bread in two of the coffee-houses, but pastry; singular enough!* Dinner: and here, as matter of curiosity, follows our bill of fare, which proves clearly that France is in a starving situation:—An excellent soup; a dish of fish, fresh from the harbour; a fore-quarter of delicate small mutton, like the Welsh; a superb turkey, and a couple of ducks roasted; pastry, cheese, and fruit after dinner, with wine *ad libitum*, but still the *pain bis* [brown bread]; provoked with the Frenchmen grumbling at the bread; made a saying: *Vive le pain bis et la liberté!* I forgot the vegetables, which were excellent; very glad to see such unequivocal proofs of famine.

Went to the Comedie in the evening: a neat theatre, and a very tolerable company; twenty performers in the orchestra: house full; several officers, very fine looking fellows: the audience just as gay as if there was no such thing as war and brown bread in the world. Supper just like our dinner, with wine, &c. N. B. *Finances.* The louis worth 5000 livres, or about 200 times its value, in assignats; the six-franc piece in proportion. My bill *per diem*, for such entertainment as abovementioned, is six francs, (five shillings), and my crimson damask bed 20 sols, or ten pence; coffee in the morning 12 sols, or sixpence; so that I am starving in the manner I have described, for the enormous sum of 6s 4d a day: sad! sad! Paid for my seat at the theatre, in the box next to that of the Municipalité 80 livres in assignats, or about fourpence sterling. Be it remembered, I lodge at the principal hotel in Havre, and I doubt not but I might retrench, perhaps, one-half, by changing my situation; but hang saving!

Recipes

~~~

To Bake a Shoulder of Mutton

Lard it with streaked bacon, and put it into an earthen pan proportioned to the size of the meat, and two or three onions sliced, a parsnip and a carrot sliced also, a clove of garlic, two cloves, half a bay leaf, and some leaves of basil, adding about a gill of water, or, which is better, broth, salt, and pepper. If the meat be larded, use less salt; then put in the meat, and set it in an oven. When it is done, strain the sauce through a sieve, squeeze the vegetables to make a lettuce cullis to thicken the sauce, and, having skimmed the whole, serve it with the meat.

To Dress Whitings

Gut, wash, and well dry them, taking care to leave the liver in the fish: Cut them slightly in five or six places on each side, roll them in flour and broil them over a very brisk fire: serve them upon a napkin, or, for a side dish, with a white sauce of capers and anchovies. If you would serve them with greater delicacy, cut off the heads and take out the middle bone, arranging the pieces with the white side uppermost upon the dish, pouring the sauce over them.
  Menon, *La Cuisinière Bourgeoise* (1793).

February 4

Dinner for Fox Films
Hotel Australia, Sydney, Australia, 1916

The movie star Theda Bara (1885–1955) became the screen's first sex symbol when she sprang to fame in 1915 in her role as the vampire in William Fox's silent movie *A Fool There Was*. The movie's popularity firmly established the success of the new Fox Films Corporation, as well as the use of the word "vamp" for a sexually predatory woman. In 1916 Bara and the famous star William Farnum (1876–1956) along with representatives of the Fox Film Corporation were in Sydney, Australia, on a promotional tour. They were entertained at dinner at the Hotel Australia.

MENU

"Carmen" Cocktails
Oysters a La—"The Devil's Daughter"
Potage "Plunderer"
Fish— "A Fool There Was" (And He Was Caught)
A Thief'S Entrée
Claret Cup Not Brewed Within the Walls of Jericho
"Princess Romanoff" Champagne
Roast (We Hope Not from the Critics)
The Sweets of "Infidelity"
Café Noir—Strong as Samson

Cigars and Cigarettes for
"The Idler"

This menu is another fine example of a "theme" menu, and, as with other theme menus, it is almost certain that the individual dishes were not especially invented for the dinner but were merely standard dishes renamed to enhance the fun and excitement of the evening. Every dish, and even the final cigars and cigarettes, were named in honor of a movie star, character or plot idea—Bara starred, for example, in *Carmen* and *The Devil's Daughter* and Farnum in *The Plunderer*. Infidelity presumably refers to the plot of *The Unchastened Woman*, another Bara movie. Several other Fox Films are also acknowledged—*The Idler, The Thief of Baghdad*, and *Princess Romanoff*.

Recipes

~~~

Claret Cup

Put 1 bottleful claret, the thin rind of a lemon, and 1 or 2 tablespoonfuls of castor sugar into a large jug, cover, and let it stand embedded in ice for 1 hour. Add 1 wineglassful of sherry, 1 liqueur glass of brandy, 1 liqueur glass of noyeau, 1 liqueur glass of Maraschino, 2 or 3 sprigs of balm, borage, or verbena (when procurable), 1 large bottle of seltzer of soda water, and serve. A few strips of cucumber may be used instead of balm, borage, or verbena.
The Australasian Cookery Book (ca. 1915).

Australia is said to have been founded "on the sheep's back"—an acknowledgement of the huge importance of the industry to the early colony. The type of "roast" at this dinner is not specified, but by far the commonest on the dinner table in Australia is roast lamb (although in the past roast mutton was even more common). The following recipe is "fancy," for its time, and certainly good enough for a restaurant version of roast lamb.

Roast Lamb
(Basted with Coffee)

5 lb. joint of lamb	3/4 tablespoon salt,
1 teaspoon dry mustard	few slivers garlic clove (optional),
1 breakfastcup coffee	cream, sugar, flour,
1/2 cup cream	1 or 2 teaspoons currant jelly.

Wipe the joint of lamb with a damp cloth and rub with the salt and dry mustard. If you like garlic, insert a few slivers of the garlic clove. Roast in a hot oven for two and a half to three hours, basting it with weak stock or water and turning occasionally. When it is half cooked, baste with the coffee to which the cream and sugar have been added. When the joint is cooked, make the gravy in the usual way, using the juices in the pan and add flour and cream to make the gravy as thick as you want it. When the gravy has cooked for ten or twelve minutes, add salt and the currant jelly.
"Australian Cookery of Today Illustrated," *The Sun News-Pictorial* (Melbourne, ca. 1930).

February 5

Debut Dinner at the New York Vegetarian Society's Vegetarian Restaurant No. 1, New York, 1895

The New York Vegetarian Society finally realized its "long cherished wish" when it opened "with some ceremony," its first restaurant at 240 West Twenty-Third Street in New York City in 1895. Vegetarianism was still far from being a common lifestyle choice at the end of the nineteenth century, and the opening dinner was described in some detail in the newspapers. *The New York Times* pointed out that "no beverage containing the smallest percentage of alcohol is countenanced" at the restaurant, but it assured its readers that "to offset this privation to those who wish to experiment with the cuisine of the vegetarians, an endeavor will be made to serve the finest coffee that it is possible to make." The only thing the restaurant still lacked was a first-class *patissière*, and it was hoped that before long a Hungarian or Italian would be engaged.

Fruit Soup.
Celery, Pickles, Olives.
White Potatoes with Asparagus, Sweet
Potatoes with French Peas.
ENTREES.
Spaghetti with Tomato Sauce, Cauliflower, Baked.
Graham Bread, Entire Wheat Flour.
Flageolette Beans.

SALADS.
Lettuce, Field Salad—French or Mayonnaise Dressing.

DESSERT.
Bohemian Cream, Fruit Sauce, Rice Pudding,
Lemon Sauce.
Fruits, Oranges, Dates, Figs, Grapes,
Assorted Nuts.
Tea, Coffee, Chocolate.

Present at this inaugural dinner were the president of the American Society, Rev. Henry S. Clubb, the president of the New York Society, Mr. J. W. Scott, and 40 or 50 members. Mr. Clubb gave the after-dinner speech in which he defended vegetarianism as taught by one of the association's founding members, Sylvester Graham (1795–1851)—a man immortalized by the cereal products that bear his name. Graham was a failed preacher turned nutrition guru who developed a huge but controversial following in the first half of the nineteenth century for his doctrine of vegetarianism, temperance, and sexual restraint. The evening's entertainment was rounded off by a vegetarian song written and sung by Mr. George Brunswick; the other guests joining in heartily for the chorus.

Recipes

~~~

Wheat-Meal Bread—Graham Bread

In every cook-book I have examined, and in all the medico-dietetical works I have consulted, I find saleratus or pearlash, and salt always in the recipe for making what those books call brown, dyspepsia, or Graham bread. Those two drugs ought always to be left out. Molasses or brown sugar is also a fixture in the ordinary receipt books, and as a small quantity—a tablespoonful to a common loaf—is not harmful, the saccharine element may be left to taste. Make the sponge of unbolted wheat-meal in the ordinary way, with either hop or potato yeast, but mix it rather thin. Be sure and mold the loaves as soon as it becomes light, as the unbolted flour runs into the acetous fermentation much more rapidly than the bolted or superfine flour, and bake an hour and a quarter of an hour and a half, according to the size of the loaf.

Russell Thacher Trall, *The New Hydropathic Cookbook* (1855).

Spaghetti Aux Tomatoes

1 lb. of spaghetti
the strained juice of one tin of tomatoes
1 oz. of butter
pepper and salt

Mix the tomato juice with 1 pint of water and let the liquid come to the boil, throw in the spaghetti, taking care to keep the contents of the saucepan boiling fast; add the butter and seasoning, and cook until tender; time from 15 to 20 minutes. Serve very hot with grated cheese.

Thomas Allinson, *The Allinson Vegetarian Cookery Book* (1915).

Lemon Sauce

Make a teaspoonful cornflour smooth in saucepan with a little cold water. Add a gill of boiling water, juice of a lemon, and 2 ozs. sugar. Let boil a minute or two. If flavour of rind is liked, grate that in. Add a little Carmine to colour.

Mrs. Mills, *Reform Cookery Book* (1909).

Rice Rudding: see January 12.
French Dressing: see June 17.

February 6

Dinner with President Thomas Jefferson
The White House, Washington, DC, 1802

Thomas Jefferson (1743–1826), the third president of the United States and one of the authors of the Declaration of Independence, was known to have a

Ice cream recipe written by Thomas Jefferson. Courtesy of Library of Congress.

passionate interest in all aspects of food, from cultivation to its appearance on the dining table. Stories abound about his gardening "firsts" (figs, dates, various nuts) and experiments (he was said to have grown sixteen varieties of peas at Monticello), his wine collection, his kitchen gadgetry (a waffle maker, a macaroni machine, and an ice cream churn), and the fancy French ideas he brought back to America after his service as minister to France (1785–1789). It is surprising in view of his interest in food that there is such a dearth of detailed descriptions of his dinner parties. The most detailed one that does exist appears in the journal of Manasseh Cutler (1742–1823), a clergyman and congressman. Cutler and several other members of the House of Representatives and the Senate dined at the White House on February 6, 1802. The entry reads

> Rice soup, round of beef, turkey, mutton, ham, loin of veal, cutlets of mutton or veal, fried eggs, fried beef, a pie called macaroni, which appears to be a rich crust filled with the strillions of onions or shallots, which I took it to be, tasted very strong and not agreeable. Mr. [Meriwether] Lewis told me there was none in it: it was an Italian dish, and what appeared like onions was made of flour and butter with a particularly strong liquor mixed with them. Ice cream very good, crust wholly dried, crumbled into thin flakes; a dish somewhat like a pudding—inside white as milk or curd, very porous and light covered with cream sauce; very fine. Many other jimcracks, a great variety of fruit, plenty of wines and good. President social. We drank tea and viewed again the great cheese.

> Life, Journals and Correspondence of
> Rev. Manasseh Cutler, LL. D, Volume II, by
> his grandchildren William Parker Cutler and
> Julia Perkins Cutler (Cincinnati:
> Robert Clarke & Co., 1888).

It is not surprising that Mr. Cutler was confused by the macaroni pie. He would hardly have been likely to have been served it elsewhere, as Jefferson (who became enamoured of it in Italy) is credited with introducing macaroni to the United States. It was often served in a pre-baked dense pastry pie shell, which served the same function as a casserole dish.

Ice cream was served regularly at Jefferson's table. It appears to have been served in a way similar to the deep-fried ice cream that we associate with Chinese restaurants—the dish that in its turn inspired the "invention" of the Bombe Alaska. One visitor to Monticello wrote "ice-creams were produced in the form of balls of the frozen material inclosed in covers of warm pastry, exhibiting a curious contrast, as if the ice had just been taken from the oven." Ice for the ice cream churn was harvested from the Rivanna River and stored in the vast ice house of Monticello, and in one year the supply lasted right through to the following October.

Cutler makes reference to the "great cheese," or "The Greatest Cheese in America for the Greatest Man in America" which was delivered to Jefferson on New Year's Day in 1802, by John Leland, a Baptist preacher. The "mammoth cheese" measured over 4 feet in diameter, was 17-inches thick, and weighed 1,235 pounds. It had been made by the Baptist citizens of Cheshire in Massachusetts who felt themselves subject to political and religious discrimination, in acknowledgement of Jefferson's support for the ideal of religious freedom.

Recipes

~~~

Thomas Jefferson's ice cream recipe was recorded in his own handwriting.

Ice Cream

2 bottles of good cream
6 yolks of eggs   1/2 lb. sugar

mix the yolks & sugar
put the cream on a fire in a casserole, first putting in a stick of Vanilla.
when near boiling take it off & pour it gently into the mixture of eggs & sugar.
stir it well.
put it on the fire again stirring it thoroughly with a spoon to prevent it's sticking
    to the casserole.
when near boiling take it off and strain it thro' a towel.
put it in the Sabottiere then set it in ice an hour before it is to be served.
put into the ice a handful of salt.
put salt on the coverlid of the Sabotiere & cover the whole with ice.
leave it still half a quarter of an hour.
then turn the Sabottiere in the ice 10 minutes
open it to loosen with a spatula the ice from the inner sides of the Sabotiere.
shut it & replace it in the ice
open it from time to time to detach the ice from the sides
when well taken (prise) stir it well with the Spatula.
put it in moulds, justling it well down on the knee.
then put the mould into the same bucket of ice.
leave it there to the moment of serving it.
to withdraw it, immerse the mould in warm water, turning it well till it will
    come out & turn it into a plate.

February 7

Mormon Ball, Social Hall
Salt Lake City, Utah, 1860

Richard Burton (1821–1890) was an English adventurer, explorer, linguist, and prolific writer. He was eccentric as well as brilliant (often traveling in disguise), with a keen interest in all sorts of cultural and religious practices, which some of his detractors interpreted as "collecting cults." In 1860, apparently on a whim, he traveled to the United States to visit Salt Lake City. He was apparently intrigued by the then Mormon practice of polygamy and discussed this at a meeting with Mormon leader Brigham Young (1801–1877). In his book about this trip, *City of the Saints* (1861), Burton described a "highly select" social event in the city, the Territorial and Civil Ball.

BILL OF FARE

FIRST COURSE.
SOUPS.

Oyster,	Vermicelli,
Ox-Tail,	Vegetable.

SECOND COURSE.
MEATS.

Roast.	Boiled.
Beef,	Sugar-corned Beef,
Mutton,	Mutton,
Mountain Mutton,	Chickens,
Bear,	Ducks,
Elk,	Tripe,
Deer,	Turkey,
Chickens,	Ham,
Ducks,	Trout,
Turkeys,	Salmon

STEWS AND FRICASSEES.

Oysters and Ox Tongues,	Chickens,
Beaver Tails,	Ducks,
Collared Head,	Turkeys,

VEGETABLES.

Boiled.	Baked.
Potatoes,	Potatoes,
Cabbage (i.e., greens),	Parsnips,
Parsnips,	Beans,
Cauliflower,	
Slaw	
Hominy.	

THIRD COURSE.
Pastry.   Puddings.

Mince Pies,	Custards,
Green Apple Pie,	Rice,
Pineapple Pie,	English Plum,
Quince Jelly Pie,	Apple Soufflé,
Peach Jelly Pie	Mountain,
Currant Jelly Pie,	Pioneer,
Blancmange.	Jellies.

FOURTH COURSE.

Cakes.	Fruits.
Pound,	Raisins,
Sponge,	Grapes,
Gypsy,	Apples,
Varieties,	Snowballs,
Candies.	Nuts.
Tea.	Coffee.

The guests had paid $10 per couple to attend. Burton was intrigued and amused that this allowed only one lady per gentleman, although he noted "for all extra $2 each must be paid.... Premiums are offered when the time draws nigh, but space is limited, and many a Jacob is shorn of his glory by appearing with only Kachel for a follower, and without his train of Leahs, Zilpahs, and Billahs."

He also made some comments about the "subtantial goodies" served to the 250 persons present:

It will be observed that the cuisine in Utah Territory has some novelties, such as bear and beaver. The former meat is a favorite throughout the West, especially when the animal is fresh from feeding; after hibernation it is hard and lean. In the Himalayas many a sportsman, after mastering an artificial aversion to eat bear's grease, has enjoyed a grill of "cuffy." The paws, which not a little resemble the human hand, are excellent *experto crede*, I can not pronounce ex cathedra upon beavers' tails; there is no reason, however, why they should be inferior to the appendage of a Cape sheep. "Slaw" according to my informants is synonymous with sauer-kraut. Mountain, Pioneer, and Snowballs are unknown to me, except by their names, which are certainly patriotic, if not descriptive.

This is certainly an interesting menu. It is entirely in English, with no French terms at all, apart from *soufflé*, which does not have an English equivalent. The menu is set out in plain style, and the food also appears to have been an unfussy mix of plain food, frontier game, and homely cakes (but, unusually for the time, no ice creams). The only real puzzle is why the caterers thought it necessary to indicate that "cabbage" was "greens."

Recipes

~~~

Gipsy cake is another name for tipsy cake, or broken cake pudding. In other words it is a trifle (or *tiramisu*). At its simplest it is made from sponge cake soaked with some sort of liqueur or spirits, with fruit, nuts, and custard. This

Mormon community would not have sanctioned the use of alcohol and would have substituted with fruit juice or syrup.

Gipsy Cake

Take a Sponge Cake (the size you wish), soak it in wine and a glass of brandy; blanch some sweet almonds; cut them lengthways in narrow chips, and stick them all over it: you may put some custard in the dish.
   William Kitchiner, *The Cook's Oracle*, (1845).

Apple Pie: September 14.
Beaver Tail: see January 3.
Blancmange: January 7.
Collared Head: see September 17.
Hominy: May 19.
Mince Pies: see January 9.
Ox-tail Soup: March 21.
Pound Cake: April 19.
Rice Pudding: January 12.

February 8

Whale Meat Luncheon
American Museum of Natural History, New York City, 1918

Thirty "selected epicures, explorers, biologists, and notables," including the polar explorer Robert Peary (1856–1920) and "men prominent in scientific, business, and professional spheres," including government food administrators and the zoologist William T. Hornaday (1854–1937) met on this day in the restaurant of the American Museum of Natural History to enjoy a luncheon featuring whale meat.

Hors d'Oeuvre—Whale
Whale pot au Feu
Celery   Olives   Radishes
Corn Pone   Nut Butter   Delmonico War Bread
Boiled Skate   Mustard Sauce
Parsley Potatoes
Planked Whale Steak, a la Vancouver
Border of Samp   Onion Sauce
Vegetable Salad
Ice Cream   Bisque of black bread, a la Delmonico
Ginger bread with raw sugar   Coffee

It was a little over 12 months since the United States had entered World War I (see April 6), and the aim of the highly publicized event was to promote whale meat as a substitute for other meats that were in short supply.

The chef, Seraphin Millon, was co-opted from Delmonico's, the most famous restaurant in New York, and he apparently worked some culinary magic on the humpback whale that was the source of the meat. Naturally, the specially selected guests waxed lyrical over the flesh, declaring it quite free from a fishy taste, and rather like venison in fact, or at least "as good as the best pot-pie," perhaps even "as delicious a morsel as the most aesthetic or sophisticated palate could possibly yearn for" (*New York Times*, February 9, 1918). There was little doubt, however, that this meat was intended for the tables of the poor—it was noted to be very cheap at 12 1/2 cents a pound, conveniently available in cans, and considerably better all round than the horsemeat being promoted for the same purpose in Britain. In spite of the enthusiasm of the guests at this event, the prediction that "within two years we shall much prefer Whale Meat to Beef" was not realized, nor was it realized the second time around, a little over two decades later in World War II, when it was again promoted vigorously.

The massive whale-hunting operations of previous times were not primarily for food, they were to supply the demand for oil and "bone" (the latter to supply corset manufacturers). The industry gradually declined during the nineteenth century as vast underground stores of oil were discovered and tapped, and fashions gradually changed.

Recipes

~~~

Whale meat was promoted through various other avenues during the war: the Bureau of Fisheries produced a booklet called, *Whales and Porpoises as Food* (which included 32 recipes furnished by the American Pacific Whaling Co.), recipes for whale meat were demonstrated at the Patriotic Food Show in Chicago in January 1918, and newspapers featured it in their cookery pages.

Nice Whale Meat Dish

Dice one cup of whale meat and boil for fifteen minutes. Add one cup of parboiled and diced carrots. Make a sauce of the stock from the meat and carrots, thickening it with rye flour. Place all of this in a greased baking dish and cover with crust of hot mashed potatoes.

Capital Times, January 3, 1918, Madison, Wisconsin; recipe from the Patriotic Food Show.

Whale Steak

Cut whale meat into individual steaks 1–2 inches thick. Dip each steak in salted milk, then in finely sifted crumbs. Rub each with onion juice. Place in an oiled pan, sprinkle with olive oil, and broil in a very hot oven for 10 minutes. When browned, serve immediately.

Daily News (Des Moines) April 26, 1919.

February 9

Archbishop's Meals
Valencia, Spain, 1568

There is little in the way of extant menus for sixteenth-century Spain. One that has survived is a description of two meals eaten by the Archbishop of Valencia and several gentlemen, dated February 9, 1568. The archbishop was Fernando de Loaces y Pérez, who died less than three weeks later, on February 29.

Europe was riven with religious turmoil in the sixteenth century, and nowhere was this more aggressive and sinister than in Spain. King Philip II (1527–1598) was a fervent Catholic, determined to enforce Catholicism on all his subjects and rid the country of every trace of Protestantism, Judaism, and Islam. The Moors (Arabs from northern Africa) entered Spain in the early eighth century and occupied a large part of the Iberian peninsula for 700 years. There were many attempts by European Christian forces to expel them, but it was not until Granada was reclaimed in January 1492 that Muslim rule finally ended. The Archbishop's congregation in 1568 included *moriscos* (forcibly converted Muslims, or "Moors") and *conversos* (forcibly converted Jews) as well as long-standing Catholic families.

The vehement determination to rid the country of every vestige of every other religion is quite ironic in view of the content of this menu. Seven hundred years of Moorish occupation had unequivocally influenced Spanish cuisine. The Moors introduced many new ingredients to the Iberian peninsula such as sugar, eggplant, oranges, rice, rose water, and pomegranates. They also influenced the style of cooking. "Spanish" dishes flavored with saffron, cumin, coriander, thick stews based on dried legumes such as broad beans,

Dinner: Eaten by His Lordship and 4 Gentlemen.

Pan vino y naranjas dulces.	Bread, wine, and sweet oranges
2 gallinas asadas.	2 hens, roasted
6 perdices asadas.	6 partridges, roasted
Costrada de medio cabrito	Half a kid goat in a pastry crust
(5 huevos en yemas, manteca y especias).	(5 egg yolks, fat, and spices)
Jabalí asado.	Wild boar, roast
Albondigas apedreadas de carnero con 8 huevos en yemas.	Mutton meatballs with 8 egg yolks
Carnero cocido, 2 libras.	Boiled mutton, 2 pounds
Nabos en tocino.	Turnips in bacon
Puerco cocido, 2 libras.	Boiled pork, 2 pounds
Peros, 4 libras.	Apples, 4 pounds
2 cardos.	2 cardoons
Aceitunas y queso, 50 nueces.	Olives and cheese, 50 nuts (probably walnuts)

Supper: Eaten by His Lordship and 2 Gentlemen.

Entrada contada.	Uncommon entrée
3 perdices asadas.	3 partridges, roasted
1 conejo.	1 rabbit
3 gazapos.	3 young rabbits
Cabezuelas de cabritos asadas.	Small heads of roast kid
Torta de queso.	Cheese pie
6 huevos.	6 eggs
Postres contados.	Uncommon desserts

chick peas, and lentils, and dishes thickened with bread all have Moorish roots. The Moors also brought their pastry-making skills with them and their love of fritters and fine pastries made with honey, nuts, rose water, and eggs. Finally, the tradition of communal dining from the same dish comes from the Arab tradition.

It is unknown whether the archbishop realized that the oranges and pastry (and no doubt the spices and pulses) he enjoyed were there thanks to his religious enemy. Had he known, would he have made a concession in the name of good eating?

Recipes

~~~

The following recipes are taken from *Libro del Coch*, published by Rupert de Nola in about 1520 and translated by Robin Carroll-Mann.

Kid Pie (Pastel De Cabrito)

And if by chance the kids are too fat to be roasted, you may cut them in pieces, and make them into pasteles or empanadas. And you may take fine spice and chopped parsley and put them in the empanadas with a little sweet oil and take this food to the oven; and a little before you remove it from the oven, beat some eggs with verjuice or orange juice and put it in the empanada through the vent hole on the top of the empanada, and then return it to the oven for the space of three Paternosters [see November 18]. And then remove it, and put this pastel before the lord on a plate, and open it and give it to him.

Marinated Mutton (Carnero Adobado)

Take a piece of mutton, and make little pieces of it, and cast it to cook in an earthen pot, with the broth of the pot. And after cooking it well, take saffron, and cloves, and pepper, and blend it with a taste of vinegar and cook it a little with that; and then take egg yolks without the whites, and beat them very well and cast them within; and stir it in one direction until it is thick; and cast in your taste of honey and then remove it.

Armored Hen (Gallina Armada)

Roast a good hen. And when it is nearly half-roasted, baste it with bacon. Then take well-beaten egg yolks, then with a spoon or with the tip of a large wooden spoon rub the hen with these yolks, little by little. And then sprinkle wheat flour well-sifted with ground salt over the eggs, turning the hen constantly and swiftly; and the crust is worth more than the hen.

   Libro de Guisados, the 1529 Spanish edition of an earlier work written in Catalan called *Libre del Coch*, published in 1520 by Rupert de Nola, trans. Robin Carroll-Mann.

The Order of Serving
According to the *Libre del Coch*, 1520

First the fruit, and after it a pottage; and then roast, then another pottage and then a stew after the pottage, unless it is blanc manger which is given at the beginning, after the fruit. Some lords eat at first all the stewed food, and then the roasted. If there are fried foods [fritters or pancakes] they must be given afterwards, as it were, and then the other fruit. And this is the way and manner in the service, according to the custom of the court of the king my lord.

February 10

Tripartite Dinner Meeting
Vorontsov Villa, Yalta, Ukraine, 1945

The "Big Three" leaders (Franklin D. Roosevelt, Winston Churchill, and Josef Stalin) met in February 1945 at Yalta on the Crimean Peninsula to discuss the management of Germany after the expected imminent allied victory. The British headquarters and de facto 10 Downing Street, while Churchill was in residence, was the Voronstov Villa, the former home of a Russian count. The Villa had been occupied for a while by one of Hitler's generals and consequently had avoided being stripped and damaged. The American diplomatic contingent were housed in the Livadia Palace, the Tsar's old summer residence, and the Soviets in the Yusupov Palace, the former home of a Russian aristocrat.

   Churchill hosted a dinner meeting at his headquarters on the evening of February 10. The menu for the historic event was a simple typewritten piece of letterhead stationery.

Caviare
Pies
White and Red Salmon
Shamaya
Salted Herrings
Sturgeon in Aspic
Swiss Cheese
Game

Sausage
Sucking Pig, Horse-radish Sauce

—

Vol-au-Vent of Game

—

Game Bouillon
Cream of Chicken

—

Wite Fish, Champagne Sauce
Baked Kefal

—

Shashlik of Mutton
Wild Goat from the Steppes
Pilau of Mutton

—

Roast Turkey
Roast Quails
Roast Partridge
Green Peas

—

Ice Cream
Fruit
Petit Fours
Roasted Almonds

—

Coffee

Churchill, Roosevelt, and Stalin at Yalta. Courtesy of Library of Congress.

Yalta was a miserably cold location in the depths of this particularly grim winter. The location had been insisted upon by Stalin (who refused to fly), to the great irritation of Churchill. Much of Europe was starving, and those responsible for catering for the conference must have had their work cut out for them. Certainly, the likes of this bill of fare—a strange blend of Turkish/Russian/English food—would never have been seen before on a British diplomatic table, nor is it likely to ever be repeated.

Many of the fish at this dinner were sourced from the Black Sea and are now endangered and subject to international conservation law. It has been estimated by the Global International Waters Assessment (GIWA) that the Black Sea fish stock has been depleted by about one third in the last two decades. Perhaps as many as 60 species (fish and plants) have become extinct, or at best are endangered. Of the fish on this menu the Caspian shemaya (*Chalcalburnus chalcoides*) also called "the Royal fish" is endangered, as is the other "royal" fish, the ancient sturgeon (various species of *Acipensiderae*), source of the finest caviar, and the Kefalor golden grey mullet (*Altinbas kefal* or *Liza aurata*) is considered vulnerable.

There are some familiar meat dishes. Kebabs in their various forms have become virtual international foods. In Turkish, *kebap* means roasted meat and *şiş* is a skewer, and shashlik, shish-kebab, doner kebab, (or even just kebab) therefore refer to meat on skewers. Variations on the theme of skewered meat occur across Eastern Europe and Asia, as they do for *pilau*, and interpretations for both started to appear in English cookbooks from the seventeenth century.

Recipes

~~~

Baked Mullet

Clean the fish and soak for an hour in salted and acidulated water. Drain, wipe dry, stuff with seasoned crumbs, sew up, rub with butter, and put into a baking pan, adding enough hot water to keep from burning. Baste as required and serve with any preferred sauce.

Olive Green, *How to Cook Fish* (United States, 1908).

There are many varieties of horseradish sauce both cold and hot, from a simple mix of the grated root with vinegar, sugar, and oil to rich cream-based or brown-sauce based versions.

Horse-radish Sauce

Take one gill of whipped cream, two tablespoons of finely-grated horseradish, one tablespoon of white vinegar, a little mustard, salt and pepper, and mix well together.

Vicomte de Maduit, *The Vicomte in the Kitchen* (London, 1937).

Kebabs and Pilau: see March 30.
Salted Herrings: see May 6.
Petits Fours: see November 14.

February 11

''Gotham's Costliest Banquet''
Waldorf-Astoria Hotel, New York, 1899

It was a freezing February night in the streets of New York when Randolph Guggenheimer (1846–1907), president of the Municipal Council, gave a dinner for 40 guests in February 1899. In the dining room of the Waldorf-Astoria, however, it was all summertime, songbirds, and roses. The dinner broke all previous standards for extravagant dining—no mean feat in a city with plenty of millionaires with a taste for conspicuous consumption.

The bill for ''Gotham's Costliest Banquet'' came to $10,000—an amount, as one newspaper pointed out, that would pay the average wages of 18 New

---

BUFFET RUSSE

Private Wine   Oyster Cocktails.
Amontillado.   Lemardelaise à la Princesse.
Pasado.   Green Turtle, Bolivar.
                        Basket of Lobster.
            Columbine of Chicken, California Style.
        Roast Mountain Sheep with Puree of Chestnuts.
                        Jelly
                Brussels Sprouts Saute
        New Asparagus with Cream Sauce and Vinaigrette
Mumm's Extra Day   Fancy Sherbet
Moet & Chandon Brut

                Diamond Back Terrapin
                    Ruddy Duck
            Orange and Grapefruit Salad
        Fresh Blueberries and Raspberries
                Vanilla Mousse
                    Bonbons
                    Fruits
                    Coffee.

York working men for a year. The man behind the planning and execution of this extraordinary dinner was the *maître d'hotel*, the famous Oscar Tschirky ("Oscar of the Waldorf"). It was his finest hour. He had created his "heroic masterpiece."

"All the fruits of the earth" were there to delight the guests. They sat in a 12-sided arbor, beside a beautiful fountain, under a canopy of vines with bunches of magnificent grapes at hand's reach; beautiful songbirds hidden among the foliage supplemented the musicians in a "woodland oratorio," and flowers of every variety—tulips, daffodils, orchids, lilies of the valley, and complete bushes of American Beauty roses "grew" where the floor should have been. An artificial sun and moon mimicked the fall of night, which was then magically lit by Venetian lanterns and scores of tiny colored electric light bulbs. There seemed to be no end to the artifice. The usual small gifts for the guests—the millionaire's equivalent of party favors—were jewelled boxes for matches, perfume, and snuff.

The dinner itself was, of course, of the best that could be provided. Wine bottled before the French Revolution was opened. The mountain sheep and ruddy duck had been rushed to New York in portable refrigerators. The raspberries were a new variety grown especially for the occasion, and were served on decorative candied sugar leaves. And as for the blueberries, Oscar recalled them in an interview long after the event. "I remember those blueberries," he said. "A man came to the hotel with some berries he said were New Jersey blueberries. I had never seen anything like them before, and I have never seen anything like them since. They were an inch long, like a blackberry" (*New York Times*, May 13, 1917).

Recipes

~~~

Brussels Sprouts Sautéd

One pound of Brussels sprouts should be thoroughly washed and boiled, and then put into a pan over the fire, together with a good-sized lump of butter, a little salt, and tossed for eight minutes. Sprinkle over them a little chopped parsley, and serve, when done.

Puree of Chestnuts

Take off the outer skins of some chestnuts, put in a pan of boiling water and boil for a few minutes with a little salt to season. Take them off, put into cold water and remove the skins. Put the chestnuts in a pan with a quart of broth, put on the fire until boiling, then move to the side and boil slowly until tender. When cooked rub the chestnuts through a wire sieve with a wooden spoon, then put them back with the remainder of the liquid to the saucepan, put in a teaspoonful of sugar and a small lump of butter, and boil them up again.

Chocolate Bonbons

Put half a pound of French chocolate in a sugar-boiler, and stand on the stove till the chocolate is soft. Dissolve half an ounce of gum arabic in a tablespoonful and a half of hot water, mix it with the softened chocolate, stir until the chocolate is smooth, then mix in two ounces of fine icing sugar. When well mixed, drop the chocolate from the spout of the sugar-boiler cutting it off with a piece of wire into pieces the size of Brazilian nuts. When the bonbons are dry, pack them in paper in cardboard boxes.

Oscar Tschirky, *The Cook Book* (1896).

February 12

Former Slave Attends a Republican Dinner
Lincoln Dinner, Waldorf-Astoria Hotel, New York, 1909

The dinner held by the Republican Club at the Waldorf-Astoria in 1909 to celebrate the birthday of President Abraham Lincoln (1809–1865) would hardly have been noteworthy on account of its menu alone. The food was standard, classic fine-dining fare of the time, and could have been provided at any similar event of a decade on either side.

Huitres de Cotuit.
Consomme Diablotin.
Tortue Vert Clair.
Radis.   Olives.   Celeri.   Amandes Salees.
Escalope de Bass a la Duchesse.
Pommes Parisienne.
Ris de Veau, Lafayette.
Tranche de Dinde Farci, Sauce Diable.
Pommes de Terre Sautees, Petits Pois Verts.
Sorbet Fantaisie.
Canard a Tete Rouge.
Salade de Saison.
Glaces Assorties.   Petits Fours.   Fruits.
Café.
Ruinart Brut.
Appolinaris.

The menu may have been predictable, but a "manifest air of curiosity" was evoked amongst the audience of 800 (which included "practically every Republican of prominence in the city") when the keynote speaker stood up to give his address. He was the African-American leader and former slave, Booker T. Washington (1856–1915). The former "piece of property," who was eight years old when slavery was abolished, paid tribute to Lincoln as his personal liberator and that of his people and also drew a wider inference from the Emancipation Proclamation:

Booker T. Washington. Courtesy of Library of Congress.

By the same act that freed my race he said to the civilized and uncivilized world that man everywhere must be free, and that man everywhere must be enlightened, and the Lincoln spirit of freedom and fair play will never cease to spread and grow in power until throughout the world all men shall know the truth, and the truth shall make them free.

It was ironic that there were no women guests at this dinner at which the main discussion topic was emancipation. Women were not only prevented from voting in elections in 1909, they were prevented from attending public dinners—even if they were members of the press. It had become an issue for female reporters as early as 1868, when the New York Press Club refused to admit them to a banquet honoring author Charles Dickens; it was still an issue in 1906 when they were likewise refused admission to a banquet at which Mark Twain was to speak. They were, however, allowed to observe the proceedings from the ladylike distance of the public galleries of the banqueting rooms, and a small number were there to listen to Booker T. Washington on this particular night.

Recipes

~~~

The following recipes are taken from *The Epicurean* (1894), by Charles Ranhofer, chef at Delmonico's in New York.

The Way to Prepare
Sweetbreads (Ris de Veau)

Sweetbread is a glandulous substance found below the calf's throat [the thymus gland] and is considered a most delicate morsel. Separate the throat sweetbreads from the hearts; the throat part is the largest of the two, the heart is whiter, of a round shape and more delicate and tender than the throat, place them in cold water to disgorge for several hours changing it each hour so as to have them very white; lay them in a saucepan with an abundant supply of cold water, set it on the fire and when the sweetbreads are firm to the touch or poached, or more properly speaking parboiled, then refresh and suppress all the wind-pipes, fibers and fatty parts, afterward lay them under a very light weight. This blanching is for the purpose of hardening the sweetbreads so as to be able to lard them more easily. Blanched sweetbreads are used for sautéing by cutting them in two through their thickness. For brochettes they are cut in slices and for garnishing in the shape of salpicon.

Redhead Ducks, Roasted

Prepare the ducks, . . . wipe out the insides with a cloth and fill the empty space with some bread dressing combined with butter or chopped suet, thyme, bay leaf, parsley, and a few finely sliced green celery leaves, adding egg-yolks; truss, and run a skewer through to fasten them on the spit, then roast basting over with melted butter or oil. . . . lay them on the spit to roast for fourteen to eighteen minutes, more or less according to their weight; salt over, remove from the spit and untruss and serve on a very hot dish, or they can be roasted in the oven, putting them into a baking pan; pour a little fat over and set them in a hot oven; they will take a few minutes longer to cook this way, then serve on a very hot dish. Hand round separately on a folded napkin some hominy or samp the same as for canvasback ducks. Cut up the ducks and serve on very hot plates. Four slices can be taken from each duck, two on each fillet and one or two of these served to one guest.

Turtle Soup: see November 10.
Petits Fours: see November 14.
Pommes Parisienne: see June 23.

February 13

YMCA Father and Son Dinner
Nyack, New York, 1918

The Young Men's Christian Association (YMCA) was founded in 1844 by an English draper concerned for the bodily health as well as the immortal souls of the thousands of young men moving away from their families and into the big cities for work. The movement spread rapidly, and within a decade there were nearly f400 "Y's" in seven countries around the world. In the early twentieth century, another type of social phenomenon developed—that of "Father and Son" nights. They were held under the auspices of many organizations—churches, schools, Masonic lodges, and so on—and were intended to foster a broader community concept of male mentoring, not just the filial.

The men and boys of the Nyack YMCA got together on February 13, 1918 for some character-building public speaking and a plain and wholesome dinner.

MENU

Olives   Pickles
Lamb, a la Lovatt
Mint Sauce
Potatoes   Green Peas
Hot Biscuits—Dr. Hoover
Coffee   Jellies
Pie

U.S. Food Administration poster for the war effort. Courtesy of Library of Congress.

America's involvement in World War I was nearing its first anniversary (see April 6), and patriotism was clearly on the agenda. The American flag graced the cover of the menu, and the after-dinner toasts were to the food problem and our country as well as the boy, the school, and the church.

Herbert Hoover (1874–1964), the wartime U.S. food administrator, was given special mention on the menu. As part of Hoover's "Food Will Win the War" campaign, he had set some regulations two weeks before this dinner that were intended to conserve vital foods for feeding the troops and assisting war-ravaged Europe. The regulations were expected to be followed by every patriotic American as well as by industry. Wheat and meat were the most vital. Hoover determined that Mondays and Wednesdays were to be observed as "wheatless" (plus one meal every day was to be wheatless), Tuesday was to be meatless (as was one meal every day), and in addition Saturday was also to be porkless. "Wheatless" did not just apply to bread, but also to crackers, pasta and cakes, and so on. The only exception was a small amount allowed for thickening soups or sauces, or as a "binder" in corn bread or other breads. Hoover also announced the introduction of "Victory Bread," effective immediately. Pure white bread was no longer allowed. Victory bread had to contain 5 percent of cereals other than wheat, with this percentage to progressively increase to 20 percent by February 24.

February 13 in 1918 was a Wednesday, so a wheatless day. It is unthinkable that such patriotic and civic-minded citizens as attended this dinner would have breached the rules, and certainly the "Hoover" hot biscuits would have been wheat-free, as would the pie crusts.

Recipes

~~~

Baking Powder Biscuits (Wheatless)

Rye 1 1/4 cup
Rolled Oats, 1 1/3 cups
Baking powder 1 1/2 teaspoons
Salt, 1/2 teaspoon
Sugar, 2 tablespoons
Fat, 3 tablespoons
Water, 2/3 cup or more

Add rolled oats to dry ingredients. Chop in shortening. Add enough water to make soft dough. Roll out to 1/3 to 1/2 inch thickness. Bake 20 minutes in a moderately hot oven. Yield: 12 biscuits.

Oatmeal Crust (Individual Pies)

2 cups finely ground oatmeal
1 teaspoon fat
1 cup boiling water

Scald the oatmeal with the water. Add fat and mix thoroughly. Roll very thin and line small pie or tart tins with the mixture. Bake in a hot oven. Fill with apricot marmalade or other thick mixture. If desired spread a meringue on top and brown in the oven.
Thetta Quay Franks, *Daily Menus for War Service* (1918).

To the Women of the United States:
Statement Issued by Secretary David Houston
U.S. Department of Agriculture, May 5, 1917

Every woman can render important service to the Nation in its present emergency. She need not leave her home or abandon her home duties to help the armed forces. She can help to feed and clothe our armies and help to supply food to those beyond the seas by practicing effective thrift in her own household.

Every ounce of food the housewife saves from being wasted in her home—all food which she or her children produce in the garden and can or preserve—every garment which care and skilled repair make it unnecessary to replace—all lessen that household's draft on the already insufficient world supplies.

To save food the housewife must learn to plan economical and properly balanced meals, which, while nourishing each member of the family properly, do not encourage overeating or offer excessive and wasteful variety. It is her duty to use all effective methods to protect food from spoilage by heat, dirt, mice or insects. She must acquire the culinary ability to utilize every bit of edible food that comes into her home. She must learn to use such foods as vegetables, beans, peas, and milk products as partial substitutes for meat. She must make it her business to see that nothing nutritious is thrown away or allowed to be wasted.

Waste in any individual household may seem to be insignificant, but if only a single ounce of edible food, on the average, is allowed to spoil or be thrown away in each of our 20,000,000 homes, over 1,300,000 pounds of material would be wasted each day. It takes the fruit of many acres and the work of many people to raise, prepare and distribute 464,000,000 pounds of food a year. Every ounce of food thrown away, therefore, tends also to waste the work of any army of busy citizens.

Clothing is largely an agricultural product and represents the results of labor on the sheep ranges, in cotton fields and in mills and factories. Whenever a useful garment is needlessly discarded, material needed to keep some one warm or dry may be consumed merely to gratify a passing fancy. Women would do well to look upon clothing at this time more particularly from the utilitarian point of view.

Leather, too, is scarce, and the proper shoeing of armies calls for great supplies of this material. There are only so many pairs of shoes in each hide, and there is a shortage of animals for leather as well as for meat. Anything that can be done to encourage adults or children to take care of their shoes and make them last longer, meaning that so much more leather is made available for other purposes.

Employed women, especially those engaged in the manufacture of food or clothing, also directly serve their country and should put into their tasks the enthusiasm and energy the importance of their product warrants.

While all honor is due to the women who leave their homes to nurse and care for those wounded in battle, no woman should feel that because she does not wear a nurse's uniform she is absolved from patriotic service. The home women of the country, if they will give their minds fully to this vital subject of food conservation and train themselves in household thrift, can make of the housewife apron a uniform of national significance.

Demonstrate thrift in your homes and encourage thrift among your neighbors.
Make saving rather than spending your social standard.
Make economy fashionable lest it become obligatory.

New York Times, May 1917.

February 14

Valentine's Day Dinner
Sherry's, New York, 1901

There was a great air of excitement and expectation among the high society in New York as Valentine's Day approached in 1901. The new millionaire and eligible bachelor James Henry Smith (d. 1907) had announced he would give an entertainment, and nothing else had been discussed for weeks. As the newspaper pointed out, it was a difficult task to give anything that was new and original during the year of magnificent entertainments. Smith, however, called upon two of the city's most famous society hostesses to assist, and Mrs.

Stuyvesant Fish and Mrs. Cornelius Vanderbilt were only too happy to oblige. These formidable women did not let the host down, and the entertainment turned out to be "one of the most lavish and perfect" ever given in the city. The second floor of the famous Sherry's restaurant was reserved for the dinner and the following *cotillion* (dance).

Huitres

Consomme de Tortue Verte.

Olives   Celari   Amandes.

Bass de Mer Normande.

Aloyau de Boeuf.
Aux de Champignons Frai.   Pommes Duchesse.

Jambon de Virginie aux Epinards.

Canard Sauvage.

Fried Hominy.   Gelee.

Salade.

Mousse de Vanille.
Gateaux.   Bonbons.

Café.

Champagne.   Appolinaris.

For the 132 especially privileged guests it was a "rose dinner" in honor of Valentine's Day. The guests stepped out of the second-floor lift not into a mere hallway, but into a magnificent palm grove from which they moved to a reception room decorated with silk rugs, the walls completely covered with flowers (including masses of roses) and pink satin ribbons. When dinner was announced, an ivy screen moved aside to reveal the rose arbor where the guests were to dine. Roses were everywhere, including the ceiling. In the center of each table was a six-foot high tree covered with American Beauty roses, the lower branches starting two feet above the tables so that the guests could converse beneath the fragrant, flowery canopy. The menus were in the form of Valentine's tied with satin ribbon.

The cotillion (to which many more guests were invited) began at 11 P.M. in a mirrored ballroom decorated with green vines and yet more spring flowers in every available space. Nor was the food finished for the evening. Two suppers were provided during the cotillion—a buffet available all evening and a later one served in a more formal manner.

The dinner itself was typical of the time, and it must have been thought unnecessary to continue the pink Valentine rose theme to the dishes served. The only strange note is the fried hominy, which seems strangely out of place in such a formal meal.

Recipes
~~~

The following recipe is from the classic fine-dining cookbook of the time, *The Epicurean*, published in 1894 by the famous chef of Delmonico's restaurant, Charles Ranhofer.

Roast Beef—Middle Short Loin—English Style
(Rosbif d'Aloyau a l'Anglaise)

Cut along the vertebra and toward the top of the back a piece containing the greater part of the tenderloin, from the end rib to the hip; this part called the middle short loin, and is the choice piece for roasting; it is used in the best houses in England and France. The meat must be selected from a young and tender beef of deep crimson color and veined with slices of fat. Cut from the center a piece weighing, ten, twenty, or thirty pounds, more or less, according to the number of guests to be supplied, cut away the fat, and a piece of the flank seasoning with salt and pepper, and fold the flank over; the meat should be the same thickness throughout. Tie it well, making a knot at each turn of the string. It can be wrapped up in several sheets of buttered paper. A piece of beef roasted on the spit is far preferable to one cooked in the oven. It suffices to place it in the middle of an English cradle spit, but sometimes it is impossible to cook it in this way. Therefore the most practical manner is to cook it as follows:

Set it in a deep pan with raised edges, and furnished with a grate slightly raised on four feet an inch and a half high. Pour into the pan a few spoonfuls of fat, put the meat on the grate, and roast it in a moderate oven allowing for a short loin weighing fifteen pounds one and a half hours, one of twenty, two hours, and one of thirty, two and a half hours, forty pounds, three and a half hours, the time always to be calculated according to the regularity of the fire and the thickness of the meat; roast the meat, basting and turning it over frequently, add a little water in case the grease threatens to burn. When nearly done salt. When the short loin is nearly cooked untie, and keep in a hot closet from fifteen to forty minutes according to the size, then serve it in a large dish; it must be cut in slices lengthwise of the meat, beginning at the sirloin and then the tenderloin. Serve on very hot plates with a sauce-boat of clear gravy passed round at the same time.

Fried Hominy

When cold hominy [see May 19] is left of the previous day, it is very good wet up with an egg and a little flour, and fried.

Catherine Esther Beecher, *Miss Beecher's Domestic Receipt Book* (1850).

February 15

Exotic Menu for New York Epicures
The Bank Coffee House, New York, 1823

William Niblo (1789–1875) of New York considered himself a gourmet, and he clearly perceived a niche market for his Coffee House in the burgeoning desire for novelty in dining. He sourced exotic and *recherché* ingredients from all over the country, and on this day presented to his customers "a bill of fare rarely equalled (at least for variety) in this country, and worthy the attention, no doubt, of all who devote their time and faculties to the important object of finding new sources of gratification in eating."

FIRST COURSE:
Green Turtle, made of Calf's Head;
Terrapin,
Ox-Tail,
Hen Soup in Scotch style,
Fish of all kind in the market, boiled, stewed, and barbecued.

SECOND COURSE:
A Bald Eagle,
a Hawk
an Owl,
an Opossum,
Bear Meat,
a Raccoon
a wild Swan.

THIRD COURSE:
Venison,
Mutton,
Wild Turkeys,
Roast Beef,
Canvas Back Duck,
Partridges,
Quails,
Snapping Turtle,
Calipash
and Calipee,
Terrapin, etc.

with the usual appendages of
puddings,
pies,
wines,
liquors, etc.

This menu was certainly varied. There were familiar dishes such as the soups and fish dishes and the puddings and pies still recognizable today.

There were the dishes that would have been less commonly eaten (at least by the urban American of the time), but not unheard of, such as bear and wild swan. Several dishes had social or racial connotations, and there were a few very unusual items.

The really strange items are the bald eagle "shot on the Grouse Plains of Long Island" and the "remarkably fine Hawk and Owl, shot in Turtle Grove, Hoboken." There is a widespread human prejudice against the eating of carnivorous animals, particularly carrion-eaters. Crows, for example are generally despised (see July 12), whereas their cousins, the rooks, are not. Perhaps the roots of this taboo lie in the ancient belief that the characteristics of the animal eaten will be taken on by the eater, or perhaps it is that the taste of their flesh, as is often alleged, is rank and offensive. The owl is particularly unusual as it has always been associated with nighttime, witches, and the underworld, and has rarely been part of the human bill of fare.

Mock turtle soup, usually made from calf's head (see July 4), had by this time become a valued dish in its own right, and was not simply a poor alternative to the real thing. Turtle flesh had been a metaphor for luxurious eating (see November 10) for well over a century, and it appeared in several forms at this dinner. *Calipash* and *calipee* refer to the upper and lower shells of the turtle and the gelatinous fatty material adjacent to them. This fat was highly desirable and was retained when the turtle was butchered, to be cut up and served in real turtle soup.

At the other end of the social scale, many references of the time associate the eating of raccoon and possum with subsistence living, particularly among certain ethnic or racial groups, as in these comments: "the Negroes eat the flesh of the raccoon, which they consider a great delicacy" (Daniel Blowe, *A Geographical, Historical, Commercial, and Agricultural View of the United States of America* [Edwards & Knibb, 1820]) and "the Negroes frequently eat the flesh of the raccoon, and are very fond of it, though it has a very disagreeable and rank smell" (Jane Loudon, *The Entertaining Naturalist* [Henry G Bohn, 1850]).

The interesting question raised by this bill of fare, and which was mooted by the newspapers of the time, is, What, exactly, defines epicurism? Is it a finely nuanced palate, a great knowledge of food, or the quest for dishes that are desirable simply because they are unusual?

Recipes

~~~

Instructions for the cookery of animals such as raccoon and possum are more likely to appear in the journals of explorers and frontiersmen than formal cookbooks.

Raccoon

Whilst some of the men were attending to this important business, the others began to prepare their dinner, and being curious to see how they would cook the racoon, I remained by their fire. A more summary exercise of the culinary art I never saw. Having made a fine blazing fire, they tied his hind feet to a piece of stick, and his head to another; two of them then held him in the blaze until all the fur was singed off, and then slightly eviscerating him, consigned him in that state to the pot, covering him over with pieces of fat pork to keep him down. They seemed to enjoy their repast immensely, for their talking and laughing was incessant.

George William Featherstonhaugh, *A Canoe Voyage up the Minnay Sotor* (1847).

Possum Roasted

Chill thoroughly after scraping and drawing. Save all the inside fat, let it soak in weak salt water until cooking time, then rinse it well, and partly try it out in the pan before putting in the possum. Unless he is huge, leave him whole, skewering him flat, and laying him skin side up in the pan. Set in a hot oven and cook until crisply tender, taking care there is no scorching. Roast a dozen good sized sweet potatoes—in ashes if possible, if not, bake them covered in a deep pan. Peel when done, and lay while hot around the possum, turning them over and over in the abundant gravy. He should have been lightly salted when hung up, and fully seasoned, with salt, pepper, and a trifle of mustard, when put down to cook. Dish him in a big platter, lay the potatoes, which should be partly browned, around him, add a little boiling water to the pan, shake well around, and pour the gravy over everything. Hot corn bread, strong black coffee, or else sharp cider, and very hot sharp pickles are the things to serve with him.

Martha McCulloch-Williams, *Dishes & Beverages of the Old South* (1913).

February 16

Banquet to Honor Neopolitan Princes
Florence, Italy, 1476

Benedetto Salutati was a wealthy merchant (perhaps an armourer or gold-smith) in Florence. On February 16, 1476, he held a banquet in honor of the four sons of the King of Naples (the Kingdom of *Aragón*) that was "a monument to excess."

The guests were received into a grand room whose walls and ceiling were covered with magnificent tapestries. A table on a raised platform was covered with several layers of tablecloth, as was the habit of the time, so that as it became soiled during each course, one layer could be removed to reveal the clean cloth underneath. A fine sideboard with nine shelves displayed a huge amount of silver and gold goblets, dishes, and other tableware—including 80 bowls of perfumed water for the guests to wash their hands before the meal. As was also usual for the time, food was served and carved by skilled attendants, and tasted for poison. Fine wines were matched to the food—Malvasia, Moscatello, Vernaccia, Greco, Trebbiano, Fianello, Falsamico, Bonagia di Trapani, vino del Cilento, Fassignano, Mazzacane, and Asprino.

Renaissance kitchen.

A fifteenth-century banquet was not just about food. It was an entire entertainment spectacle, and the food itself was part of the entertainment. It was colored, gilded, jellied, and decorated in many ways. There were birds in their plumage, and even a pie from which live birds flew out.

The first set of offering consists of seventeen different dishes, each guest is offered gilded ornaments, cream, layered dishes made with the flesh of the upper body of kid, blanche manger, plus eight dishes of jellied capons with the duke's coat of arms moulded on top, and a fountain which spurts perfume, and four dishes of veal, mutton, capons and boiled ham.

The second set of offerings consists of groups of four dishes with roasted peacocks which have been covered again with their own feathers, their tails fanned open, these followed by dishes of veal, mutton, capons, partridges, roasted pheasants and flavourings.

This continues with chicken pies accompanied with a sauce made with egg yolks, rose water and spices and sugar, pies with their pastry lids shaped like a bells and filled with live birds, once opened, the birds escape and fly freely in the room. Once the second tablecloth is removed the third set of offerings are presented, small pies made with puff pastry, sweet batters shaped like lamps (?), milk tortes, sugar confectionary, tortes made of marzipan perfumed with musk, wafers.

Giulio Bertoni, *Biblioteca dell' archivum romanicum* (1921), translated by Marisa Raniolo Wilkins.

The entertainment included eight young men dressed as hunters, complete with game, dogs, and bugles. And finally, at five in the morning, sweetmeats were presented in 17 silver dishes whose lids were decorated with all sort of figures and the coats of arms of all the guests.

Recipes

~~~

The spectacle of a pie containing live birds that flew out to the astonishment and delight of the guests was a favorite form of feast food entertainment right up into the seventeenth century. The following recipe is from *The Italian Banquet* (1598), an English translation of an earlier work, *Epulario*, first published in 1516, but itself a plagiarized version of a previous book.

To Make Pies that Birds May Be Alive in Them and Fly Out When It Is Cut Up

Make the coffin of a great pie or pastry, in the bottome thereof make a hole as big as your fist, or bigger if you will, let the sides of the coffin bee somewhat higher then ordinary pies, which done put it full of flower and bake it, and being baked, open the hole in the bottome, and take out the flower. Then having a pie of the bigness of the hole in the bottome of the coffin aforesaid, you shal put it into the coffin, withall put into the said coffin round about the aforesaid pie as many small live birds as the empty coffin will hold, besides the pie aforesaid. And this is to be done at such time as you send the pie to the table, and set before the guests: where uncovering or cutting up the lid of the great pie, all the birds will flie out, which is to delight and pleasure shew to the company. And because they shall not bee altogether mocked, you shall cut open the small pie, and in this sort you may make many others, the like you may do with a tart.

February 17

British Royals Dine at Mount Nelson Hotel
Capetown, South Africa, 1947

When King George VI with Queen Elizabeth and their daughters the Princesses Elizabeth (the future Queen Elizabeth II) and Margaret Rose visited the Union of South Africa in 1947, it was the first visit of a reigning British sovereign to the former Dominion of the Empire. The royal family arrived on February 17 aboard HMS *Vanguard* and the diplomatic dining routine began immediately with a private luncheon at the governor general's residence outside the city. In the evening of the same day they attended a state dinner in Capetown. *The Times* proclaimed that "characteristic South African dishes and wines were served at the banquet," although they are certainly not obvious from the menu.

Hors d'oeuvres.

Melon Frappé au Curacao.

Consomme Grande Bretagne.   Crème a la Reine.

Filet de Sole Africaine.   Lamb Cutlets Margaret Rose.

Duckling George VI.   Turkey English–Style

Green Peas a la Menthe.   Pommes Croquettes.

Iced Aparagus with Sauce Elizabeth

Plum Pudding.   Peaches Princesse.

Macaroon Royale with Camperdown
Sauce

Certainly the royal family was honored in the names of the dishes, and it was common at the time for a chef to slightly alter a classic dish and rename it for a special guest. Most "South African" dishes have a Dutch Indonesian heritage, reflecting the early Dutch colonization of both countries, and none of these are apparent here. The only obvious concession to the continent is the "*à l'Africaine*" garnish for the fish. This is a traditional garnish from the classic French repertoire and consists of marble-sized balls of a black (or dark purple) variety of potato briefly cooked in boiling water then gently braised in butter with small marrows or zucchini—a dish that appears to have decidedly racist roots.

Recipes

~~~

Potage à la Reine is a classic soup that put in a regular appearance at fine dinners throughout the nineteenth century. It is made from a puree of chicken, but, as usual, there are many variations on the basic theme.

Potage à la Reine

This is a delicate white soup, said to be a favourite with Her Majesty [Queen Victoria]. Skin and wash carefully three young chickens or two large fowls, and boil them in five pints of nicely-flavoured veal stock for about an hour. Lift them out, pick off all the white meat, put the bodies of the birds again into the stewpan and let them simmer an hour and a half longer. Season the broth with salt and cayenne, and when it is sufficiently simmered, pour it out, let it cool, and

thoroughly take off the fat which rises to the surface. Pound the white flesh of the birds to a perfectly smooth paste, and with it a tea-cupful of finely grated white breadcrumbs. Mix gradually with this paste a small quantity of the boiling stock and press it through a fine hair sieve. Add the rest of the stock, and stir the whole over a gentle fire in a clean saucepan until it boils. Add from a pint to a pint and a half of boiling cream. Serve very hot.
  Cassell's Dictionary of Cookery (London, ca. 1870s).

Wafer paper is also called rice paper. It is made from rice starch, is edible, and becomes part of the base of the macaroon.

Macaroons

1/4 lb. Ground Almonds
1/2 lb. Castor Sugar
3 or 4 Whites of Eggs
A Squeeze of Lemon Juice
Wafer Paper.

  Put the almonds and sugar into a basin, and add the lemon juice and the white of eggs very gradually, beating well with a wooden spoon or spatula. Beat thoroughly and make the mixture just moist enough to drop from a spoon. Put it into a forcing-bag with a plain pipe at the end, and force out small portions onto rounds or squares of wafer paper. This quantity should make twelve. Dust over with icing sugar, which will make the macaroons crack on top, and place a half-blanched and split almond on the top of each. Bake in a very moderate oven until nicely browned, dry, and well risen. Lift onto a sieve to cool, and break off any scraps of wafer paper that extend beyond the edges.
  The Woman's Book (London, 1911).

Melon Frappé (melon water ice): see June 20.

February 18

French Royal Supper
Château de la Muette, Paris, 1749

Louis XV (1710–1774) was King of France from the age of five. At the age of nine he inherited the Château de la Muette on the death of his aunt the Duchesse du Berry. The *château* was in the Bois de Boulogne, the forest on the outskirts of Paris, and it had grown out of a sixteenth-century royal hunting lodge. Louis completely rebuilt the *château* and spent a great deal of time there entertaining his mistresses and also holding sessions of the Council of State. The cuisine, of course, was as elegant as unlimited wealth and power could make it. On February 18, 1749, the bill of fare for the royal supper offered the following choices:

DEUX GRANDES ENTREÉS.
Un râble de mouton de montagne.
Un quartier de veau, une blanquette dans le cuisseau.

DEUX OILLES.
1 au riz.
1 à la jambe de bois.

DEUX POTAGES.
1 à la faubonne.
1 aux choux fleurs.

SEIZE ENTRÉES.
1 de côtelettes mélées.
1 de petits pâtés à la Bèchameil.
1 de lange de moutons à la duchesse.
1 de petits pigeons aux truffes entières.
1 de haricot de mouton aux navets.
1 de boudins d'écrivesses.
1 de filets de poularde à la d'Armagnac.
1 de matelelot à la Dauphine.
1 de noix de veau aux épinards.
1 de membres de faisan à la Conty.
1 de filets de perdreux à la Périgueux.
1 de petits poulets à l'Urlubie.
1 de ris de veau à la Sainte-Ménéhould.
1 sarcelles à l'orange.
1 lapereaux en crépines.
1 poules de Caux en escalopes.

QUATRE RELEVÉS.
1 dindonneau à la peau goret, sauce Robert.
1 pâte de bécassines.
1 quartier de sanglier.
1 noix de bœuf aux chou-fleurs.

DEAUX GRANDS ENTREMETS.
1 pâté de jambon.
1 gâteau de Savoie.

QUATRE MOYENS.
2 de boissons d'écrivisses.
2 gâteau au fromage.

HUIT PLATS DE RÔTS NON MENTIONÉS.—SEIZE ENTREMETS.
1 de cardes au jus.
1 de crêtes au bouillon.
1 d'amourettes.
1 de foies gras grillés.
1 de ragoûts mêlés à la crême.
1 de crême au chocolat.
1 d'abbaise de massepain.

1 d'œufs à l'Infante.
1 d'huitres au gratin.
1 de pattes de dindon à l'espagnole.
1 d'asperges.
1 de truffles à la cendre.
1 de crême glacée.
1 de canelons meringués.
1 de chou-fleurs.
[one entremet appears to be missing]

The menu was arranged in the typical French haute cuisine style of a balanced, even number of dishes and courses, with many classic dishes.

Recipes

~~~

D'amourette means an affair of the heart, but this dish was no romantic or aphrodisiacal dish. Strangely, the word also refers to the spinal marrow or "pith" of a beast. Today we would consider it offal, to be tossed aside (or disguised in sausage meat perhaps), but it was not always so. In keeping with other animal parts not favored today, it could be, and was, regularly turned into favored dishes, and the following recipe shows how the most unpromising body part can be made into a gourmet dish fit for a king.

Des Amourettes du veau Frites

Piths, or marrow of the back, or chine of a calf, fryd.

Cut your piths in length about three or four inches, blanch them in water, and take off the outermost skin, lay them an hour in a marinade of white wine and vinegar, &c. dry them in a cloth, make a batter of ale or small beer, pour in a little oil or oiled butter, stir it well together, put in your piths, and give them a toss, and fry them of a beautiful yellow, and dish them up on a heap of fry'd parsley. Piths of mutton or lamb make as pretty a dish.
William Verral, *A Complete System of Cookery* (1759).

Robert Sauce is one of the most enduring classic dishes. Recipes for it appear in the mid-sixteenth century, although the sauce was being made for at least 200 years. In *Le Viander de Taillevent* (a cookbook of the late fourteenth century) it appears as *taillemaslée*.

Robert Sauce

Slice several Onions and fry them in Butter, turning often until they take Colour, then add a little Cullis and good Broth, Pepper, and Salt; let them boil half an Hour and reduce to a Sauce; when ready add Mustard: you may sift it for those that only like the Flavour of Onions.
François Menon, *The Professed Cook* (1769).

Des meringues
Whites of Eggs Batter

This is done with Whites of Eggs well beat up, and as much Sugar as will make it the Consistence of a thick Batter; put a little rasped Lemon-peel in it; drop it in small Drops upon white Paper; strew Powder-sugar over; bake in a very moderate Heat; when done, glue two drops together with Caramel-sugar, and put a Bit of Sweet-meat betwixt: this is made of what size is most agreeable.
    François Menon, *The Professed Cook* (1769).

February 19

Creole Dinner for the New Orleans Press Club
The Atheneum, New Orleans, Louisiana, 1898

The New Orleans Press Club showcased the regional cuisine, folklore, and culture at *Un Petit Dine Creole* when the city hosted the annual convention of the League of Press Clubs in 1898. This is the menu in English: it was also given in "Negro patois." It was designed and executed by George G. Voitier, the Steward of the New Orleans Press Club.

They boast of their terrapin,

Tattered rags are better than to go naked.

But once taste Cacene,

Absinthe and Anisette.

And you taste something which is fine.

Fricassee Cacene (pig skin).

In Louisiana they find good calas (cake eaten with coffee).

Oysters, Choupique and bamboula (national dance).

Don't tie your dogs with sausages.

Oysters from Mosquito Bayou.

Jambalaya Tchourisses (rice and blood puddings).

With a good gombo prepared by Silvie,

A Creole dinner is not complete

Without ever scolding I would pass my life.

Without a little suckling pig.

Gombo filé, Bisque 'crébiches.

A runaway pig, stuffed and roasted.

Small vegetables with salt.

Sweet salad with chickory.

When I was a little boy

A bird in the hand

My mother would say

Is better than all the birds flying in the woods.

This stewed fish, my son,

Is mighty good.

Courtbouillion Patassa from Bayou Patassa.

HAUT SAUTERNE 1878— Calvet & Co.

A cockroach never holds its own before a hen.

Chicken Paté.

A crawfish is a darned beast!

Boiled crawfish.

Everyone knows what boils in his own pot.

Red beans with rice ("Hopping John").

SAINT JULIEN 1876— Calvet & Co.

Snipes with laurel leaves en baguette.

Watercresses from Bayou des Herbes.

CHAMPAGNE—G. H. Mumm & Co.

Lagniappe is something very good (a corruption of a Spanish word which means thrown in a market basket *over and above*).

Popcorn, Sugared pecans,

Sweet potato bread, Thick molasses.

The last drawn from the pots in the sugar-house before it turns to sugar.

A fourth of an ice cream. A fourth of a piece of cake.

Ice cream biscuit. Mulatto stomach (gingerbread).

Tante Zizine's poundcake.

There are no Skipenon grapes and no persimmons,

But we'll give you what there is.

Bananas, Oranges, Sugar cane, Mandarins.

Black Creole coffee ("Morning Joy").

A singed cat fears the fire.

Brulo.

Cigarettes perique—corn paper.

Creole cigarettes—yellow paper.

When you have no horse, you ride a donkey;

When you have no donkey, you ride a goat;

When you have no goat, you go on foot.

A discussion of this menu would naturally start with a definition of "Creole" cuisine, which inevitably requires it to be compared or contrasted with "Cajun" cuisine. Therein lies a problem because the debate, although long-standing and frequently heated, will never reach consensus. They may once have been completely distinct, but there has been much blending over time, and there is huge regional variation across the state of Louisiana. It is probably true to say that they have more similarities than differences.

One dish in particular crosses the divide. It is gumbo, a generic name for a soup or stew or soupy stew made with whatever meat or shellfish is available (usually a mixture) and given its unique texture by the use of okra or *filé* powder. There is an almost infinite number of variations depending on local tradition and available ingredients. Over 20 different sorts of gumbo were served at a famous society dinner in New Orleans in 1803.

Recipes

~~~

Gumbo Filé

Put into a casserole (saucepan) a spoonful of pure lard and one of flour, stir it well until it is of a light brown. Chop an onion into small pieces and throw them in. Cut up a fat capon or chicken into small pieces and put these in the casserole with the flour and lard. Stir it all the while until the chicken is nearly done. When the whole is well browned, add a slice of ham, cut up small. Throw in two or three pods of red pepper, and salt to your taste. Now add a quart of boiling water, and leave it on the fire for two hours and a half. A quarter of an hour before dinner is served add three dozen oysters with their liquor. Just before taking the soup off the fire, put in a tablespoonful of filet, stirring it all the while. Let it boil one minute and then serve. Do not put in too much filet; the spoon should not be full. Indeed, half a tablespoonful is enough.

Célestine Eustis, *Cooking in Old Créole Days* (New York, 1904).

Jambalaya of Fowls and Rice

Cut up and stew a fowl; when half done, add a cup of raw rice, a slice of ham minced, and pepper and salt; let all cook together until the rice swells and absorbs all the gravy of the stewed chicken, but it must not be allowed to get hard or dry. Serve in a deep dish. Southern children are very fond of this; it is said to be an Indian dish, and very wholesome as well as palatable; it can be made of many things.

Lafcadio Hearn, *La Cuisine Creole* (New Orleans, ca. 1885).

Calas or Callas: see March 12.

February 20

Wartime Luncheon
Stork Club, New York, 1943

The Stork Club was once "New York's New Yorkiest place," according to columnist Walter Winchell. The nightclub was opened in 1929 as a front for mobsters by former bootlegger Sherman Billingsley and quickly became *the* place to be for the rich, powerful, famous, and beautiful. Anybody who was anybody came here, and came to be seen here, and almost anything could happen. The Vanderbilts, the Kennedys, the Roosevelts came, as did the Duke and Duchess of Windsor (who were famously snubbed here by Winchell). Movie stars came—Charlie Chaplin, Errol Flynn, Rita Hayworth, Grace Kelly, Marilyn Monroe, and many others. The writer Ernest Hemingway came and got into a scuffle with the warden of Sing-Sing prison, knocking him down.

In 1943 the club was in its third and final location (it closed in 1965) at 3 East 53rd Street, just off Fifth Avenue, now the location of Paley Park. For such a glamorous place with such wealthy clientele, a place about which the writer Lucius Beebe said "There is no food or time of the day and night when the service of Champagne is not both appropriate and agreeable," the luncheon menu for February 20, 1943, seems quite austere.

SPECIAL LUNCHEON $1.50

Fruit Cocktail
*

Omelette Au Fromage
or
Minced Chicken Curry, Rice Pilaw
*

Pie or Raspberry Sherbet
*

Demi Tasse

This was of course a small selection from the very comprehensive menu for the club. Why would the millionaire clients need a "special" menu for a $1.50 luncheon? Perhaps it simply made the dining decision easy, leaving energy to be better spent on people-watching and partying? Perhaps it was a discreet way of allowing those who had gained entry on account of their beauty rather than their money—the starlets and dancers hoping to snare a millionaire—to buy lunch?

This was wartime, and there were rationing restrictions in place (although a former bootlegger who kept company with mobsters may not have had trouble finding his way around a few laws). Sugar in particular was in short supply and rationing regulations were put in place in early 1942. The shortage was due to a number of factors. Production in the Phillipines and Hawaii had been severely affected by the war; imports from Cuba were reduced because more was being diverted to the allies, and a "heavy diversion" was being made to the production of molasses for conversion to industrial alcohol, which was used in the manufacture of explosives. In January 1942, the household consumption of sugar was restricted to 50 pounds per capita (a reduction from 74 pounds in 1941) by the Office of Price Administration, and a comparable reduction for "industrial purposes" from 47 to 27 pounds was being contemplated. Patriotic citizens did not shop around and hoard supplies, and patriotic restaurants and hotels found various ways to reduce sugar consumption. Most dining establishments appealed to the patriotic instincts of their patrons, and many found indirect disincentives such as removing sugar bowls entirely from tables and having staff sweeten drinks "at the customer's discretion," or keeping the bowls deliberately almost empty to discourage "souveniring" of individually wrapped cubes.

Recipes

~~~

The "special luncheons" at the Stork Club at this time commonly started with fruit cocktail, ended with pies and sherbet, and had an egg choice for the main. The sugar used in the fruit cocktail and desserts in 1943 would have had to come from the club's industrial allowance.

Frozen Fruit Cocktail

1/2 cup crushed pineapple
2 cups orange pulp
3/4 cup grapefruit pulp
1/4 cup powdered sugar
1 cup lemon or lime carbonated beverage or ginger ale

Add the sugar to the fruits and stir gently until sugar is dissolved. Add carbonated beverage. Set into freezing tray of automatic refrigerator. Freeze to slush. Serve as appetizer. Serves 6.
The Lily Wallace New American Cookbook (1946).

Cheese Omelet

One or two eggs for each person, 1 tablespoon of milk for each egg, and salt to taste. Beat the eggs and milk. Have ready and hot a smooth heavy omelet pan containing 1 tablespoon butter or other fat, and pour the egg mixture into the pan. As soon as the omelet has browned slightly on the bottom, sprinkle 1/2 cup grated cheese on it and place in a very hot oven until the omelet is cooked and the cheese melted. Fold and turn out on a hot platter.
Adapted from *The Lily Wallace New American Cookbook,* (1946).

Pilau: see March 30.
Sherbet: see April 29, June 10.

Menu Notice at Fred Harvey Restaurants, 1942

Sugar, Tea, and Coffee Conservation.

Because of the Government's dramatic reduction in our allowance of the above items,
we are now compelled to ask our guests to observe the following restrictions.

Sugar.
For Breakfast: Not to exceed two level teaspoons
Luncheon or Dinner: Not to exceed one level teaspoon

Coffee.
One cup of hot coffee, one glass of iced coffee.

Tea.
One cup of tea, hot or iced.

February 21

Business Dinner
Hotel Lutetia, Boulevarde Rapail, Paris, 1947

The beautiful art deco Hotel Lutetia was built on the Left Bank of Paris in 1910. The name of the hotel comes from that given to the settlement by the conquering Romans in 53 BCE—*Lutetia Parisiorum*, which loosely means the marshy location inhabited by the local tribe, the Parisii. In the first few decades of its existence the fashionable hotel played host to many of the rich or famous of the time, including Picasso, Matisse, J. D. Salinger, Josephine Baker, and Charles de Gaulle (who honeymooned there). These early guests were not to know that the hotel would play a far more active role in the history of the city in the 1940s.

When the Germans entered Paris in June 1940, the Lutetia became the headquarters of the Gestapo. In August 1944 when the city was liberated it was requisitioned by the Allies, and in a nicely ironic turn became the repatriation center for returning prisoners of war, prison camp returnees, and displaced persons. By 1947 the Lutetia was well and truly back in business as a fine hotel, indulging its guests and arranging fine dinners such as the following one for a commercial textile company on February 21, 1947.

Potage Darblay
Truite Saumonée au Chablis
Jambon braisée au Madère
Petits Pois à la Française
Poularde de Bresse rôti au cresson
Salade
Fromages
Bombe Nélusko
Sablés
Corbeille de Fruits

```
                          —
                        VINS
                      Sylvaner
                     Beaujolais
                    Vougeat 1937
                  Champagne frappé
                        Café
                      Liqueurs
```

This was a fine menu with fine wine served in typical French style. The salmon was cooked in white wine, the ham in Madeira wine, and the chicken (from Bresse, which is said to produce the finest chicken in the world) prepared with watercress, a favorite method of serving poultry since the early nineteenth century.

Young, tender, fresh peas have been a favorite in France since the seventeenth century. Tiny, hard, dry "field peas" were a staple food of the peasants of Europe for centuries, eaten in the form of pease porridge, pottage, or pudding (see November 1, December 21). In the seventeenth century Dutch horticulturists developed the "garden pea," which could be eaten fresh. It is difficult to imagine any new vegetable causing great excitement nowadays, but when these sweet, tender *petits pois* came on the scene, the aristocracy of seventeenth-century France went wild for them. Mme de Maintenon (1635–1719), the mistress and then second wife of Louis XIV, wrote in 1669 "The impatience to eat them, the pleasure of having eaten them, and the joy of eating them again are the three points of private gossip ... it is both a fashion and a madness." The ladies of the court of Louis XIV ate the peas straight from the pod as if they were candy, but various ways of cooking them soon developed.

Recipes

~~~

Potage Darblay

This is essentially a *Potage Parmentier* (see January 12), a potato and leek soup named for Antoine Parmentier (see October 21) with a *julienne* (matchstick sized slips) of vegetables, lightly cooked in butter and added just before serving.

Poulet Rôti (au Cresson)

Cover your fowl with a buttered sheet of paper or with slices of bacon, roast, and a few minutes before taking off the spit, remove the paper or bacon. When a good colour, dish up the fowl, and garnish with watercress.
366 Menus and 1200 Recipes of the Baron Brisse (1896 [1868]).

Bombe Nélusko

This popular dessert was named for a character in the grand opera *L'Africaine*. It is made by lining a mould with praline ice cream, filling it with chocolate mousse, and freezing.

February 22

George Washington's Birthday Celebration
Hotel Cecil, London, 1897

The American Society in London was founded in 1895 by a group of eminent expatriates with the dual objectives of fostering good relations between the United States and Great Britain and celebrating the heritage and traditions of their home country. Both objectives were served by inviting prominent English men and women to celebrate events such as Independence Day, Thanksgiving, and on February 22—the birthday of George Washington.

Instead of the customary dinner, in 1897 the Society decided to hold a reception followed by a collation, at the Hotel Cecil. In other words, a formal "receiving" was to be followed by an informal light meal. The "receiving" on this occasion was by the U.S. Ambassador Thomas Bayard and his wife and daughter who formally greeted about 300 guests, including the President of the Society, Henry Wellcome, founder of Wellcome Pharmaceuticals, and Moncure D. Conway, the controversial clergyman and abolitionist and

---

MENU.

CHAUD.

Consommé en Tasse.
Stewed Oysters.
Fried Oysters.
Scalloped Oysters.
Croquettes de Volaille.

FROID.

Mayonnaise de Homard.
Chaudfroid de Mauviettes.

MENU.

Salade de Légumes.
Salade Italienne.
Salade Romaine.
Punch à la Romaine.

Foie Gras
Sandwiches   Lettuce and Egg
Ham and Chicken

Petite Pâtisserie Française assortie.
Babas au Rhum

Terrine de Foie Gras.	Gelées variées.
Galantine de Volaille	Petites Glaces assorties.
Salade de Volaille au Céleri.	Café glacé.
Langue.	
Bœuf Pressé.	
Côte de Bœuf.	———
Boned Turkey.	Tea Coffee
Jambon d'York.	Chocolate

supporter of women's suffrage. The *New York Times* was sufficiently interested to note the event, referring to it as "brilliant."

The informal nature of a collation is obvious from this menu. There were only a few warm dishes—tiny cups of consommé, several dishes of cooked oysters, and some croquettes—perhaps to welcome the guests on the winter evening. The remainder of the meal was in the form of a cold buffet, which included that most informal of snacks—several varieties of sandwiches (see November 25).

Recipes
~~~

Scalloped Oysters

6 quarts oysters	6 cups cracker crumbs
1 1/2 cups oyster liquor	3 cups melted butter
3/4 cup milk or cream	Salt
3 cups stale bread crumbs	Pepper

Mix bread and cracker crumbs and stir in butter. Put a thin layer in bottom of buttered baking dishes, cover with cleaned oysters, sprinkle with salt and pepper; repeat. Dip oyster liquor and cream over top, cover with remaining crumbs. Bake thirty minutes in hot oven. A little finely-chopped celery is an improvement. There should never be more than two layers to a dish for scalloped oysters.

Pressed Beef

12 pounds beef from flank	2 cups onion
brisket, or round	2 cups carrot
1 tablespoon salt	1 teaspoon peppercorns
Sweet herbs to taste	1/4 cup vinegar

Wipe and trim meat, cover with boiling water, bring to boiling point, simmer until meat is in shreds. Add vegetables and seasonings one hour before it is done. Remove meat and pack in long, narrow pans. Reduce liquor to three cups, strain and pour over meat. Cover and press with a heavy weight. Serve cold in thin slices.

Reception Chocolate

1 pound chocolate	1 1/2 pounds sugar
2 quarts boiling water	8 quarts hot milk

Melt chocolate in double boiler, add boiling water, stir until smooth. Boil ten minutes, or cook one hour in double boiler, add sugar and one-fourth teaspoon of salt. Turn into hot milk, beat until foamy, and serve with whipped cream.
Frances Lowe Smith, *Recipes and Menus for Fifty* (Boston, 1913).

Salade Italienne

Cook in salted water one pint of green peas, half a pint of string beans, half a pint of carrots and as much turnips, both of these pushed through a tin tube; they should be a quarter of an inch in diameter, and three eighths of an inch long. First blanch the carrots and turnips, then cook them in broth with salt and sugar, and when done drain and leave them to get cool. Put into a salad bowl the carrots, green peas, some green peppers, string beans, turnips and finely cut-up chervil, tarragon, chives and finely chopped parsley; season with salt, pepper, vinegar and oil, mixed well together. Cut some beets and potatoes in an eighth of an inch thick slices, remove some rounds from these with a vegetable cutter three-quarters of an inch in diameter, then season; set the beetroots alternated with the potatoes around the base; near the top place a row of round slices of pickles half an inch in diameter; divide the height between the potatoes and the pickles with fillets of anchovies into six panels; in the center of these place a round slice of mortadelle and on the top lay some small channeled mushrooms.
Charles Ranhofer, *The Epicurean* (1894).

Croquettes of Poultry: see August 21.
Mayonnaise de Homard (Lobster mayonnaise): see March 31.
Chaud-Froid: see July 25.
Punch Romaine (Roman punch): see July 1.

February 23

Coronation Feast of Queen Catherine
Westminster Hall, London, England, 1421

The marriage of Henry V of England to Catherine of Valois (the daughter of Charles VII of France) was intended to seal the conditions of the Treaty of Troyes in 1421 in which Henry was recognized as heir and regent of France.

Catherine's coronation ceremony was followed by the traditional feast—
which was no less spectacular for its occurrence during the season of Lent,
when "ye shall understande, that this feaste was al of fyshe."

FIRST COURSE.	SECOND COURSE.	THIRD COURSE.
Brawne and mustard	Gely	Dates in compost
Ded ellys in Burneur	White potage or crème of almandes.	Creme motle
Frument with Balien	Counger	Carpe deore
Pyke in Erbage	Solys	Turbut
Lamprey powdered	Cheuen	Tenche
Trout	Barbyll with Roche	Perche with goson
Codlyng	Freshe Samon	Fyrshe sturgeon with welkes
Playes fryed, Marlyng fryed	Halybut	Porperis rosted
Crabbys	Gurnarde	Mennes fryed
Leche Lumbard floryshed	Rocket broiled	Creuys de eawe douce
A bake mete in paste	Smelth fryed	Pranys
Tartys.	Creuys or lobster	Elys rosted with lamprey
	Leche Damaske	Poudrid welkys
A soltetie (a Pelican and St Katherine)	Lamprey freshe baken	Datys
	Flampeyne	Rede schryppys
		A leche called the whyte leche etc.
	A soltetie (A Panther and St Catherine).	A march payne garnyshed
		A soltetie (A Tiger and St. George leading him)

The number of "fish" and "fast" days on the Christian calendar varied
from one to three days a week over many centuries, and the strict observance
of Lent required forty days of avoiding not just flesh-meat but also dairy
products and eggs.

The inclusion of whale and porpoise on the fish-day menu is usually attributed to ignorance, but their inclusion made perfect sense to the medieval

cook, cleric, and physician. The prevailing "theory of everything" at the time had been inherited from the ancient Greeks. Humoral theory was based on the belief that every single thing in the natural world arose from the four basic elements (fire, earth, water, air), each of which had a particular quality (hot, dry, moist, cold). In the human body these were represented by the "humours" (sanguine, choleric, phlegmatic, and melancholic). Imbalance in the humors resulted in disease, and both disease and mood could be manipulated by diet—which therefore required a knowledge of the "temperaments" of various foods.

To turn away from earthly things and consider one's mortal soul could be assisted by turning towards foods that would cool and calm the earthly passions. The prohibition was not about "fish" as understood today, but instead about animals that lived in the water, which were considered "cool" in temperament, and so would transmit this quality to the eater. Another useful characteristic of "fish" was that there was no visible evidence that they reproduced sexually, so fish flesh would be less likely than meat to *provoke to venery.*

The food restrictions of Lent had other benefits that came into increased prominence after the Reformation. Lent in the Northern Hemisphere occurred at the end of winter or in early spring when food supplies were low, but new-season crops were still some way off. A prohibition on eating meat and eggs at this time made eminent sense as it preserved the breeding stock. An economic rationale also became important. A demand for fish reduced the drain on agricultural resources and supported the fishing industry. This in turn produced trained seamen and stimulated shipbuilding, which assisted the development of naval power and encouraged voyages of exploration. It is little wonder that fish days and fast days were enforced by secular as well as religious powers for many centuries.

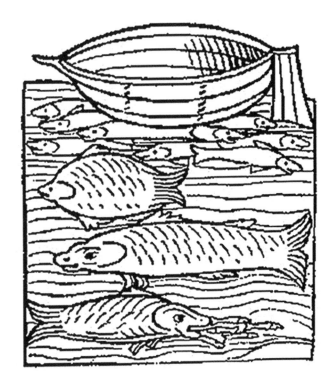

One apparent problem on this menu is the "brawne and mustard." Brawn is almost always assumed to refer to "swine's flesh" (usually in a dish that can be sliced), and it would be nigh on impossible to justify an aquatic origin for a pig. An older sense of the word referred to the flesh of

Fish. Med Life Illustrations.

any animal, and there are medieval references to such things as "brawn of lobster" and recipes for Lenten brawn made from fish.

The white pottage, custards, tarts, and "leaches" were all egg-free in this menu, and the primary substitute was almond milk, which was required in vast quantities for an event such as this and must have been incredibly labor intensive to prepare without the labor-saving devices in use today.

Recipes

~~~

Furmenty (frumenty) is a sort of porridge made from boiled wheat. In its simplest form (boiled in water) it was the staple food of the peasants. For the rich it formed a side dish for venison—or on fish days, for whale or porpoise—and was often enriched with wine or ale, or as in this version, with almond milk.

Furmente with Porpeys

Take clene whete and bete it small in a morter and fanne out clene the doust, þenne waisthe it clene and boile it tyl it be tendre and broun. þanne take the secunde mylk of Almaundes & do þerto. boile hem togidur til it be stondyng, and take þe first mylke & alye it up wiþ a penne. take up the porpays out of the Furmente & leshe hem in a dishe with hoot water. & do safroun to þe furmente. and if the porpays be salt. seeþ it by hym self, and serue it forth.
   Form of Cury (1390).

Compost

A "compost" was a "stew" or preserve of fruit and sometimes vegetables. It is essentially the same as what is now called a "compôte."

Brawn: see April 28.
Lamprey Freshe Baken: see March 9.

February 24

State Dinner
The White House, Washington, DC, 1999

President Bill Clinton (b. 1946) and Hilary Rodham Clinton (b. 1947) were hosts to his Excellency Flt. Lt. Jerry John Rawlings, president of the Republic of Ghana and Nana Konadu Agyeman-Rawlings, at a White House State Dinner on Wednesday, February 24, 1999. The menu was as follows:

Five Spice Roasted Duck over Marinated Pears and Papaya
Scallion and Vegetable Salad
Gingered Red Pepper Dressing

Grilled Yellowtail Snapper
Butternut, Celeriac, Gold Potato Hash
Truffled Lobster Fricassèe
Roasted Pumpkin Sauce
Mâche, Spinach and Winter Greens Salad
Tomatoes and Herbed Goats Cheese Baked in Brioche
Basil Vinaigrette

DESSERT
Sweet Kente Wrapped Mango
and Golden Pineapple Ice Cream
Exotic Roses
Raspberry Sauce
Gold Bars and Ghana Coco Beans

WINES
Etude Pinot Blanc 1997
Wild Horse Pinot Noir 1997
Domaine Carneros "Le Reve" 1992

This is a thoroughly modern menu, but there are still traces in this event of old traditions of diplomatic dining, and of dishes with very old histories. The organizers of state dinners have to negotiate several sometimes competing principles when it comes to entertaining important international visitors. There is a natural wish to showcase their own national cuisine (see May 11, October 11, June 10) and often a desire also to acknowledge that of the visitor. To complicate matters, there may be religious requirements (see April 29) to be considered, as well as the personal tastes and preferences of the guest. A great deal of international discussion takes place beforehand, and the proposed menu is usually discussed and agreed upon well in advance. "Forbidden" ingredients in particular are notified to the host nation. Queen Elizabeth II, for example, does not eat garlic (because it is inappropriate for the royal breath to be offensive), nor does she eat raw seafood such as raw oysters (because of the food poisoning risk) or berries, which might leave seeds in the teeth, and potentially "splashy" dishes such as spaghetti are also not favored.

Vinaigrette dressing has French roots, as can be deduced from its name, which refers to the vinaigre (vinegar) it contains. References to it appear in English in the seventeenth century, but it does not appear to have become popular (in England and the United States) until late in the nineteenth century. In its basic form it consists of oil and vinegar (usually in the proportions of 3:1) and salt. Many other things are added to the basic mix, as in this menu where it is flavored with basil.

Brioche is a cake or loaf made from a yeast dough enriched with eggs and butter. The name comes from *broyer or brier* meaning to knead. It has been made in Europe since at least the early fifteenth century, but its roots can be traced back to Roman times. It is the same dough as makes *savarin, kugelhopf,* and *babas* and lends itself as a base to many dishes both savory and sweet.

Recipe

~~~

Brioche

For the yeast, take four ounces of finely sifted flour, twelve grammes of yeast, and two and a half fluid ounces of water; make this into a soft paste; put it in a dish in a warm place and cover it; keep it until it has risen to three times its former size; the yeast should jut be right, or the brioche will be heavy or bitter; take twelve ounces of sifted flour, place it on the table, make it up to a heap, and then open a hole in it; use twelve grammes of perfectly fresh butter, eight grammes of salt, a half-tumbler of milk or cream, and nine eggs; work all well together, introducing the yeast; dust a cloth with flour, put it in an earthenware bowl, and place your brioche paste in that, covering it with another cloth: let it remain twelve hours in a warm place; then the paste ought to be neither too hard nor too soft: if too soft, add more flour; if too hard another egg. The consistency ought to be about that of bread. Take the dough and turn it in from the edges, working it some half a dozen times. Put it aside again for four hours. Then work it twice as before. Make it into a round ball. Take a sheet of tin, with butter, and put the brioche on it in an oven with brisk heat. If it shows a tendency to run or spread, it must have a piece of buttered paper placed around it. Several brioches of small size can be made from this receipt. Time of baking from one-half to three-quarters of an hour. Paper forms are made expressly to bake brioches in.

From *Cuisiniere de la Campagne*, first published in 1816, the 67th edition in 1887. Quoted in *The New York Times*, 1881.

February 25

Dinner with the British Prime Minister
No. 10, Downing St., London, England, 1983

Margaret Thatcher (b. 1925), the Conservative Party prime minister of the United Kingdom from 1979–1990, was known for her tough, unyielding approach to many issues of the day, and as a result she attracted several unflattering nicknames, such as "The Iron Lady" on account of her dealings with the Soviet Union, and "Thatcher Milk-Snatcher" for her decision to end the free milk program in schools. As the country's leader, however, she did have to play the welcoming hostess to visiting dignitaries and heads of state. In February 1983 one of her guests was Amintore Fanfani (1908–1999), the prime minister of Italy. Thatcher entertained him at Number 10, Downing Street, the official residence of the First Lord of the Treasury (and later the English prime minister) since 1735. The dinner was elegant in its simplicity.

Lamberhurst Priory, 1979
Château Talbot, 1971
Port – Brandy – Liqueurs

Avocado Mousse
with Waldorf Salad

Sautéed Breast of Chicken
with Rosemary
Mixed Salad
New Potatoes

Hazelnut Ice Cream
with Strawberries

Coffee

The perhaps slightly surprising item on this menu is the presence of an English wine alongside the French, particularly in view of the guest being from a country also noted for its wines. England is hardly famous for its wine, but English wines have been appearing increasingly often on English diplomatic and royal occasions and have been achieving some success in wine competitions.

Wine-making was introduced to England by the Romans when they conquered the country in the first century BCE. Since then, it has undergone several renaissances and relapses but has never completely disappeared. The Middle Ages is cited as England's great era of wine-making, and it is often quoted that the success of the industry at this time was due to a warmer climate, and its decline to a progressive cooling in the later medieval era. Its relatively modern resurgence is by the same argument attributed to global warming. Climatologists continue to debate whether or not the "Medieval Warm Period" and the following "Little Ice Age" actually happened, but in reality there were other reasons for the decline of wine-making at this time. When Henry II married Eleanor of Aquitaine in 1152, the country gained access to the fine wines of Bordeaux, and English wine could not compete with the quantity and style of those wines. Then, in the fourteenth century, the plague swept across England and Europe, depopulating entire areas and causing decline in many agricultural industries. Another blow was the dissolution of the monasteries by Henry VIII between 1536–1541. The monasteries had always been the center for wine-making because of the need for sacramental wine.

There have always been a few enthusiasts who have continued to grow grapes in the south of England, and there were brief periods in the sixteenth and seventeenth centuries when the industry flourished on a small scale. Samuel Pepys (1633–1703), while writing his diary in the mid-seventeenth century, saw his first vineyard in Greenwich on the outskirts of London on May 1, 1665, and mentions tasting English wine on a number of other occasions. Since the 1950s interest in wine-making has gradually increased. The Lamberhurst Priory in Kent, which provided the wine at the prime minister's dinner, was one of the pioneering vineyards in the revival of the British wine industry.

The French wine served at the dinner, the Château Talbot, was from Bordeaux, which has in fact been "English" for much of its history. This particular wine has a close connection with Britain—it is said to be named for John Talbot, Earl of Shrewsbury.

Recipe

~~~

Avocado Mousse

Serves 6
1/2 oz. (or 1 slightly rounded tablespoon) powdered gelatin
1/4 pint cold water
1/4 pint chicken stock
3 small or 2 large ripe avocado pears
1 level teaspoon salt
pinch pepper
1 teaspoon onion juice, taken from finely grated onion
2 teaspoons Worcestershire sauce
1/4 pint mayonnaise
1/4 pint double cream

Measure water into small saucepan, sprinkle over gelatin and leave for 5 minutes. Then warm gently until gelatin is dissolved and mixture clear, but do not boil. Draw pan from heat, stir in stock, and set aside.

Halve avocados and remove stones; scoop out flesh into basin and mash until smooth. Add onion juice (finely grate small onion on to a saucer, and spoon out juice), add to the avocado pulp with salt, pepper and Worcestershire sauce. Add gelatin mixture and stir over iced water until just beginning to thicken. Then quickly fold in mayonnaise and lightly whipped cream. Pour into 1 1/2 pint mold (or individual molds) rinsed with cold water and chill until set firm. When set, unmold and serve.

Adapted from *The Times*, May 2, 1968.

Waldorf Salad: see October 7.

February 26

German-American Press Honors Prince Henry of Prussia
Waldorf-Astoria Hotel, New York, 1902

When his Royal Highness Prince Henry of Prussia (1862–1929) was sent on a visit to the United States in 1902 by his brother Kaiser Wilhelm II, it was promoted as a purely friendly visit designed to foster goodwill between the two countries. The events and celebrations planned for his stay were of course anything but lacking in formality or politics. The large-distribution German language newspaper of New York, the *Staats-Zeitung*, tendered a dinner in honor of the prince. It was "the largest gathering of newspaper makers that ever sat down at one board in the history of the United States," as well as "an opportunity for the Prince to get in touch with one of the principal bulwarks of a Republic" according to *The New York Times*.

MENU

Oysters.
Rudesheimer, 1889.
Clear Green Turtle.
Amontillado pasado
Mousse of ham, Venetian style.
Zeitinger Schlossberg, 1893.
Terrapin, Philadelphia style.
Champagne.
Sweetbread, new century.
Breast of chicken, Finoise.
New peas, sauté.
Canvasback Duck.
Sherbet Admiral.
Lettuce Salad.
Chambertin, 1878.
Fancy Ices
Cakes.   Fruit.
Coffee.
Liqueurs.

It was a fine menu, as would be expected. It started with the usual oysters, moved through several choice entrees including the increasingly rare terrapin, ended with the expected fancy ices and cakes, and was accompanied by a fine selection of international beverages. The format, too, was standard for the time. Many mutually congratulatory toasts and speeches were made. Women did not grace the table but were allowed to "grace the function" in a decorative capacity by being allowed to bedeck themselves in their finery and observe the proceedings from the galleries.

The decorative finery also extended to the table. As the punch was being served the guests were delighted to receive as souvenirs (the ancestors of modern party favors) small plaster busts of the prince. When it came time to serve the obligatory ices, there was an even greater and more clever spectacle, as *The New York Times* reported:

The army of waiters filed in with miniatures of the German Emperor, Prince Henry, President Roosevelt, the latter both in civilian attire and as a Rough Rider; Liberty, Columbia, Germania, crowns and mitres, and many huge German coats of arms—all done in ices. There were also reproductions of the yacht Meteor and of the Hohenzollern. The last two craft and the sugary statuette of President Roosevelt were placed before Prince Henry, and he clapped his hands with the rest.

Recipes

~~~

Mousse of Ham in Cases

Finely mince one pound lean cooked ham, place it in a mortar with the yolks of two eggs and pound to a paste; then press through a sieve into a bowl. Season with a saltspoon grated nutmeg, a saltspoon cayenne pepper, adding one tablespoon sherry wine; mix well with a spoon, then gradually add one gill cold cream, continually mixing meanwhile. Beat to a stiff froth three egg whites and gently mix with the preparation. Fill up six small paper cases. Place the cases in a tin and bake in the oven for fifteen minutes. Remove, dress on a dish with a folded napkin and send to the table.

Alexander Filippini, *The International Cook Book* (1914).

Terrapin, Philadelphia Style

Terrapins should be boiled, or rather thrown alive into boiling water for twenty minutes, and then taken out, carefully skinned, and the toe-nails taken off. This first water in all cases should be thrown away, as all the solvents of the body are contained in it, otherwise the terrapin will have a strong taste. Boil it for two hours in fresh water, or, if the terrapins are large, until the legs can be taken off easily, or the shells become detached. Take off first the two hind legs, and then carefully take out the sand bad and the end of the alimentary canal, which generally contains the last digested food. Then break off the forelegs, clean the head, and break up the neck; cut up the entrails fine, and carefully detach the eggs. Have a bowl of cold water ready to wash off the liver in case the gall should be broken in boiling. If not broken, detach it with a sharp knife from the liver, and should it break in handling, plunge the pieces stained by it in cold water.

The Dressing. For a full count terrapin: The yolks of four hard-boiled eggs should be rubbed up with one quarter pound of butter, one-half teacupful browned flour, one tablespoonful mustard, salt, cayenne pepper, and black pepper to taste. When the dressing is boiling, add the terreapin, stirring all the time to prevent scorching. Just before taking from the fire, add a tumblerful of Sherry wine an boil up once. Serve hot.

Mrs. C. H. Gibson, *Mrs. Charles H. Gibson's Maryland and Virginia Cook Book* (1894).

February 27

Dinner at a ''Gentlemen's Ordinary''
Brown's Hotel, Washington, DC, 1847

Brown's Hotel no longer exists on Pennsylvania Avenue in Washington. It replaced a previous establishment called The Indian Queen, and was replaced in turn by the Metropolitan Hotel, which survived until the 1930s.

BILL OF FARE

SOUP.

Macaroni.

FISH.

Boiled Rock.

ROAST.

Beef, Mutton, Turkey, Duck, Goose.

ENTREES.

Common Duck, stewed,   Beef Steak Pie,
Braised Lamb, farcie,   Veal Liver Pique,
Kidneys, au Madeira,   Pig's Feet, Piquant sauce,
Bouilli Beef,   Wild Duck, en salmi,
Mutton Chops, Panees,   Stewed Chicken, Madeira,
Fricasee of Veal,   Calf's Brains, Tomato sauce,
Macaroni, au fromage,   Chicken, a la mode,

GAME.

Wild Ducks.

BOILED.

Ham,   MUTTON, Caper sauce,
Chicken,   ROUND OF CORNED BEEF.

VEGETABLES.

Boiled Potatoes, Cabbage, Carrots,
Mashed Potatoes, Parsnips, Hominy,
Celery, Rice

DESSERTS.

Fritters.   ORANGE PUDDING, in pastry.

PASTRY.

Grape Pie, Mince Pie, Peach Pie, Apple Pie.

FRUIT.

Shellbarks, Apples, &c.

*Boarders inviting friends to their meals, will please make it
known at the office.*

BREAKFAST, 8 ½—DINNER, (Daily) 3.—TEA, 7.

SUNDAY—Dinner at 2 o'clock.

WINE BILL ON THE OTHER SIDE.

The hotel, in its various incarnations is only a few blocks from the Capitol, and has born witness to some significant moments in American history. "The Star-Spangled Banner" was composed at the site (when it was still The Indian Queen) in 1814. President John Tyler took his oath of office at Brown's in 1841. Abraham Lincoln stayed at Brown's while he was in Washington in the 1840s as a Congressman.

Why then, with this illustrious history, did the owner of Brown's in 1847 consider it a "Gentlemen's Ordinary"?

An "ordinary" used to mean a regular daily meal or allowance, and by extension came to apply to the inn or tavern serving such a meal at a fixed price. In seventeenth- and eighteenth-century England, the name was often associated with gambling houses frequented by aristocratic and well-off "men of fashion," but this seems to have been less of a connection in the United States. The correct name for the "menu" at an ordinary was *table d'hôte*—meaning the host's table, not a "bill of fare." A *table d'hôte* suggested a common table, a more public meal, at a stated hour (as does this menu) and fixed price. A bill of fare on the other hand used to mean a list of dishes, each individually priced, from which a guest could order at will. Before it was rebuilt as Brown's Hotel, The Indian Queen Tavern was indeed an "ordinary." The story is that outside the hotel was a tall pole with a bell. At the fixed mealtime, a slave summoned the guests by ringing the bell, which could be heard for many blocks away.

The word "menu"—a French word referring to the small list or size, gradually took over from "bill of fare" in the nineteenth century. The change was vigorously resisted by some English gastronomes, and to this day, the famous Simpson's on the Strand in London still provides a "bill of fare."

Recipes

~~~

Beef Bouilli

Take part of a round of fresh beef (or if you prefer it a piece of the flank or brisket) and rub it with salt. Place skewers in the bottom of the stew-pot, and lay the meat upon them with barely water enough to cover it. To enrich the gravy you may add the necks and other trimmings of whatever poultry you may happen to have; also the root of a tongue, if convenient. Cover the pot, and set it over a quick fire. When it boils and the scum has risen, skim it well, and then diminish the fire so that the meat shall only simmer; or you may set the pot on hot coals. Then put in four or five carrots sliced thin, a head of celery cut up, and four or five sliced turnips. Add a bunch of sweet herbs, and a small table-spoonful of black peppercorns tied in a thin muslin rag. Let it stew slowly for four or five hours, and then add a dozen very small onions roasted and peeled, and a large table-spoonful of capers or nasturtians. You may, if you choose, stick a clove in each onion. Simmer it half an hour longer, then take up the meat, and place it in a dish, laying the vegetables round. Skim and strain the gravy; season it with catchup, and made mustard, and serve it up in a boat. Mutton may be cooked in this manner.

Miss Leslie, *Directions For Cookery, In Its Various Branches* (Philadelphia, 1840).

Orange Pudding

Stir to a cream six ounces of white powdered sugar, with four of butter then add a wine glass of wine, the juice and chopped peel of a couple of large fresh oranges. Beat eight eggs to a froth, the whites and yolks separately mix them with a quart of milk, a couple of ounces citron, cut in small strips, and a couple of ounces of pounded crackers. Mix all the ingredients well together, line a pudding dish with pastry, put a rim of puff paste round the edge of the dish, and then turn in the pudding, and bake it in a quick oven about half an hour.

The American Housewife (1841).

February 28

Banquet in Honor of Ferdinand de Lesseps, Panama, 1886

The Anglo-American Association of the Isthmus of Panama held a banquet on February 28, 1886, in honor of Count Ferdinand de Lesseps (1805–1894). On the basis of de Lesseps's success in Suez, the French had begun the building of a canal across the Isthmus of Panama in 1880, with de Lesseps in charge. The French team seriously misjudged both the engineering and environmental challenges. Digging across the rocky Isthmus of Panama was quite different from across the sands of Egpt, and the manpower toll wrought by malaria, cholera, and yellow fever was devastating.

By the time of this banquet in 1886 it must have become apparent to those in the know that the project was in trouble and that a sea-level canal was not feasible; yet de Lesseps (who was not an engineer) remained committed to the idea. Ultimately work came to a halt in mid-1889. It was eventually resurrected by an American team and the canal finally opened in 1914. At the banquet, however, to judge from the list of toasts, it was optimism and mutual admiration all around. As was usual for such banquets held by eminent expatriates, the food in no way reflected their colonial postings, but was styled exactly as it would have been in the finest New York or London restaurant.

POTAGE.
Printanier.

HORS D'ŒVRE.
Radis, Saucisson de Lyon, Olives, Beurre, Cornichon.

RELEVÉ.
Corbine Sauce aux Huitres.

ENTRÉES.
Croquettes de Volaille.
Filets de Boeuf Financiere.
Canard aux Petits-Pois.

PIECES FROIDES.
Galantine de Dinde à la Moderne.
Jambon de York Glacé.

PUNCH GLACÉ.

LEGUMES.
Asperges Sauce Mousseline.
Haricots-verts Sautés.

ROTIS.
Dindon Truffé, Marcassin, Mouton.

SALADES DE SAISON.

ENTREMETS.
Crème Anglo-Americaine.
Biscuits de Savoie monté.
Genoise Glacée à la Vanille.
Pieces en Nougat.

DESSERTS.
Petits gateaux glacés et Fruits.

LIQUEURS ET CAFÉ.
VINS.
Bordeaux.
Xeres,
Chateau Leoville.
Sauternes Chateau Rieussec.
Bourgogne.
Pommard.
Champagne.
Veuve Clicquot.

Recipes

~~~

The following recipes, except for the nougats, are taken from *The Table: How to Buy Bood, How to Cook It, and How to Serve It* (1889) by Alessandro Filippini, one-time chef at New York's famous Delmonico's restaurant.

''Printanier, means ''spring,'' and recipes in this style contain fresh vegetables.

Consomme Printanier

Cut out, with a vegetable scoop, two carrots and one turnip; simmer them for twenty minutes in water and with a tablespoonful of salt, then drain and throw them into a quart of consomme in a saucepan with two tablespoonfuls of cooked green peas, and two tablespoonfuls of cooked string beans cut into small pieces. Add a handful of chiffonade, cook five minutes more, and serve in a hot tureen.

Chiffonade for Soups. Chop well together half a head of lettuce, half a handful of sorrel, a few branches of chervil, and a little parsley. Use it in soups five minutes before serving.

The classic garnish *Financière* which appears in a number of dishes in this book was so called because of its extravagance. As with many ''haute cuisine'' dishes of the time, it required multiple prior steps.

Garnishing Financiere

Cut a blanched, throat sweetbread into dice-sized pieces, put it in a saucepan with two truffles, six mushrooms, twelve stoned olives, six *godiveau* quenelles, and two blanched chicken livers cut in pieces. Moisten with half a glassful of sherry or Madeira wine, and season with half a pinch each of salt and pepper, and a quarter of a pinch of nutmeg; add a pint of Madeira sauce, cook again for ten minutes, skim off the fat, and serve when required.

Godiveaux Forcemeat

Remove the stringy tissue from half a pound of veal suet, pound it in a mortar; take the same quantity of lean veal, chopped in the machine, a quarter of a pound of very consistent *pate-a-chou* [choux pastry, see June 1], omitting the eggs, and pound all together. Season highly with a tablespoonful of salt, a teaspoonful of pepper, and half a teaspoonful of nutmeg. Add four raw egg yolks and two whole ones, and when well incorporated strain through a sieve, and put it on ice to be used when required in other recipes. Poach it for three minutes before serving.

Quenelles: see December 9.

Sauce Madeira (Demi-Glace)

Add one small glassful of mushroom liquor to one pint of good Espagnole sauce [see January 18]; also a small glassful of Madeira wine, a bouquet [of herbs] and a scant teaspoonful of pepper. Remove the fat carefully and cook for thirty minutes, leaving the sauce in a rather liquid state; then strain and use when needed. This takes the place of all Madeira sauces.

Modern *nougat* is an intensely white confection containing nuts, and the recipe usually includes beaten egg whites. The idea came to Europe from Arabia, where honey was used in the sweetmeat. Many early English recipes were made from a caramelized sugar syrup and were more like *praline*. This recipe is closer to the original idea but does not include the more recent addition of egg whites.

Honey Nougat

4 tablespoons strained honey.
2 ounces almonds, blanched.
1 pound flour of sugar, or icing sugar.

Make the honey hot without boiling, stir in the sugar a little at a time until it becomes too firm, then turn out on the table and knead in more sugar and also the almonds, which must be dry. When the nougat is firm enough to keep its form in a square bar like a brick split lengthwise, sugar the outside, roll it in wax paper, and keep it a day before slicing it up.

Jessup Whitehead, *Cooking for Profit* (1886).

March

63rd Annual Dinner of the St. David's Society
Hotel Savoy, New York, 1898

The St. David's Society of New York was founded in 1835, and every year it celebrated the national day of Wales with a fine dinner. In 1898 the British consul general was invited, as were representatives of other national heritage organizations such as the Friendly Sons of St. Patrick, the St. Nicholas Society, the St. George Society, the New England Society, and the Holland Society.

St. David was a revered sixth-century bishop and teacher credited with many miracles. He has been the patron saint of Wales since early medieval times, and in the eighteenth century his feast day (March 1) was adopted as the national day of the country. People of Welsh heritage have formed St. David's societies around the world, and the day is usually celebrated with dinner, songs, and speeches. A very ancient traditional symbol of the day is the leek, although the reasons given are varied and much disputed. The leek has been proudly worn (as a cockade in the hat, for example) by the Welsh on this day for many centuries, and in more recent times a tradition has developed of eating dishes containing them. On the whole, however, there is less emphasis on traditional Welsh foods on this day than there is on many other national days such as the Irish St. Patrick's Day (see March 17).

The twin goals of most national heritage societies is to keep their tradition alive at the same time as reinforcing their allegiance to their adopted country. The traditional toasts at St. David's society dinners were to the president of the United States and the Queen of Great Britain, "The Land We Live In," "The Literature and Music of Wales," "The Land of Our Fathers," "The Ladies," and "Our Guests." In response to the toast to "The Land We Live In," the journalist and Republican politician Charles Emory Smith (1842–1908) took the opportunity to "uphold the President's attitude toward Spain." He was referring to the sinking of the battleship USS *Maine* two weeks previously—the event that precipitated the Spanish-American war.

On this particular occasion in 1898, the menu was written in Welsh, but the dishes themselves were from the established international classic repertoire (such as Chicken with Cress, see February 21) or unequivocally

BWYDLEN	MENU
Wystrys y Glasbywnt	Blue Point Oysters
Isgell Tyfolion Gwalia	Consomme, Chancelier
Maesrin Ifres Crwst-huliedig	Fresh Mushrooms in Crust a la Bordelaise
Gwangeniaid Cyffeithiedig y Werdd-don	Planked Shad, Vert Pré
Cucumerau Darparedig	Cucumbers
Rhost-gig Oen Gwarnwyn a Sibr Sur	Spring Lamb with Mint Sauce
Cloron y Bermo Dringol Ffa Ffrengig	String Beans Panachee Bermuda Potatoes
Gwydirol Grwbein y Fair-Dalaeth	Terrapin, a la Maryland
Surrfed Sant Daffyd	Sorbet St. David
Gwanwyn Gywrion Berwedig	Broiled Spring Chicken, Water Cress
Dawr-ffres	Mixed Salad
Bwydlys Cymsyg	
Hufen-boten Rhewedig	Ice Cream
Cacenau Amrywiol Sugrgestu	Mixed Cakes Candy
Efrwythau Coffi	Fruit Coffee
Marwth 1, 1898	Tuesday, March 1, 1898

American (such as the "planked" fish). "Planking" was developed by Native Americans of the Pacific Northwest as a way of cooking food in the absence of metal baking dishes. Fresh meat or fish is slowly grilled above the coals of an open fire (or today in an oven) on specially prepared wooden planks. The technique is also a way of adding flavor to the food, as it becomes infused with the wood's oils and smoke.

Recipes

<div align="center">~~~</div>

Vert-pré is a green garnish (herbs, watercress) that sometimes includes potatoes.

Planked Fish

A white fish weighing between three and four pounds is the most satisfactory to plank. If your plank is new, oil all over very well; put it into a warm oven and gradually increase the heat until the oven is very hot, to prevent warping. Have cracker crumbs, finely chopped greens, such as parsley, onion and green peppers, at hand, and all kinds of vegetables, shrimps, mushrooms, etc. Clean and season the fish well, inside and out, and on the plank put small pieces of butter, scattering cracker crumbs and chopped greens over. On this place the fish, and after flaking with butter, scatter more greens; add seasoning, such as tomato catsup, Worcestershire sauce, one-quarter cup of sherry and strained tomato juice, keeping some of the latter for basting later on. Prepare some creamed potatoes and just before putting the fish into the oven place them around the edge of the plank in tablespoonfuls, using a fork to fashion them like roses, and flaking same with small pieces of butter. Have the oven very hot, and allow the fish to bake from one-half to three-quarters of an hour, according to the size of the fish. While the fish is baking prepare the vegetables, slicing cucumbers, peppers, tomatoes, etc. Watch the fish, occasionally basting with the tomato juice. Ten minutes before removing the fish from the oven garnish with the vegetables, boiled peas (if you have some on hand), shrimps, mushrooms, truffles, etc. Do not disturb the fish or garnishings, but put the plank on a large tray and serve. It is a most attractive dish.

The Neighborhood Cookbook, Council of Jewish Women (Portland, Oregon, 1914).

Terrapin: see March 1.

March 2

Prince Ernest's Dinner
Germany, 1778

The British royal family has strong German ancestry, and between 1714 and 1837 many royal members had both English and Hanoverian titles. King William IV (1765–1837) of England was also King of Hanover (the connection was through his grandmother Austusta of Saxe-Coburg). When he died in 1837, the Crown of England went to his niece, Princess Victoria. In most parts of Europe, however, traditional Salic Law pertained and this forbade the inheritance of the crown by a woman. The Crown of Hanover was passed to his brother, His Royal Highness Prince Ernest Austustus (1771–1851).

Before he became King of Hanover, the young prince sat down to the following dinner on March 2, 1788.

Clear Gravy Soup
Brown Cabbages and Boiled Jack Trouts
Round of Beef
Fricandeau of Veal
Young Pigeons
Pudding
Asparagus
Fricassee of Sweetbreads
Roast Mutton from Schmalkalden
Wild Boar's Head
Cakes
Pineapples
Oranges
Dessert

This menu is for an everyday meal, not a state or official dinner. There are some obvious German dishes: the mutton was from the region of Schmalkalden in central Germany, and the boar's head most likely also came from the forests of that region. There is cabbage—a vegetable inextricably linked to Germany, and one of the oldest vegetables eaten by humans. The "brown cabbage" may refer to either the variety of cabbage or the method of cooking. It may have been *Braun-Kohl* (literally "brown cabbage"), which has a dark purplish-green, small head. A less likely possibility is that it is a well-known Scandinavian dish in which the cabbage cooked with brown sugar or molasses.

The menu also includes one of the newest fruits to be enjoyed in Europe—the pineapple. The first people from the Old World to see the pineapple were some of Christopher Columbus's men, on the island of Guadeloupe, on November 4, 1493. Unlike several of the other New World findings (potatoes and tomatoes, for example), the pineapple was an immediate success in Europe—for those who could obtain it—because it was sweet and exotic. The pineapple is a tropical fruit, and (unlike the potato and tomato) did not grow in the temperate and cool climate of Europe. It may have been first grown in Europe in Leyden in the mid-seventeeth century, and in 1712 in England—in hot-houses of course. In 1746 the writer and Earl of Orford Horace Walpole (1717–1797) noted in a letter that he had paid a guinea for two pineapples—equivalent to 141 (USD $255) today—a phenomenal price by any standards.

Recipes

~~~

Braun—oder Winterkohl
(Brown or Winter Cabbage)

These must be washed and cut small. Make a quarter of a pound or a little more pork lard or other fat hot, and fry the sliced cabbage, stirring until it is soft. Add sugar and meat broth. Chestnuts can be added. Before serving, stir in a little flour.
Adapted from Friederike Louise Löffler, *Neues Kochbuch* (1806).

A Fricandeau of Veal: see August 29.

March 3

Final Voyage of the HMY *Britannia*
Karachi, Pakistan, 1997

The British royal family had a yacht at their disposal from the mid-seventeenth century until HMY *Britannia* was decommissioned in December 1997. The *Britannia* was the 83rd royal yacht, and she had served Queen and country for over four decades. She was a floating residence for the royals, a hotel for up to 250 privileged guests, a venue for diplomatic dinners, and if the need had arisen could have been quickly converted into a hospital ship. Her last and longest voyage began in January 1997, when she set off from Portsmouth bound for Hong Kong, to take part in the celebrations that accompanied the handover of the region from Britain back to China, in June later that year. The opportunity was taken for a number of commercial and diplomatic visits at various ports en route. On March 3, the day of her scheduled arrival in Karachi, Pakistan, the following meal was served on board.

Terrine of Vegetables

Honey Roast Duck Breast
Sole Fillets with Tarragon

Assorted Salads
Hot New Potatoes

Lemon Mousse in Filo Pastry
Cassis Sauce

Cheese

The royal yacht was in Karachi for "commercial events," so it does not seem likely that this dinner was held in the magnificent state dining room with its magnificent mahogany table capable of seating 56 guests.

Staff in charge of provisioning, catering, and cooking aboard the *Britannia* did not just have to be prepared for the particular preferences of the royal family members who happened to be aboard at any one time, and the state or diplomatic dinners that were to be held; the admiral, 20 officers, and 220 yachtsmen who manned the ship also had to be fed. There was a personal royal chef aboard (on this voyage it was Robert Irvine), but the overall responsibility fell to the Supply Department. In addition to a number of stewards, accountants, and others, the Supply Department included one chief petty officer caterer (CPO) in charge of catering and menu planning, two CPO cooks (one in charge of the Royal and Wardroom Galleys, one in charge of the Ship's Galley), two petty officer cooks (one each in charge of the Wardroom Galley and the Ship's Galley), two Wardroom leading cooks, two Ship's Galley leading cooks, four Wardroom cooks, four Ship's Galley cooks, and one royal Marine butcher.

Recipes

~~~

Lemon Mousse

4 tablespoons water
1/2 oz. powdered gelatin
8 oz. caster sugar
finely grated rind and juice of 3 lemons
1/2 pint single cream
1/2 pint double cream

Measure water into small saucepan and sprinkle in the gelatin. Set aside for 5 minutes to soften. Stir over low heat to dissolve gelatin, but do not allow to boil. Draw off heat.

In mixing basin, combine sugar, rind, and strained juice. Stir in both creams, and whisk till thick and light. Gradually whisk in the gelatin. Hold the pan high above the basin and pour in a thin steady stream whilst mixing all the time. Continue whisking for a few minutes until the mixture shows signs of thickening up, then pour into a serving dish. Chill until firm. Remove from refrigerator for an hour before serving.

The Times, January 6, 1968.

Royal Picnics

Everything is kept in readiness aboard the HMY *Britannia* in case the royal family wishes to go ashore for a picnic. The boatswain is responsible for coordinating the trip to shore and the preparation of the equipment once the picnic ground is reached. Individual items of equipment are provided and maintained by different departments, as follows:

The Royal Barge Crew: tents, poles, guys, pegs, and groundsheets.

Royal Apartment Staff: food and drink hampers, blankets, games, sports equipment.

Engine Room: barbeques, fuel, utensils, lamps.

Communications: portable radio and radio operator.

March 4

Irish Revolutionary Veterans Dinner
Central Opera House, East Sixty-Seventh Street, New York, 1894

When the veterans of the Irish Revolutionary Brotherhood held their eighth annual banquet to commemorate the 27th anniversary of the doomed Irish nationalist ("Fenian") uprising of 1867, they sat down to a menu that was both a homage and a history lesson. There were four courses representing the four provinces of Ireland, and 32 individual dishes representing the number of counties. Many of the dishes were named for revolutionary heroes, battle sites, and political events; many were propaganda statements in themselves; and many were simple tongue-in-cheek self-mocking humor.

Oyster Paddies.
Ox Tail a la John Bull.
Whisky Straight from a Ram's Horn.
Wexford Pike.
Lough Erne Sparkling Fizz.

ENTRÉES.
Spuds in their Jackets.
Agitation Fricasee.
Federation Hush, a la McCarthy.
Leinster Hall Crow Pie.
Saddle of Far-down Mutton.
Home Rule Extra Dry.

ROAST.
Treason Felony Shanghai, with Penal Servitude Sauce.
Irish Boned Turkey, Connemara Sprouts.
Parliamentary Pot Roast, a la Redmond.
Ribs of Radical Beef, with Union Gravy.
Wild Goose, with Raparee Sauce.
Irish Lame Ducks.
Old Port, Brian Boru's Cellars.

DESSERT.
Parliamentary Pudding, with Government Plums.
Orange and Green Marmalade.
Kilmainham Gruel.
Mountjoy Meringue.
Millbank Mince.
Chatham Corn Starch.
Potteen.
Scaldteen.
Usquebaugh, ad lib.
Phenix Park Perfectos, Limerick Twist.
Deoch-a-Dhorish.

As it turned out, not all the dishes were served, the delinquency being due to a conspiracy on the part of the chef, who was announced on the card as "a culinary suspect, late cook in her Majesty's service at Hotel Kilmainham." No doubt this little joke was itself an acknowledgement that one of the reasons for the dreadful failure of the uprising was that the Fenian ranks were full of informers. In perhaps another nod to the confused start of the abortive revolt, the dinner was held a day early (the anniversary was on March 5), by one hour—at 11 P.M. on the night of March 4.

There were of course many concessions to the reported liking of the Irish for hard liquor. Whiskey appears in several guises—as as *Usquebaugh*, the Gaelic word from which we get the word "whiskey," and which means "water of life," as *Poteen*, homemade "whiskey" illicitly distilled on a huge scale, and as *Scalteen*, a "drink that would make a corpse walk" based on hot sweetened whisky. The final menu item—*Deoch-a-Dhorish*—or the Irish version of the parting drink no doubt contained whiskey too.

Recipes
~~~

Baked Potatoes (in Their Jackets)

Select smooth, medium sized potatoes. Scrub with a small vegetable brush and bake in a hot oven for about forty minutes or until soft. Remove from the oven, break the skin slightly in order that the steam can escape and serve as quickly as possible. (Properly baked potatoes are more easily digested than potatoes cooked any other way. They are, however, better cooked in boiling water than baked in a slow oven.)

If there is no oven in the school room equipment the potato may be baked in an outdoor fire. For this purpose a pit is dug and a fire built in the pit. When the fire has burned well down, bury the potatoes in the ashes and allow them to bake for about forty-five minutes. They bake with less danger of burning if wrapped in damp clay or wet paper before being put into the fire.

Jessie Pinning Rich, *The Irish Potato* (1914).

There are a number of dishes going by the name of parliament pudding, but this one seems particularly appropriate for this dinner, as it fits with the "orange" theme.

Parliament Pudding

Cream 1 tablespoonful of butter with 3/4 cup of sugar, add the beaten yolks of 6 eggs, 1 cupful of fine bread crumbs which have been soaked in milk, and the juice and the grated rind of 1/2 an orange; stir this until very smooth, then add the beaten whites of 2 eggs. Have a pudding mould thickly buttered and dusted with dry crumbs, line with macaroons which have been moistened with orange juice; put in a layer of the batter, then a layer of sponge cake spread with orange marmalade and alternate the layers until the mould is full, having batter at the top. Cover and steam for three-quarters of an hour, unmould carefully and serve with hard sauce.

Mrs. J. L. Lane, *365 Orange Recipes: An Orange Recipe for Every Day in the Year* (ca. 1909).

Scolsheen or Scalteen

Made by boiling a mixture of whiskey, water, sugar, butter and pepper (or caraway seeds) in a pot: a sovereign cure for a cold. Sometimes the word *scalteen* was applied to unmixed whiskey burned, and used for the same purpose. From the Irish *scall,* burn, singe, scald.

Old Dublin Society, *Dublin Historical Record* (1941).

March 5

Dinner for the Bushmen's Corps
Adelaide, South Australia, 1900

When the British took on the Boers (Dutch farmer-colonists) in South Africa in the nineteenth century, it was ostensibly to protect British citizens in that country. As with most wars, however, it was ultimately over resources, and the gold of the Transvaal was a powerful drawcard. Britain called on its other colonies for assistance, and its citizens responded magnificently even if they had never set foot on the shores of "Home." In Australia, each individual colony (for it was before Federation) raised contingents of "Bushmen"— amateurs supported by public conscription—from the ranks of young men eager for the excitement of battle. On the eve of their departure for South Africa, the mayor of Adelaide gave a farewell banquet for the South Australian Bushmen's Corps.

Soup
Cronje
Roast Turkey a la Joubert
Roast Chicken – Modder River
Roast Vondam Duck
Roast Goose Kruger
Saddle of Transvaal Mutton
Sirloin of Commandeered Beef
Ox Tongue Albrecht.
Pretoria Ham

Sweets
Kimberley Jelly a la Boer
Mafeking Pudding
Pastry a la Africander

Fruits in Season

The soldiers at this dinner would have been well aware that the siege of the town of Mafeking (now Mafikeng) was now almost five months old, and that that of Kimberley had been relieved only a fortnight before, after 124 days. Perhaps as they dined they were reminded of desperate food shortages and the terrible stories of desperate measures being taken to feed everyone in the besieged towns. The man in charge in Mafeking was Colonel Robert Baden-Powell (of Boy Scout fame). A little over a week before the farewell dinner for the Bushmen, Baden-Powell noted in his diary:

> Our soup kitchen in town is working most successfully. Today's work with it goes as follows: Half a horse 250 lbs.; mealie meal, 15 lbs.; oat husks, 47 lbs. This made 132 gallons. The soup was of the consistency of porridge. Fifty pounds of above will feed 100 natives.

Ironically, the Bushmen were blissfully unaware as they were banqueted that the glory of war would devolve for many of themselves into a struggle for food (and against disease). Rations were often halved, or not forthcoming, and they were frequently forced to live off the land, pillaging and foraging as they went.

Recipes
~~~

The names of the dishes on this menu were clearly given to evoke some of the celebrities and events of the conflict. No doubt they were standard dishes renamed for the occasion, and it is impossible to know what the actual recipes were. A dish called Mafeking pudding did come to be popular, however, one joke being that it was a pudding so hard and gluey with thick custard that it formed (or would have formed) a suitable missile for throwing at the enemy. It is a steamed pudding, occasionally containing marmalade, but in this particular version it is the great British favorite of "golden syrup." Golden syrup is made during the process of refining sugar; it is a golden colored syrup similar in consistency to molasses but of a very mild caramel flavor.

Mafeking Pudding

Butter a basin and line thickly with golden syrup. Take about 1/2 lb. stale breadcrumbs, 1 tablespoonful self-raising flour, 1 egg, sugar to taste, 1 tablespoonful chopped suet. Mix all together with a little milk and use to fill the basin. Steam for one and a half hours.
   The New Magazine, 1911.

Siege Food in Mafeking

Colonel Robert Baden-Powell, in his memoir, *Lessons from the Varsity of Life,* described, the siege food.

> we learned to economise very rigidly in the matter of food, and also to devise food substitutes. When a horse was killed ... His skin, after having

the hair scalded off, was boiled with his head and feet for many hours, chopped up small, and with the addition of a little saltpetre was served out as "brawn". His flesh was taken from the bones and minced in a great mincing machine and from his inside were made skins into which the meat was crammed and each man received a sausage as his ration. The bones were then boiled into a rich soup, which was dealt out at the different soup kitchens; and they were afterwards pounded up into powder with which to adulterate the flour ....Our flour was made from the horses' oats, pounded and winnowed. ... We managed thus, however, to issue every man daily a big biscuit of oatmeal. The husks of the oats were put to soak in large tubs of water for a number of hours, at the end of which the scum formed by the husks was scraped off and given as food to the hospital chickens, while the residue formed a paste closely akin to that used by bill-stickers. This was called sowens, a sour kind of mess, but very healthy and filling .... Amongst other things we supplied for the invalids in hospital a special blancmange which was made from the *Poudre de Riz* from the hairdressers and chemists shops.

March 6

Abraham Lincoln's Inauguration Ball
Patent Office, Washington, DC, 1865

President Abraham Lincoln (1809–1865) was reelected for a second term of office in 1864 and was formally inaugurated on March 4, 1865. Five weeks later the Civil War ended. A further week and Lincoln was dead, assassinated by John Wilkes Booth during a theater performance.

The festivities began immediately after Lincoln's formal inauguration. The traditional ball was planned for March 6, and it was rumored that the "supper was to be something extraordinary."

Judging from this bill of fare, the guests' expectations must have been well met. In addition to the "select and tasteful variety" of viands, there were three "leading and conspicuous pieces from the confectioner's hands"— impressive decorative pieces representing the Capitol building, "the heroic deeds of the gallant army," and "the proud achievements of the navy." The guests too were an impressive sight. *The New York Times* listed and described in great detail the important attendees—the "leading men of politics" and the "lovely, graceful and intelligent women" with their elegant toilette and sumptuous jewels, noting that "There were not, however, any colored persons present, as the Washington Secessionists insisted would be the case."

The event itself became anything but elegant. In retrospect, the conditions were not auspicious. The grand corridor in the West Wing was set up for supper, with a table in the center, and standing room for 300 people. The

Oyster Stews
Terrapin Stews
Oysters, pickled

BEEF
Roast Beef
Filet de Beef
Beef à la mode
Beef à l'anglais

VEAL
Leg of Veal
Fricandeau
Veal Malakoff

POULTRY
Roast Turkey
Boned Turkey
Roast Chicken
Grouse, boned and roast

GAME
Pheasant
Quail
Venison

PATETES
Patète of Duck en gelée
Patète de foie gras

SMOKED
Ham
Tongue en gelée
do. plain
SALADES
Chicken
Lobster

CAKES AND TARTS
Almond Sponge
Belle Alliance
Dame Blanche
Macaroon Tart
Tart à l'Orleans
do. à l'a Portugaise
do. à la Vienne
Pound Cake
Sponge Cake
Lady Cake
Fancy Small Cakes

JELLIES AND CREAMS
Calf's Foot and Wine Jelly
Charlotte à la Russe
do. do. Vanilla
Blanc Mangue
Crème à la Nelson
do. Chateaubriand
do. à la Smyrna
do. do. Nesselrode
Bombe à la Vanilla

ICE CREAM
Vanilla
Lemon
White Coffee
Chocolate
Burnt Almonds
Maraschino

FRUIT ICES
Strawberry
Orange
Lemon

ORNAMENTAL PYRAMIDES

Nougate

Orange

Caramel with Fancy Cream Candy

Cocoanut

Macaroon

Croquant

Chocolate

Tree Cakes

DESSERT

Grapes, Almonds, Raisins, etc.

---

problem was, there were 5,000 people in attendance. *The New York Times* reported the debacle with some disgust:

> The crush which followed can be better imagined than depicted . . . in less than an hour the table was a wreck; a few ornaments not destroyed were removed, and the array of empty dishes and the debris of the feast were positively fright-ful to behold. . . . many only succeeded in ruining their toilets. . . . a demolition in a twinkling of an eye of all the confectioner's handiwork, the frantic snatch-ing of viands from the tables, the brandishing aloft of wine cup, and plate, and cutlery, and laden with articles alike dangerous to toilet and stomach: of munch-ing and crunching sans ceremonies: of defilement and ruin to precious apparel, the result perhaps of weeks of the dressmaker's effort; of the loss of temper and the loud cries of complaint.
>
> As much was wasted as was eaten, and however much there may have been provided, more than half the guests went supperless . . . the fact remains that the supper was a disaster, and detracted from the otherwise pleasant aspect of the occasion.

The newspaper sadly concluded, "The American people, we are ashamed to say, have not yet learned to behave at table: and that species of etiquette, not too prevalent in private, is certainly always absent at public suppers," adding, rather snobbily, that "Doubteless the shoddy and petrolia family were represented, to a limited degree; but 'oil' will tell very soon, as it spreads so rapidly, and cloth not infrequently makes the man."

Recipes

~~~

Almond Sponge Cake

Ten eggs, one pound of sugar, half pound of flour, a few drops of lemon. When these ingredients are well beaten, add half-pound of sweet almonds, blanched, and pounded in a white mortar or stout bowl. To blanch them—that is, skin them—pour boiling water upon them. Add a little peach extract, and bake in a brisk oven. This is very rich.

Jennie June's American Cookery Book (New York, 1870).

Macaroon Tarts

Commonly miscalled macaroni tarts. Patty pans lined with sweet paste, partly filled with almond macaroon mixture and baked.

Sweet Tart Pastry

8 ounces of flour
3 ounces of butter
1 tablespoonful of powdered sugar
1 egg
Little salt
Quarter cupful of water

Rub the butter into the flour as in making short paste, add the egg, sugar and salt with the water, mix and knead it smooth. Roll out very thin, cut out pieces and line the patty pans.

Almond Macaroon Mixture

8 ounces of granulated sugar
4 whites of eggs
8 ounces of almonds
1 teaspoonful of lemon juice

Put the sugar and two of the whites in a deep bowl together, and beat with a wooden paddle about fifteen minutes, then add another white and beat again, then the lemon juice and then the last white. Crush the almonds by rolling them with the rolling-pin on the table. They need not be blanched (freed from the skins) unless so preferred. When they are reduced to meal mix them with the contents of the bowl. This mixture, as well as the cake icing, should always be started with bowl and ingredients all cold, for if warm they cannot be beaten to the requisite degree of firmness.

The patty pans or gem pans being already lined with the tart paste, half fill with the macaroon paste, smooth over and bake in a very slack oven The baking is the most difficult part, for with too much heat the macaroon mixture melts away to candy. These tarts, when right, rise smooth and rounded in the crusts, and are partly hollow underneath.

Jessup Whitehead, *The Chicago Herald Cooking School: A Professional Cook's Book for Household Use* (1883).

Charlotte Russe: see September 4.
Blancmange: see January 7.
Pound Cake: see April 19.
Fricandeau: see April 29.

March 7

Dinner for the New York Association of Union Prisoners
Murray Hill Lyceum, New York City, 1895

Three decades after the end of the Civil War, over 100 former Union soldiers who had been held prisoners of the Confederacy sat down to a menu specifically designed to remind them of "Libby and other prisons."

Pea Soup—Old Belle Isle Style
Gherkins—Pemberton
Olives—Libby and Sons
Table Celery—à la Saulsbury
Boiled Salmon—Same as was served to the
colored troops when captured.
Roast Turkey—Sauce on march to the sea.

SIDE DISHES
Cornmeal Mush—Nigger peas
Mule-hoof jelly, very nice
Roast Beef—the kind that the officers did not have at Macon.

RELISHES
Poke Greens—Boiled with mule corned beef.
Claret—on tap by all Southern prison keepers.

DESSERT
Cornmeal Cake—Sweetened with molasses.

FRUIT
Bad luck.

BONBONS
In boxes from Andersonville,.
Ice-Cream—Very best Florence style.
Genuine old Confederate coffee.
Frosted cornbread.

The guests will help themselves and bring their own knife and fork.
P.S. A deposit will be required on tin cups and plates.

The men who ate and exchanged reminiscences over this meal were the lucky ones. Although the exact number of casualties of the war will never be known, most estimates put the total number of deaths at above 600,000. Of these, perhaps 60,000 died in prison camps. They died from malnutrition in one or other of its manifestations—starvation, scurvy (vitamin C deficiency), "dropsy" (edema, probably due to vitamin B1 deficiency), and the associated problems of diarrhea and other infections.

The menu makes reference to many places and events of the war, including two of the most notorious prisons—Andersonville in Georgia, where almost 13,000 prisoners died, and Libby Prison at Richmond, Virginia. The exact

Libby Prison, Richmond, Virginia. Courtesy of Library of Congress.

ration served to prisoners varied according over the time, but it was always grossly insufficient. One Andersonville prisoner described the daily ration as consisting of half a pint of meal, a teaspoonful of salt, two ounces of meat, and half a pint of old, bug-ridden beans. The beans were often called—as they are in this menu—"nigger peas." The name is clearly an ethnic slur, and refers to beans (probably a variety of black bean) grown in the South specifically for the feeding of slaves.

Recipes

~~~

Plain Pease Soup

To a quart of split peas, and two heads of celery, and a large onion, put three quarts of broth, or soft water; let them simmer gently over a slow fire for three hours. Stir them up every quarter of an hour, to prevent the peas sticking at the bottom of the pot, and burning.
  J. M. Sanderson, *The Complete Cook* (1864).

Poke

The young stalks and leaves of the poke-berry plant when quite small and first beginning to sprout up from the ground in the spring, are by most persons considered very nice, and are frequently brought to market. If the least too old they acquire a strong taste, and should not be eaten, as they then become unwholesome. They are in a proper state when the part of the stalk nearest to the ground is not thicker than small asparagus. Scrape the stalks (letting the leaves remain on them) and throw them into cold water. Then tie up the poke in bundles, put it into a pot that has plenty of boiling water, and let it boil fast an hour at least. Serve it up with or without toast, and send melted butter with it in a boat.

Eliza Leslie, *Directions for Cookery, in its Various Branches* (1840).

Hotel de Yankee

First Lieut. William C. Harris spent some time in "the Tobacco Warehouse" (Libby Prison), and his memoir (*Prison-life in the Tobacco Warehouse at Richmond*, 1862) shows clearly that even in the midst of hunger, soldiers could retain their sense of humor about food.

It is one o'clock, and dinner-hour. As we draw near our "mess-table," we find that a jovial wag has pasted on the wall the following bill of fare:

HOTEL DE YANKEE.

BREAKFAST.
Fried Liver, "with crumbs."
Liver Fried.
Coffee, when purchased by boarders.
Tea—ditto
Bread
Black Bread.
Water-Soakers.
Dry Toast "over gas-light."

DINNER.
Boiled Beef.
Beef Boiled, "Secesh à la mode."
Hoe-Cake, made with boarder's meal.
Roast Beef, if you can beg any from outsiders.
Tomatoes and Potatoes,—if you purchase them.
White Bread.
Stale—ditto
Annual Pudding, "only made once a year."

SUPPER.
Codfish Fried, if bought and sent to cook.
Cold Boiled Beef.

Boiled Beef, turned over seven or eight times.
Cold Coffee, warmed over.
Bread, sure.
Water, sure.

Gentlemen will find this a first-class hotel; and it is kept on a Southern plan. The beds are well aired, if taken care of by the boarder himself. All extra meals can be sent to the boarder's room, if purchased by him outside of the hotel. The proprietor earnestly requests that no money be given to servants, as he pays and clothes them liberally for their services.
JEFFERSON DAVIS, Proprietor.

March 8

Dinner Given by the ''Chinese Delmonico''
Lenox Lyceum, New York, 1891

The opening of the Food and Health Exposition in New York in 1891 was celebrated with a dinner that was "as novel as it was informal," according to *The New York Times*, which reported the event with interest. The dinner was given at a meeting of the Directors of the Exposition and was an elaborate affair arranged by Soo Kin, the proprietor of the King Hong Low restaurant in Mott Street. Soo Kin was referred to as "the Chinese Delmonico," a reference to the famous Delmonico's family and the restaurant of the same name that had been a New York fine dining institution for decades.

The venue for the dinner was a small dining room in the lower hall of the Lyceum, which was decorated with beautiful embroideries and valuable bronze ornaments, the doors replaced with beaded curtains "of great antiquity and beauty." The host and translator for the evening was K. P. Lee, described patronizingly as "a Yale graduate who speaks English without an accent." *The New York Times* reporter thought that the dinner, "barring the chopsticks, was a delightful affair from soup to soup," and described it thus:

1. Birds' nest soup, that famouse Chinese delicacy, was the first course, or course of honor, according to Celestial etiquette, and with it were served thimble-sized cups of pear wine ... a little porcelain scoop was used to eat the delicacy with and the diners got along very well with it ... every portion was promptly dispatched.

2. Chicken and Birds'Nest Stew: the chopsticks were in order, and the trouble began. Only Mr. Lee was able to make the food stay between them long enough to get it to his lips. The other diners distributed their portions with pleasing impartiality on their own and their neighbors' apparel and finally had to beg for a return of the soup scoops in order to taste the stew. The chopsticks for the rest of the meal were placed among the ornaments of the table.

3. Stewed Dragon's Beard: a preparation of shark's fin, seaweed, and Chinese ham. Pretty generally left alone. Banana wine with 2 and 3

4. Palm Flower Duck Fricassee: small slices of breast of this rarest of Chinese ducks, placed and piled in alternate layers with bamboo shoots, ham, black mushrooms, and dried fish: was the pièce de resistance of this dinner. With it were handed round pots of rose wine, one of the strongest and most expensive of Celestial liquors. . . . The diners were so abstemious at this point that the waiters' faces became quite wrinkled with contempt.

5. Seaweed Soup was the last course, and then the table was cleared and the dessert brought on.

6. This consisted of a dozen kinds of sweet cakes, several varieties of Chinese nuts, including the sacred dragon nut, water chestnut which tasted very much like our horseradish, grape fruit, and small Chinese oranges which were as sweet as honey and were stamped in black with the sign of the Emperor's approval.

7. The pots of tea that ended the dinner were the real treat of the whole affair. They were filled with a light yellow brew from the leaves of "Water Fairy" tea, which was radically different from any the Americans had ever tasted and enough of it was drunk to last a sewing society for a year.

Recipes

~~~

Birds' Nest Soup

. . . is even more of a luxury in China than turtle soup is in England . . . it forms the first dish at all grand dinners. Here is a receipt for preparing *Potage aux Nids d' Hirondelles*, translated from the Chinese:

"Take clean white birds' nest shreds, or birds' nests, and soak thoroughly. Pick out all feathers. Boil in soup or water till tender, and of the colour of jade-stone. Place pigeons' eggs below, and add some ham shreds on top. Boil again slowly with little fluid. If required sweet, then boil in clear water till tender, add sugar-candy, and then eat. This is a most clear and pure article, and thick (or oily) substances should not be added. It should be boiled for a long time; for, if not boiled till tender, it will cause diarrhoea."

Steamed Sharks' Fins

Sun-dried sharks' fins are to be washed clean [as follows]: First take the fins [as bought] and place in a cooking pan, add wood-ashes and boil in several waters. Then take out and scrape away the roughness [on the fins]. If not clean, boil again, and scrape again, until properly clean. Then change the water and boil again. Take out, remove the flesh, keeping only the fins. Then boil once again. Put in spring water. Be careful in changing the water, and thoroughly soak them, for it is necessary that the taste of lime should be taken out of them. Then put the fins into soup, stew three times till quite tender. Dish in a bowl, placing meat of crabs below them, and add a little ham on the top. The taste is clear, neither tender nor tough, something like the taste of pomeloes at times.
James Dyer Ball, *Things Chinese: Or, Notes Connected with China* (1904).

Frumentie: see February 23.

March 9

Inthronization Feast of the Archbishop of Canterbury
The Archbishop's Palace, Canterbury, England, 1504

William Warham's (ca. 1450–1532) enthronement took place during Lent, the period when the devout were expected to refrain from all meat and animal products. A "fast" day by no means implied abstinence or frugality, however. It was still three decades before King Henry VIII's historic break with the established Church, the Church was extraordinarily wealthy, and the Church hierarchy (mostly drawn from the powerful families of the land) were used to good living.

The archbishop sat alone at this feast, there being none of sufficient rank to share the high table. Two lesser bills of fare were served to the clergy and lower officials. The feast was introduced by a "warner"—a person or a mechanical device that "warns" or heralds an imminent event.

A Warner

PRIMUS CURSUS.

Frumentie ryall and mammonie
to pottage.

Lynge in foyle.

Cunger p. in foyle.

Lampreys with galantine.

Pyke in latmer sauce.

Cunger r·

Halibut r·

Samon in foyle r·

Carpe in sharpe sauce.

Eeles rost r·

Samon baked.

Custard planted.

Leche florentine.

Fryttor dolphin.

A Subtyltie

2. CURSUS.

Jolir Ipocras and prune Orendge
to pottage.

Surgion in folye with welkes.

Turbit.

Soles.

Breame in sharpe sauce.

Carpes in armine.

Tenches florished.

Crevettes do.

Lamprons rost.

Roches fryed.

Lampreys baked.

Quince and Orenge baked.

Tart melior.

Leche Florentine.

Fryttor ammell.

Fryttor Pome.

A Subtiltie with three stages.

IN THE THIRDE COURSE PLATE.
Wafers and Ipocras.

Confertes.
Sugar Plate.
Fertes with other subtilties.
Ipocras.

Feasts such as this ended with wafers and sweet wine, and later also nuts and candied fruit and other sweetmeats. Eventually these end-of-meal digestives became a separate course called "the banquet," which evolved into our modern dessert course, as the word itself came to refer to the whole feast. Sugar was phenomenally expensive at the time of this feast and was imported as an exotic spice. The almonds too were imported. They were used in huge quantities at feasts to make the almond milk (essential at Lent), and *marchpane* or marzipan, essential at all great dinners (see January 15). It was reported that "all the Archbishop's honours were drawn, depicted, and delineated after a strange manner, on gilded marchpane upon the banquetting dishes." The gilding of these marzipan shapes would have been with real gold leaf.

The sumptuousness of this bill of fare is also demonstrated by the type of fish served. Dolphin, being an aquatic animal, was allowed (see February 23), and rich oily fish—desirable for their meaty taste—are prominent. There were several dishes of conger (and eel), and three dishes contain lamprey. The lamprey is a primitive eel-like fish which lives a parasitic life on the blood of other fish to which it attaches itself by means of its powerful sucker-like mouth. It has always been associated with royalty—Henry I (1068–1135) was said to have died from eating "a surfeit of lampreys," and Queen Elizabeth II received the traditional coronation gift of a lamprey pie in 1953.

Recipes
~~~
A dish "baked" at this time meant essentially a pie. A very thick pastry crust or "coffin" functioned as a cooking container in the days before shaped metal baking dishes were developed. There are many examples of bake-metes in the other medieval menus in this book. "Meat" could also mean any sort of "flesh," including fruit, as in the "Quince and Orenge baked" offered at this feast, which were therefore in the form of a pie.

The following recipe for *lamprey bake*, taken from *A Noble Boke Off Cookry ffor a Prynce Houssolde or Eny Other Estately Houssolde* (ca. 1500) includes two instructions that are not found in a modern cookbook—how to stop the lamprey from leaping out of the pot before he is dead, and how to "blow up" the lid of the coffin to raise it above the contents. A galentyne was a sort of sauce for fish, although it later came to mean a jellied savory dish.

---

### To Mak a Freshe Lamprey Bake

To bak a freche lampry tak and put a quyk lampry in a pot put ther to a porcyon of red wyne then stop the pot close that he lep not out and when he is dyinge tak him out and put hym in skaldinge water then tak hym in your handes with alyn clothe and a handfull of hay in the tother hand and strik hym so that the skyn go away and saue him hole then weshe hym and cut hym out whart a straw brod from the naville so that the stringe be lowse, then slitt hym a litill at the throt and tak out the string and kep the blode in a vesselle and it be a female thrust in your hand from the naville upwards so that the spawn com out ther as ye tak out the stringe and ye will boile it salt it a littill in the same place within that ye may cum and lowse the bone with a prik from the fische and brek it a litill from the hed and slit hym a litill from the taille then put the prik betwene the bone and the fische and drawe the bone from the taille as esly as ye may that it cum out all hole from the taile then wind the bone about thy finger and drawe it out softly for breking and so ye shall tak it out hole then chope the lampry o twhart the bak eury pece iij fingers brode and let them hold to gedure and toile them welle in the blod, and ye will mak your galentyn of crust of white bred cutt it in schyves and toiste it on a gredirne that it be somdelle broun and tak a quart of good red wyne for the bakinge of the lampry and put the bred ther in and drawe it and mak it not chargaunt and ye will ye may grind a fewe of raissins and mak it up ther with and let the fyft part be venygar put ther to pouder of cannelle a gretdele, pouder galingalle pouder lombard pouder of guinger sugur saffron and salt and let it be be tweene braun and yallowe and mak thy colour of sanders then mak a large coffyn of pured floure and put thy lampry ther in and put in the galentyn that it stand as highe as the lampery and let it haue a good lide and wet the bredes round about and lay it in the coffyn and close it round about to the pen for ye must haue a pen betweene the lidd and the coffyne to blow the pen that the lid may rise welle and luk the ovene be hoot and set it in to it.

---

## March 10

### Dinner at Sea
### SS *New York*, 1928

In spite of her name, the SS *New York* was a thoroughly German ship. She was built for the Hamburg-America Steamship line as part of its trans-Atlantic fleet, and named for her major destination. The magnificent ship was launched on April 1, 1928 and was not yet a year old when some of its passengers sat down to the following dinner, which was built around four of the cornerstones of German cuisine—goose, potatoes, cabbage, and cherries.

The wild cherry probably originated somewhere in Asia but by prehistoric times was widespread in Europe. It became particularly favored in Germany,

| ABSCHIEDSESSEN | FAREWELL DINNER |
| --- | --- |
| Ochsenschwanzuppe | Oxtail Soup |
| Gebackene Sunderschnitte | Fried Fillet of Perch Pike |
| Kartoffelsalat | Potato Salad |
| Gebratene Gans | Roast Goose |
| Rotkohl      Kartofflen | Red Cabbage      Potatoes |
| Kirschenkompett | Compote of Cherries |
| Rahmeis, Waffeln | Ice Cream, Wafers |
| Kaffee | Coffee |

which is still the world's largest producer. A German cookbook written in 1553 by a woman called Sabina Welserin contains amongst its 205 recipes, four specifically for cherries—one pudding, two tarts, and one for sour cherry puffs, as well as several that use cherry syrup or jam.

The cabbage is another ancient vegetable which has been eaten across Europe (where it appears to have originated) for millenia. The very earliest forms were leggy, leafy plants similar to kale—the round "head" was not developed until about 2,000 years ago. Welserin only mentions cabbage once, in passing, in a recipe for a "green tart," but it was common in Germany as revealed in another sixteenth-century book, *Ein New Kochbuch* (1573), by Marx Rumpolt. He has multiple recipes for white, green, brown, and "sour" cabbage—the last we would recognize as sauerkraut. Red cabbage was developed somewhere about this time, and is very popular on account of its deep bright color. Rumpolt also mentions a dish of dried cherries soaked in water and wine and served warm or cold—essentially a cherry compôte (see August 11).

The goose has also been a favorite food of humans across Europe and Asia since very ancient times. It was eaten by the ancient Egyptians, Greeks, and Romans—all of whom prized the liver of the goose and force-fed their birds to make them fat—hence *"foie gras"* ("fat liver"). The goose is a very fatty bird, and until very recent times this was a very desired feature—the calorie density being all important at a time when food supplies were often very precarious indeed. Sabina Welserin's book has four recipes for goose. In one for "a well roasted young goose" she suggests stuffing it with its own liver and "ten plums" before roasting it on a spit, when "it will be good." In her other version of roast goose, the bird is stuffed with a delicious-sounding mixture of onions, quince, pears, and bacon—a recipe that truly gives a lie to the common belief that food at this time was stodgy and unimaginative.

Only the potato is "new" in German cuisine. It is a New World food, not known in Europe until it was brought back from the Americas by early sixteenth-century explorers. It is commonly repeated that the first European recipe for potatoes appeared in the Rumpolt cookbook under the heading *Erdtepfel* or Earth Apple, but historians now believe this was a variety of squash. The potato was only very slowly adopted in Europe, but there is no doubt that the Germans were amongst the first to make a lot of use of it, and it was while a prisoner of the Prussians that the potato's greatest eighteenth-century advocate, Antoine Parmentier (see October 21) was converted to its value.

## Recipes

~~~

German Potato Salad

Boil one dozen small potatoes without paring. Remove the skin and cut potatoes size of dice, also a small onion, finely minced. Put small pieces of bacon in a pan and fry brown and crisp. Add a large tablespoonful of vinegar and a pinch of salt. Pour the hot bacon fat and vinegar over the diced potatoes, toss them up lightly with a fork and serve hot.
   Mary at the Farm and Book of Recipes Compiled during Her Visit among the "Pennsylvania Germans" (1915).

The pigment in red cabbage acts in exactly the same way as litmus paper in the laboratory, and in the presence of alkali turns an unappetizing blue or grey. For this reason it is always cooked with an acid ingredient, often with apples and/or vinegar as in the following recipe. It was also commonly preserved by pickling in vinegar (see March 29).

Red Cabbage, German Style

One sliced red cabbage, one-half glass of vinegar, three sliced apples, two cups of bouillon, and a small piece of salt pork or bacon. Put in oven and cook as for two hours.
   Victor Hirtzler, *The Hotel St. Francis Cook Book* (1919).

Ox Tail Soup: see March 21.

March 11

Ironmongers' Company Dinner
Ironmongers Hall, Fenchurch Street, London, 1687

The Ironmongers of England were already an established "brotherhood" by the early fourteenth century, and by 1515 they were listed as tenth in the

A Bill of Faire for View and Search Day, being ye 11th of March 1686/7.

A sirloyne of beef.	4 barrels of oysters.
A breast of veale.	Oranges and lemmons.
A double pole of ling.	2 gallons of Canary
Five dishes barrell codd.	4 gallons of clarrett.
A side of salmon.	1 gall. of white wine.
Twelve dabbs, twelve whitings.	Sallads, 1 quart of oyle.
2 quarts of oysters.	Some gudgeons or smelts.
1 quart of shrimps.	

order of precedence of the twelve great livery companies (see October 28). Each year the company exerted its right to an annual inspection of its properties at the "View and Search Day." When the inspection was completed and the notices issued to tenants where repairs were required, the warden and members retired to enjoy a dinner. The following bill of fare for the dinner is dated according to both the "old style" and "new style" calendars (see December 22), so the year is given as 1686/7.

As was normal at the time, the cooking methods were not necessarily specified on the bill of fare. "Fancy" or "made" dishes would have been particularly mentioned, but other meats etc. are usually assumed to be plainly roasted or boiled and served with the standard sauces.

There is far more fish and seafood on this menu compared to meat than would be expected, probably reflecting the fact that this was the Lenten season. Oysters were very popular at all levels of society and are listed twice on the menu, probably representing fresh and pickled versions. Shrimps were a little more unusual at formal dinners, as they were often considered food for the poor. A "pole," or "poll" of ling was the head and shoulders (the most desirable part) of the fish, which was also commonly dried and salted.

All forms of dried, salted fish such as the "Barrel Cod" on this menu were indispensible staples for fast days and for long sea voyages. They were also important as a virtually indestructible standby at a time when there were few other methods of preservation—a use reflected in its other common name of *stockfish*. Dried cod was so vital in early medieval times that the search for it drove many early voyages of exploration.

Recipes

~~~

The method of preparing dried salt fish has not changed for centuries, and neither has the traditional garnish. Salt cod is still served with egg sauce, as in this eighteenth-century recipe. Ling was commonly served with mustard, or butter and mustard.

Poor Jack and Baccalao are alternative names for dried cod.

How to Boil Salt Fish,
as Poor Jack or Baccalao, Tusk, Barrel Cod, Ling, etc.

Salt-fish of all kinds, to be boiled, must be steeped in fresh water at least eighteen hours, or longer, according to the thickness and dryness of the fish. Let it be twelve hours in the first water, then scraped and clean it well from all dirt and loose bits that hang about it. And use a hand-brush to scrub the *baccalao* or *poor jack*, *ling*, and the *tusk-fish*; with this caution, not to break the skin so as to slip it off; for the skin of the tusk and ling especially is accounted the most delicious part of the fish. *Barrel cod* are generally boiled whole: the larger sort of salt fish are split down the back, and then cut into pieces of about four or five inches square. Put them in as much cold water as will cover the pieces to be boiled, and take care that the water does not come a-boil, it must only wallop or simmer, and that not above ten or fifteen minutes for barrel-cod and tusk, five or six minutes for whitings and small haddock, and not above twenty-five minutes for ling and large cod, for if the water is made to boil furiously, or the fish be kept simmering in the water longer than ten or fifteen minutes, it will eat wooly. Take it up piece by piece with a slice, and dish the fish with the skin uppermost: and garnish the dish with hard eggs quartered. Serve it up with egg-sauce, parsnips and potatoes, and with melted butter and mustard.

James Jenks, *The Complete Cook: Teaching the Art of Cookery in All Its Branches* (1768).

Egg Sauce

Boil your eggs hard, chop them up, put them into some good melted butter, and just boil them up.

Elizabeth Price, *The New Book of Cookery* (ca. 1780).

March 12

Antebellum Riverboat Menu
Robert F. Ward, Mississippi River, 1853

Accommodation for first-class passengers of the riverboats that traveled the Mississippi in the nineteenth century could be very luxurious and the dinner choices extensive, as the bill of fare for this day aboard the *Robert F. Ward* shows.

SOUP
Green Sea Turtle

FISH
Redfish, Baked, Browned Oyster Sauce   Sheepshead, Boiled
Broiled Trout Mad. [Madeira]. Wine Sauce

BOILED

Ham   Mutton [Capers]   Corned Beef   Turkey with Oyster Sauce

Tongue

Chicken Eggs   Spiced Round of Beef

ENTREES

Knuck[le] of Veal, Green Peas   Turkey Wings, Celery Sauce

Crabs,   Stuffed Pigs Head, Tomato Sauce   Oyster Pie   Shoulder of Lamb

Green Peas   Turtle Cutlets, Mad[iera]. Wine sauce

Macaroni à la Neapolitaine

ROASTS

Beef   Pork   Pig   Mutton   Turkey   Chicken   Veal   Duck

VEGETABLES OF THE SEASON

GAME

Saddle of Venison with Cranberry Sauce   French Duck with Currant Jelly

Black Duck Smothered in Wine Sauce Grouse   Stuffed, with Lemon Sauce

PASTRY AND DESSERT

Orange, Coconut, Lemon, Green Apple, Mince, Cherry, Cranberry and Gooseberry Pies

Apple, Grape, and Whortleberry Tarts   Pineapple Cream Puffs

Fruit, Citron and Tapioca Puddings   Prune, Fruit, Sponge and Jelly Cakes

Calle Fritters   Lady Fingers   Charlotte Russe

Blanchemange English Coconut Cream   White Wine and Rum Jellies

Pineapple Sherbert   Rose and Lemon Ice Creams

FRUIT

Oranges, Bananas, Figs, Grapes, Prunes, Raisins, Apples

Almonds, Walnuts, Pecans, Filberts

Sauternes and Claret Wines

Coffee

If the cooks aboard this vessel were aiming to please everyone, they probably succeeded. There were dishes of great elegance: turtle soup—the metaphor for fine dining (see November 10), fish and meat with classical sauces, and an adequate selection of game. There were plenty of roasts and simple fruits for those with plain palates. There were pies, tarts, and cakes galore for the sweet tooths, and for those with nursery palates—jellies, creams and ices, as well as *blanchemange* with its medieval heritage (see January 7).

The only concessions to local cuisine are the *calle fritters* and lady fingers. Callas (or calas) are rice fritters—traditional Creole snacks popular as a breakfast dish which used to be sold *toutes chaud* (all hot) in the streets of New Orleans. What is meant by "lady fingers" depends where in the world one is. They may be a variety of banana or okra, or Middle Eastern filo pastry rolls with a savory filling of minced lamb or a sweet one of honey and nuts. In the context of this menu they are sweet treats somewhere between sponge cakes and cookies, very similar to the eighteenth-century Naples biscuits, or *savoiardi* biscuits used in trifles.

Recipes

~~~

Callas

A Creole cake eaten hot with coffee.

One teacup of rice well boiled and mashed, one small coffee cup of sugar, two tablespoons yeast, three eggs, and flour sufficient to make a thick batter; beat the whole well together and fry in hot lard. Be careful not to have the batter too thin, or it will not fry well.

Lady Fingers

Mix into a half pound of confectioner's sugar the yolks of six eggs. Work this mixture with a spoon until very light and frothy; then mix into it the whites of six eggs that have been beaten stiff, adding at the same time a quarter of a pound of flour, dried and sifted. Place this batter into a meringue bag, and squeeze it through in strips two and one-half inches long, sprinkle over some fine sugar and bake in a moderate oven twelve to fifteen minutes.

Carrie V. Shuman, *Favorite Dishes: A Columbian Autograph Souvenir Cookery Book* (1893).

Tapioca Pudding: see September 26.
Caper Sauce: see December 8.
Madeira Wine Sauce: see February 28.

March 13

Dinner at Sea, Tourist Class
RMS *Majestic*, 1928

The White Star Line RMS *Majestic* left New York on March 10, 1928, on its regular voyage to Europe and England with some illustrious passengers on board. George Gershwin, the famous American composer was there, accompanying his lyricist brother Ira and his family on a trip that would be the inspiration for his orchestral composition *An American in Paris*. Lord Brabourne, a peer of the United Kingdom, was traveling home, as were an assortment of Austro-Hungarian aristocrats. Other celebrities included the opera star Maria Jeritza, the French tennis player Pierre Etchebaster, and Emil Ludwig, the German author.

The *Majestic* carried over 2,500 passengers in three classes—first, tourist, and third. Presumably the celebrity guests enjoyed better fare than the tourists, who sat down to this mid-Atlantic dinner.

Ox Tail Soup
Poached Codfish, Sauce Paloise
Duckling en Casserole
Roast Beef, Yorkshire Pudding
Fried Egg Plant
Boiled and Roast Potatoes
Salad: Ninette
Chesterfield Pudding
Ice Cream with Wafers
Pineapple   Oranges
Dinner Rolls
Tea   Coffee

The 1920s and 1930s were a golden age for ocean liner travel. As many as a dozen huge ships left New York harbor each day, and there was great competition for passengers. Naturally the food was expected to be superb—and it usually was, with each shipping line trying to provide popular international choices while at the same time demonstrating its national identity. The SS *New York* (see March 10) was plying the trans-Atlantic route serving its very German menu at the same time as this very British meal was being served aboard the RMS *Majestic*.

The only slightly atypical dish, for a British menu of this era, is the fried eggplant, which is more commonly associated with French and Italian cuisine. One comprehensive cookbook, *Cassell's New Dictionary of Cookery*, published in 1910 says, "This delicate and delicious vegetable is rapidly coming into favour in this country." Frying them in batter was a popular method of preparation.

Recipes

~~~

Aubergines Fried in Batter

Peel the aubergines and cut them in slices. Make a frying batter with flour, water, one egg, salt, and olive oil instead of butter.
   Dip each piece of aubergine in batter, and fry them in boiling fat.
   The Gentle Art of Cookery (London: Leyel & Hartley, 1925).

The Chesterfield pudding is a classic moulded iced pudding, one of the enduring favorites invented during the Victorian era.

Iced Pudding, à la Chesterfield

Grate one pound of pine-apple into a basin, add this to eight yolks of eggs, one pint and a half of boiled cream, one pound of sugar, and a very little salt. Stir the whole together in a stewpan over a stove-fire until the custard begins to thicken; then pass it through a tammy, by rubbing with two wooden spoons, in the same manner as a *purée*, in order to force the pine-apple through the tammy. This custard must now be iced in the usual manner, and put into a mould of the shape represented in the annexed wood-cut; and in the centre of the iced-cream, some *Macédoine* of red fruits, consisting of cherries, currants, strawberries, and raspberries in a cherry water-ice, must be introduced; cover the while in with the lid, and immerse the pudding in rough ice in the usual way, and keep in a cool place until wanted.

When about to send the pudding to table, turn it out of the mould on to its dish, ornament the top with a kind of drooping feather formed with green angelica cut into strips, and arranged as represented in the wood-cut; garnish the base with small *gauffres,* filled with some of the ice-cream reserved for the purpose, place a strawberry on the top of each, and serve.

Charles Elmé Francatelli, *The Modern Cook* (London, 1860).

Sauce Paloise

This is a Bearnaise sauce (see May 31) with fresh mint instead of tarragon. It is named after the town of Pau in the French province of Béarn, on the border with Spain.

Yorkshire Pudding: see December 24.
Ox-Tail Soup: see March 21.

March 14

Dinner at Sea
SS *Prince Rupert,* 1922

The SS *Prince Rupert* was a steamship owned by the Grand Trunk Railway of Canada and traveled the sea route between Vancouver and Alaska. The food aboard the ship leaned toward the traditional and substantial, as befitted the era and the weather, and there was plenty of choice at each meal, as steamship passengers would have expected.

DINNER.

Oysters on Half Shell
Queen Olives   Celery en Branch
Consomme Italienne   Puree of Split Pea
Boiled Filet of Salmon Colbert Sauce
Harico Ox Tail   Macedoine
Breaded Veal Cutlets   Tomato Sauce
Welsh Rarebit
Boiled Fowl with Bacon   Bread Sauce
Baked Premium Ham au Bourgeoise
Roast Prime Ribs of Beef with Yorkshire Pudding

—
Shrimp Salad, Mayonnaise
Brussels Sprouts   Yellow Turnips
Mashed & Boiled Potatoes
*
Steamed Marmalade Pudding   Fruit Sauce
Deep Apple Pie   Prince Rupert Triffle
Strawberry Ice Cream   Assorted Cakes
Canadian, American, and MacLaren's Cheese
Fresh Fruits
Tea   Coffee   Cocoa

The only clearly Canadian dish on the menu is the MacLaren's Cheese, a very popular Canadian product developed by Alexander Ferguson MacLaren, one-time M. P. for North Perth, Ontario. MacLaren learned cheese-making as a young man, and eventually became president of the Ontario Dairymen's Association. He introduced his cheese in distinctive tubs in 1892 under its full title of "MacLaren's Imperial Cheese," and it was indeed sold throughout the Empire and beyond, before being eventually sold to Kraft in 1920.

The most intriguing dish on this menu is without doubt Welsh rarebit. The dish basically consists of cheese on toast, and these are the two absolutely essential ingredients in a myriad of variations. There has been a great deal of vociferous and opinionated debate over many decades as to whether the correct name is "rarebit" or "rabbit," and an equally vigorous debate as to how the dish got its name. The Oxford English Dictionary traces Welsh rabbit to 1725, with Welsh rarebit appearing 60 years later, so clearly the latter is the upstart usurper. The eminent lexicographer H. W. Fowler (author of *Fowler's Modern Language Usage* in 1926) brooked no argument on the issue, stating that "Welsh Rabbit is amusing and right. Welsh Rarebit is stupid and wrong." It seems likely that the change to "rarebit" is an example of folk etymology. The word "rabbit" pronounced in a effete, upper-class English accent does rather sound like "rarebit," and thus in the ears of an eighteenth-century scholar, this is what it became.

There are many theories about the connection between the Welsh, rabbit, and cheese, ranging from the possible to the ridiculous. It seems most likely that it is an ethnic slur disguised as a joke, and indicates that the Welsh are too poor to buy rabbit or too stupid to catch it. Alternatively it may be an ironic joke on the part of the Welsh themselves, and it demonstrates their good humor in times of adversity. A bizarre extension of the name confusion turns up on some French menus, where Welsh rabbit is literally translated as *Lapin Gallois*. The ethnic slur aspect has also been thoroughly worked over since the dish was named. Cookbooks contain many variations of the dish which have become specialties in their own right, for example Scotch woodcock (with anchovies), Yorkshire buck rarebit (with eggs), and English monkey (a sort of cheesy bread sauce thickened with an egg).

Recipes

~~~

Welsh Rarebit

1/4 lb. grated cheese	1 egg
1/4 c. cream or milk	2 tsp butter
1/2 tsp mustard	few grains cayenne
1/2 tsp salt	Toast

Place the cheese, mixed with the cream or milk, in top part of double-boiler and heat until the cheese is melted. Then add the beaten egg, to which the mustard, salt, and cayenne have been added, then add the butter. Cook until it thickens, stirring constantly. Pour over toast. Welsh rarebit is often made in the chafing dish.

Mary Lockwood Matthews, *Elementary Home Economics: First Lessons in Sewing and Textiles, Foods and Cookery, and the Care of the House* (1922).

Marmalade Pudding

One-half pound of breadcrumbs, one-half pound of brown sugar, one-half pound of beef suet cut very fine, four eggs and one small can of marmalade. Mix all together, put in a close shape [i.e., in a basin or mold] and boil for three hours.

Everyday Cook Book (Good Housekeeping, 1903).

Colbert Sauce: see April 17.
Yorkshire Pudding: see December 24.

March 15

Breakfast on the ''42nd Street Special''
Chicago to Los Angeles by Rail, 1933

The promotional campaign run in 1933 for the Warner Brothers movie musical *42nd Street* was a publicist's wildest dream come true. President Franklin D. Roosevelt (1882–1945) himself invited the cast and crew to Washington to celebrate his inauguration, in gratitude for their support during his California campaign. A seven-car "42nd Street Special" train was put together and traveled across the country from Hollywood to Washington and back, inviting headlines wherever it went. By any standards the trip was a success. The movie (released on March 9) was a smash hit, the musical genre revitalized, and Warner Brothers saved from the possibility of bankruptcy.

The train left Hollywood on February 21 and arrived in Washington, DC, on March 4, stopping at a hundred towns along the way to simultaneously celebrate and promote President Roosevelt's "New Deal" for America and the "New Deal in Entertainment." Townsfolk turned out in the thousands hoping to catch a glimpse of one of the movie celebrities aboard the train, and special stops were made in the towns that were the homes of the twelve chorus girls specially chosen for the trip. The chorus girls no doubt had their own agenda and were hoping to be "discovered," but for this trip they were decorative promotional aids—almost all the same height and build, but with different colored hair, but all examples of "American girlhood at its loveliest." The newspapers took care to note that their loveliness would not be put at risk, and, according to the *Charleston Gazette*, "To enable them to retain their health and shapely grace on the long journey their meals will be scientifically prepared for them by a famous chef in an all-electric health kitchen."

Scientific preparation, a famous chef, and an all-electric health kitchen would not, in themselves, maintain the shapely grace of these American lovelies. Some personal discipline would have been required, as this extensive breakfast menu from the return trip demonstrates.

Grapefruit   Baked Apple
Orange Juice
Rolled Oats   Shredded Wheat
Calf's Liver and Bacon
French Toast, Apricot Marmalade
Grilled Ham   Grilled Bacon
Eggs as Desired
Wheat Cakes with Maple Syrup

Rolls   Toast   Muffins

Coffee   Tea   Chocolate

There are two dishes on this menu of particular historic interest. French toast has a long history. It is essentially bread dipped in egg and fried, and in many old manuscripts and cookery books it is called *pain perdu* which is usually translated as *lost bread* (for the very obvious reason that *perdu* means lost in French). An alternative explanation is that the bread has so wonderfully enriched that it is *pain pour Dieu*, or *God's bread*. Today bread is not treated with any particular reverence on a daily basis, but in previous times when it was the absolute staple for all classes, to throw it away was sinful as well as wasteful. There were many ways of using up stale bread; it was dipped in soup or wine, it was used to thicken stews and sauces, and it could be dipped in egg and fried. Almost every country with a bread-based diet has a version, and the names are legion. It is sometimes called Spanish toast or German toast. More poetically it goes by the names of poor knights, golden bread, bread fish, gypsy toast, gilded slices, and nun's toast for example, and in Estonia it is called "duckling," perhaps with a similar rationale to the idea of Welsh rabbit (see March 14).

Muffins are interesting from a historic perspective because the name indicates how a meaning can change when migrants and colonists adapt to their new country. A muffin (or crumpet) in England used to be a small flat "cake" made from a yeast dough or batter (like bread) cooked on a griddle and often served split, toasted, and buttered. The muffin in America became a sweet cake, more like a conventional cake, cooked in small cups, like cup cakes.

Recipes

~~~

Fried Toast or French Toast

12 slices bread 1/2 inch thick
1/2 teaspoon salt
3 eggs
2 cups milk

Beat the eggs, add the milk and salt. Dip slices of bread into the mixture and saute in a little hot fat until a delicate brown on both sides. Serve hot. Sprinkle with powdered sugar or serve maple sirup with the toast.

Raised (``English'') Muffins

1 cup scalded milk
1 yeast cake softened in 1/4 cup warm water
3/4 teaspoon salt
4 tablespoons sugar
2 tablespoons shortening
3 1/2 cups flour
1 egg

Add the scalded milk to the salt, sugar and shortening. When lukewarm, add the yeast and one and one-half cups flour. Beat thoroughly. When very light, add the beaten egg and the remaining flour. Mix well and let the dough rise until double in bulk. Shape into portions small enough to fit into muffin-tins. Brush the top with egg-white slightly beaten and sprinkle with chopped nuts. Let rise in a well-oiled tin and bake in a hot oven (400–425°F).
Ruth Berolzheimer, *The American Woman's Cookbook* (1939).

March 16

Bill of Fare
Virginia Hotel, St. Louis, 1858

The Virginia Hotel on the corner of Green, Main, and Second streets in St. Louis was reopened in 1853 after extensive additions and renovations. Management had the express intention of providing "all of the luxuries and conveniences of home" to traveling businessmen visiting the city. A contemporary book about the city by Jacob N. Taylor (*Sketch Book of Saint Louis* [M. O. Crooks, 1858]) noted that "all will concede the fact that the table of the Virginia Hotel is always provided with the best the market affords''—a justifiable claim, if we are to judge from the menu provided on March 16, 1858.

SOUP.
Spring.

—

FISH.
Fresh Cod Fish boiled à la Hollandaise.

—

Leg of Mutton, Caper Sauce.
Beef Tongue.   Ames' Sugar Cured Ham.
Corned Beef and Cabbage.

—

COLD DISHES.
Corned Beef.   Roast Beef.
Ames' Sugar Cured Ham.   Beef Tongues.

—

ROAST.
Beef.   Ribs of Beef.
Ham, Champagne Sauce.   Leg of Veal.
Saddle of Mutton.   Chickens.   Pork.

—

ENTREES.
Langue de Boeuf a la Flamande.
Blanquette de Veau.
Emince de Dindon Friccasse.
Cerville de Veau en Marinade.
Salt Pork fried with Onions.
Corned Beef Hashe with Fried Eggs.
Coeur de Veau a la Sauce Piquante.
Calves Feet a la Vinnegarette.
Roll of Beef Braise au Jus.
Veal Pot Pie.
Kidneys Fried with Salt Pork.
Scrambled Eggs with Cod Fish.
Escollope de Cochon a la Sauce Robert.
Ailerons de Dinde a l'Italienne.
Foil de Veau Braise a l'Espagnole.
Pork and Beans Baked.

—

RELISHES.
Pickles.   Horse Radish.
Cheese.   Worcestershire Sauce.   Pickled Beets.
Cranberry Sauce.

—

VEGETABLES.
Potatoes Boiled.   Potatoes Mashed.   Boiled Rice.
Stewed Oyster Plant.   Sauer Kraut.   Mashed Turnips.
Fried Parsnips.   Hominy.   Onions.

—

PASTRY.
Honey Comb Pudding, Brandy Sauce.
Madeira Wine Jelly.   Peach Marengues.
Mince Pie.   Cranberry Pie.   Cocoanut Pie.

—

DESSERT.
Apples.   Pecan Nuts.
Layer Raisins.   Coffee.

—

HOURS FOR MEALS.
Breakfast from 6 1/2 to 10 o'clock.
Dinner 12 to 3 o'clock.

—

Tea from 6 to 9 o'clock.

—

Each Waiter has a Wine Card and Pencil.

The hotel menu also included an extensive wine list, and the following set of regulations.

Transient Boarder's bills collected weekly.

Seats for families are reserved for dinner only.

Meals served in rooms will be charged extra.

Families will not be called to meals except for Dinner.

Persons inviting friends to meals will give notice at the office that seats may be reserved for them.

Regular boarders, on leaving will register their names as absent, that proper credit may be given.

Guests intending to depart during the night or at early hours will please give notice at the office, that they may be called in time and prevent delays.

This menu is an example of a *table d'hôte* (see February 27), hence the advice to guests about notifying the office should they not be present for a meal. The food itself is the substantial fare of the time. It seems that hotel managements of the time could not avoid listing the *entrées* in French, even without any knowledge of their correct spelling.

Recipes

~~~

Honey Comb Pudding

One-half cupful flour, one-half cupful of sugar, one half-cupful of milk, one half cup-full of butter, one-half pint New Orleans molasses, four eggs, one teaspooful

soda. Mix flour, sugar, butter, and milk warm enough to dissolve the butter, all together; add the beaten eggs, and last, the molasses and soda beaten to a froth. Bake half an hour. Serve with cream, or foamy sauce.
Mrs. Hattie Burr, *The Woman Suffrage Cook Book* (Boston, 1886).

Cocoanut Pie

One cocoanut fresh, draw off the milk, then place the nut in a hot oven and let it stay long enough for the shell to pull off; then grate with the nut juice one tea-cup of powdered white sugar, one tablespoonful of butter and lard rubbed together until creamed, then take the yelks of four eggs and beat into sugar and butter until perfectly light; grate the rind of one lemon into it, and squeeze the juice of the lemon into the creamed butter and sugar; beat the white of four eggs light, and add also to creamed butter and sugar, and stir them well, add also one-half tea-cup of sweet milk. Will make three pies. Use a half pound of flour for the pastry, one tablespoonful each of butter and lard—you only want crust at the bottom of plate, and bake in quick oven.
What Mrs. Fisher Knows about Old Southern Cooking (San Francisco, 1881).

Champagne Sauce: see May 27.
Caper Sauce: see December 8.
Hominy: see March 20, May 19.

March 17

St. Patrick's Day Banquet
The White House, Washington, DC, 1959

President Dwight D. Eisenhower (1890–1969) invited the president of Ireland Seán Thomas O'Kelly (1882–1966) to visit the United States in 1959. It was the first official visit of a President of Ireland to the country and was planned to coincide with the traditional St. Patrick's Day celebrations. President O'Kelly arrived on March 16 "radiating Gaelic charm," to a green carpet welcome—the traditional red one being specially replaced for the day. President Eisenhower wore a green tie, other officials wore green socks, and U.S. congressmen sported green carnations in their lapels. The green theme even extended to the St. Patrick's Day banquet on the following evening.

Historically, much political business has been facilitated over the banquet table. A potentially embarrassing diplomatic situation loomed before this event when it was realized that President O'Kelly's visit would coincide with that of Harold Macmillan (1894–1986), prime minister of the United Kingdom—a country with a long history of unpopularity in Ireland. Some strategic rescheduling averted the problem, and President O'Kelly's visit was a lighthearted affair. President Eisenhower joked that "everybody was Irish today," to which the Irish President responded with "I salute my most distinguished subject."

	DINNER	
	Prosciutto Ham and Melon	
	Cream of Watercress Soup	
Dry Sack	Melba Toast	
	Celery Hearts	Assorted Olives
Chateau	Seafood Newburg	
Climens	Vol-au-Vent	
1950	Cucumber Sandwiches	
Beaune	Roast Stuffed Long Island Duckling	
Greves	Applesauce	
1952	Casserole of Eggplant	
	French Beans Almondine	
	Tossed Greens in Salad with Anchovy	
	Cheese Crusts	
	Frosted Mint Delight	
	Lady Fingers	
Pol Roger		
1952	Assorted Nuts Bon Bons Demitasse	
	Mints	

There had been a vogue for color-themed dinners in the previous century, with some creativity needed to have an "all-white" or "all-pink" meal. Green food is not such a challenge, however, and it would not have been difficult to plan this meal. The dishes themselves are not remarkable, and one assumes there was plenty of parsley to garnish the savory dishes. The cucumber sandwiches are a little unexpected at a formal state dinner. They are usually associated with English afternoon tea parties and garden parties—perhaps because only the upper class could afford the hot-houses to grow them, or perhaps their lightness and lack of substance symbolized their leisured and frivolous lifestyle.

State dinner for the Irish president. From left, Mamie Eisenhower, President Sean O'Kelly, Mrs. O'Kelly, and President Eisenhower. (AP Photo)

Recipes

~~~

Cucumber Salad Sandwich

Mix sliced cucumber with mayonnaise and spread between bread.
    Mrs. C. F. Leyel and Miss Olga Hartley, *The Gentle Art of Cookery* (1925).

Mint Ice

2 cups sugar
1 quart water
1 cup slightly bruised fresh mint leaves
Juice of two lemons
Green food coloring
16 crystallized mint leaves.

Place the sugar and water in a pan and bring to the boil, stirring until the sugar dissolves. Boil five minutes. Add the fresh leaves, cover and cool. Strain. Add the lemon juice and color it a delicate shade of green. Pour into a

refrigerator tray and freeze until mushy. Stir well. Freeze until firm. Serve in sherbert glasses or with fruit. If desired, garnish with the crystallized leaves.
New York Times, August 4, 1962.

Cream of Watercress Soup

2 cups milk
Leaves from one stalk celery
2 slices onion
2 tablespoons butter or margarine
2 tablespoons flour
3/4 teaspoon salt
dash pepper
1 bunch watercress.

Heat milk to scalding with celery leaves and onion. Remove vegetables. Cream together fat, flour, salt, and pepper. Add to milk and cook, stirring, until thickened. Grind watercress or chop it very fine. Add to sauce and heat.
New York Times, May 31, 1951.

Vol-au-vent: see September 17.
Lady Fingers: see March 12.

March 18

Dinner for the New King, Alfonso XIII
Royal Palace, Madrid, Spain, 1902

Alfonso XIII (1886–1941) was proclaimed King of Spain on the day of his birth, his father having died before he was born. Until he attained his majority, Spain was ruled by his mother Queen Maria Christina. When the time of his coming of age dawned (on his sixteenth birthday), all of Spain participated in a week of feasts, parties, and bullfights. The day after his birthday, the King sat down to the following dinner.

DINER DE S.M.

Consommé brunoise au Tapioca
Frito à l'Espagnole
Filets de bœuf à la Richelieu
Fricandeau de veau aux Epinards
Petits pois à la Flamande
Poulets à la Broche
Salade de mâche et betteraves
Pain de Gênes
Glace Abricotine

There is nothing on this menu that is distinctly Spanish. It could have been a dinner at any fine-dining establishment or palace in any country of Europe at the time. The ruling families of Europe had intermarried for centuries, and in spite of their frequent and bloody conflicts had developed a cuisine which was quite generic and pan-European in nature. By the nineteenth and twentieth centuries this meant that it was firmly based in the classic French tradition.

The only apparent concession to Spain is the *Frito à l'Espagnole*, which is hardly any concession at all given that menus of the time were full of dishes styled *à l'Allemande, à la Française* or *à l'Anglaise* and so on. These names were bestowed not by the countries themselves but by others attempting to determine the quintessential ingredients or techniques of each nation. Sometimes the connection is obvious—in dishes styled *Hollandaise*, for example, which always contain a lot of butter on account of the good, early reputation of the Dutch dairy industry. Some are more tenuous—*Polonaise* (Polish style), indicating a garnish of buttered breadcrumbs and hard boiled eggs, or *Allemande* (German style), a white or *blond* sauce possibly named after the fair-headed people of that country. The dish of peas at this dinner was styled *à la Flamande*, meaning in the Flemish style, and the *Pain de Gênes* is "bread" from Genoa—actually *Genoese* cake.

Frito means fried. It comes from the Latin *frigere*, hence the word is recognizable in all of the Latin-based languages—*fritto* (Italian), *frito* (Portuguese and Spanish), and *frit* (French). Italy has its *fritto misto*, so perhaps this *Frito à l'Espagnole* was a variation of the same idea—a number of small morsels of a variety of foods, battered and deep fried.

Recipes

~~~

Richelieu Sauce

This is a rich brown game sauce, reduced with Madeira or Marsala wine, then work in a little liquefied meat extract and some finely chopped truffles.

Game Sauce (Sauce Gibier)

Some game bones and trimmings,
1 pint espagnole or brown sauce,
1/2 gill sherry,
onion,
carrot,
turnip,
parsley,
thyme,
marjoram,
bay-leaf,
mace,
clove.

> The trimmings, carcasses, etc., of any kind of game may be used for this sauce; those of grouse or woodcock are preferable. Chop small the trimmings of game, put them in a stew-pan with a small onion, a piece of carrot, and a piece of turnip all cut in slices, a few sprigs of parsley, a sprig of thyme, one of marjoram, a bay-leaf, a small piece of mace, and one clove, moisten with the sherry, cover and put on the fire to cook for five minutes. Now add the espagnole or brown sauce, let it come quickly to a boil, and keep simmering for fifteen minutes longer. Pass through a tammy cloth, return to a clean stew-pan, season with a little salt if necessary, and keep hot in the bain-marie until required for serving.
> Charles Herman Senn, *The Book of Sauces* (1915).

Pain de Gênes, or Genoa Bread or Genoese Cake: see January 20.
Fricandeau de veau: see April 29.
Sauce Gribiche: see June 23.

March 19

Luncheon to Celebrate Opening of Sydney Harbour Bridge
RMS *Maloja*, Sydney Harbour, Australia, 1932

The Sydney Harbour bridge has become an iconic image of the Australian city—its outline against the sky giving it the affectionate nickname of "The Coathanger." It had another name during its construction—"The Iron Lung," because it saved many lives during The Great Depression by providing work for thousands of construction workers. Proposals for a bridge between the central business district and Sydney's North Shore had been discussed on and off since the earliest days of the colony, but it was not until 1925 that construction began.

Eight years later the bridge was officially opened at a ceremony that was not without a short, unpleasant drama. Just as the Premier was about to perform the usual tape-cutting ceremony, he was preempted by a fanatic called Francis de Groot (an Irishman, in spite of his name), who rode up on horseback, wearing full military dress and brandishing a sword, and slashed the ribbon himself, declaring the bridge open "in the name of the decent and respectable people" of New South Wales. De Groot was part of a paramilitary group called the New Guard which was convinced that the country was in danger of sliding into communism, and was planning a right-wing revolution. He was quickly taken into custody and further action averted, and no doubt the dignitaries and special guests (including Bradfield) were especially relieved to relax aboard the P&O ship RMS *Maloja* for the official luncheon.

MENU

Oyster Cocktail
Hollandaise Soup
Sole Colbert
Roast Pheasant

CURRIES
Prawn   Chicken

COLD SIDEBOARD
Mayonnaise of Salmon
Sardines
Asparagus tips en Aspic
Raised Game Pie   York Ham
Roast Ribs of Beef   Galantine of Capon
Boar's Head   Pressed Ox Tongue
Salad Marquise

SWEETS
Macedoine of Fruit
Neopolitan Cream Ices

CHEESE
Gruyere   Cheddar   Stilton
Dutch Cream   Old Blue Cheshire

Although it was 24 years after Federation, the country was still strongly tied to its British roots, and the designer, John Bradfield, hoped and planned that the bridge would confirm the city as the "shining diamond in Britain's empire." The bridge was "all British engineering feat," built with British finance and British steel. The menu of the official luncheon too was resolutely British—as was usual for official functions of the time, even to the extent of including the medieval flourish of the boar's head (see January 4).

Recipes

~~~

Marquise Salad

3 firm tomatoes
1/2 cup chopped onion
1/2 cup chopped parsley
2 tablespoons salad oil

Peel tomatoes and cut in half. Mix onion and parsley, add oil; let stand two hours before using. When ready to serve line salad bowl with lettuce, place tomatoes on it and on each half put 1 tablespoon onion and parsley mixture. Pour on French dressing. Everything should be ice cold.
Dr. Price, *The New Dr. Price Cookbook* (1921).

Curried Prawns

1 1/2 pints Prawns.	1 tablespoonful sliced Onion.
1 oz. Butter.	1 dessertspoonful Curry Powder.
1/2 oz. Flour.	1 dessertspoonful Lemon Juice.
1 1/2 gills Milk, 1/2 gill Stock.	1 dessertspoonful Chutney.
1 apple	Salt and Pepper.
Boiled Rice.	

Peel and slice the apple and onion. Melt the butter in a saucepan, add the sliced onion, and fry till transparent but not coloured. Then add the apple, curry powder and flour, and keep stirring while the mixture comes to the boil and boils for 2 minutes. Now gradually thin down with the milk, and add the stock—white for preference, stir till the sauce is smooth and boiling, then simmer in a covered pan for 1/2 hour. Season to taste, add the prawns, and when piping hot, the chutney, and stir in the lemon juice. Serve at once in a hot dish with a border of boiled rice.

New Standard Cookery Illustrated, edited by Elizabeth Craig (1933 Australian ed.).

Oyster Cocktail: see January 24.
Neapolitan Ice-Cream: see December 20.
Sole Colbert: April 17.
Raised Pies: see October 25.

March 20

American Maize Banquet
Hotel King of Denmark, Copenhagen, Denmark, 1893

A huge international publicity campaign was put in place during the lead-up to the 1893 Columbian Exposition in Chicago, to encourage foreign participation. The theme of the exposition was the celebration of the 400th anniversary of the discovery of the New World by Christopher Columbus.

To Charles Murphy, the United States' agricultural corn agent in Europe, what better way to celebrate Columbus than via his most useful gift to the Old World? Murphy held a dinner to the "prominent citizens of Copenhagen" at which maize was put firmly in the spotlight by being the major ingredient in all dishes.

The *Chicago Times* was sure that the banquet "impressed the Danish guests with some enlarged ideas as to American food products," and noted that according to Murphy "the banquet has been made the theme of considerable favorable comment by the press." The real agenda of course was economic. The U.S. Secretary of Agriculture J. Sterling Morton stressed this in saying

	"Economy in food is the wealth of all nations"
	Mush (Maize) & milk.
	Grilled Oysters, rolled in Maize, mixed rye maize bread, mixed maize wheat bread.
California Wines	Fried (Maize) Mush with maple syrup.
	Roast Turkey, Hominy (Maize) croquettes
Reisling (White)	California Fruit
Claret	Corn Flour (Maize) Pudding and California Fruit
	Cheese & butter with corn (Maize) bread.
Champagne	Cerealine Flake (Maize) Pudding
	Ices, California Raisins, Figs and assorted Fruit.

There is no doubt whatever of the importance to this country of opening up foreign markets for every product of which we are capable of raising a surplus above and beyond our own needs. This would do much to save the discouragingly low prices, which, without such an outlet, invariably attend an extra large crop. Our policy should be, however, to encourage as much as possible the export of the finished products of maize, doing the milling and keeping the offal in our own country.

Recipes

~~~

Charles Murphy, the man who gave this banquet, wrote a treatise called *American Indian Corn (maize) a Cheap, Wholesome, and Nutritious Human Food* in 1890 in which he included 130 "formulas" for the preparation and cooking of corn, and the use of maize for brewing.

Hominy Croquettes

1 coffee cup of (fine) cold, boiled hominy.
1 table-spoonful of butter.
1/2 cup rich milk.

Work these together until all are quite smooth and a soft paste; place the pan used for mixing in another of hot water, and heat, but do not boil, then carefully add

1 tea-spoon sugar.
2 yolks of eggs well beaten.

Stir while they thicken, and when cold and stiff flour your hands and form into oval balls, dip in the beaten white of the two eggs to which you have added

1 table-spoon cold water.
(1 table-spoon olive oil if liked.)
1 salt spoon salt.

Then roll in fine cracker crumbs (the rolled cracker having been sifted), and fry in boiling lard.

Mrs. Henderson's Corn Starch (Corn Flour) Pudding

(Three formulas in one.)
1 pint rich milk.
2 large table-spoons corn starch.
1/2 cup sugar.
4 whites of eggs, beaten stiff.
1 salt spoon salt.

Dissolve the corn starch in a little of the milk; stir the sugar into the remainder of the milk, then place on the fire. When it begins to boil, add the dissolved corn starch. Stir constantly for a few minutes, when it will become a smooth paste. Now stir in the beaten whites and cook for three minutes; remove from the fire and flavour with vanilla, turn into a wet pudding mould, and set to cool; or, you may add one-half cocoa-nut, grated, before putting it into the mould.

Serve with whipped cream around it, or a sauce of boiled custard made with the yolks, thus:

1 pint rich milk.
4 yolks of eggs, very well beaten.
1/2 cup sugar.
1 tea spoon corn starch,

Wet in cold milk. Boil all together and watch carefully. Flavour with one tea-spoon of vanilla.

Always flavour after you have taken it from the stove.

If the milk is boiled first before it is added to the other ingredients, there is less danger of the custard curdling.

With still the same formula for corn starch pudding, first flavour the whole with vanilla, then take out a third of the pudding and flavour it with half a bar of chocolate, which has been grated; stir in till smooth and perfectly blended. Then put one-half of the white part into a mould (which has been wet with cold water), and smooth the top. Next put the dark part in; smooth again, and finish by putting the remaining white part in, and put away to get firm.

Or, with the same formula for corn starch pudding, you may flavour with fresh fruit—strawberries, raspberries, or pine-apples.

Serve with whipped cream, or boiled custard as given above.

March 21

Dinner for the Rifle Volunteers
Auckland, New Zealand, 1871

In common with many other indigenous peoples around the globe, the Maori of New Zealand believed that the land belonged to the tribe, not to individuals. They resisted strongly the allocation of land to the white settlers who began arriving after the British declared sovereignty in 1840. The prolonged period of fighting (1845–1872) over the issue became known as the Maori Wars. The colonists protected themselves as best they could, forming volunteer companies to supplement the Militia. On this day, the Provincial

Superintendent of Aukland gave a dinner to thank the Rifle Volunteer representatives for their efforts.

The evening was declared "the utmost success," the rifle band performed a "happy selection" of music, and the caterer did a creditable job. The bill of fare was described by the *Daily Southern Cross* newspaper the next morning.

> Soups: Ox tail soup, oyster soup. Fish: Fried cutlets of mullet, soles au gratin. Entrees: Stewed pigeons, sweet bread, lamb cutlets and tomato sauce, oyster patties, curry of chicken, stewed ducks, rissoles. Joints: Roast beef, roast ribs of lamb, braised ham, boiled turkey, roast fowls, saddle of mutton, ox tongue, roast ducks, roast turkey, boiled fowls. Sweets: Plum pudding, almond pudding, apple pie and custard, maccaroni au gratin, Maraschino jelly, orange jelly, raspberry cream, trifle, cabinet pudding, lemon pudding, tourte preserves, mayonnaise of lobster, curaçoa jelly, vanilla cream, almond cream, rhubarb souflet. Dessert.

This bill of fare could equally have been served at any similar event anywhere in Her Majesty's Empire. Maintaining the style and standards of "home" was the guiding principle of every aspect of life. There was no thought of deliberately seeking out local ingredients or the culinary ideas of indigenous ignorant savages—in fact to do so would have been tantamount to treason. This was a staunchly British menu, and perhaps the only clue to its colonial origins comes from the fact that it was written in unpretentious English, not French.

The climate of New Zealand was not much different from Britain, so new settlers were not forced to make creative substitutions for familiar ingredients. Colonists and migrants have always taken their familiar cookbooks with them, and at this time without doubt, one of the most popular was the Isabella Beeton's household manual, first published in 1861. The entire dinner on this day could be prepared with the guidance of this classic text.

Recipes

~~~

The following recipes are taken from *Beetons's Book of Household Management* (1861), the amazingly comprehensive manual organized by Isabella Beeton (1836–1865) and taken to all corners of the British Empire by its colonists.

Ox-Tail Soup

2 ox-tails,	1 bunch of savoury herbs,
2 slices of ham,	1 bay-leaf,
1 oz. of butter,	12 whole peppercorns,
2 carrots,	4 cloves,
2 turnips,	a tablespoonful of salt,
3 onions,	2 tablespoonfuls of ketchup,
1 leek,	1/2 glass of port wine,
1 head of celery,	3 quarts of water.

Cut up the tails, separating them at the joints; wash them, and put them in a stewpan, with the butter. Cut the vegetables in slices, and add them, with the peppercorns and herbs. Put in 1/2 pint of water, and stir it over a sharp fire till the juices are drawn. Fill up the stewpan with the water, and, when boiling, add the salt. Skim well, and simmer very gently for 4 hours, or until the tails are tender. Take them out, skim and strain the soup, thicken with flour, and flavour with the ketchup and port wine. Put back the tails, simmer for 5 minutes, and serve.

Sweet Macaroni Pudding

2 1/2 oz. of macaroni,
2 pints of milk,
the rind of ½ lemon,
3 eggs,
sugar and grated nutmeg to taste,
2 tablespoonfuls of brandy.

Put the macaroni, with a pint of the milk, into a saucepan with the lemon-peel, and let it simmer gently until the macaroni is tender; then put it into a pie-dish without the peel; mix the other pint of milk with the eggs; stir these well together, adding the sugar and brandy, and pour the mixture over the macaroni. Grate a little nutmeg over the top, and bake in a moderate oven for 1/2 hour. To make this pudding look nice, a paste should be laid round the edges of the dish, and, for variety, a layer of preserve or marmalade may be placed on the macaroni: in this case omit the brandy.

Cabinet Pudding: see June 30.
Oyster Soup: see January 4.
Plum Pudding: see June 28.
Mayonnaise of Lobster: see March 31.

March 22

Fine Dining Experience
Verrey's Restaurant, Regent Street, London, 1899

Lieutenant-Colonel Nathaniel Newnham-Davis (1854–1917) was one of England's first restaurant critics. He had had a distinguished military career before retiring in 1894 to enjoy and write about *La Vie de Luxe* (The Life of Luxury), which he made the title of one of his newspaper columns. Newnham-Davis was a prolific writer as well as enthusiastic gourmet, and in 1897 he was commissioned by the editor of the *Pall Mall Gazette* to write a dining guide to London. The book, entitled *Where and How to Dine in London*, was published in 1899, and in the preface the editor says,

I knew I was availing myself of the services of a thoroughly experienced, trustworthy, and capable commissioner, who would deal with the task entrusted to him in a pleasantly mixed anecdotal and critical spirit, while at the same time supplying useful guidance to persons wanting to know where to dine and what they would have to pay.

In March 1899, the colonel received a phone call from an American friend who was briefly in London, and their subsequent dinner (which costs him £2:4:2; equivalent to approximately USD 261 today) was perfect material for one of his stories.

Myra Washington ... knows most people who are worth knowing in Europe, has been to most places worth seeing, and is in every way cosmopolitan ... She had come to London from Cannes to meet John [her husband], who was running over from America for a couple of days on business, and wanted to do as much as possible in the shortest time ... now I was to be responsible for her evening's amusement on the third evening.

... so it was with a full sense of the responsibility I had incurred that I sought Mr. Krehl, the elder of the two brothers in whose hands Verrey's now is ... I am a very strong believer myself in small dinners, but it was difficult to make up a menu which would be sufficiently substantial, without appearing gluttonous, for two.

This was the dinner that we settled on before I started home to dress:

Petite marmite.
Oeufs à la Russe.
Soufflé de filets de sole à la Verrey.
Timbale Lucullus.
Noisettes d'agneau à la Princesse.
Petits pois à la Française.
Pommes Mirelle.
Aiguillettes de caneton à l'Orange.
Salade Vénétienne.
Pouding Saxon.
Salade de fruits.

The *oeufs à la Russe,* with their attendant *vodkhi,* met with Mrs. Washington's approval: there were no flies on them, was her expression. We did not quite agree as to the *soufflé,* I daring to say that though the fish part of the dish was admirable I thought the soufflé covering might have been lighter, a statement which my guest at once countered, and, by her superior knowledge of culinary detail reduced me to silence, overcome but certainly not convinced. As to the *timbale,* with its savoury contents of quenelles, foie gras, cocks'-combs, and truffles, there could be no two opinions; it was excellent, and the same might be said of the noisettes, each with its accompanying *fond d'artichaut,* and the new peas with a leaf of mint boiled with them. Mrs. Washington would have preferred *pommes soufflées* to *pommes Mirelle,* but I could hardly have known that when ordering dinner. The Venetian salad, a little tower of many-coloured vegetables, looking like poker chips, Mrs. Washington said, peas, beans, truffles, potatoes, beetroot, flavoured by a slice of *saucisson* and dressed with whipped white of eggs, was one of the triumphs of the dinner, and so was the *salade de fruits.*

For Mrs. Washington to praise a fruit salad is a high honour, for she is one of the favoured people for whom François, late of the Grand Hotel, Monte Carlo and now of the Hotel Cecil, deigns to mix one with his own hands. . . . I was told that the *pouding Saxon* was an unnecessary item, and I was rather glad, for I had shied at it when ordering dinner.

Recipes
~~~

Eggs à la Russe

6 eggs
2 tablespoonfuls of caviar
1/2 pint of stock
1 teaspoonful of onion juice
1 dash of pepper.

Hard-boil the eggs, remove the shells, cut them into halves lengthwise; take out the yolks without breaking the whites, and press them through a sieve, then add caviar, onion juice and pepper. Heap these back into the whites. Boil the stock until reduced one-half, baste the eggs carefully, run them into the oven until hot, pour over the remaining hot stock, and send to the table.
Sarah Tyson Rorer, *Many Ways for Cooking Eggs* (1910).

There are several dishes that go by the name of Saxon pudding. One is similar to a trifle, with custard and layers of cake and macaroons. Another is a brown bread pudding with almonds and crystallized fruit. The following is a light and elegant version baked, as the Victorians loved to do, in a mold.

Saxon Pudding

According to high authority this is one of the best puddings of Germany. Boil a gill of milk, put into a stewpan half a pound of flour. Gradually dilute the flour with the milk so as to obtain a fine smooth paste. Add four ounces of butter, and salt to taste. Place the saucepan on a moderate fire, stir the preparation till it begins to thicken, then take it off the fire, but still continue working it. When the paste is smooth, place it again on the fire, working it still, and gradually introduce into it the yolks of ten eggs, four ounces of oranged sugar, four ounces of butter, and a little salt. When the preparation is frothy, introduce seven or eight whipped whites of eggs. Pour the preparation into a dome or cylinder mould which has been buttered or glazed with sugar and potato flour. Set the mould in a stewpan with boiling water reaching to half its height. Bake in a slack oven for forty minutes.
Cassell's New Dictionary of Cookery (London, 1910).

Petits pois à la Française: see July 11.

March 23

Queen's Guard Dinner
St. James' Palace, London, 1855

The Queen's Guard is the infantry regiment charged with the responsibility of guarding the person of the monarch and the official royal residences of St. James' Palace and Buckingham Palace. Their headquarters are at the former, and the Changing of the Guard ceremony so popular with tourists in London begins with a march from there to Buckingham Palace.

On March 23, 1855, there was a ceremonial dinner at St. James'.

LES HUÎTRES.

POTAGES.
A la Créci aux croutons.   De macaroni au consommé.

POISSONS.
La merluche sauce aux œufs.
Les truites grillées à la Tartare.
RELEVÉS.
Saddle of mutton.
Les poulets garnis d'une langue et des chouxfleurs.

ENTRÉES.
Les cotelettes de mouton à la Soubise.
Le vol au vent aux ecrévisses.
Les Kromeskys de ris de veau.
Les filets de bœuf piqués sauce poivrade.

ROTS.
Les pigeons, and la pintade piquée.

RELEVÉS.
Les pommes au riz.   Les fondus en caisses.

ENTREMETS.
La gelée au noyau.   Les epinards au jus.
Les meringues à la Chantilly.   La moelle aux croûtons.

Whether or not they knew it, in this standard Victorian menu, there is a fine acknowledgement of one of the greatest English military victories in history. *Potage Crécy* is most commonly (at least in modern times) a soup made from a purée of carrots. It is said to be named for the famous Battle of Crécy on August 26, 1346, at which a vastly outnumbered small English force defeated the huge French army of Philip V, thanks to the superb skill of the English longbowmen. Crécy is a village in northern France. Like so many stories of the origin of well-known dishes, this one is more myth and folklore than history. The most fanciful variation of the story is that in the post-battle pillaging the victorious English feasted upon the carrots growing luxuriantly in the region. The soup is undoubtedly named for the region and the root crops which are grown there, but it was certainly not invented on the battle field any more than was chicken Marengo (see July 14). Earlier versions of the recipe did not specify carrots alone. *Potage à la Cressy* in an eighteenth-century French cookbook by Françoise Menon is a mix of "all sorts of roots," and Isabella Beeton (1836–1865) gives a combination of vegetables and lentil in her version.

Recipes

~~~

Soup A La Crecy

4 carrots,	2 sliced onions,
1 cut lettuce,	and chervil;
2 oz. butter,	1 pint of lentils,
the crumbs of 2 French rolls,	half a teacupful of rice,
2 quarts of medium stock.	

Put the vegetables with the butter in the stewpan, and let them simmer 5 minutes; then add the lentils and 1 pint of the stock, and stew gently for half an hour. Now fill it up with the remainder of the stock, let it boil another hour, and put in the crumb of the rolls. When well soaked, rub all through a tammy. Have ready the rice boiled; pour the soup over this, and serve.

Beeton's Book of Household Management (1861).

Pommes au Riz

Peel eight russet apples, not very large ones, and rub them over well with a lemon cut through the middle, to keep them white; take out the cores and rub the insides with a lemon; then put them in boiling water with a little cinnamon; cover the pan, and let the apples boil very slowly so as not to break. At the same time boil some rice in milk with a little sugar and a few drops of orange-flower water. When it is well swollen and very thick, keep it warm, and see whether the apples are tender; if so, take them out of the pan, skillfully, without breaking them, and dip them in pounded sugar. Arrange them on a dish (a silver one if possible) and fill up the insides with the rice. Sift pounded sugar over the tops of the apples and put them in a hot oven until they are of a light brown; serve immediately.

Cookery for English Households, by a French Lady (1864).

Sauce Poivrade: see December 19.
Kromeskies: see August 4.
Meringues: see February 18.

March 24

Breakfast at Sea
RMS *Queen Elizabeth,* 1953

When she was launched in 1938 the Cunard ship RMS *Queen Elizabeth* was to be the largest passenger liner ever built. With the breakout of World War II she was immediately fitted out as a troop transport ship, only picking up her intended career after the war ended. From this time on she regularly and faithfully criss-crossed the Atlantic for over 20 years, carrying mail and passengers between New York and Southampton (via Cherbourg in France).

There was something for everyone amongst the meal choices aboard the *Queen Elizabeth* on a return trip to Southampton in 1953, as this breakfast menu shows.

BREAKFAST
Tuesday, March 24, 1953

Juices: Pineapple, Orange
Apples   Grapefruit   Oranges
Compote of Fruit   Purée of Apples   Compote of Figs
Rolled Oats   Oatmeal Porridge
Bran Flakes   Puffed Rice   Weetabix

Fried Butterfish, Tomato Sauce   Kippered Herrings
Eggs: Fried, Turned, Poached, Boiled
Omelettes (to order): Plain, Parsley
Broiled Breakfast Bacon
Corned Beef Hash Cakes
Purée Potatoes

COLD   Ox Tongue   Roast Beef
Radishes   Sliced Tomatoes

Griddle and Buckwheat Cakes
Maple and Golden Syrup
Breads: Wholewheat   Vienna   Sultana   Carmalt
Hovis   Rye   White and Graham Rolls   Toast
Bath Buns
Preserves   Honey   Marmalade

Teas: Ceylon, China
Coffee   Chocolate   Nescafé   Ovaltine
Instant Postum   Milk   Horlick's Malted Milk
Chase and Sanborn
Instant Coffee

Even those who are very adventurous about food tend to be conservative at breakfast. The catering manager aboard the liner had gone to a deal of trouble to ensure that every passenger could start their day as they were accustomed, even down to the choice of maple syrup (for the Americans and Canadians) or golden syrup (for the British) for the pancakes. There are all the ingredients of a continental, an American, and an English breakfast here. The cereal choices range from simple unadulterated oat porridge to modern processed and packaged cereals with well-known brand names. Those with robust British stomachs could have kippers, those with robust American stomachs could have corned meat hash cakes. There are eight different breads, plus Bath buns (a traditional fruit bun from the English town of the same name) and, of course—toast.

The beverage choices are perhaps the most interesting. To have a product named on the menu of a luxury liner is, to put it mildly, a marketing triumph. There are three well-known cereal-based processed beverages here— the Instant Postum and Horlick's (familiar to American passengers), and their English cousin, Ovaltine. The unqualified "coffee" is presumably the ordinary brewed variety, but discerning passengers could specify the Chase and Sanborn brand ("roasted and sold in sealed tins") and others could chose instant coffee of the Nescafé brand if they wished.

Recipes

~~~

Corned Beef Hash

There is no elaborate receipt to follow . . . the necessity in the case is not to put things in, but to keep things out. Keep out the cold turnips. Keep out the cold mashed potatoes even, if they are not uncommonly good and fresh. Keep out the black and hard scraps and ends of meat, they will give a color and appearance and stale taste that will cause the mess to be thrown out, the good to be lost with the bad. Keep out the onions. This is the last thing that will be agreed to. Cooks of hotels have been known to quit the house rather than they would leave the onions out of the hash. But the people who live in the expensive class of hotels will leave the dish alone if you do not, and if they despise it who else is going to bring hash in fashion again? It is in the interest of true economy to make hash popular, because it uses up corned beef, which is too plentiful. To make "dry hash" that will be eaten and enjoyed, take

1 pressed-in cup minced corned beef.
4 medium potatoes—1 pound.
1/2 a level teaspoon good black pepper.
1 level teaspoon salt.
1 ounce fresh butter.
A spoonful of hot water.

Shave off all discolored outside of meat. Chop as fine as pepper-corns or wheat in a wooden bowl with a chopping knife, add the pepper, salt and butter to it. Pare the potatoes raw, steam or boil them, put them to the meat boiling hot

---

and mash together. It is not of much consequence whether it is to be baked or not but it looks better browned over and can be served hottest that way. Leave out the butter when there is plenty of fat to the meat. Those who study to make this almost forgotten dish good take care to corn fat pieces of brisket and calves udder for the purpose.

Buckwheat Cakes

2 cups buckwheat flour.
2 cups water and yeast mixed.
1 level teaspoon salt.
1 tablespoon golden syrup.
2 tablespoons melted lard.

Make a sponge or batter over night of the warm water, yeast and flour. In the morning add the enriching ingredients; beat up well, and bake thin cakes on a griddle.

Most people like buckwheat cakes with a little cornmeal mixed in the batter. Eggs are not needed except when accidentally the batter ferments too much, when an egg will bind and make the cake easier to bake. Serve with butter and syrup.

Jessup Whitehead, *Cooking for Profit. A New American Cook Book Adapted for the Use of All Who Serve Meals for a Price* (Chicago, 1893).

March 25

Charles Dickens Eats aboard
an American Canal Boat, 1842

English author Charles Dickens (1812–1870) was at the height of his popularity when he traveled to America for the first time in 1842. He was revelling in his success, which must have seemed particularly precious and poignant in view of his background. Dickens had experienced great hardship as a child when his father spent time in debtor's prison, and the experience sharpened his social conscience and gave him much fodder for his novels. It also sharpened his appreciation of food and dining anecdotes and metaphors, and there are few writers who have as successfully and delightfully woven these themes throughout their stories and journals.

On this day in 1842, he was aboard a canal boat, en route from Harrisburg to Pittsburgh, and he clearly took great delight in the experience.

At about six o'clock, all the small tables were put together to form one long table, and everybody sat down to tea, coffee, bread, butter, salmon, shad, liver, steaks, potatoes, pickles, ham, chops, black-puddings, and sausages. "Will you try," said my opposite neighbour, handing me a dish of potatoes, broken up in milk and butter, "will you try some of these fixings?" At eight o'clock [next morning], the shelves [i.e. bunks] being taken down and put away and the tables joined together, everybody sat down to the tea, coffee, bread, butter, salmon, shad, liver, steak, potatoes, pickles, ham, chops, black-puddings, and sausages, all over again. Some were fond of compounding this variety, and having it all on their plates at once. As each gentleman got through his own personal amount of tea, coffee, bread, butter, salmon, shad, liver, steak, potatoes, pickles, ham, chops, black-puddings, and sausages, he rose up and walked off. When everybody had done with everything, the fragments were cleared away: and one of the waiters appearing anew in the character of a barber, shaved such of the company as desired to be shaved; while the remainder looked on, or yawned over their newspapers. Dinner was breakfast again, without the tea and coffee; and supper and breakfast were identical.

American Notes for General Circulation (1842).

Recipes

~~~

One of the most famous cookbook writers in America at the time of Dickens's visit was Eliza Leslie. The following recipes are taken from her best seller, *Directions for Cookery, In Its Various Branches*, published in 1840.

Common Sausage Meat

Having cleared it form the skin, sinews, and gristle, take six pounds of the lean of young fresh pork, and three pounds of the fat, and mince it all as fine as possible. Take some dried sage, pick off the leaves and rub them to powder, allowing three tea-spoonfuls to each pound of meat. Having mixed the fat and lean well together, and seasoned it with nine tea-spoonfuls of pepper, and the same quantity of salt, strew on the powdered sage, and mix the whole very well with your hands. Put it away in a stone jar, packing it down hard; and keep it closely covered. Set the jar in a cool dry place. When you wish to use the sausage-meat, make it into flat cakes about an inch thick and the size of a dollar; dredge them with flour, and fry them in butter or dripping, over rather a slow fire, till they are well browned on both sides, and thoroughly done. Sausages are seldom eaten except at breakfast.

Baked Shad

Keep on the head and fins. Make a force-meat or stuffing of grated bread crumbs, cold boiled ham or bacon minced fine, sweet marjoram, pepper, salt, and a little powdered mace or cloves. Moisten it with beaten yolk of egg. Stuff the inside of the fish with it, reserving a little to rub over the outside, having first rubbed the fish all over with yolk of egg. Lay the fish in a deep pan, putting its tail to its mouth. Pour into the bottom of the pan a little water, and add a jill of port wine, and a piece of butter rolled in flour. Bake it well, and when it is done, send it to table with the gravy poured round it. Garnish with slices of lemon.

A Diary in America

Frederick Marryat (1792–1848) was an English novelist and friend of Charles Dickens. He spent time in Canada and America in 1837–39, and also published an account of his impressions.

In the West, when you stop at an inn, they say—"What will you have? Brown meal and common doings, or white wheat and chicken fixings?"—that is, "Will you have pork and brown bread, or white bread and fried chicken?" Also, "Will you have a feed or a check?"—"a dinner or luncheon?"

I must descant a little upon the mint julep, as it is, with the thermometer at 100, one of the most delightful and insinuating potations that ever was invented, and may be drunk with equal satisfaction when the thermometer is as low as 70. There are many varieties, such as those composed of claret, Madeira, &c.; but the ingredients of the real mint julep are as follows. I learned how to make them, and succeeded pretty well. Put into a tumbler about a dozen sprigs of the tender shoots of mint, upon them put a spoonful of white sugar, and equal proportions of peach and common brandy, so as to fill it up one-third, or perhaps a little less. Then take rasped or pounded ice, and fill up the tumbler. Epicures rub the lips of the tumbler with a piece of fresh pineapple, and the tumbler itself is very often incrusted outside with stalactites of ice. As the ice melts, you drink. I once overheard two ladies talking in the next room to me, and one of them said, "Well, if I have a weakness for any one thing, it is for a mint julep!"—a very amiable weakness, and proving her good sense and good taste. They are, in fact, like the American ladies, irresistible.

But what was most remarkable, Broadway being three miles long, and the booths lining each side of it, in every booth there was a roast pig, large or small, as the centre attraction. Six miles of roast pig! and that in New York city alone; and roast pig in every other city, town, hamlet, and village, in the Union. What association can there be between roast pig and independence?

March 26

Grand Dinner Given by the Duke and Duchess of Cornwall aboard HMS *Ophir,* Malta, 1901

The planned extended voyage of the Duke of Cornwall (1865–1936) and his wife Princess Mary of Teck (1867–1953) to the farthest reaches of the British Empire (Australia) in early 1901 had to be postponed because of the death of his grandmother, Queen Victoria, on January 22 of that year.

It was not until mid-March that the Duke (the future King George V) and Princess Mary set off on their tour. For over seven months their "wandering home" was the specially refitted yacht *Ophir*, aboard which "they made the grand tour of the Empire in a fashion never so much as dreamed of before" (*The Times*, March 9, 1901).

Sherry—Amorosa	Consommé Lavalette
Madeira—1834	—
	Paupiettes de Soles à la St. George
Hock:	Whitebait à la Diable
Marcobrunner 1893	
	Epigrammes d'Agneau Italienne
Champagne:	Aspic de Mauviettes Bellevue
Moët et Chandon, 1893	—
	Dinde Braisé et Jambon au Champagne
	Epinards et Pommes
Claret:	—
Château Lafitte, 1888	Perdreaux Rôti au Cresson
	Pommes Pailles
Port—Royal White	—
Port—1878	Cordons à l'Espagnole
	—
Brandy—1840	Timbale de Fruits
	Glace Maltaise
	—
	Croustade de Foie Gras

The Duke and Duchess left London on March 15 by train for Portsmouth. The following morning they set sail, escorted by the cruisers *Diadem* and *Niobe*. By the 19th they were in the Bay of Biscay, which lived up to its reputation and gave the ships a rough time and the Duchess a bout of seasickness. There was an overnight stop in Gibraltar before the next port of Gozo in Malta, which they reached on the morning of the 25th. The following day the Duke and Duchess gave a grand dinner aboard the *Ophir* for various honored guests, dignitaries, and representatives of the military.

The extensive remodeling of the Orient Line vessel the *Ophir* to convert it into a royal yacht had not included the grand dining room, which was already perfect for its illustrious guests. The chairs were upholstered in red leather, and the tables could be arranged in a horseshoe pattern to seat 56 guests. The saloon was panelled in rosewood and satinwood, and according to *The Times*, its "principal decoration might have been expressly designed for the occasion, for under the arched spaces at each end of the dome are the shields of Great Britain and the four leading Australian colonies."

Malta is an island with a very strategic location in the Mediterranean and has been part of many nations at different times in history. It became part of the British Empire in 1814 after the end of the Napoleonic Wars, and finally gained its independence in 1964.

A common diplomatic device at state and official dinners was to pay homage to both host and guest nation by giving special names to dishes on the menu (even if the recipes themselves were little altered). St. George is the patron saint of both England and Malta, so the fish dish would appear to signify a cultural bond between the two countries. The consommé should probably have been written "La Valette" in honor of Jean de Valette—a Knight of St. John and a hero of the fight against the Ottoman Turks at the siege of Malta in 1565, for whom the Maltese capital of Valette is named. Finally, there is the ice cream (one of the most common dishes to be adapted with honorary names on diplomatic menus)—named obviously for the island of Malta.

The urge to impress guests was not confined to political and diplomatic banquets. There is an apocryphal but amusing story behind the intriguingly named dish of *epigrammes*. An epigram is a short, witty inscription or poem which turns on an clever or paradoxical thought. The impromptu invention of epigrams was a favorite game at the gatherings of seventeenth-century poets and literati. From a culinary point of view, *epigrammes* are pieces of lamb breast and lamb cutlets breaded and plated (without sauce) in an alternate arrangement on a platter. The story about their origin takes place in the mid-eighteenth century, in France. A very young aristocratic wife was entertaining a number of guests when she overheard one of them remark that the previous evening he had partaken of "a feast of excellent epigrams." The young hostess, keen to impress her guests the next evening, ordered her chef to prepare a dish of *epigrammes*. The chef had no idea what they were and was unable to find any reference to them, but not wanting to admit ignorance he simply invented a new dish. The hostess, at the insistence of her guests, proudly announced the name of the dish—*Epigrammes d'Agneau* (epigrams of lamb). The worldly guests were most amused, and the young lady puzzled by their amusement—but the name and the dish instantly became classics.

Recipes

~~~

Epigrammes of Lamb, Italian Style

Prepare and cook the epigrammes as [in next recipe]. Meanwhile cook a pound of macaroni, Italian style [second recipe], lay the half of it on a dish; dress the epigrammes on it in the form of a circle; fill up the centre with the remainder of the macaroni, and serve with some Tomato sauce apart.

Epigrammes of Lamb
(Basic Preparation)

Saw off the breast of a neck of lamb in the same manner as for mutton cutlets; remove the tendon of the breast and boil in some stock with an onion and a small "bouquet garni." When the lamb is done drain it, and take out all the bones; keep these, as they will be required later on. Sprinkle some salt and a little pepper over the meat; lay it flat on a dish; press, with another dish and a weight at the top of it, till cold. Then cut the breast of lamb in pieces the size and shape of cutlets, pass these through some melted butter and bread-crumbs, and through two or three beaten eggs and bread-crumbs again. Cut the bones kept for that purpose with a large knife or chopper to a point at one end, stick one in each cutlet, and fry them in hot fat to a nice golden colour.

Macaroni, Italian Style

Put one pound of cooked and strained macaroni into a stewpan with two ounces of butter, three spoonfuls of tomato sauce, and as many of beef gravy: toss up the lot on the fire to mix and warm it well together, then sprinkle two handfuls of grated cheese over it, season with a little white pepper, toss it up again and turn it into a hot dish, sprinkle again a little grated cheese on the top, with three tablespoonfuls of good beef gravy and serve.

  E. Duret, *Practical Household Cookery* (London, 1891).

Whitebait a' la Diable (Whitebait, devilled): see August 14.

March 27

Gay Rugby Dinner
Hotel Lutetia, Paris, 1957

On the anniversary of the very first international rugby game in 1871, the French Rugby Federation entertained the Welsh rugby team at the magnificent Hotel Lutetia in Paris during the Five Nations competition of 1957. The dinner was as fine as would be expected from a hotel such as the Lutetia (see February 21).

Le Saumon de l'Adour au
Champagne

Le Carré d'Agneau Périgourdine
Les Bouquets de Primeurs

Le Chaud-Froid de Vollaile Rose de Mai

Coeurs de Laitues Mimosa

Le Plateau de Fromage

L'Ananas Voilé a l'Orientale

Les Friandises

VINS

Chablis 1er Cru Fourchaume 1954

Chateau Montrose
Saint-Estephe 1954

Mercurey Clos du Roi 1953

Magnums

Le Taittinger Blanc de Blanc 1950

Café, Liqueurs

The dinner was clearly very formal and elegant, with classic dishes accompanied by fine wines. The paper menu, however, has a most unexpected illustration and caption. Above a drawing of what appears to be two rugby players holding hands, there is the phrase "gay rugby." In the 1950s the word "gay" did not have the connotation that it does today, and the menu demonstrates how dramatically language usage can change. "Gay," according to the Oxford English Dictionary has many meanings that have nothing to do with sexual orientation, but can mean for example "noble, beautiful, excellent, fine" as well as "lighthearted, carefree, exuberantly cheerful, merry, sportive"—all of which could apply to keen sportsmen.

The dinner itself was certainly "gay" in the sense of "bright or lively-looking, esp. in colour; brilliant, showy." *Bouquets de Primeur* (new season) sounds far more colorful than simple "vegetables"; the aspic of the *chaud-froid* (see July 25) was colored delicate rose pink by the addition of tomato puree, and the lettuce salad was garnished with fluffy yellow egg yolk. The dessert of

Gay Rugby menu.

L'Ananas Voilé a l'Orientale would have been very showy indeed—a real masterpiece of the *patissier's* art made from pineapple (or pineapple ice) decorated with a spun sugar "veil."

Recipes

~~~

The name of this salad comes from the garnish of egg yolks which mimics the fluffy yellow flowers of the mimosa.

Salade Mimosa

Make a salad dressing by mixing two parts of olive oil with one part wine vinegar and adding a little chopped parsley, chervil, chive and tarragon. Stir a tablespoonful of raw cream into every gill of dressing.

Dress the small yellow leaves from the hearts of fresh lettuces with the mixture given above. Pass 1 or 2 hard-boiled eggs—yolk and white together—through a fine sieve and scatter on top of the lettuce.

Rene Roussin, *Royal Menus* (London, 1960).

Périgourdine: refers to dishes containing truffles, or with a sauce perigord (perigeaux): see April 14.

Champagne Sauce (for the salmon): see May 27.

March 28

Dinner for the Duke of Orléans, France, 1690

The city of New Orleans is named in honor of Phillipe, Duke of Orléans (1674–1723), brother to the Sun King Louis XIV, and regent until Louis' great-grandson and heir Louis XV came of age. The Duke was known to enjoy the good life (to the extent of being considered dissolute), and this included the pleasures of the table. One of the most famous independent cooks of the time, François Massialot (1660–1733) cooked for many of the royal and aristocratic families, and in one of his cookbooks he describes a meal arranged for the Duke on March 28, 1690.

The First Course

Side-Dishes

For the first Course, An hot pye of young Rabbets and Partridges, in which may be put, during the time of serving, some good Cullise of Partridge or other Ragoo's.

A *Poupeton* farced with twenty or thirty young Pigeons, according to the number of Guests entertained; with all sorts of Garnitures.

A Dish of *Brusolles*, broiled upon the Coals, with a Cullise pour'd upon it.

A Dish of farced Sweet breads of Veal, broiled upon Coals, with a Ragoo.

A *Marinade* of fryed Chickens.

A large fat Pullet roasted after the English Way, with a Ragoo put thereupon in serving it up.

A Dish of *Filets* cut in slices, with Gammon.

A Dish of *Croquets*.

One of *Filets* of a young fat Hen with Cucumbers.

One of farced *Fricandoe's* in a Ragoo.

The Second Course.

Side-Dishes

Let there be three great Dishes of all sorts of wild Fowl that are in season, and four Sallets in the Cornere; proportionably to the Courses that are served up, and the Guests that sit at Table.

For the Intermesses.

Twelve dishes; *viz.* One of Gammon, garnish'd with dry'd Tongues, and *Bolonia*-sausages.

A Cream-pye garnish'd with little Tarts.

A *Blanc-manger* of Gellies of divers Colours.

A Dish of Asparagus in Cream.

One of *Morilles* in Cream.

One of Sweet-breads of Veal and Cocks-combs farced in a Ragoo.

One of Capons-livers *à la Crêpine*, broil'd upon the Grid-iron.

One of the Kidneys of Capons.

One *Pain au Jambon*.

A Dish of *Truffles* in a *Court-bouillon*.

A Ragoo of the Sweet-breads of Veal, white Mushrooms and *Morilles*.

This was a typical dinner for an aristocratic household. In addition to the huge number of rich and elegant dishes, Massialot wrote that "There was for the Duke himself *Potage de Santé* prepared of a fat Pullet with Eggs in her, and of a Capon." A *Potage de Santé* is "a soup of health," and elaborate recipes for it abound in cookbooks of the time. *Croquets* are *croquettes*, which are essentially the same as *kromeskies*.

Recipes

~~~

Potage de Santé

After having caus'd some good Broth of Buttock-beef, a Knuckle of Veal and Mutton, to be put into a Pot, with Capons, fat Pullets, or other Fowls proper for the Potage *de Santé*, and having made the same Broth very savoury; let the Crusts be soaked with it, whilst some Herbs are boiling in another Pot, such as Sorrel, Purslain, Chervil, &c. all cut up very small. These Herbs may serve to garnish your Potage and Fowls; or they may be strain'd, so as nothing be put into the Dish, but the Broth and good Gravy, when served up to Table.

Another sort of *Potage* de Santé, is made quite clear, of a Chicken or Pullet, and a piece of a Fillet of Veal, without any Garniture; only it may be brought to a colour, by passing the red-hot Fire-shovel over it.

Croquets

Croquets are a certain Compound made of a delicious Farce, some of the bigness of an Egg, and others of a Walnut. The first sort may be us'd for Side-dishes, or at least for Out-works, and the others only for garnishing. To that purpose, take the Breasts of large fat Pullets, Chickens and Partridges, and mince this Meat with some Bacon, Calves-udder, Veal sweet-breads, all parboil'd, *Truffles*, Mushrooms, Marrow, the crummy part of a Loaf, steept in Milk, and all sorts of fine Herbs, as also a little Cream-cheese, and as much Milk-cream, as shall be judg'd requisite: When the whole Mixture is well minc'd and season'd, let four or five Yolks of Eggs be put into it, and one or two Whites. With this Farce, the Croquets are to be form'd of a round Figure, then roll'd in a beaten Egg, breaded at the same time, and set by in a Dish, in order to be fried afterwards with sweet Lard, and served up hot to Table.

François Massialot,*The Court and Country Cook*, English translation (London, 1702).

Blanc-manger: see January 7.

March 29

Luncheon Crossing the Equator
SS *Orontes,* 1937

There is a very long tradition amongst seafaring nations of holding a special ceremony to "initiate" any new sailors on board when they cross the equator for the first time. It takes the form of a mock court held before "King Neptune" and his assistants at which the initiate is "tested" by being submitted to various humiliating (and sometimes brutal) procedures. Tourist ships have long held a very watered down version of the "Crossing the Line" ceremony purely for the amusement of civilian passengers. It is to be assumed that the tourist class passengers aboard SS*Orontes* were not too traumatized to enjoy their luncheon after the early morning crossing of the equator.

LUNCHEON

Grape Fruit

Potage Brunoise

Fresh Herrings en Marinade

Lancashire Hot Pot with Pickled Red Cabbage

Poonah Curry

Grill: Lamb Cutlets
Chipped Potatoes

Potatoes: Creamed, Steamed, Jacket
Braised Onions

COLD SIDEBOARD:

Roast Mutton   Chantilly Sauce
Chicken and Tongue Roll   Divine Sauce

SALADS:
Lettuce, Egg & Tomato, Beetroot, Radish, Cucumber,
Spring Onion, Potato

Pickles

Sauces: Worcester, Tomato, Burmah

Tapioca Milk Pudding
Fruit Sandwich Pastry

Cheese: Gouda & Danish Blue

Tea

Coffee will be served in the public rooms

The *Orontes* regularly traveled the England to Australia route, with occasional springtime cruises in the Mediterranean. This was a good, solid luncheon that clearly demonstrates its British roots.

Regional dishes which derive from some common theme are often only distinguished by small details such as a garnish or accompaniment. The Lancashire hot pot at this meal was served with its traditional accompaniment of pickled red cabbage, otherwise it could have been mistaken, perhaps, for Irish stew or any one of a myriad of variations on the mutton and potato theme.

The origin of the name "hot pot" comes ultimately from the French verb *hocher,* meaning to shake. It means, therefore "a shaken pot," and in a culinary sense by medieval times came to mean a jumble or mish-mash of whatever ingredients were available. Sometimes it takes the form of *hotch-potch*, or *hodge-podge, hochepot* (French) or *hutspot* (Dutch). As the name suggests, the range of ingredients is almost infinite. Mrs. Beeton's *Book of Household Management* (1861) has a recipe for hodge-podge using up minced leftover cold mutton, lettuce, and green peas. Another Victorian classic cookery book suggests that a hotch-potch may be made with a sheep's head or feet, old green peas (soaked the night before), turnip, carrot, and leeks. There is a fish hoche-poche on the menu of August 9.

Lancashire hot-pot—in the sense of the regional name—appears to be a nineteenth-century phenomenon, although meat and vegetable stews have existed there as they have everywhere, ever since there have been pots and cooks. Mutton is claimed to be the authentic meat in this "traditional" regional variation, and the traditional accompaniment is pickled red cabbage. It is said that the essential difference between Lancashire hot pot and other mutton and potato stews is the overlapping layer of thinly sliced potatoes on the top, but the reality is, there is no "authentic" Lancashire hot pot, just as there is no single authentic Irish stew or French pot-au-feu. One recipe for Lancashire hot pot from *Cassell's Dictionary of Cookery* (ca. 1870s) contains oysters and curry powder!

Recipes

~~~

Lancashire Hot Pot

3/4 lb. meat
2 carrots
1 onion or leek, if possible
3 lbs. potatoes
1/2 pint vegetable stock
1 dessertspoonful of fat from the meat, or dripping
1 dessertspoonful flour
pepper and salt.

Cut up meat into small pieces and place in a fireproof dish or casserole. Add sliced carrots and onion or leek, and pepper and salt. Add half the potatoes. Instead of slicing potatoes, crack off lumps with a knife. Place the fat from the meat or dripping on top. Put in a moderate oven with the lid on for half an hour. Take out, add stock, blend 1 dessertspoonful flour in a little water, pour into casserole. Add remainder of potatoes and sprinkle with salt and pepper. Cook in a moderate oven. Remove the lid for the last 20 minutes and cook until the potatoes are brown.
Food Facts Leaflet No. 119 (London: Ministry of Food, 1941).

Red Cabbage Pickle

1 large red cabbage	Whole white peppers
Salt	Ginger
Vinegar	Bay leaves
Cloves	Sugar

Remove the coarse outside leaves from the cabbage, and wash the remainder, searching for any insect life. Cut the cabbage into a large dish or platter, and sprinkle with salt; add more cabbage and salt in alternate layers; leave for three or four days, turning it several times during that interval. Drain away the moisture which the salt has extracted, put the cabbage into jars, and cover with vinegar in which two cloves, six white peppers, one small piece ginger root, bay leaf, and one teaspoonful of sugar to every pint of vinegar, have been boiled.

Cover with muslin, and when cold tie down. A few slices of cooked beets improve the color.

Marion Harris, *Canning, Preserving and Pickling* (1914).

Potates, Jacket: see March 4.

March 30

Dinner in a Harem
Thebes, Egypt, 1851

Very little is known about the Victorian Englishwoman and intrepid traveler Caroline Paine (ca. 1820–1850). Her sole claim to fame is the book of her travel adventures across Egypt, North Africa, and Turkey in 1850–51—*Tent to Harem: Notes of an Oriental Trip.*

She and her companions were staying in Luxor, and while on a sightseeing visit to the ruins of El Karnak, they received an invitation that they accepted with enthusiasm—to visit the harem of the governor. Paine had visited a harem in Turkey and was most interested to compare. Her account of the visit is interesting not only from her description of the local traditions of hospitality and the details of the meal they were served, but also for its insight into the lives of the harem women.

we were here refreshed in the midst of our laborious task of sight-seeing by a delicious cup of coffee kindly sent us by the Harem of the Governor. Cups, covered with a red napkin richly embroidered with gold, were brought on a waiter, followed by coffee in a silver urn suspended over a blaze by delicate chains of silver. Before taking coffee, we were offered sherbert, presented, as usual, in large lemonade glasses, with covers. Not being thirsty, I merely sipped at it, a fault which called forth a rebuke from my friend R., who was versed in the customs of the Arabs, and said that politeness required one to drink freely. Later in the day, while the rest of our party were seated around a stone spread with hard boiled eggs, bread and tea, that had been sent to us from the boat . . . we were informed that the Harem had honored us with an invitation to visit them that afternoon. Here was an adventure, and a dilemma too [they were dusty from exploring the ruins, and had to send for clean collars and gloves].

[After coffee and sherbet] We made several attempts to take our leave; but our obliging hostess insisted upon our dining with her. Curious, as we were, to see the customs of these people, we yielded, nothing loth, to her entreaties. A crumb-cloth was spread at one end of the room, a small table of dark wood, inlaid with pearl, about the size and height of one of our ottomans, was placed upon it, and upon that was deposited the large round waiter that serves for a table. Cushions were properly arranged, and we were invited to partake. Great care was taken to make the invalid comfortable. Then we all seated ourselves, *a la Turque*. Our hostess would not sit until we were all disposed of, and the daughters stood through the dinner. There were no plates, but there were spoons, and, stranger than all, there were forks, which, it will be remembered, the Turks never use, to which she directed our attention with evident pride, and certainly she had shown a kind and delicate regard to our wants in procuring them; and we never ceased to wonder where and how she had managed to obtain such an unoriental article of luxury.

Bread of excellent quality was placed, with napkins, for each person. I forgot to mention that water was brought in a ewer, with a basin, previous to our going to the table, and it should be borne in mind that this cleanly custom is never omitted by the Mohammedans. As usual, the basin was borne by an attendant, another poured water upon the hands, while a third followed with a napkin of embroidered muslin. We made these necessary preparations for the table as one would who felt it to be rather a form than an essential purifying, while our hostess engaged in it as if conscious of the nature of the duties she was about to perform.

The first dish was kabobs, a favorite dish of the Turks, made of bits of mutton, one or two inches square, roasted separately on spits until quite dry and hard, and seasoned very highly with garlic. And now how should we manage in the absence of knives and plates? The manners of our hostess were gentle, courteous, almost polished, and we would not have consciously transgressed the rules of etiquette which prevailed at this board; and so we did very much as all wise persons do who wish to avoid blunders under similar circumstances—we waited for an example, and followed the one given by taking some of the kabobs with our fingers; and it was really nice, as the garlic had been omitted, and fresh green peas had been substituted. A pair of plump, finely browned chickens were next served. The mystery was, how they were to be carved without a knife. This was soon solved by our sultana, who rather gracefully commenced a demolition with her fingers. When it was in a condition to be eaten, she took a leg, and, biting off a piece of it, handed the remainder to Mrs. –, which was an act of extreme politeness. The rest of us were then urged to partake, which we did, of course.

A dish of pilav, which is rice and chicken stewed together, a favorite dish with the Turks, was then brought in. When suited to their taste, like almost every thing, it is highly seasoned with garlic. But here, again, was a regard for our comfort; the garlic was omitted. It was savory, and we ate of it with spoons. Our hostess, in the mean time, was busy, picking up with her fingers delicate titbits of chicken, which she added to the pilav. She ate nothing herself, but talked all the while she was thus occupied. A dish of garlic and gumbo followed, into which we dipped pieces of bread and choked them down. With a dish of sweets and clotted milk, (yaourt) our repast was finished; and again, bathing our hands, we arose from the table with grateful, contented hearts, and wiser than when we sat down.

. . . Many a hearty regret was expressed by her that we had not made her house our home while at Luxor, and some of our party regretted it also. At length, we *must* go. It had been a point with our kind hostess that we should remain until sundown. That time had come, and there was now no excuse for detaining us longer. She followed us down stairs, with many expressions of good will and hearty blessings. We were at the gate, the hand of the black porter rested upon the latch, and we were wondering why he did not open it, when the "imsheh, imsheh," (go away! go away!) which he uttered to his mistress, reminded us that we were quitting a prison, and our hearts sickened at the thought of leaving this woman, who had so graciously and agreeably entertained us, a prisoner within her own walls.

Early travelers to the "orient" were often more intrigued by the rituals of dinner than the actual food, although recipes for kebabs and pilau did appear in English cookbooks from the eighteenth century.

Recipes
~~~

Pilau of Rice

Wash, pick, and dress, in the same manner as for plain rice, observing only, that before setting in the oven, a little pounded mace must be added to the rice; then put into a stewpan a chicken half boiled and a piece of pickled pork three parts boiled, and cover with the rice. On serving, place the fowl and pork at the bottom of the dish, with the rice over, and garnish with boiled or fried button onions and halves of hard eggs, hot.

John Mollard, *The Art of Cookery* (1836).

Accounts by early travelers to faraway places are often a source of "recipes" for exotic foreign dishes.

Yaourt

Put into a bason a spoonful of beer yeast, or wine lees; pour on it a quart of boiling milk; when it is formed into a curd, and is become sour, take of it a table spoonful and a half to serve as a ferment to a fresh quart of milk, in the same manner of the yeast. This after a few repeats, will bcome good yaourt, and lose the taste of the yeast by degrees.

William Eton, *A Survey of the Turkish Empire* (1801).

Kababs

A dish common in Arabia called kabob or kab-ab, which is meat cut into small pieces and placed on thin skewers, alternately between slices of onion and green ginger, seasoned with pepper, salt and kian [cayenne], fried in ghee, or clarified butter, to be ate with rice and dholl [dhall], a sort of split-pea boiled with rice.

James Forbes and Eliza Rosée Montalembert, *Oriental Memoirs* (1834).

March 31

Tiffin at the Cricket Club
Cinnamon Gardens, Colombo, Ceylon, 1906

Cricket was introduced to Ceylon (now Sri Lanka) virtually immediately after the country was ceded to the British Empire in 1815. By the time Sri Lanka won its independence in 1948, the game had become firmly entrenched in the culture of the country. It is often jokingly said that in return for "curry," England gave India the game of cricket, the bureaucracy, and a national language. This menu, from a "tiffin" catered for the Colombo Cricket Club by the famous (but no longer existing) Bristol Hotel, shows that the culinary and linguistic exchange between the two continents was rather more complex.

Cold Tiffin.

Lobster Mayonnaise
Pigeon & Steak Pie
Cold Lamb and Mint Sauce
York Ham & Rolled Tongue
Beetroot   Potatoes   Lettuce   Salads
Iced Macedoine of Fruits
Sultana Cakes and Marsalla
Cheese
Fruits

The word "tiffin" came into use in English at the tail-end of the eighteenth century and referred to a light, informal meal, usually presented buffet style —the "glowing Asiatic cousin" (according to Thomas de Quincey) of the English luncheon. In many parts of the Indian subcontinent, workers' lunches (prepared freshly by their wives at home) were delivered in stacking containers called "tiffin-boxes" by *dabbawalas* or "tiffin-wallahs" on bicycles. The word "tiffin" is, however, of northern English origin, and originally meant "to take a little drink." Its adaptation in this way has no doubt preserved a dialect word that was already dying out in its home country.

Tiffin often included a number of curries (another intriguing word, see January 1) with their traditional sambals or accompaniments. At the Colombo Cricket Club on this particular day, however, the meal was as British as the heritage of the hotel that prepared it. It could just as easily have been called "luncheon" and served at any cricket club on English soil, with no one questioning its origins at all.

Recipes

~~~

Lobster Mayonnaise

Take out the meat of a freshly-boiled hen lobster, and cut it into small neat squares. Trim and wash two large fresh lettuces, or any other salad, taking great care that they are quite *dry* before being used. Cut or tear these into neat pieces, and arrange a layer of them at the bottom of a large dish, place several pieces of lobster upon them, and repeat until the materials are finished. Just before serving pour over them a sauce made as follows: Beat the yolks of two raw eggs for two or three minutes, until they begin to feel thick, add, by drops at first, ten table-spoonfuls of best salad-oil, and four of tarragon vinegar. The mixture should be as thick and smooth as cream. The secret of making a mayonnaise is to add the liquid gradually, and to beat well between every addition. Season the sauce with half a teaspoonful of dry mustard, half a salt-spoon of salt, and half a salt-spoonful of white pepper. Cover the salad with the liquid. At the last moment, sprinkle over the lobster coral, which has been powdered and well sifted, and garnish the dish with sliced beetroot and hard-boiled eggs.
    Cassell's Dictionary of Cookery (London, 1910).

Pigeon pie was often made with the feet of the pigeon sticking out of the top crust, to indicate its prestigious contents.

Pigeon Pie

Cut two pigeons into pieces of convenient size and fry them in two ounces of clarified dripping. Take them out of the pan and put them aside to cool. Fry a small onion (sliced) until lightly browned in the dripping used to cook the birds. Then stir in a small bunch of sweet herbs and parsley (tied together), one teaspoonful of tarragon vinegar and season with pepper, salt and nutmeg. Let the sauce boil up, and then simmer for fifteen minutes, color it with browning, and strain it into a bowl. Cut one pound of rump-steak into small pieces which should be almost square, dust them with pepper and salt, and roll them up. Place the rolls of meat in a pie-dish, together with the pieces of pigeon. Sprinkle over them some chopped parsley and a little lean minced bacon, fill up the dish with the prepared sauce, cover it closely and put it into a moderately hot oven for one hour. Let the meat get cold, add some pieces of hard-boiled egg, and cover it with pastry, leaving a small aperture in the middle of the crust, to be filled in with an ornamental rose of pastry (the latter should be baked separately) after the pie is finished. Brush the crust over with beaten egg, and bake the pie in a moderately hot oven.
    Nicolas Soyer, *Soyer's Standard Cookery* (1912).

Sultana Cake can be made by adding sultanas to Pound Cake mixture: see April 19.

April

April 1

One-Dollar Lunch
Hotel Agua Caliente, Tijuana, Mexico, 1931

The Mexican town of Tijuana is just across the border from California, and no distance at all for those who wished to avoid the restrictions of Prohibition (see December 6, December 27, August 20, October 8, and November 25) during the 1930s. The thirsty tourist trade was a gold mine for the town, the well-to-do being quite happy to buy a $5 champagne cup to wash down their bargain-priced $1 meal.

Boiled Celery Heart Salad

—

Petite Marmite Parisienne
or
Cream of Fresh Artichokes, Mercedes

—

Selection of:
Gulf Shrimps Saute en Cassolette, Timbale of Rice Provencale
Potted Mock Venison with Home made Noodles, Polonaise
Braised Leg of Spring Lamb with Glazed Onions and
Potatoes, Boulangere

Mexican Specialty:
Machaca con Huevos Revueltos
(Mexican Dried Beef with Scrambled Eggs)

Veal Cutlet Fried in Butter, Sauce Merland
Selection of Fresh Vegetables with Baked Stuffed Tomato
Cold Boiled Fresh Lobster Mayonnaise
Cold Roast Prime Beef Ribs, String Bean Salad

—

Minced Browned Sweet Potatoes Cubaine
Summer Squash Sauté in Butter

—

Creme Bavarois Panache
or
Cherry Ice or Ice Cream with Wafers

—
Café
—

TODAY'S BAR SPECIAL:
Clicquot Champagne Cup 5.00

In spite of its location, this was unequivocally an American hotel serving American food with the usual mangled menu language. The hotel saw no reason to explain the French *Petite Marmite Parisienne*, or *Potatoes, Boulangere*, yet thought it necessary to translate for its over-the-border guests the token Mexican dish on offer of *Machaca con Huevos Revueltos*.

There is always a debate about "authenticity" when dishes are adapted from one culture to another. In reality, however, as long as humans have been around they have been on the move, either peacefully migrating or conquering and colonizing, and wherever they have gone they have taken their ingredients and their cooking methods with them. These have had to be adapted according to local ingredients and conditions, and it is usually impossible to pin down the origin of a specific dish. Dried beef is said to be a traditional dish from Mexico—but there were no beef cattle in Central or South America until they arrived with the conquistadores.

The drying of meat is a very old method of preservation around the world, and it was inevitable that in the South American continent, a local variation (and name) would be developed. In the frozen wastes of the far north, dried meat was mixed with a large amount of fat and dried berries to make *pemmican*. In South Africa, antelope and buffalo meat became, under the influence of the Dutch language, *biltong*, referring to it being cut from the buttock (*bil*) of the animal but resembling the tongue (*tong*) when dried. In South America, the flesh had chili added and became jerky—from the Peruvian word for dried meat—*charqui*. *Machaca* as it is called in this menu is from the Spanish word meaning crushed or pounded, referring to its preparation before cooking.

Recipes

~~~

Here is one American take on the mexican dried beef with scrambled eggs on this menu.

Buey Ahumando (Ahumado) y Huevos

To a cupful of chipped beef soaked in hot water and chopped fine, add a cupful of strained tomatoes, two hard-boiled eggs cut fine, one tablespoonful of grated cheese, one grated onion, a chile pepper chopped fine and a big lump of butter. Beat all these together, break in two raw eggs and scramble in a frying-pan.

   May E. Southworth, *One Hundred and One Mexican Dishes* (San Francisco, 1906).

The Preparation of Charqui

Described in *A Journal Written on the Coasts of Chili, Peru, and Mexico, in the Years 1820, 1821, 1822,* by Captain Basil Hall of the Royal Navy.

The three men who had been employed in cutting up the bullock now commenced an operation, peculiar, I believe, to South America, namely, the preparation of what is called by us jerked beef, a term, probably derived from the local name *charqui*. The men seated themselves on low stools in the different cells, and began cutting each of the detached portions of meat into long strips, or ribbands uniform in size from end to end; some of these which were cut from the larger pieces, being several yards in length, and about two inches in width. To perform this operation neatly requires considerable expertness. The piece of meat is held in the left hand, and at each slice is hitched round so as to offer a new place to the knife; and in this way the strip of meat seems to unwind itself, like a broad tape from a ball, till at last nothing remains. We tried to perform this ourselves, but continually cut the strip across before it had attained any length. When the whole has been treated in this manner, it is allowed to hang under cover for a certain time, during which it acquires a black colour; and owing to the heat and dryness of the air, speedily loses much of its moisture. The meat is afterwards exposed to the sun till thoroughly dried, and being then made up into great bales, strongly tied around with a net-work of thongs, becomes the dried beef of commerce.

Lobster Mayonnaise: see March 31.
Bavarois: see May 18.

April 2

First Dinner, RMS *Titanic*, 1912

The very first meal served aboard RMS *Titanic* was considerably more modest than the well-known and much-written about final dinner.

Hor's D'oeuvre Varies

Consomme Mirrette
Cream of Chicken

Salmon

Sweetbreads

Roast Chicken
Spring Lamb, Mint Sauce
Braised Ham & Spinach

Green Peas   Cauliflower
Bovin & Boiled Potatoes
Golden Plover on Toast

Salad
Pudding Sans Souci
Peaches Imperial
Pastry

Dessert Coffee

The famous last dinner on the *Titanic* was served to first-class passengers on the night of April 14, just hours before the "unsinkable" ship hit an iceberg and went down with the loss of over 1,500 lives. It was enjoyed by the fabulously wealthy passengers who could afford the $4,350 (equivalent to $93,000 today) for a one-way fare from Southampton, England, to New York. This very first meal, on the other hand, was served to the crew of the ship on its one and only day of sea trials. The menu was preserved thanks to 5th Officer Harold Lowe (whose monthly wage was about $20), when he posted it to his fiancée as a memento.

There are a few small mysteries and one tragic irony in this menu. The dishes are for the most part instantly recognizeable. Consomme Mirrette (Mirette) is a classic clear soup with chicken *quenelles*, shredded lettuce, chervil, and cheese croutons. The peaches have been presented in a manner elegant enough for the ruler of an empire, although there are no clues to their exact preparation. The bovin and potatoes is the greatest mystery. In the *Oxford English Dictionary* there are some similar words, which may either be clues or red herrings. "Bovinia" are a type of large potato, but one reserved for use as cattle fodder. "Boivin" is a name for several sorts of the herb meadow rue, which hardly seems to be the reference here. Boivin is also

Titanic grand dining room.

the name of a character in Guy de Maupassant's short story *Old Mongilet*—and Mme. Boivin does serve up "an earthenware dish containing warmed-up boiled beef and potatoes"—but there is no obvious connection between this story and the dish appearing aboard ship several decades later. The surname "Boivin" is said to derive from a nickname meaning a wine drinker (from the French words *boivre*, to drink, and *vin* for wine). Some food historians have suggested that the potatoes are cooked in wine, and the name is a corruption of *beau vin* (good wine), which seems very unlikely from either a culinary or linguistic point of view. Finally, there may be a connection with the commercial preparation Bovril—a beef extract popular in Britain since the mid-nineteenth century which was included in military and naval rations. It is likely that many of the sailors aboard the *Titanic* were trained in the Navy, and perhaps some of their Bovril ration was used to pep up their potatoes. Bovril and potatoes could easily have been abbreviated to bov 'n potatoes and then interpreted as bovin and potatoes.

The tragic irony is in the name of the pudding. "Sans souci" means "carefree." Many dishes are named "sans souci," without any consistent set of ingredients, so the exact nature of this pudding cannot be certain. No doubt the name summed up the feelings of the crew and passengers aboard the luxurious, unsinkable *Titanic* on this day of sea trials.

Recipes

~~~

Braised Ham

Take a ham and pare the under part; cut off the knuckle, and pare off the yellow lard; bone it without injuring the ham; *dessallez* it, that is to say, steep it to take out the salt; tie it up in a cloth, and put it into a *braisière* of a size to fit it; after having put in the braising ingredients as above, moisten with water, and when about half done, put in a bottle of Madeira or a glass of brandy and a bottle of champagne; leave the cover of the *braisière* off, that the seasoning may reduce; sound to know if it is enough; drain and put it upon a cover; take off the skin; glaze with a reduction of veal. If there is none sift a little sugar over it, and glaze in the oven or with a hot poker; give it a good colour; serve it upon spinage or any other vegetable.

Antoine Beauvilliers, *The Art of French Cookery* (London, 1827).

April 3

Spelling Reform Dinner
Waldorf-Astoria Hotel, New York, 1907

An article in *The New York Times* on April 4, 1907, announced that "The prospect of extending the campaign for simpler spelling into all English-speaking lands grew brighter at the dinner of the board at the Waldorf-Astoria last night." The newspaper was referring to a dinner held by the

Simplified Spelling Board on its first anniversary. The aim of the board was "to bring spelling into closer accord with our pronunciation," and ultimately make it easier for children to learn to read. A new list of words was published at this anniversary feast, and the menu card itself was a witty expression of the project.

S.S.B.

CONSEIL D'ORTHOGRAPHE
SIMPLIFIÉE

BANQUET (à la simplicité spartiate)

MENU

Clovisses du moyen âge (anti-réformistes)

Ne soyez pas une clovisse
LE SAGE,
Frequemment en vain, 23

POTAGE
Potage à la Squibeau
Je vis de bonne soupe et non de beau langage
MOLIÈRE, *Les femmes savantes*, 2:7

HORS D'ŒUVRE (quel spectacle!)
Radis radicaux. Olives conservatives. Céléri simple.
Amandes salées. Bon mots frais (et confits)

POISSON (d'Avril)
Filet de bar (aquatique)
Pommes de terre à la langue du mode (c'est à dire potatoes)
Longum iter est per praecepta, breve et efficax per exempla
SENECA, Epist. 6:5

PIÈCE DE RESISTANCE (quelle folle!)
Tournedos de filet de bœuf, sauce des arlequins journalistes
Pommes de terre (encore!) simplicissimes, à la Conseil d'Orthographe
Simplifiée
Haricots verts (nous connaisons les fèves!)
Pamplemousse à la Biguestique (sans rabais,—mais avec permis de circulation)

RÔTI
Poitrine de pintade rôti en casserole. S.S.B. grillé, en son rôle
Salade des Trois Cents Paroles.

ENTREMETS DE DOUCEUR (à la fin!)
Glacés de Fantaisies Phonétiques
Petits fours (à six et sept). Fruits (de réforme)
Marrons de l'Ancienneté (sans recours)

Café sans phrase. Postum hygiénique (à supplications)
Vins (et orthographes) à la chance

Rira bien qui rira le dernier

It seems odd for an organization promoting a simplification of the spelling of English words that the organization retained the standard French for the menu. Nevertheless, with many *bon-mots frais* (fresh good words) it acknowledged the battle between the "radical reformists" (radishes, fruits) and the "medieval" conservative (olives, clams). It was also a celebration of language itself. There are several puns and word-plays (the *petits fours* were "at sixes and sevens"), the *Poisson d'Avril*, or April fish, is the French equivalent of the April fool, and the *Marrons de l'Ancienneté* represent the metaphor of the "old chestnut." To judge by the final phrase on the menu—*Rira bien qui rira le dernier* (he laughs well, who laughs last)—the reformists also clearly believed that they would get the last laugh.

The campaign extended to the souvenirs given at the dinner which were miniature reproductions of the New England primer of the middle seventies. These had "The paper cover, the color and texture of the pages, and the style of type were like those of the age that has gone, but the spelling was that which the Simplified Spelling Board recommended last year, and some modern verses were put in place of the old-fashioned rhymes."

Recipes

~~~

Salted Almonds (Amandes Salées)

Select fine, whole almonds, peel and lay them on a paper-covered baking sheet. Push this into a hot oven and when roasted to a fine golden brown throw them into a basin and sprinkle with a little water, slightly thickened with gum arabic, then dredge with very fine salt through a salt box having a perforated lid. Stir the almonds from time to time until dry, then leave to cool.

Hazel-nuts, walnuts, and pistachios can also be salted; these are generally dressed in crimped paper cases or small fancy boxes; they are passed around with the desert, or at the same time as the hors d'oeuvre, and then left on the table during the entire length of the dinner. It is an improvement to mix these nuts and serve them together.

Fresh Fruits (Fruits Frais)

Choose ripe fruits; arrange them either in baskets, fruit stands or plates garnished with green grape leaves and fresh moss. The base must be solid so that when carried they will not be dislodged; place the handsome part of the fruit on the outer side. Early fruits are always appreciated as they foretell those that are to follow in their season. Fruits for dressing are apricots, pineapples, pears, peaches, oranges, lady apples, grapes, cherries and strawberries. In case no

> fresh green leaves are procurable, use artificial ones made of muslin and dipped in wax. If a pineapple is to be arranged in the center of a basket, stand it on a cardboard cylinder four inches high by three inches in diameter.
>
> Charles Ranhofer (of Delmonico's in New York), *The Epicurean* (1894).

April 4

Good Friday Dinner
Tuileries, Paris, France, 1828

Charles X (1757–1836) acceded to the throne of France on the death of his brother Louis XVIII in 1824 and ruled the country until he was forced to abdicate during the revolution of 1830. Charles was a personally devout man, but even if he had not been, the prevailing culture would have made it impossible for him to ignore the Catholic Church's dietary rules for fast days.

Vendredi Saint (or Good Friday) fell on April 4 in 1828. It is the Friday before Easter Sunday, and therefore, during Lent, when the strictest rules applied. No animal products at all were to be eaten—no butter, milk, eggs, or cheese. Cooks since the Middle Ages became extraordinarily creative when it came to working within the rules, and some of their successes are shown in the menu for the royal family dinner on this day.

Autour de plateau dormant.

Quatre Potages,
Riz au lait d'amandes,　　Gruau de Bretagne à la noisette,
Mitonnage à la provençale,　　Panade à 'orgeat.

Deux buissons de pâtisseries à l'huile.
en forme et coulers d'écrivisses et d'éperlans frits.

Quatre salade cuîtes.

De chou-fleurs à l'huile,　　D'une macédoine des septs racines,
De lentilles à la reine et de haricots-riz,　　Des patates d'Espagne et de truffes
de Piémont.

Deux salades crues.
Macédoine verte au soya,　　Chicorée blanche et piment,

Rôties au vin d'Alicante.

Croûtes gratinées au chocolat.

Quatre corbeille de fruits crus.
Vingt-quatre assiettes.
garnis de fromages secs et de fruit secs, de massepains sans beurre et sans œufs,
de confitures, compotes,
conserves, et autres sucres nommés de jeûne ou d'*abstinence.*

The pastry and *massepain* (marzipan) dishes were made without butter or eggs, but a wonderful illusion was created by a basket of pastries made in the shapes and colors of crayfish and smelts (small fish). The soups were particularly inventive. Almond milk stood in for meat broth, and hazelnuts graced the "British gruel." A *mittonage* and a *panade* are both bread-based. The *macedoine* (a dish composed of small pieces) of "seven roots" may be an allusion to the "Tree of Life" whose seven roots keep it firmly earthbound, and the seven roots of medieval Jewish thought—the fundamental roots of Christian biblical faith.

The only puzzle is the "fromages secs" on this menu. Cheese in all forms was forbidden to devout Catholics during Lent, but "fromage" could also mean anything compressed or molded like cheese (see April 4) and this may have referred to what would now be called "fruit cheese"—a dense fruit puree dried and cut into strips or decorative pieces.

Recipes

~~~

Almond Soup

Take a pound and a half of sweet almonds and twelve bitter ones; skin them as usual, by putting them in water over the fire; pound them, putting in from time to time a drop of water to prevent their oiling; when they are quite smooth they are sufficiently done: put into a stewpan six pints of water; when it boils infuse half an ounce of coriander and half a lemon, keeping out the skin and seeds; moisten the almonds with this infusion; rub it several times through a napkin or tammy till it takes the appearance of milk; salt and sugar it properly; put it into the *bain-marie*; take very thin slices of bread, glaze them in the oven and throw them into the almond soup when it is going to table.

Crust Soup—Mittonage

Take a household loaf and rasp it lightly, cut out the crumb without breaking it, which will answer for frying to garnish spinage dishes or soups, or for a charlotte or a panade; round the crusts handsomely, and let them simmer for a few minutes; before serving, put any vegetables on them, and pour over an empotage; serve it as hot as possible.

Antoine Beauvilliers, *The Art of French Cookery* (1827).

April 5

State Dinner
The White House, Washington, DC, 1960

President Alberto Lleras Camargo (1906–1990) of Colombia made a 13-day visit to the United States in 1960 and was entertained at a the obligatory

---

DINNER

Minted Hawaiian Pineapple

Dry Sack   Consomme with Marrow Balls

Melba Toast

Hearts of Celery   Queen and Ripe Olives

Chateau   Filet of Sole Veronique

Climens   Cucumbers Marinated

1950   Boston Brown Bread Sandwiches

Roast Stuffed Duckling Marnier

Orange Sauce

Beaune   Tomato Pudding

Greves

1952   Spinach Souffle

Bread Sticks

Endive and Bibb Lettuce Salad

Green Goddess Dressing

Toasted Chippers

Pol

Roger   Nesselrode Pudding

1952   Brandied Marron Sauce

Petits Fours

Salted Nuts   Candies   Demitasse

---

state dinner in the White House by President Dwight D. Eisenhower (1890–1969).

There are some interesting contrasts in this menu. There is a combination of classic and "local" dishes common to diplomatic dinners. A sophisticated diner anywhere in the world would have recognized *Sole Veronique*—a classic French dish attributed to the famous Auguste Escoffier (1846–1935), the favorite Victorian dish of nesselrode pudding (see June 30), and the very old combination of duck with orange (see January 21). In contrast to the elegant, classical dishes, there are several that sound quite homely, such as the

Boston brown bread (see June 11) and the tomato pudding, although no doubt these were dainty versions of the recipes.

There was clearly some attempt to feature specifically American produce: bibb lettuce was developed in Kentucky, and the pineapple, although native to central South America, certainly made its home in Hawaii. The green goddess dressing is a modern-era American invention. The most widely accepted story of its origin is that it was developed at the Palace Hotel in San Francisco in 1923, in honor of the actor George Arliss, the star of the play *The Green Goddess*, which was showing in the city at that time. The "green goddess" in the play is the deity of the fictional Indian Princedom of Rukh, and the dressing, naturally, is green, by virtue of the large amount of parsley and green onion tops. The dressing had a resurgence of popularity in the late 1950s and 1960s and appears on several state dinner menus of the time, including that for Soviet Premier Nikita Khrushchev (1894–1979) in 1959.

Recipes

~~~

Green Goddess Dressing

1 cup mayonnaise
1 clove garlic, crushed
3 anchovies, chopped
1/4 cup finely chopped chives or green onions with tops
1/4 cup chopped parsley
1 tablespoon fresh lemon juice
1 tablespoon tarragon vinegar
1/2 teaspoon salt
ground pepper
1/2 cup sour cream, whipped.

Combine the ingredients, folding the sour cream last when the other ingredients have been well blended.
Sheboygan Journal (Wisconsin), March 3, 1952.

Tomato Pudding

No. 2 can of tomatoes
1 cup brown sugar
1 tsp salt
3/4 cup boiling water
3 cups white bread crumbs
1/2 cup butter

Strain tomatoes through a sieve, crush pulp thoroughly to get all of it. Add boiling water and let it all bubble away on stove for 5 minutes. Heat oven to 375, while above mixture cooks, cut bread in 1/2 inch squares. Put in casserole

and pour melted butter over crumbs, and stir well. Then add boiling mixture. Stir again and bake for 50 minutes.
  The News and Tribune (Jefferson City, Missorui), February 26, 1961.

Melba Toast: see November 15.
Sole Veronique: see August 13.
Nesselrode Pudding: see June 30.
Petits Fours: see November 14.

April 6

Anniversary Luncheon of the Entry of the United States into World War I
Mansion House, London, England, 1918

On the first anniversary of the entry of the United States into the war the Lord Mayor of London gave a luncheon for 400 people at his official residence, the Mansion House. Among the guests were many officers of the U.S. Army and Navy (including Vice-Admiral Sims), the Archbishop of Canterbury, numerous diplomats from both countries, (including Winston Churchill, the minister of munitions), as well as "representatives of the Dominions and of the banking and commercial interests of the City; men of letters, actors, scientists, artists, journalists, and members of Parliament" (*The Times*, April 8, 1918). The guest of honor was Walter Hines Page, the American ambassador.

At the end of the meal proper, the usual toasts were made. Arthur Balfour, (who had been prime minister between 1902–05), began with the chief toast "The Day We Celebrate," after which Page presented to the mayor, to accept on behalf of the City of London, an American Flag, giving rise to an "enthusiastic outburst of applause" on behalf of all present.

London Lord Mayoral luncheons and banquets were traditionally the epitome of civic dining, with vast amounts of food spread across multiple courses, but rationing had been in force in England to one degree or another, since early 1917. The public were reassured that the meal "was in conformity with the demands of the Food Controller. It was probably the most frugal that has ever been served at the Mansion House on a public occasion. It consisted only of soup, fish, eggs, vegetables, and fruit."

Clear Turtle

—

Salmon Souché Cucumber

—

Devilled Whitebait

—

Eggs Florentine

—

Fruit Salads
Baked Custards

—

Anchovy Toast

—

Dessert

Even in deepest darkest wartime it had been found possible to provide turtle soup, the absolute staple and symbol of the Lord Mayor's official table. The other dishes, though hardly "frugal," were certainly extremely modest.

The salmon was lightly poached and served in its own liquor, a style called *souché, souchy, souchet, zoochi* or some other variation of the abbreviated form of *water-souchy*, which is an interpretation of the Dutch *waterzootje*— which means, essentially, fish poached and served in its own liquor. As was traditional, it was served with a cucumber salad. The eggs florentine were (and still are) a popular way of serving eggs, atop a pile of creamed spinach.

Recipes

~~~

Water Souchy

Fish, Perch or Flounders.
Fish Liquor.
Four Parsley plants, roots and leaves.
One teaspoonful of grated Horse-radish.
One teaspoonful of Shalot vinegar.
One teaspoonful of Cayenne sauce.
One teaspoonful of Walnut ketchup.

Stew the fish slowly, in just enough fish liquor to cover them, with the parsley, the horse-radish, and above sauces. When the fish are done, lay them in a deep dish, with a teaspoonful of chopped parsley; strain the liquor over them, and serve, adding a little more fish liquor if there is not enough left after the cooking to cover them.

Mrs. Charles Clarke, *High Class Cookery Recipes* (1893).

Poached Eggs, Florentine

Remove the stalks and thoroughly wash a pint and a half very fresh spinach, and plunge in a quart boiling water with half a teaspoon salt and boil for fifteen minutes. Drain on a sieve, press out all the water and chop very finely. Place in a saucepan with half ounce butter, half a gill cream, two saltspoons salt, half teaspoon sugar, two saltspoons pepper and a saltspoon grated nutmeg. Mix well and let cook for five minutes. Dress the spinach on a hot dish.

Prepare twelve poached eggs without toasts. Lay them over the spinach and serve.

Alexander Filippini, *The International Cook Book* (New York, 1906).

Turtle Soup: see November 10.
Anchovy Toast (Croûtes): see December 11.
Devilled Whitebait: see August 14.

April 7

Cooking Class Dinner
Cooking Academy, Fourth Avenue, New York, 1865

Pierre Blot (ca. 1818–1874) was one of America's first celebrity chefs, yet his time in the spotlight was short-lived. Details of his early life in France remain mysterious, and in the end he died in relative obscurity. In the 1860s, however, the self-styled professor of gastronomy was the "benevolent missionary of civilization" heaven-sent to confer the blessings of good cuisine upon the United States. He had had an inauspicious start for such fame, apparently arriving in the country in the 1850s as a political refugee, with little or no command of the language. He set about cooking in private homes and improving his language skills, and in 1863 published his first book, *What to Eat and How to Cook It*. Two years later, in March 1865, he opened the New York Cooking Academy.

At each class the cooking of a full meal was demonstrated (it was not a "hands on" course), and at the end of the session, the pupils enjoyed the fruits of the lesson. On April 7, the bill of fare was as follows:

Pot au Feu.
Shad au gratin.
Vol au vent de poulet.
Salsify, Bechamel Sauce.
Pommes de terre en croquettes.
Tourte Francaise.

The New York Times reported on the opening of the academy with great enthusiasm. Sixty-two students were enrolled when it opened. There were three classes—two for servants and one for "ladies," each class meeting twice a week for ten weeks. The ladies were mostly drawn from "the families of our most distinguished and wealthy citizens"—ladies who were intelligent as well as wealthy and were "determined not only to know how dishes should be prepared, but also how to cook them themselves." They were observed to take copious notes of every step of that art "which has so much to do with the temper of the sterner sex."

The newspaper eulogized Blot, reporting him as "a person of refinement and education" who "combines the chemistry of cooking thoroughly with the art" and spoke with "simplicity and clearness of style." The academy was, it said, deservedly a success, and "an institution much needed by our American housewives."

The *Pot-au-feu* was an exception to the general rule in that it had to be started in advance of the class, as it took five hours to cook. Blot stressed its importance in France by telling his students that "nothing can be done without the broth or *pot au feu* or soup, or whatever you please to call it," and that "The French army is fed on this *pot-au-feu* three hundred and sixty days in the year."

Recipes
~~~

Salsify, or Oyster-Plant (in Bechamel)

Scrape them, and throw one by one as they are scraped into cold water, with a few drops of vinegar; when they are all scraped, move them a little, take out of the water, and throw them in boiling water with a little salt, boil till tender, and drain; place them warm on a warm dish, and serve with brown butter, a *maître d'hotel*, or white sauce.

While the salsify is boiling as directed above, make a Bechamel sauce; drain the salsify when done, and turn it into the Bechamel sauce as soon as the latter is finished; keep on the fire for about two minutes, stirring the while, and serve warm.

Pierre Blot, *Handbook of Practical Cookery for Ladies and Professional Cooks* (New York: D. Appleton and Company, 1868).

Fish au Gratin

Bone and skin the fish as directed. For a fish weighing about two pounds, spread one ounce of butter on a tin plate or baking-pan, spread over it half an onion, chopped ; place the pieces of fish on them; add salt, pepper, a tablespoonful of vinegar or a wine-glass of white wine, and half an ounce of butter; spread over and bake.

While it is baking, put in a small saucepan one ounce of butter, and set it on the fire ; when melted, add half a tablespoonful of flour, stir, and, when it is turning yellow, add also about one gill of broth, two tablespoonfuls of meat-gravy, the juice of the fish when baked (if the fish be not done when the time comes to put the juice in the pan, keep the pan in a warm place, and wait), salt, and pepper; boil gently about five minutes, stirring occasionally. Place the fish in a tin or silver dish, spread three or four mushrooms sliced over it; turn the sauce gently over the whole, dust with bread-crumbs; put half an ounce of butter, in four or five pieces, on the whole; bake ten or twelve minutes, and serve in the dish in which it is.

Pot au Feu

The word *pot-au-feu* means the meat, vegetables, seasonings, spices, and the "pot" or soup-kettle itself, ie., every thing made use of in making broth. The popular meaning of the term in France is, the soup and the beef and vegetables served as releves and, with the working-classes, the only thing (with bread, wine, and fruit) composing the family dinner.

Vol-au-vent: see September 17.
Bechamel Sauce: see January 18.

April 8

Dinner for Peace and Goodwill Mission
SS *Abangarez*, Puerto Barrios, Guatemala, 1929

The SS *Abangarez* was one of the 13 banana carriers built for the United Fruit Company between 1908–11. On one occasion while she was in the Guatemalan port of Puerto Barrios, she was the venue for a dinner to the delegates of one of the peace and goodwill missions sent to Nicaragua in the 1920s.

Martini
Crabmeat Cocktail
Cream of Celery   Essence of Tomato
Iced Celery   Queen Olives
Redfish au Gratin

Veuve Cliquot
Breaded Calf's Brains
Roast Partridge, St. James.
Baked Sugar Cured Ham
Roast Potatoes   String Beans
Lettuce Salad, Mayonnaise
Peach Melba   ButterCream Pastry
Banana Ice Cream
Walnuts   Apples   Cluster Raisins

Benedictine
Brie Cheese Toasted Crackers
Demi Tasse

Bananas were a rare and exotic fruit in the United States until the 1870s, because their inherent softness and rapid ripening made importation (even from so close as the Caribbean) virtually impossible. *A Domestic Cyclopaedia of Practical Information* published in 1877 described the banana as being "the fruit of the palm tree found in the West Indies and South America" and thought it necessary to give instructions as to its use:

> It is eaten raw, either alone or cut in slices with sugar and cream, or wine and orange juice. It is also roasted, fried, or boiled, and is made into fritters, preserves, and marmalade. It is dried in the sun and preserved as figs; meal is extracted from it by pounding and made into something resembling bread, and the fermented juice affords excellent wine. With us it is brought to the table as dessert, and proves universally acceptable.

The United Fruit Company was formed in 1895 and became incredibly powerful. At its peak it controlled 90 percent of the banana market, and in the process it controlled the government of several Central South American countries such as Guatemala, Honduras, and Nicaragua. This inextricable association between a poor developing country dependent on a single crop, a corrupt minority leadership, and a large corporation with huge economic power is the origin of our phrase "banana republic."

Recipes

~~~

Crabmeat Cocktail

A half cupful of tomato catsup, a quarter cupful of horseradish, a tablespoonful of lemon juice, a desertspoonful of Worcestershire sauce, eight drops of Tabasco sauce, a saltspoonful each of sugar and salt, ten drops of garlic vinegar and a saltspoonful of paprika. Mix the ingredients well. Allow a heaping tablespoon full of the crabmeat to each cocktail, well moistened with sauce. Garnish with a spray of fresh watercress.

The Amarillo Globe, February 14, 1919.

Banana Ice Cream

1 quart of cream
6 large bananas
1/2 pound of sugar
1 teaspoonful of vanilla

Put half the cream and all the sugar over the fire and stir until the sugar is dissolved; take from the fire, and, when perfectly cold, add the remaining half of the cream. Freeze the mixture, and add the bananas mashed or pressed through a colander. Put on the lid, adjust the crank, and turn until the mixture is frozen rather hard.

This quantity will serve ten persons.

S. T. Rorer, *Ice Creams, Water Ices, Frozen Puddings Together with Refreshments for all Social Affairs* (1915).

Peach Melba

This classic dessert was invented by August Escoffier (1846–1935) in the 1890s. It was inspired by the performance of the opera singer Dame Nellie Melba (1861–1931)—as was Melba toast (see November 15)—in Wagner's *Lohengrin*. The opera is based on the German folktale of the "Knight and the Swan," and in Escoffier's original presentation, the dessert consisted of vanilla ice cream and peaches decorated with spun sugar and served in an ice sculpture of a swan. Later Escoffier added the raspberry sauce (or puree) in place of the spun sugar, and this is the recipe recognized today.

April 9

Emperor Wilhelm's Lunch
Royal Palace, Berlin, Germany, 1909

Wilhelm II (1859–1941) was the last German Emperor and the last king of Prussia. He was forced to abdicate in November 1918 and immediately went into exile in the Netherlands, where he remained for the rest of his life. With World War I still several years away, it is doubtful that the Kaiser had any concern about his fate when he sat down to the following luncheon on April 9, 1909.

Windsorsuppe.
Windsor Soup.

Steinbutten mit Colbertsauce.
Turbot with Colbert Sauce.

Gedaempftes Roastbeef, garnit.
Steamed (boiled) Beef, garnished.

Kleiner Schinken Auflauf.
Small Ham Pudding.

Gefuelleite Wachtetbrueste.
Stuffed Quail.

Kapaunen, Fruechte, Palat.
Capon, Fruit, Palate.

Frische gruene Bohnen.
Fresh green Beans.

Ananaspeise.
Pineapple on skewers.

Kaesestagen, Gefrorenes.
Cheese Platter, Ices.

Nachtisch.
Dessert.

There is little on this menu that identifies it as German. The royal families of Europe formed their own international clique by virtue of their intermarriage, and they ate very similarly. The "steamed roastbeef" seems an odd description until one realizes that roast beef was so strongly identified with the British that in Europe any large piece of meat, however cooked, became "roastbeef" (*rosbif* in French)—even if it was mutton (see January 18).

Windsor soup was a standard dish on English menus in the late Victorian and Edwardian eras. There were several forms, but it was the "brown Windsor soup" that became simultaneously a required dish that was symbolic of the sophisticated table, and a joke. One theory is that the name is a pun on

Brown Windsor Soap, a fragrant dark brown soap introduced at the Great Exhibition of 1851, and supposedly a favorite of the Queen herself. The original form of Windsor soup appears to have been invented by the man who was Queen Victoria's chef for a short while in the 1840s—Charles Elmé Francatelli. His version is a complicated but ultimately very elegant white soup (see recipe here) and appears to be a far cry from the infamous thick brown sludge which was often described later in the century. There is no recipe for it in Mrs. Beeton's extraordinarily comprehensive *Household Manual* (1861), so it was clearly not a well-known dish at that time.

Recipes
~~~

Calf's Feet Soup à la Windsor

Place in a two gallon stock-pot a knuckle of veal, a pound of raw lean ham, four calf's feet, and an old hen minus the fillets; which reserve for making quenelles with, for further use. To these add two carrots, two onions stuck with four cloves, celery, a bouquet of parsley, green onions, sweet basil, and lemon thyme, tied neatly together, moisten with half a bottle of light French white wine, and put the stock-pot on a moderate fire to boil for ten minutes or so; then fill it up from the common stock, or any white broth you may have ready, set it to boil on the stove, skim it well, and after four hours gentle ebullition, take the calfs feet out and put them in water to clean them; then take all the bones out, and lay them on a dish to cool, to be trimmed afterwards so as to leave the inner part of the feet only, all the outer skin being thinly paired off, that the feet may have a more transparent appearance; cut them into inch lengths, by half an inch in width, and put them by in a small soup pot till required. Strain the *consommé* through a napkin, thicken it moderately with a little white *roux* (going through the regular process for making white *velouté*), then add thereto a little essence of mushrooms, and finish by incorporating with the sauce thus prepared, a leason of six yolks of eggs mixed with a little grated Parmesan, and half a pint of cream; squeeze the juice of half a lemon into it, and season with a little crystallized soluble cayenne. Pour the soup into the tureen containing two dozen very small quenelles (made with the fillets of the old hen,) some boiled macaroni cut into inch lengths, and the tendons of the calf's feet, previously warmed in a little consomme, with the addition of half a glass of white wine. Stir the soup gently in the tureen to mix these ingredients together, and send to table.

Charles Elmé Francatelli, *The Modern Cook* (London, 1860).

April 10

Dinner for President Harry S. Truman
The Gridiron Club, Hotel Statler, Washington, DC, 1948

The Gridiron Club was founded in Washington in 1885 for journalists of that city and immediately became prestigious by virtue of the fact that membership was (and still is) by invitation only. It is famous for its annual spring dinner, a glamorous white-tie affair at which the current president is invited as the honored guest and speaker.

The motto of the club is "The Gridiron singes but never burns,"—referring not merely to the way that the customary steak is cooked, but to the politicians who are customarily "roasted" during the speeches and general hilarity that accompany the evening. The "roasting" on this night began with the menu cover, which featured a political cartoon that was a spoof on John Bunyan's *Pilgrim's Progress*—the "author" on this occasion being John "Bunion," and the pilgrims a number of major political figures of the time (including Joseph Stalin) and presidential candidates racing towards the "delectable mountain," at the top of which is the White House.

Seafood in Aspic

—

Consomme Indienne
Hearts of Celery   Olives   Rose Radishes

—

Terrapin Maryland
Hot Corn Sticks

—

Sirloin Steak Bordelaise
New Asparagus Hollandaise   Potatoes Delmonico

—

Smoked Turkey and Smithfield Ham
Hearts of Endive   French Dressing

—

Baba Ring au Rum with Fresh Strawberries
Bavarian Cream

—

Demi Tasse

Duff Gordon Amontillado
B. V.Burgundy
San Benito Champagne
Villaton Cigars
Cigarettes

The motif of the Gridiron Club is—of course, a gridiron, the same motif as the original "Sublime Society of Beef-steaks" founded in England in 1735. A long line of such clubs with similar names followed. They were always very masculine organizations whose dining experiences focused on the simple and manly art of putting away as many steaks as possible in the evening, accompanied by as much wine and other liquor as was required to wash them down.

Naturally, the menu on this night included a simple sirloin steak with Bordelaise sauce, a brown sauce with a concentrated wine base traditionally served with grilled meat, the dish being then garnished with slices of poached bone marrow. To make a classic Bordelaise sauce according to the true French tradition is a very complex, time-consuming process requiring several prior steps such as preparing a sauce espagnole (January 18) and is rarely done today outside of high-class restaurants.

Recipes

~~~

Shrimps in Aspic

Cover bottom of mould with layer of aspic 1/4 inch thick. When solid, garnish with pimiento and whites of hard-cooked eggs cut into shapes of fish, flowers or animals. Fill mold with [cooked] shrimp a few capers, and chopped nuts. Pour aspic over shrimp (just dissolved, not warm). Place in refrigerator until firm. Serve on lettuce leaves, garnished with radishes cut into rose shapes, sliced hard-cooked eggs and tomatoes. Serves 6.

Aspic Jelly

1 tablespoon gelatin	1/8 teaspoon pepper
1 pint stock	Juice of 1/2 lemon
1 teaspoon salt	1 egg white
1 teaspoon mixed spices	1 egg shell

Put gelatin in 1/2 cup cold water. Soak 30 minutes. Dissolve over hot water. Add stock, salt, spices, pepper, and lemon juice. Heat slowly, stirring constantly, almost to boiling point. Add egg white and egg shell. Bring to boil while beating. Boil 1 minute. Strain through cheesecloth. Pour in mold. Chill until set.
The Lily Wallace New American Cookbook (1946).

Delmonico potatoes are named for the famous New York restaurant of the same name and became a popular dish very early in the restaurant's history. The original recipe was eventually published in a book by Alexander Filippini, the man who predated the chef most usually associated with the restaurant—the famous Charles Ranhofer.

Delmonico Potatoes

Place four good-sized boiled and finely hashed potatoes in a frying pan with one and a half gills cold milk, half gill cream, two saltspoons salt, one saltspoon white pepper and a saltspoon grated nutmeg; mix well and cook on the range for ten minutes, lightly mixing occasionally. Then add one tablespoon grated Parmesan cheese, lightly mix again. Transfer the potatoes into a gratin dish, sprinkle another light tablespoon grated Parmesan cheese over and set in the oven to bake for six minutes, or until they have obtained a good golden colour; remove and serve.
Alexander Filippini, *The International Cook Book: Over 3,300 Recipes* (1906).

Bordelaise Sauce: see July 13.
Terrapin Maryland: see April 10.
Bavarian Cream: see May 18.

April 11

Good Friday Wartime Lunch
Barrow-in-Furness, Cumbria, England, 1941

Nella Last was a f49-year-old English housewife when she began keeping a diary in September 1939. She had volunteered to take part in the Mass Observation Project in which thousands of ordinary people agreed to record the day-to-day details of their lives. Her diary is a wonderful record of life on the home front and of the trials of managing under rationing. Rationing reached its peak in the second half of 1940; and the first months of 1941, until food started to arrive from the United States, were grim. A few days after her diary entry on this day in 1941, her town was extensively bombed.

Good Friday. . . . I rested and read until lunch. It was easily prepared, for I made the vegetable soup yesterday, and opened a wee tin of pilchards, heated them and served them on hot toast. They were only 5 1/2 d., and yet were a better meal than two cod cutlets costing at least 2s. I feel it would be better value if, instead of bulky, flabby cod and other white fish from America, the Government brought in only dried and tinned fish. So much can be made up from a 1s. tin of salmon or tuna, and so little from the same value of white wet fish. Besides there's the "keeping" value too. I packed up tea, greengage jam in a little brown pot, brown bread and butter, a little cheese and a piece of cake each, and we set off after

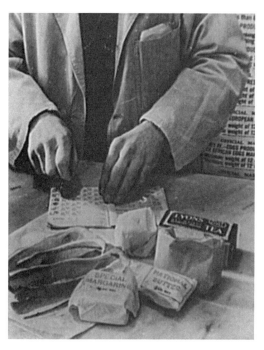

lunch. I have been longing and yet dreading to cut this particular cake for some time now. I made it last June, when butter was more plentiful. It was one of two: and one was for Christmas, and one to be shared between Cliff and my husband for their birthdays on 11 and 13 December. I cut only one, made it do over Christmas and thought I'd cut the other at New Year. With my "squirrel's love" of a little in reserve, I made do and kept putting off until it got to Easter! It's a "perfect cake in perfect condition," as my husband said. I wrapped it in grease-proof paper—four separate wrappings—then tied it and put it in an air-tight tin. I expect it's the last good cake we will ever have—at least for years—and I do so love baking cakes and watching people enjoy them (I myself prefer bread and butter on the whole).

Grocer cancelling ration book. Courtesy of Library of Congress.

Rationing began in Britain on January 8, 1940, with restrictions on butter, bacon, and sugar and did not end until July 3, 1954—nine years after the end of the war. As the war went on, more foods were rationed, although the amounts fluctuated according to supply. At the peak, in late 1942, the ration per person, per week was

- One shilling and two pence worth of meat (which bought very little, and the housewife had no choice, she simply accepted what the butcher had available)
- Eight ounces of sugar
- Eight ounces of fat
- Four ounces of bacon or ham
- Two ounces of tea
- Two ounces of cheese
- One egg

Home baking was particularly difficult, as the sugar and fat allowances for the family had to stretch to making the jams, preserves, cakes and puddings —a job that was a normal part of a housewife and mother's role. The Ministry of Food produced regular leaflets advising on substitutes (soy beans and flour for meat and wheat, syrup and honey for sugar, grated carrots for dried fruit in puddings, and so on), and the use of the despised dried eggs.

Recipes

~~~

Easter Pie

1 lb. mixed root vegetables,
1 1/2 oz. dripping or lard,
quarter pint of water,
salt and pepper,
quarter lb. sausage meat,
3 dried eggs, reconstituted.

Cut vegetables into small dice and fry in the fat until well browned—about 15 minutes. Add the water, season well and bring to the boil. Place in a piedish. Roll the sausage meat into small balls and place amongst the vegetables and bake in a moderate oven for 15 minutes. Season eggs and beat. Pour over the vegetables, return to the oven and bake for a further 10–15 minutes. until the egg is set and browned.

Soya Marzipan Paste

2 oz. margarine,
2 tablespoons water,
1–2 teaspoons almond essence,
4 oz. soya,
4 oz. sugar.

Melt margarine in water. Draw saucepan off heat, stir in almond essence, sugar and soya. Turn out, knead well, and shape into little eggs and chicks.
Food Facts Leaflet No. 247 (Ministry of Food, March 1945).

Britain: WWII Rationing Timeline

September 8, 1939	Ration cards issued.
January 8, 1940	Rationing of butter, bacon and sugar.
March 11, 1940	Rationing extended to include most other meats.
July 1940	Ban on making or selling of iced cakes
September 1940	Ban on manufacture of candied and crystalized fruit.
December 3, 1940	Extra Christmas rations of 4 oz sugar and 2 oz tea announced.
February 1941	The standard "National Wheatmeal" loaf introduced.
March 1941	Jam, marmalade, treacle, and syrup rationed.
May 5, 1941	Cheese rationing.
May 28, 1941	Lord Woolton announced egg rationing.
November 1941	Milk rationed.
December 1, 1941	Points based rationing introduced.
1942	Dried egg powder introduced.
April 6, 1942	It becomes illegal to sell white bread.
July 1942	Tea ration for those under five years old removed.
July 26, 1942	Sweets (candy) are rationed.
August 1942	Rationing peak.
1946	After the war has ended, reduction in the ration of bacon, poultry, and eggs are announced, and dried egg is no longer available.
July 1946	Bread rationed.
1947	Rationing was more severe than during the war. Potatoes are rationed.
January 1948	Bread is de-rationed.
December 1948	Jam is de-rationed.
October 1952	Tea rationing ends.
February 4, 1953	Sweets rationing ends.
March 1953	Egg rationing ends.
April 1953	Cream rationing ends.
September 26, 1953	Sugar rationing ends, after almost 14 years.
May 8, 1954	Fat (including butter) is de-rationed.
July 3, 1954	Meat de-rationed.

Good Friday Buns

"Major Lloyd George, Parliamentary Secretary to the Minister of Food . . . informed Mr. Banfield . . . that the Minister of Food had placed no prohibition on the manufacture of Good Friday buns, and bakers could make them if they wished; but they would not be given any extra fat."
The Times, April 3, 1941.

April 12

First Meal in Space
Vostok 1, 1961

The first person to eat in zero gravity was the Russian cosmonaut Yuri Gagarin. He orbited the earth once, at an altitude of a little over 187 miles (302 km), and a speed of 18,000 mph. The flight only lasted 108 minutes—hardly long enough to warrant much in the way of catering, but no one knew whether it would be even possible to chew and swallow in space. Thirty minutes into the flight, Gagarin made his experiment. He successfully consumed three 160 gm aluminium tubes of specially prepared space food of different consistencies.

Meat Puree

Coffee

Blackcurrant Marmalade

Gagarin got a little distracted by the experience, and noted:

> When I was eating my food, drinking water, I let go of the [note]pad, and it floated right in front of me with the pencil. Then I had to record the regular report. I took the pad, but the pencil wasn't where it had been. It flew off somewhere. . . . I closed the log and put it in my pocket.

Yuri Gagarin. (AP Photo/Tass)

There was more food (and water) on board, in case of an emergency. It had been calculated that in the case of retro-rocket failure, it would take ten days for the spaceship to return "naturally." Nine different foods had been developed for this first flight, although the shelf life was very limited compared to later versions. All of the food came in aluminium tubes, and the calorie allowance per day was about 2800 Kcal, made up of 100 gm of protein, 118 gm of fat, and 308 gm of carbohydrates.

Recipes

~~~

Whether it is made for breakfast or for a space flight, marmalade is marmalade. It is simply fruit boiled with sugar until it gels. In previous times it was often made so thick that it could be cut into slices or shapes—similar to the "fruit leather" or "fruit cheese" that we can buy today. The marmalade (or jam) that Gagarin ate in space was essentially no different from that made from the following recipe.

Blackcurrant Marmalade

Take the currants when they are fully ripe, strip them from the stalks, bruise them a little in the preserving pan, and stew them gently, keeping them turned until they are tender, which they will generally be in from ten to fifteen minutes. Pour off about three parts of the juice, which will make excellent jelly, and rub the remainder with the currants through a sieve. Weigh the pulp, boil it rapidly for a quarter of an hour, or for twenty minutes if there should be a large quantity of it; then, for each pound, stir into it, until dissolved, nine ounces of white sugar rolled or pounded fine; boil the marmalade quickly for ten minutes, stirring it often, and pour it into small pans. If well made it will cut out in firm slices.

James Robinson, *The Whole Art of Curing, Pickling, and Smoking Meat and Fish* (1847).

The meat puree would have been like meat paté, similar to this version, suitable for a fancy dinner party.

Purée De Volaille

Stew a fowl in stock with the meat of any boiled poultry or game, and pound it in a mortar with three or four yolks of hard eggs; beat it to a paste. Then take a piece of bread, soaked in either stock or milk, and a dozen of sweet almonds; pound with the meat again until well mixed; then add by degrees some stock with a spoon, and stir it strongly; observe that it is neither too thick, nor yet too thin, but of the consistence of thick cream; pass it through a tamis, and put it in a basin to keep hot; place it in a pan of boiling water till you serve.

Frances Crawford, *French Cookery Adapted for English Families* (1852).

April 13

Dinner for the Bonapartes
Tuileries Palace, Paris, France, 1811

When Napoléon Bonaparte (1769–1821) dined with his family at the Palais de Tuileries (Tuileries Palace) on April 13, 1811, it was a very new family

indeed. Desperate for an heir, he had divorced his wife Joséphine de Beau-
harnais in January 1810, and on April 1 he married Marie-Louise of Austria
(1791–1847). Marie-Louise fulfilled the role required of every royal wife and
gave him an heir, also called Napoléon, on March 20, 1811.

Deux Potages.
Au macaroni et purée de marrons.

Deux relevés.
Une pièce de bœuf bouillie, garni de légumes,
Un brochet à la Chambord.

Quatre entrées.
Côtelettes de mouton à la Soubise,
Perdreaux de Monglas,
Fricassée de poulet à la chevalière,
Filets de canard au fumet.

Deux rôts.
Un chapon au cresson,
Un gigot d'agneau.

Deux plats de légumes.
Des choux-fleurs au gratin,
Du céleri-navet au jus.

Quatre entremets au sucre.
Crème au café,
Gelée d'orange,
Génoise decorée,
Gauffres à l'Allemande.

This must have been a very satisfying time for Napoléon. He was Emperor
of the French. He had a son and heir and a newly renovated palace, he had
great plans for Europe, and he was blissfully unaware of what lay ahead. A
little over 12 months later was the disastrous campaign in Russia, which
was followed by his exile, first to Elba in 1814, then to St. Helena in 1815.

By all accounts Napoléon was not interested in food, and it is not likely
that he paid any particular attention to this meal. It is interesting, however,
that the menu includes a soup made from a puree of chestnuts. Chestnuts
were a staple food in Corsica, the childhood home of Napoléon. The French,
when they took control of the island in 1770, tried to destroy the chestnut
industry. It was, they said, "the food of laziness," providing "bread" for the
peasants and fodder for their livestock without any effort. The seventeenth-
century horticulturist John Evelyn referred to chestnuts as a "lusty, and
masculine food for Rustics at all times," but the wealthy enjoyed them too,
in the form of extravagant sweetmeats known as *marrons glacées*.

Recipes

~~~

Potage à la Purée de Marrons

Take boiled chestnuts, skin and pick out all the bad ones; put them in a frying-pan, with a little bit of butter, and toss them till the inner scurf comes easily off; when it is rubbed off, put them in a pot with a little stock or *consommé* and let them cook; drain, and pound them in a mortar, put them through a search, wetting them with the stock in which they were cooked; when they are thus prepared, put them in a stewpan with two spoonsful of stock; mix it well with purée; leave it to simmer three or four hours; take off the fat and add a little sugar, season it properly, and serve it with bread fried in butter, or a mittonage.

Beauvilliers give two versions of crème au café. The first uses gizzards (the muscular stomach of a bird, usually a chicken) to thicken the custard-like mixture. He does give an alternative, which is a more acceptable variation for modern tastes.

Crème au Café Blanc
(without Gizzards)

Take a pint and a half of cream; add to it the zest of a lemon and some sugar; roast two ounces of coffee; throw it into your boiling cream; cover, and let it infuse for half an hour; take out the coffee [place the cream over hot water and thicken with six egg yolks], fill the cream quickly into pots, having care to stir it; put them into hot water; leave them to take in the bain-marie without allowing it to boil; put a cover on the pot and lay fire upon it; when it has taken, take out the pots, and put them into cold water without covering them: when ready wipe, and serve.

Antoine Beauvilliers, *A Complete System of French Domestic Cookery* (1837).

Chapon au cresson: see February 21.
Gauffres: see January 31.

April 14

Stanley Club Dinner in Honor of Louis Pasteur
Continental Hotel, Paris, 1886

When the members of the Stanley Club—one of the "American" clubs of Paris—gave a dinner to honor the French scientist Louis Pasteur (1822–1895) on this day in 1886, they made special recognition of "the services he has rendered to the Americans afflicted with or threatened with hydrophobia (rabies), who came here for his treatment." As they sat down to enjoy the following menu, they could not have realized the enormity of the debt that would ultimately be owed to him by the eating public whose food he made safe and whose wine he prevented from spoilage.

POTAGES
Consommé à la Royale
Mock Turtle.
Hors d'oeuvre variée

RELEVÉS
Croustades à la Parisienne
Saumon sauce à la Daumont

ENTRÉES
Filet de Boeuf, sauce Chevreuil, garni de Croquettes
et de Champignons farci
Caneton de Rouen à la Bigarade
Timbale à la Financière
Punch à la Romaine

RÔTS
Chapone de Houdan farcie sauce Périgueux

SALADE
Langouse à la Russe

ENTREMETS
Asperges en branches, sauce Hollandaise
Pudding sauce Sabayon
Bombe Vanille et Fraises
Dessert varié

VINS
Madère   Château Grand Moussas
Haut Barsac 1878   1871
Médoc en carafes   Champagne frappé
Richebourg 1874   Ch. Heidsieck

CAFÉ ET LIQUEURS

Pasteur's early work was on fermentation, and it was supported by the wine and beer industries who wanted a solution to the souring malady that sometimes affected their product. He ultimately proved that microorganisms were responsible, convincing him of the truth of germ theory (many of his opponents did not believe that microscopic organisms could create such havoc), allowing improvements in the manufacture of wine and beer, and ultimately also leading to his medical breakthroughs. Pasteur's investigations also showed him that heating then cooling a liquid destroyed these "germs"—a process that became known as Pasteurization and which was (and still is) widely applied to milk in particular.

Recipes

~~~

There are several classic sauces in this meal, and they occur in many other menus in this book. Many sauces are variations of the four classic foundation sauces of the French repertoire (see January 18) as the Perigueux sauce recipe demonstrates.

The Périgord region of France is famous for its truffles, and a dish styled *Périgueux*, *Perigourdine*, or something similar always contains truffles.

Perigueux Sauce

1 gill brown sauce
1 gill tomato sauce
1 glass sherry
1 teaspoonful anchovy essence
1 oz. butter
3 truffles

Chop finely three large truffles, put them in a small stewpan with the sherry, reduce to one-half (covered); add the brown and tomato sauce; boil for a few minutes, finish with a teaspoonful of anchovy essence and the butter.
Charles Herman Senn, *The Book of Sauces* (Chicago, 1915).

Brown Sauce

Espagnole Sauce is an example of a brown sauce (see January 18).

Tomato Sauce

Cut half a pound of ripe tomatoes into slices, also half a small peeled onion, and cook them for about 20 minutes with a teaspoonful of castor sugar, a few peppercorns, half a bayleaf and half a teaspoonful of salt. Rub through a sieve or strainer, and add a pint of brown stock. Fry in an ounce of butter 1/2 ounce of flour, and stir until well browned, then pour in gradually whilst stirring, the hot tomato liquid. Boil up, skim, and let simmer for about 15 minutes, then serve.

Holland was noted for its dairy industry and its high-quality butter, and it is this that gives Hollandaise sauce its name.

Hollandaise Sauce

Crush about a dozen peppercorns, put them in a saucepan with 2 tablespoonfuls of French wine vinegar and 4 tablespoonfuls of water. Cover the pan and place it on the fire, boil fast to confuse the contents of the pan. It should be reduced to about one-half its volume. Stir or whisk in 4 yolks of eggs, then by degrees whisk

in 4 to 6 oz. of fresh butter, and lastly add about a gill of hot water. Season with salt and the juice of 1/2 a lemon. Pass the sauce through a fine tammy cloth. Return it to a clean saucepan, which must stand in a pan of hot (not boiling) water. Keep it thus till required for table.
  Charles Herman Senn, *The Book of Sauces* (Chicago, 1915).

"Sabayon" is related to the Italian word *zabaglione*, a frothy dessert sauce which is somewhere between a custard and an old-fashioned "posset" (see January 13).

Sauce Sabayon

Put half a pound of sugar and eight egg-yolks in a bain-marie, set it on the fire, and whip the preparation until it becomes frothy, then add half a pint of Madeira or other wine, and continue to whip until the sauce is very light and begins to thicken, then remove it at once from the bain-marie, and serve.
  Charles Ranhofer, *The Epicurean* (1894).

Mock Turtle: see July 4.
Punch à la Romaine (Roman Punch): see July 1.

April 15

Week's Menu for the First Family
The White House, Washington, DC, 1973

In 1973, the "outraged housewives" of America made a political issue out of rising food prices—or, as the newspapers called it, "the great supermarket stick-up." The man behind much of the campaign was Democrat Representative William R. Cotter who proposed a nationwide meat boycott, to start on April 1, 1973. The aims were to force an immediate price freeze on meat at December 1972 levels, a Congressional investigation of food prices, repeal of the Meat Import Quota Act to allow more meat into the country from overseas, and a temporary halt to the export of scarce foods. There were the usual campaign rallies, marches, and meetings, and meatless recipes were promoted and circulated. There was also a specific and very personal focus on President Richard M. Nixon (1913–1994). Housewives were asked to send their grocery receipts to him and to ask what was going onto the table at the White House. In response to the pressure, the White House released the week's menus for Monday 9 to Sunday 15.
  On Sunday 15, the First Family were to sit down to a modest dinner of

---

Meat Loaf

Baked Potato, Green Beans

Tossed Green Salad

Naturally, the immediate question was raised as to whether or not this week's menu was typical. A number of people supposedly in the know were canvassed, and comments that Pat Nixon was "always a careful shopper" and that the First Family had always been modest in their food tastes and "big on vegetables" were published.

The boycott was widely supported, and campaigners ultimately claimed a qualified success and continued to promote meatless meals twice a week. Some farmers retaliated by withholding stock from the markets, but they were unable to stop the president from putting a ceiling on meat prices.

Recipes

~~~

What was purported to be Pat Nixon's authentic recipe for her husband's favorite meal—her "swell meatloaf"—was widely distributed in the newspapers. It also appeared in *The White House Family Cookbook* by the chef of the time, Henry Haller, in 1987.

Pat Nixon's Meatloaf

2 tablespoons butter	1 cup finely chopped onions
2 garlic cloves minced	3 slices white bead
1 cup milk	2 pounds lean ground beef
2 eggs, lightly beaten	1 teaspoon salt
Ground black pepper, to taste	1 tablespoon chopped fresh parsley
1/2 teaspoon dried thyme	1/2 teaspoon dried marjoram
2 tablespoons tomato puree	2 tablespoons bread crumbs

Grease a 13-by-9-inch baking pan. Melt butter in a sauté pan, add garlic and sauté until just golden, do not brown. Let cool.

Dice bread and soak it in milk. In a large mixing bowl, mix ground beef by hand with sauteed onions and garlic and bread pieces. Add eggs, salt, pepper, parsley, thyme and marjoram and mix by hand in a circular motion.

Turn this mixture into the prepared baking pan and pat into a loaf shape, leaving at least one inch of space around the edges to allow fat to run off. Brush the top with the tomato puree and sprinkle with bread crumbs. Refrigerate for 1 hour to allow the flavors to penetrate and to firm up the loaf.

Preheat the oven to 375 degrees. Bake meatloaf on lower shelf of oven for 1 hour, or until meat is cooked through. Pour off accumulated fat several times while baking and after meat is fully cooked. Let stand on wire rack for five minutes before slicing. Makes 6 servings.

White House Menus
April 9–14, 1973

Monday: Broiled chicken, Chinese cabbage, macaroni and cheese, spinach salad.

Tuesday: There was a State Dinner on this day, so it was necessarily more elaborate: supreme of seafood, roast tenderloin of beef aux champignons, bouquetiere of vegetables, bibb lettuce salad with brie cheese, crepes suzettes flambé.

Wednesday: Roast pork, Spanish rice, zucchini squash, watercress and tomato salad.

Thursday: Beef stew casserole, cucumber and pea salad.

Friday: Roast duckling, wild rice, mixed vegetables, grapefruit and orange salad.

Saturday: Boiled ham, parslied potatoes, cabbage, carrots and turnips, and cornbread.

April 16

Testimonial Banquet for Boxer Robert Fitzsimmons
Hotel Bartholdi, New York, 1897

Robert Fitzsimmons (1863–1917) was the first boxer in the world to become champion in three weight divisions (middle, heavy, and light-heavyweight). His New York friends and admirers gave a great testimonial banquet in his honor a few weeks after he became world heavyweight champion in Carson City, Nevada. The "Champion of Champions" won that particular fight with his famous "solar plexus" punch. The opportunity for word play was irresistible for the Hotel Bartholdi catering staff, although they spelled "plexus" incorrectly.

Blue Points.

Sherry, Orange Bitters.

Celery.   Tomatoes.   Olives.

Clear Green Turtle.

Baked Striped Bass.   Bartholdi Sauce.

Cucumbers.

Potato Hollendaise.

Sauternes.

Petit Bouchée of Chicken, with Mushrooms.

Pontet Canet.

Small Tenderloin Saute, Stuffed Tomatoes.

Lobster Newburg, en Casse.

SOLAR PLEXIS PUNCH.

Egyptian Cigarettes.

Golden Quail, En Canapè.

Pommery Sec.

Water Cress.

G. H. Mumm E. dry

Irroy.

Chicken Mayonnaise.

White Seal (Moet & Chandon)

Boned Turkey—Decorated.

White Rock Water
(Frank T. Huntoon)

Neapolitan Ice Cream.
Fancy Cake.
Roquefort Cheese.   Toasted Water
Biscuits.
Coffee.
Perfectos.   Fruit.

Dewers Scotch.

The word "punch" meaning a drink does not come from the idea that it "packs a punch." The two meanings of the word appear to come from different origins, although the *Oxford English Dictionary* admits that the etymology of both is uncertain. "Punch" meaning a blow appears to derive from "pounce" meaning a prick or sting (or the talon of a bird). "Punch" referring to a drink is usually explained as coming from *panch*, meaning "five" in several Indian languages, because it has five basic ingredients: alcohol, water, sweet (sugar), sour (usually lemon juice), and spice (or "bitter"). This is probably too fanciful an explanation, as there have never been five fixed ingredients. A second and intriguing possibility is that it is related to *puncheon*, meaning a cask for liquids—specifically the one holding the sailors' rations.

Punch was a given at a certain point at every nineteenth-century, upper-class hotel or restaurant banquet. This menu was typical in many other ways. Turtle or terrapin in one form or another—especially soup—was the indication of a high-class banquet in England or the United States. Oysters were a virtually obligatory starter, and more often than not they

Fitzsimmons's boxing pose. Courtesy of Library of Congress.

were the famous "Blue Point" variety—Atlantic oysters originally from Blue Point, Long Island, New York. Inevitably in the case of a prized delicacy, substitution frequently took place, and it is doubtful if many diners were aware of the counterfeit.

Substitution of another type took place with the American classic dish lobster Newburg. The traditional story is that the concept of the dish (essentially lobster in a cream sauce) was given to Charles Ranhofer of Delmonico's restaurant by a sea captain called Ben Wenberg. Ranhofer put the dish on the menu—naming it after Wenberg—and it was an immediate success. Ranhofer removed the dish from the menu when he and Wenberg had a disagreement, but patrons insisted on its return. Ranhofer compromised by slightly rearranging the letters of the name, and the dish became lobster Newburg.

One outstanding difference between nineteenth- (and early twentieth-) century formal dinner menus is that it was fairly common for tobacco to make an appearance, as it does in the form of the Perfectos cigars. Today they seem particularly out of place at a dinner celebrating a sportsman.

Recipes

~~~

Lobster à la Newburg

2 lb. lobster.	1 tablespoon sherry.
1/4 cup butter.	1 tablespoon brandy.
1/2 teaspoon salt.	1/3 cup thin cream.
Few grains cayenne.	Yolks 2 eggs.

Slight grating nutmeg. Remove lobster meat from shell and cut in slices. Melt butter, add lobster, and cook three minutes. Add seasonings and wine, cook one minute, then add cream and yolks of eggs slightly beaten. Stir until thickened. Serve with toast or Puff Paste Points.

Potatoes à la Hollandaise

Wash, pare, soak, and cut potatoes in one-fourth inch slices, shape with French vegetable cutters; or cut in one-half inch cubes. Cover three cups potato with White Stock, cook until soft, and drain. Cream one-third cup butter, add one tablespoon lemon juice, one-half teaspoon salt, and few grains of cayenne. Add to potatoes, cook three minutes, and add one-half tablespoon finely chopped parsley.

Fannie Merritt-Farmer, *The Boston Cooking-School Cook Book* (1896).

Neapolitan Ice Cream: see December 20.

April 17

New York Society of Restaurateurs Dinner with ``Diamond Jim'' Brady
Terrace Garden, New York, 1916

When the New York Society of Restaurateurs held their third annual dinner they invited as their guest speaker the millionaire philanthropist James Buchanan Brady (1856–1917). They had reason to honor "Diamond Jim," for he was a restaurateur's dream—a man of spectacular wealth and prodigious appetite, famously referred to by the owner of one of his favorite restaurants as "the best 25 customers I ever had."

On this particular evening, the menu was a modestly elegant collection of typical dishes of the time. It was accompanied by a list of fine wines (or "lubricants"), including an impressive selection of imported and American champagnes at $2.50 to $5.00 a quart, although the honored guest himself never touched the stuff. His beverage of choice was his "golden nectar"— orange juice, which he consumed in almost unbelievable quantities.

Fruit Cocktail

—

Ox-tail Clear

—

Assorted Relishes

—

Yama Yama Brook Trout with Fines Herbes
Cucumbers Garnished

—

Saddle of Spring Lamb, Colbert Sauce
Garnished Fresh Mushrooms
Potatoes Rissolées

—

New Asparagus, Hollandaise

—

Roast Jumbo Squab, Stuffed
Field and Beet Salad

—

Strawberry Ice, Fantaisie
Assorted Fancy Cakes

—

Coffee

Brady's appetite was the stuff of legend. A light breakfast was reported to consist of steak, chops, eggs, flapjacks, fried potatoes, hominy, corn bread, muffins, and a large volume of milk. A more substantial lunch was routinely followed by a pound or two of candy—to make the food settle better in his stomach, he said. Dinner was his main meal, and he made sure it ended with candy and was washed down with a gallon or more of his "golden nectar." Stories of the dinners he gave or attended became exercises in hyperbole. He was said to routinely order double servings at a 15-course dinner. At one dinner party he gave for 50 friends (in honor of a race horse), the eating lasted from 4 P.M. to 9 A.M., and cost $100,000. At another, after several years of international culinary espionage, he finally got to eat a dish he had longed to try since first hearing of it. The dish was *Filet de Sole Marguery*, and it was the specialty of Café Marguery in Paris. The sauce recipe was a well-kept secret, but Brady was determined to try it. He threatened the owner of Rector's—his favorite restaurant—that his patronage would be withdrawn if he could not be served the dish. The story is that not wishing to lose his "25 best customers," Charlie Rector pulled his son out of college and sent him to France under an assumed name. The young man started as a dishwasher at Café Marguery, and slowly worked his way up through the restaurant hierarchy until he was privy to the secret recipe and could prepare it perfectly. The process took two years, and Diamond Jim was on the waterfront as the son's ship sailed into New York, not even waiting until the young man had disembarked before calling out "Did you bring the sauce?" Finally, nine servings later, Brady was reported to have said. "If you poured some of the sauce over a Turkish towel, I believe I could eat all of it."

Recipes

~~~

Roast Saddle of Lamb (adapted)

Remove the red skin from a small, tender, fat saddle of lamb, fold up the flanks underneath, firmly tie it all around, then lay it on a roasting pan, spread a little melted butter over the surface, pour two tablespoons water in the pan, season with teaspoon salt and half teaspoon pepper, set in the oven for one hour, turning and basting it once in a while. Remove, untie, dress on a dish.

Potatoes Rissolees

Peel, wash and drain well twelve peeled sound new potatoes. Heat two tablespoons good lard in a frying pan, add potatoes and fry on the fire until a nice golden colour, turning once in a while. Sprinkle over a teaspoon salt, toss again, set in a moderate oven for twenty-five minutes. Remove, drain and serve.
   Alexander Filippini, *The International Cook Book,* (ca. 1906).

Sole, Colbert

Cut off the head of a large sole, and pull off the black skin. Lift off the four fillets complete, spreading the two sides apart with two toothpicks, so they will not touch. Dip in milk, then in flour, and then in beaten eggs and fresh bread crumbs, the lower side only. Dip the top side in milk and flour. Season well with salt and pepper, and place in a pan with butter, and two ounces of butter on top of the fish. Bake in the oven, basting continually until done. Then put the sole on a platter, remove the toothpicks and fill the space with two ounces of butter that has been mixed with salt, pepper, a little chopped parsley, one spoonful of meat extract, and the juice of one lemon. Place the platter in the oven just long enough to melt the butter. Garnish with parsley in branches and lemons cut in half. The whole sole may be fried in swimming lard instead of baking, if desired. This way is easier, but is not the correct one.

Victor Hirtzler, *The Hotel St. Francis Cook Book* (1919).

Filets de Soles à la Marguery

As interpreted by Charles Ranhofer, chef at Delmonico's, in his book *The Epicurean* (1894).

Raise the fillets from two clean, skinned soles; fold in two, pare nicely and season, range them on a buttered baking dish and bestrew the surface with shallots and mushroom peelings: moisten to cover with a white wine court bouillon and allow the liquid to come to a boil, then finish cooking the fillets in a slow oven. Drain them off singly, and dress on a dish; garnish one side with shrimp tails, and the other with blanched oysters, from which the hard parts have been removed, or mussels. Keep the whole very warm. Strain the broth the soles were cooked in, reduce it to a half-glaze, thicken with a mere spoonful of Normande sauce and finish with a piece of fresh lobster butter; pour this over the fillets and garnishings, then glaze the sauce with a gas salamander; two minutes will suffice for this. When the fish is ready to be served, brush the surface with thin lines of red butter.

April 18

Confederate Soldier's Dinner
Army Camp, near Pensacola, Florida, 1861

Two days after the beginning of the American Civil War a Confederate sergeant wrote to the editor of the *Daily Constitutionalist* newspaper in Augusta, Georgia. He described the conditions and the food in his camp "near Pensacola, Florida."

April 18th, 1861.

We go to bed at nine o'clock, and rise at half-past-four o'clock; drill at seven —we have breakfast; at one we have dinner; and at seven supper. Our bill of fare for to-day was as follows: mess pork, mess beef, rice, white beans, middling bacon, sea biscuits, coffee and sugar, and we get a plenty. Each Sergeant receives one bar of soap and two candles—these articles to last five days.

The sergeant could hardly have realized that the food situation for most ordinary soldiers and citizens was going to get a whole lot worse over the next few years as the war created hardship and chaos across the country. There were many instances when soldiers on both sides had to rely on the "sea-biscuit" alone for sustenance, and many occasions when even these were in short supply.

"Sea-biscuit" was the staple "bread" or "hardtack" of military and seafaring men for centuries. It was known by many names in many countries, most of them unflatteringly accurate, such as teeth dullers, flour tiles, concrete

Confederate camp. Courtesy of Library of Congress.

macaroons, ammo (ammunition) reserves, sheet iron crackers, worm castles (referring to their usual weevil population), and dog biscuits. The word "biscuit" means twice cooked (*bis* = twice, *cuit* = cooked), but the sea-biscuit variety were often baked up to four times to drive out every last drop of moisture. Their keeping powers were legendary, and it was widely believed that some biscuits made during the Civil War were reissued during the Spanish-American War 35 years later, the equivalent British rumor being that hardtack made in the 1850s was resupplied in World War I. Often the only way to eat the biscuits was to soak them in stew, or coffee, or if nothing else was available, in water, to make a sort of porridge. They were made from two ingredients only—flour and water, but no salt because it increased the potential for dampness by causing water absorption.

Recipes

~~~

Sea-Biscuit

Sea-biscuit can be made by mixing about six parts flour to one part water, kneading the dough well, rolling it out to about 1/8 thick, cutting it into squares, pricking it all over, and baking it until dry (about an hour); turn it once during baking.

Sea-Biscuit for the Royal Navy

The following passage taken from *The Engineer's and Mechanic's Encyclopædia* (1836) by Luke Hebert describes how sea-biscuit was manufactured on a large scale for the Royal Navy in Plymouth, England.

> The baking establishment consists of 9 ovens, each 13 feet long by 11 feet wide, and 17 ½ inches in height. . . . The first operation in making the biscuits consists in mixing the flour, or rather meal and water; 13 gallons of water are first introduced into a trough, and then a sack of the meal, weighing 280 lbs. . . . An apparatus, consisting of two sets of what are called knives, each set ten in number, are then made to revolve amongst the flour and water by means of machinery. This mixing lasts one minute and a half, . . . The next process is to cast the lumps of dough under what are called the breaking-rollers—huge cylinders of iron weighing 14 cwt. each, and moved horizontally by the machinery along stout tables. The dough is thus formed into large rude masses, 6 feet long, by 3 feet broad, and several inches thick. . . . These great masses of dough are now drawn out, and cut into a number of smaller masses . . . and again thrust under the rollers, . . . they fold it up, or double one part upon another, so that the roller, at its next passage, squeezes these parts together, and forces them to mix . . . which is repeated until the mixture is so complete that not the slightest trace of any inequality is discoverable in any part of the mass. . . . the dough only requires to be cut into biscuits before it is committed to the oven. The cutting is effected by what is called the cutting-plate, consisting of a net-work of 52 sharp edged hexagonal frames, each as large as a biscuit. . . . does not actually cut it through, but leaves sufficient substance to enable the workman at the mouth of the oven to jerk the whole mass of biscuits, unbroken, into the oven. . . . One quarter of an hour is sufficient to bake the biscuit, which is afterwards placed for three days in a drying room, heated to 85°, or 90°, which completes the process.

April 19

Coming-of-Age Party
Wynnstay Hall, Denbighshire, Wales, 1770

Sir Watkin Williams-Wynn, 4th Baronet, came into his title a few days before he was born due to the death of his father in an accident. He was from of the great landed families of Britain, and his mother continued to add to the family estate during his minority. By the time the 4th Baronet came of age, the family laid claim to over 100,000 acres spread across five Welsh counties and into the adjacent English county of Shropshire.

The grounds of the park surrounding Wynnstay Hall itself were eight miles in circumference, and it was here that Sir Watkin held his coming-of-age (21 years old) party in 1770. Everyone was invited from his estates and the surrounding area, and "it is thought there were at least 15000 people at dinner in Sir Watkin's park, all at the same time" (John Askew Roberts, *Wynnstay & the Wynns* [1876]).

The bill of fare for the entertainment was as follows:

30 Bullocks	166 Hams
1 ditto roasted whole	100 Tongues
50 Hogs	125 Plumb puddings
50 Calves	108 Apple pies
80 Sheep	104 Pork pies
18 Lambs	30 Beef pies
70 Pies	34 Rice puddings
51 Guinea Fowls	7 Venison pies
37 Turkeys	60 Raised pies
12 Turkey Poults	80 Tarts
84 Capons	30 pieces of cut pastry
25 Pie fowls	24 Pound cakes
300 Chickens	60 Savoy cakes
360 Fowls	30 Sweetmeat cakes
96 Ducklings	12 Backs of bacon
48 Rabbits	144 Ice creams
15 Snipes	18000 Eggs
1 Leveret	150 Gallons of milk
5 Bucks	60 Quarts of cream
421 Pounds of salmon	30 Bushels of potatoes
30 Brace of tench	6000 Asparagus
40 Brace of carp	200 French beans
36 Pike	3 Dishes of green peas
60 Dozen of trout	12 Cucumbers
108 Flounders	70 Hogsheads of ale
109 Lobsters	120 Dozen of wine
96 Crabs	Brandy, rum, and shrub
10 Quarts of Shrimps	Rock-work shapes, landscapes, in
200 Crawfish	jellies, blanchmange, &c.
60 Barrels pickled oysters	A great quantity of small pastry
1 Hogshead of rock oysters	One large cask of ale, which held
20 Quarts of oysters for sauce	twenty-six hogsheads

Not every dish would have been available to every guest. The substantial hearty food such as the whole roasted ox and plum puddings would have been for the farm workers and village folk. The family and elite guests would have enjoyed the delicate meats such as the guinea-fowl and the fashionable sweetmeats. Ice cream was a great delicacy as it required a large amount of ice (not easy in spring, before refrigeration), and was laborious to make, requiring plenty of servant power.

Dishes are not "invented"; they develop slowly over long periods of time, always built on some previous idea. Someone did not simply "invent" ice cream one day out of the blue; the idea evolved slowly. Drinks chilled with snow evolved into sherbets (see April 29, June 10) which became "ice cream" when milk or cream (and eggs) were added. Cookbooks always lag behind real practice, and although ice cream as we know it appears to have been made in Italy and France in the seventeenth century, the first written recipe in English appears in *Mrs. Mary Eales's Receipts* in 1718.

A similar story applies to pound cake. Baking powder-type rising agents did not appear until the early nineteenth century. Prior to this cakes were leavened with yeast (so they were like sweet fruit breads), or eggs, well beaten to incorporate air and develop the right protein "structure" to hold up the cake. The first mention of pound cake according to the *Oxford English Dictionary* was in 1743, and the first known recipe for it appears in Hannah Glasse's *Art of Cookery* in 1747.

Recipes
~~~

To Make a Pound Cake

Take a pound of butter, beat it in an earthen pan with your hand one way, till it is like a fine thick cream, then have ready twelve eggs, but half the whites; beat them well, and beat them up with the butter, a pound of flour beat in it, a pound of sugar, and a few carraways. Beat it all well together for an hour with your hand, or a great wooden spoon, butter a pan and put it in, and then bake it an hour in a quick oven. For change, you may put in a pound of currants, clean washed and picked.

Hannah Glasse, *The Art of Cookery Made Plain and Easy* (1747).

To Make Ice Cream

Take Tin Ice-Pots, fill 'em with any Sort of Cream you like, either plain or sweeten'd, or Fruit in it; shut your Pots very close; to six Pots you must allow eighteen or twenty Pound of Ice, breaking the Ice very small; there will be some great Pieces, which lay at the Bottom and Top: You must have a Pail, and lay some Straw at the Bottom; then lay in your Ice, and put amongst it a Pound of Bay Salt; set in your Pots of Cream, and lay Ice and Salt between every Pot, that they may not touch; but the Ice must lye round 'em on every Side; lay a good deal of Ice on the Top, cover the Pail with Straw, set it in a Cellar where no Sun or Light comes, it will be froze in four Hours, but it may stand longer; then take it out

just as you use it: hold it in your Hand and it will slip out. When you wou'd freeze any Sort of Fruit, either Cherries, Rasberries, Currans, or Strawberries, fill your Tin Pots with the Fruit, but as hollow as you can; put to 'em Lemmonade, made with Spring-Water and Lemmon-Juice sweeten'd; put enough in the Pots to make the Fruit hang together, and put 'em in Ice as you do Cream.
   Mrs. Mary Eales's Receipts (1718).

Raised Pie and Pork pie: see October 25, November 3.
Savoy Cakes: see August 1
Rice pudding: see January 12.
Blanchmonge (Blancmange): see January 7.

April 20

Vicar's Dinner
East Tuddenham, Norfolk, England, 1796

James Woodforde (1740–1803) became the parson in the village of Weston Longville in Norfolk, England, in 1773. For 40 years he kept a diary, and it is a marvelous source of information about everyday village life in the second half of the eighteenth century. He never married (having been jilted once he never put himself at risk again), and his unmarried niece came to live with him as his housekeeper. The parish provided him with a comfortable living, and much of the food came from the farms that went with his curacy. He kept pigs, caught fish in his own ponds, and brewed his own ale. He obviously enjoyed his food and recorded details of many of the meals in his own household. He was also, in spite of his single status, quite sociable, entertained often, and was entertained in turn by friends.

On April 20, 1796, he dined at the home of a friend, Mr. Mellish, the vicar of East Tuddenham, a village about four miles away. The Mellish's he notes in his diary, are "People of great Fortune . . . and live quite in Style."

Dinner was soon announced after our Arrival, which consisted of the following things, Salmon boiled and Shrimp Sauce, some White Soup, Saddle of Mutton rosted & Cucumber &c., Lambs Fry, Tongue, Breast of Veal ragoued, rice Pudding and the best part of a Rump of Beef stewed immediately after the Salmon was removed. 2nd Course. A Couple of Spring Chicken, rosted Sweetbreads, Jellies, Maccaroni, frill'd Oysters, 2. small Crabs, & made Dish of Eggs. N.B. No kind of pastrey, no Wheat Flour made use of and even the melted butter was thickened with Wheat-Meal, and the Bread all brown Wheat-Meal with one part in four of Barley Flour. The Bread was well made and eat very well indeed, may we never eat worse.

The lack of pastry and the brown bread made with part barley flour reflects the repeated severe wheat shortages that affected Britain in the second half of the eighteenth century. The harvest in 1794 was poor, and it was far worse in 1795. Just how critical the situation was is shown by the fact that in April 1795 an excise was placed on hair powder. So, while the poor rioted for bread, the rich were not able to powder their wigs to perfection. Most of the well-to-do, like the Mellish and Woodforde families, however, did voluntarily reduce their wheat consumption, and even the royal household stopped using flour in 1800.

There were two other interesting results of the wheat shortages. Pies were a mainstay at every level of society at this time, as they were a way of storing food for long periods (as long as the thick crust did not crack or get damp, it stayed reasonably airtight). When there was not enough wheat for pastry, the pie fillings were cooked in crocks or dishes, becoming terrines, patés, and dishes such as cottage and shepherd's pies with their potato "crusts." Naturally the pottery industry received a stimulus, but it went one step further than mere pragmatism. For the houses of the wealthy, where illusion was all-important, crocks were made in the same shape and color of raised pies, complete with decorative edges, such as the famous Wedgwood pie crust ware.

Recipes

~~~

To Make Shrimp Sauce

Put half a pint of shrimps, clean picked, into a gill of good gravy; let it boil with a lump of butter rolled in flour, and a spoonful of red wine.

   Susannah Carter, *The Frugal Housewife, or Complete Woman Cook* (London, ca. 1800).

To Ragoo a Breast of Veal

Take your breast of veal, put it into a large stew-pan, put in a bundle of sweet herbs, an onion, some black and white pepper, a blade or two of mace, two or three cloves, a very little piece of lemon-peel, and just cover it with water: when it is tender, take it up, bone it, put in the bones, boil it up till the gravy is very good, then strain it off, and if you have a little rich beef gravy, add a quarter of a pint, put in half an ounce of truffles and morels, a spoonful or two of catchup, two or three spoonfuls of white wine, and let them all boil together: in the meantime flour the veal, and fry it in butter till it is of a fine brown, then drain out all the butter, and pour the gravy you are boiling to the veal, with a few mushrooms: boil all together till the sauce is rich and thick, and cut the sweetbread into four. A few force-meat balls are proper in it. Lay the veal in the dish, and pour the sauce all over it. Garnish with lemons.

   Hannah Glasse, *The Art of Cookery* (London, 1796).

April 21

Banquet of the French Vegetarian Society
Rue St. Honoré, Paris, France, 1881

France did not completely avoid the trend of enthusiasm for the vegetarian way of life that developed in Britain and America in the nineteenth century.

The *Société Végétarienne de France* was founded in 1880. At their second annual banquet, members sat down to the following bill of fare.

MENU VÉGÉTARIEN DU 21 AVRIL.

POTAGES
Purée de lentilles,
soupe printanière.

Hors D'Œvre
Beurre,
radis,
olives.

ENTRÉES
Œufs à la coque,
asperges en branches.

QUATERMAINS [ENTREMETS]
Macaroni au blanc de poule,
petits pois.

SACCHARINS
Crême à la vanille,
ruches d'amygdaline,
savarin.

DESSERT
Fromage Suisse,
compote de pommes,
confiture de fraises,
dattes,
oranges,
gaufrettes.

VINS
Maçon vieux,
Saint Emilion.
Pain de Graham.

The New York Times reported its founder, Hureau de Villeneuve, as suggesting that vegetarianism should be popular in France "where many members of the lower and middle classes are already vegetarians, largely by necessity." History has not generally demonstrated that a dietary regime followed out of sheer necessity becomes popular on that account alone, so his words are more a reflection of De Villeneuve's enthusiasm for the cause.

French vegetarians were by no means committed to the teetotalism that often affected their colleagues elsewhere, and the menu included two classic wines from France. Wine was much more deeply embedded in the culture of France, and was still affordable even for the less well-off. It is also interesting that the menu specifically mentions Graham bread (see February 5), a decidedly American recipe invented by the nutrition campaigner, Sylvester Graham.

Recipes

~~~

Lentil Soup

Take a breakfastcupful of green lentils and put them to soak in cold water over-night. In the morning throw away any floating on the top. Drain the lentils and put them in a stew-pan or saucepan with some stock or water, and add two onions, two carrots, a turnip, a bunch of parsley, a small teaspoonful of savoury herbs and a small head of celery. If you have no celery add half a teaspoonful of bruised celery seed. You can also add a crust of stale bread. Let the whole boil, and it will be found that occasionally a dark film will rise to the surface. This must be skimmed off. The soup must boil for about four hours, or at any rate till the lentils are thoroughly soft. Then strain the soup through a wire sieve, and rub the whole of the contents through the wire sieve with the soup. This requires both time and patience. After the whole has been rubbed through the sieve the soup must be boiled up, and if made from green lentils it can be col-oured green with some spinach extract (vegetable colouring, sold in bottles). If made from Egyptian (red) lentils, the soup can be coloured with a few drops of Parisian essence (burnt sugar). In warming up this soup, after the lentils have been rubbed through a sieve, it should be borne in mind that the lentil powder has a tendency to settle, and consequently the saucepan must be constantly stirred to prevent it burning. In serving the soup at table, the contents of the soup-tureen should be stirred with the soup-ladle before each help.

Cassell's Vegetarian Cookery (London, 1891).

Macaroni au Blanc de Poule

Macaroni au blanc de poule is a Swiss dish, quite suitable for invalids entering upon convalescence. To make it a sufficient quantity of medium-sized macaroni should be boiled for an hour over a gentle fire. Meanwhile, melt in a saucepan a piece of butter, about an ounce, if the dish be for one person, and add to it a des-sertspoonful of flour, mixing well. Pour on this gently a breakfast-cup full of milk; add a little salt and pepper, and when these are well mingled, cook the whole in a saucepan for about ten minutes. Now, if the macaroni be well done, take it out of the water, put it in a saucepan, and cover it with the dressing you have prepared, then cook it, without boiling, another ten minutes. When ready for serving, beat up one or two eggs in a cup with a very little hot milk, and pour them over the macaroni in the dish. And here permit me a word on the subject of macaroni. Properly dressed, it is an invaluable and most delicious food (to be aware how delicious, one must have eaten it, as I have done, in Italy), but unskilfully and ignorantly prepared, it is insipid, and even worse. "Never," says the sapient author of Dinners and Dishes, "never ask me to back a bill for a man who has given me a macaroni pudding." Macaroni is not meant for puddings; it is alien to sugar and jam, but it is bosom friends with pepper, salt, butter, and Parmesan, and as a savoury dish dressed with grated cheese and cream, or tomatoes, it is ambrosia. Very few invalids can digest cheese, so in cooking macaroni for them you must get as near only to the right thing as circumstances will permit.

Anna Kingsford, M.D., "A Letter to Lady Pomeroy," in *Health, Beauty, and the Toilet. Letters to Ladies from a Lady Doctor* (1886).

Potage Printanier: see February 28.
Graham Bread: see February 5.

April 22

State Dinner for King George V and Queen Mary
British Embassy, Paris, France, 1914

Just before the outbreak of World War I, King George V (1865–1936) and Queen Mary (1867–1953) of England traveled to France, on a visit designed to give a clear international message indicating the improved relations between the two countries that had developed since the signing of the *Entente Cordiale* in 1904.

When heads of state travel to another country, a formal state dinner is usually given to them by the host country on the first evening of their visit. The hospitality is then returned on a subsequent evening, the responsibility falling to the ambassador of the visiting country. The King and Queen arrived in Paris on April 21, and attended the usual luncheon and the obligatory state dinner on the same day. The following evening they gave the return dinner at the British Embassy. The menu for the dinner—written in French as it would have been at any official dinner on English soil—was as classic as was expected.

Consommé de Volaille à la Sévigné

—

Truites Saumonées à la Norvégienne.

—

Longes de Veaux à la Nivernaise.   Pommes Fondantes.

—

Poulardes Soufflées au Champagne.

—

Parfait de Foie Gras au Porto.   Salade Rachel.

—

Asperges Vertes, Sauce Mousseline.

—

Œufs de Vanneaux au Nid.

—

Mousses au Fraises.   Gauffrettes Pralinées.

—

Pailles au Parmesan.

—

Dessert.

Even though the number of courses and dishes is quite different from the medieval era, one element of those times remains at state dinners to this day—the enormous issue of seating protocol. At the Paris dinner in 1914, there were two tables. The royal table (the equivalent of the medieval high table) was set in the vast banqueting hall of the embassy, the "second table" in the adjacent ballroom. Many of the guests, particularly at the second table, could hardly have had time to glimpse Their Majesties, for at 9:30 the dinner was over (the toasts were dispensed with) and the royal party was off to the opera.

Protocol extends to every single aspect of a banquet, and it is fraught with potential diplomatic incidents. There are two recent examples. In 2002 there was a potentially difficult situation between Iran and Spain on two issues—the serving of wine (absolutely essential to a Spanish meal, but anathema to their Muslim guests) and the covering of the hair by the women present (absolutely essential to the Iranian Muslims). The other was in January 2008 when the divorced President of France, Nicolas Sarzoky, wanted his girlfriend to accompany him on a diplomatic visit to India. Protocol rules have generally been in place for a very long time, and there is no precedent for accommodating unmarried partners in any country. Would the girlfriend be accompanied in to dinner on the arm of the Indian president, as would be usual? Where would she be seated? In the end, Carla Bruni avoided a diplomatic incident, and did not travel with her boyfriend—no doubt to the great relief of a number of state officials.

Recipes

~~~

Fondante Potatoes

Cut a quart of small potatoes to the size of pigeons' eggs, put in a casserole and cover with cold water, add a pinch of salt, and bring to a boil. Then drain off the water and put the potatoes in a flat sauté pan with two ounces of butter, and simmer very slowly until they are golden yellow. Then add a spoonful of chicken broth and simmer again until nearly dry. Sprinkle with fresh-chopped parsley, season with salt and pepper.

Victor Hirtzler, *The Hotel St. Francis Cook Book* (1919).

Rachel Salad

Cut some artichoke bottoms, boiled celery, potatoes and asparagus tips, and two truffles, in Julienne shape. Arrange the vegetables in a salad bowl in bouquets, place the truffles in the center, and pour some French dressing over all.

Victor Hirtzler, *The Hotel St. Francis Cook Book* (1919).

Pailles au Parmesan (Cheese Straws)

Although called straws the paste is better looking and better to bake if cut with a paste cutter into strips 1/4 inch wide. Equal quantities of butter, cheese and flour are pounded together to make it, but one or two yolks and a sprinkling of water improves it.

   Jessup Whitehead, *The Steward's Handbook and Guide to Party Catering* (1903).

Plover Eggs in a Nest: see April 29.

April 23

Shakespeare Tercentenary Banquet
Stratford-upon-Avon, England, 1864

On the 300th anniversary of William Shakespeare's birth, the civic leaders and good citizens of his birthplace paid homage to their most famous son with a great festival. The streets were decorated with banners, and a huge tented pavilion was erected in a nearby field to serve as a banquet hall, ball-room, and theatre. At 3:00 in the afternoon, the Earl of Carlisle, president of the festival, and other important guests began arriving for the opening banquet. As they entered the pavilion, the local Rifle Volunteers struck up the old country air "The Warwickshire Lasses," and by half-past three "the work of eating began." *The Times* newspaper correspondent included the bill of fare in his report, noting that it was "too characteristic not to merit insertion."

BILL OF FARE.

"Ladies, a general welcome"—*Henry VIII., I.,4*
"Pray you bid these unknown friends to us welcome, for it is a way to make us better friends, more known." *Winter's Tale, IV., 3*

Roast Turkeys.
"Why, here he comes, swelling like a turkey-cock." *Henry V.,V.,1.*

Pea-Fowl.
"A very, very, pea-cock." *Hamlet., III., 2.*

Roast Fowls.
"There is a fowl without a feather." *Comedy of Errors., III, 1.*

Capons.
"Item, a capon, 2s.2d." *I. Henry IV., II., 4.*

Ducks.
"O dainty duck!" *Midsummer Night's Dream, V., 7.*

Boar's Head.
"Like a full-acorned boar." *Cymbeline, II., 5.*

York Hams.
"Sweet stem from York's great stock." *I. Henry VI., II., 5.*

Tongues.
"Silence is only commendable in a neat's tongue dried." *Merchant of Venice, I.,1*

French Raised Pies.
"They are both baked in that pie." *Titus Andronicus, V.,3.*

Mayonnaise of Salmon.
"Epicurean cook sharpen with cloyless sauce his appetite." *Antony and Cleopatra, II., 2.*

Mayonnaise of Lamb.
"Was never a gentle lamb more mild." *Richard II.,1.*

Braised Lamb and Beef.
"What say you to a piece of beef and mustard, A dish that I do love to feed upon." *Taming of the Shrew, IV.,3.*

Roast Lamb.
"Come you to seek the lamb here?" *Measure for Measure, V.,1.*

Galantines of Turkeys and Fowls.
"The Turkish preparation." *Othello, I.,3.*

Lobster and Mayonnaise Salads.
"Salad was born to do me good." *II. Henry IV, IV.,10.*

Dressed Lobsters and Crabs.
"There's no meat like them, I could wish my best friend at such a feast." *Timon of Athens, I.,2.*

Potted Meats.
"Mince it sans remorse." *Timon of Athens, IV.,3.*

Potted Lamperns and Lampreys.
"From the banks of Wye, and Sandy-bottom'd Severn." *I. Henry IV., III.,1.*

Aspics of Eels, Soles, and Salmon.
"Cry to it, as the Cockney did to the eels when she put them i' the paste alive." *Lear, II.,4.*

Dessert Cakes, Jellies, and Creams.
"The queen of curds and cream." *Winter's Tale, IV., 3.*

Tourtes, Meringues, and Charlottes de Russe.
"They call for dates and quinces in the pastry." *Romeo and Juliet, IV., 4.*

Bee Hives.
"For so work the honey bees." *Henry V, I.,2.*

Fruit.
"Hercules did shake down mellow fruit." *Coriolanus, IV., 6.*

Dinner Rolls.
"The Roll! Where's the Roll?" *II. Henry IV, III.,2*

Dressed Potatoes.
"Let the sky rain potatoes." *Merry Wives, V.,5.*

Bitter Ale.
"And here's a pot of good double beer, neighbor: Drink, and fear not your man."
II. Henry VI., II.,3.
Champagne, Hock, Claret, Port, and Sherry.
"He calls for wine; 'a health,' quoth he." *Taming of the Shrew, III., 2.*

Shakespeare would have recognized almost everything on this menu in spite of the lapse of 300 years. Mayonnaise would have been an exception, for its invention was at least two centuries away. He would have been surprised when the potatoes arrived, for when Shakespeare mentions "potatoes" he is referring to the sweet potato (*Ipomoea batatas*). The 700 guests at the banquet in 1864 would have expected, and got, the ordinary white potato (*Solanum tuberosum*).

Both plants are native to the South American subcontinent—the New World—whose colonization followed Christopher Columbus's arrival in 1492. By Shakespeare's time, the sweet potato had become very popular, but it was more than 200 years before the ordinary white potato started to be eaten on any scale in England and Europe. Shakespeare may have been aware of the white potato as a horticultural curiosity, but it is clear he is referring to the sweet potato in his plays because of the context.

The potato quotation in the menu comes from *Merry Wives of Windsor*, and the lines are spoken by Falstaff, "the fat knight," just as he is about to embrace Mistress Ford. He says "My Doe, with the blacke Scut? Let the skie raine Potatoes: let it thunder, to the tune of Greensleeves, hail kissing Comfits, and snow Eringoes: Let these come a tempest of provocation, I will shelter me here." This is Falstaff's call to lust: he is invoking a deluge of aphrodisiac sweetmeats to assist his "tempest of provocation." Comfits were small sugar-coated seeds, used as digestives and—for Falstaff's purpose, to sweeten the breath. Eringo is the sea-holly, *Eryngium maritimum*, whose succulent root was candied and used as a sweetmeat, as medicine (for broken bones, snake-bites, and a multitude of diseases) and was believed also to "promote venery." Sweet potato was also reputed to "incite to venery," perhaps on account of its phallic shape, and was commonly candied. Shakespeare uses "potato" again in this context in *Troilus and Cressida* when he has Thersists comment as he watches Cressida's betrayal of Troilus "How the devill Luxury with his fat rump and potato finger, tickles these together: frye lechery, frye."

Recipes

~~~

Potted Beef

2 lbs. of lean beef,
1 tablespoonful of water,
1/4 lb. of butter,
a seasoning to taste of salt,
cayenne,
pounded mace,
and black pepper.

Procure a nice piece of lean beef, as free as possible from gristle, skin, &c., and put it into a jar (if at hand, one with a lid) with 1 tablespoonful of water. Cover it closely, and put the jar into a saucepan of boiling water, letting the water come within 2 inches of the top of the jar. Boil gently for 3 1/2 hours, then take the beef, chop it very small with a chopping-knife, and pound it thoroughly in a mortar. Mix with it by degrees all, or a portion, of the gravy that will have run from it, and a little clarified butter; add the seasoning, put it in small pots for use, and cover with a little butter just warmed and poured over. If much gravy is added to it, it will keep but a short time; on the contrary, if a large proportion of butter is used, it may be preserved for some time.
Beeton's Household Manual (1861).

Charlotte Russe: see September 4.
Raised Pies: see October 25,November 3.
Lobster Mayonnaise: see March 31.
Boar's Head: see January 4.

April 24

Opening Banquet
Woolworth Building, Broadway, New York, 1913

The opening of the Woolworth building on Broadway was *the* social event of 1913. At an amazing 57 stories it was the world's tallest office building (and the second tallest structure in the world, after the Eiffel Tower), so New Yorkers had reason to be proud. Frank W. Wooloworth, the man who had planned, executed, and paid for it all, invited 900 privileged guests to a special dinner in honor of the architect of the building, Cass Gilbert.

The dinner was held on the 27th floor, and the menu was classical for the time: French influenced, elegant, everything of the highest quality, but nothing strange, exciting, or innovative.

Caviar.
Oysters.
Turtle soup.
Turban of Pompano with Austrian potatoes.

Breast of Guinea hen with Nesselrode sauce.
Terrapin Baltimore style.
Royal Punch.
Roast Squab.
Walnut and Grapefruit Salad.
Frozen Bombe.
Fancy Cakes.
Coffee and Wine.

Everything else about the evening was, however, quite unbelievably spectacular. The dinner guests, as well as thousands of members of the general public waiting expectantly in the streets outside, were witness to an amazing feat of technology. A Western Union telegrapher installed in the building sent, at the appropriate moment, a signal to the White House in Washington,

Woolworth Building, New York City. Courtesy of Library of Congress.

200 miles away, where President Woodrow Wilson was waiting. The president himself then pressed the button that lit up the entire Woolworth building instantly, "bringing daylight to Broadway." The man who had made all this part of the evening possible—Thomas Edison, inventor of the electric light bulb—was also present as a guest of honor.

Even though the meal was eclipsed by the fantastic light show, the guests were not, of course, disappointed. The measure of a fine chef at the time was the ability to reproduce accurately, and with great consistency, the classic dishes. In complete contrast to today, when chefs at top-end restaurants are expected to keep on coming up with new ideas, novelty for its own sake was definitely eschewed by sophisticated diners of the time. The guests on this night would have expected oysters, turtle in some form or other, several classic entrees, a glass of chilled punch before the roast to cleanse the palate, and a dessert that included ice cream and cake.

Recipes

~~~

A "turban" in culinary terms refers to certain preparations of food arranged in a circle on a dish, or to specific dishes cooked in turban-shaped molds.

Turban of Fish

2 1/2 cups cold flaked fish (cod, haddock, halibut, or cusk).

1 1/2 cups milk.	1 slice onion.
Blade of mace.	Sprig of parsley.
1/4 cup butter.	1/4 cup flour.
1/2 teaspoon salt.	1/8 teaspoon pepper.
Lemon juice.	Yolks 2 eggs.

2/3 cup buttered cracker crumbs.

Scald milk with onion, mace, and parsley; remove seasonings. Melt butter, add flour, salt, pepper, and gradually the milk; then add eggs, slightly beaten. Put a layer of fish on buttered dish, sprinkle with salt and pepper, and add a few drops of lemon juice. Cover with sauce, continuing until fish and sauce are used, shaping in pyramid form. Cover with crumbs, and bake in hot oven until crumbs are brown.

Fannie Farmer Merritt, *The Boston Cooking-School Cookbook* (Boston, 1896).

Grapefruit Salad

Cut three grapefruit in halves, crosswise, and scoop out the pulp; add one cup of English walnuts, broken in pieces, and mix lightly together. Serve on crisp white lettuce leaves, with mayonnaise.

The Times Cookbook, by California Women (Los Angeles, 1905).

Royal Punch

Take two quarts of water, three pounds of sugar, juice of six lemons, two oranges, the contents of half a can of pineapples, one wineglassful of brandy, and one-half pint of white wine. Grate the rinds of one lemon and one orange into a bowl and add the juice of all the fruit. Set the water and sugar on to boil with the juice of the pineapple and boil until thick like syrup, then pour the syrup while hot on the grated rind of the lemon, etc., and juice to draw the flavor. Chop up the pineapple, add to the strained juice and freeze. Use red wine if you would have it pink, instead of white.
   Aunt Babette's Cookbook (Cincinnati, 1889).

Turtle Soup: see November 10.

April 25

Japanese Tiffin
Fujiya Hotel, Miyanoshita, Japan, 1907

The Fujiya Hotel opened in 1878, only 24 years after Japan was officially opened up to the West. It was Japan's first resort-style hotel, in a beautiful location with magnificent views, and it was designed and built specifically to cater for Western tourists and expatriates living in Tokyo and Yokohama. Over its history the hotel has played host to the Imperial family of Japan, foreign diplomats and dignitaries, and many celebrities, including John Lennon and Yoko Ono.

   A brochure from 1897 advised that "the cuisine is under the supervision of an experienced chef and meals are served at all hours" and "wines and liquors of the best qualities and brands only are supplied." There was clearly no intention to showcase Japanese cuisine—presumably because that was not what the guests wanted.

BILL OF FARE

TIFFIN   Thursday 25th April 1907

1. . . . . . .Soup
2. . . . . . .Tinned Sardines
3. . . . . . .Fried Fish
4. . . . . . .Irish Stew
5. . . . . . .Quails and Mushrooms
6. . . . . . .Chicken à l'Africaine
7. . . . . . .Beefsteak and Fried Potato Chips
8. . . . . . .Veal Curry and Rice
9. . . . . . .Brussels Sprouts
10. . . . . . .Boiled Potatoes
11. . . . . . .Cold Chicken

12. . . . . . .Cold Salt Tongue
13. . . . . . .Cold Roast Beef
14. . . . . . .Cold Salt
15. . . . . . .Cold Duck
16. . . . . . .Salad
17. . . . . . .Pickles Tomato Chutney
18. . . . . . .Olives   Pearl Onions
19. . . . . . .Sliced Beetroot
20. . . . . . .Horseradish
21. . . . . . .Custard Pudding
22. . . . . . .Stewed Fruits
23. . . . . . .Assorted Fruits
24. . . . . . .Sweet Grapes
25. . . . . . .Gruyere Cheese Cream Cheese
26. . . . . . .Tea and Coffee

Any dishes desired and not on the bill of fare will be charged extra.

Gentlemen are requested not to Smoke in the Dining Room before 1.

This was nominally "tiffin" (see March 31), but far removed geographically and culinarily from its origins. Many tiffin menus from various countries and menus from Japanese hotels and ships have a numbered format such as this, presumably to make ordering simple and avoid the inconvenience or embarrassment of language problems. There is a very strange mix of dishes indeed on this menu, and the tinned sardines hardly seem the sort of fare that a high-class hotel would serve. The Japanese, however, are masters in the art of preserving and cooking seafood, so perhaps it is not as strange as it first appears.

Recipes

~~~

Poulet a l'Africaine

Take half a pound of red peppers and three chili peppers. Dry them in the sun, or if impossible, in the oven. When they are dry pound them in a mortar, add a quarter of a pound of shallots, two cloves of garlic, six cloves, a small piece of ginger, and two bay leaves. Pound this well together till you obtain a kind of paste.

Take a chicken, cut it in five or six pieces, and brown them in butter on all sides. Add salt, two or three tablespoonfuls of the pepper paste prepared, and cook it very slowly for about ten minutes. Then dilute with hot water, so that it just covers the pieces of chicken. Let it simmer till the chicken is well cooked by which time there should be very little sauce left.

This is a recipe from North Africa. In our countries the preparation of the paste could be simplified by using cayenne pepper, powdered ginger, which could be added in the mortar to the other peppers , the garlic, the shallots. This dish should be very highly spiced.

X. Marcel Boulestin, *What Shall We Have Today* (1931).

Tomato Chutney

One peck of green tomatoes;
six large green peppers;
six onions;
one cup of salt.

Chop onions and peppers fine, slice the tomatoes about quarter of an inch thick, and sprinkle the salt over all. In the morning drain off all the salt and water, and put the tomatoes in a porcelain-lined kettle. Mix together thoroughly two pounds of brown sugar; quarter of a pound of mustard-seed; one ounce each of powdered cloves, cinnamon, ginger, and black pepper; half an ounce of allspice; quarter of an ounce each of cayenne pepper and ground mustard. Stir all into the tomatoes; cover with cider vinegar, about two quarts, and boil slowly for two hours. Very nice, but very hot. If wanted less so, omit the cayenne and ground mustard.

Helen Campbell, *The Easiest Way in Housekeeping and Cooking* (1903).

April 26

Royal Wedding Breakfast
Buckingham Palace, London, England, 1923

When King Edward VIII's brother, the Duke of York (1895–1952), proposed to Lady Elizabeth Bowes-Lyon (1900–2002), she initially turned him down, apparently fearing that life in the royal family would be too restricting. The Duke did manage to persuade her, however, and they were married in 1923. Then, in 1936, her life turned down a path she could hardly have predicted. All of a sudden she became Queen Consort when Edward abdicated (see December 12), and her husband inherited the throne as King George VI. She took to the role with great grace and charm, and eventually became Britain's most loved member of the royal family—particularly as "Queen Mother" when her daughter inherited the throne as the current Queen Elizabeth II.

In 1923 the couple was popular, young, and happy—and their wedding was a welcome event to a British public still recovering from the First World War. It was an opportunity to celebrate, and it was the first royal wedding to be recorded on film. The wedding ceremony took place in Westminster Abbey, and the wedding breakfast was held at Buckingham Palace before the couple left for the train that was to take them to their honeymoon.

Consommé à la Windsor

—

Suprêmes de Saumon, Reine Mary

—

Côtelletes d'Agneau, Prince Albert

—

Chapons à la Strathmore

—

Jambon et Langue decoupes à l'Aspic
Salade Royale

—

Asperges, sauce Crème Mousseuse

—

Fraises, Duchesse Elizabeth
Paniers de Friandises

—

Dessert

—

Café

It was very common at the time to honor special persons or guests by naming dishes for them. Occasionally a new dish was created, but more often a minor alteration would be made to a classic dish—perhaps the garnish might be changed slightly, or a different herb substituted in a sauce. These alterations were no doubt noted in the chef's personal recipe book, but without being privy to their contents, it cannot be known for sure how most of them were made. The *Reine* (Queen) Mary was Mary of Teck, the mother of the groom, the Duchesse Elizabeth was the bride, and Prince Albert was the groom who became King George VI. His full name was Albert Frederick Arthur George, and he was always called "Bertie" by his family.

Recipes
~~~

Côtelletes d'Agneau Grilles
(Grilled Lamb Cutlets)

Cutlets of half-grown lamb are best for this dish, *not* chops. They must be very carefully trimmed of all gristle and superfluous fat and present a neat appearance.

Each cutlet should be dusted with salte and pepper, lightly brushed with olive oil, and grilled for about 2 1/2 minutes (according to size) on each side.

Sauce Albert

Wash, scrape and grate 3 oz. of horseradish. Put in a saucepan with one gill of *consommé blanc* and simmer gently for 15 minutes. Add a large wineglass of cream, 3/4 pint of béchamel sauce and a dessertspoonful of breadcrumbs. Stir and thicken over a brisk heat. Remove and force through a sieve with a wooden spoon. Replace in a saucepan and over a very gentle heat stir in the yolks of 2 eggs. Season to taste with a little salt and white pepper. Mix a coffeespoonful of fresh mustard with a dessertspoonful of vinegar and, before serving, stir into the sauce.

Asperges, Sauce Mousseuse

This dish consists of hot boiled asparagus with a warm, fluffy sauce [mousseuse means "frothy"]. The cooked vegetable should be well-drained and served at once—hot.

Sauce Mousseuse is made by carefully folding in one part of whipped cream into two parts of Sauce Hollandaise. This sauce must be carefully and completely mixed but *not* beaten.

Rene Roussin, Chef-de-cuisine to King George VI, *Royal Menus* (1960).

Consommé à la Windsor: see April 9.
Sauce Hollandaise: see April 14.

April 27

Soviet Leaders Luncheon
aboard the Train to Portsmouth, England, 1956

Nikita Khrushchev (1894–1971), first secretary of the Communist Party of the Soviet Union, and Marshal Nikolai Bulganin (1895–1975), the prime minister of the Soviet Union, visited Great Britain in 1956. The visit was

British Prime Minister Sir Anthony Eden shakes the hand of Russian Communist Party Chief Nikita Khrushchev at London's Victoria Station, April 18, 1956, as Soviet Premier Nikolai Bulganin, center, watches. (AP Photo)

intended to promote friendly relations and improve trade "without prejudicing British relations with any other countries" because, in the words of Bulganin, "We have to live together."

Ukrainian exiles in England did not feel so friendly towards their old enemy, however, and on April 18, the day of the Soviet leaders' arrival, they had staged a fast day in protest. Nevertheless, on the whole the visit went smoothly, and on April 27, accompanied by the Foreign Secretary, they left London amongst "expressions of warm goodwill." They traveled by train aboard the Simplon-Orient Express to Portsmouth where they were to rejoin the Russian cruiser *Ordzhonikidze* for their journey home. En route they enjoyed a fine, very British luncheon, accompanied by a selection of excellent wines and cigars.

WINE LIST	MENU
Cocktails, Sherry	Fruit Cup Cocktail
Pouilly Dry Reserve (Bouchard Aine)	Grilled Salmon from the Tay
	Roast Saddle of Southdown Lamb
Chateau Lafitte Rothschild 1950 (Chateau bottled)	Mint Jelly Redcurrant Preserve
	Parsley New Potatoes
	French Beans
Liebfraumilch Klosterdoctor 1952	Baby Carrots
	Norfolk Garden Peas
Bisquit Doubouché V.S.O.P. Cognac	Apple and Blackberry Pie
	Whipped Dairy Cream
Kummel Benedictine	
Drambuie	English Cheese Tray
Havana Cigars, Cigarettes	Coffee

Recipes

~~~

Mint has been a traditional accompaniment to lamb (in Britain) for a long time. The best known form is mint sauce, made with vinegar and sugar, but mint jelly is an alternative. It is made on a base of apple jelly. Adding chopped mint at the same time as the lemon juice in the following recipe will make mint jelly.

Apple Jelly

9 lbs. apples,
4 quarts water,
4 1/2 lbs. sugar,
the strained juice of 3 lemons.

Pare, core, and quarter the apples. Put them in a preserving-pan with the water, and boil together until the fruit is quite tender, and forms a smooth, but not thick, pulp. Strain this through a jelly-bag or fine sieve, and, should the juice not look clear, strain a second time.

Return the juice to the saucepan, and boil it rapidly for 20 minutes, add the sugar, and continue boiling for 15 minutes, stirring all the time, and removing carefully any scum which may arise from the sugar. Add the lemon juice, and boil for another 5 minutes, or until a little of the jelly, poured on a plate, will set.

Red or White Currant Jelly: see January 5.

April 28

Lunch at Sea
RMS *Aquitania*, 1921

The RMS *Aquitania*—the "Ship Beautiful" of the Cunard Line—regularly traveled the North Atlantic route between Southampton and New York during her working life.

April 28, 1921, was the last night of a westward journey; she was bringing 600 first-class passengers, 730 second-class passengers, and 1,724 third-class passengers to New York. The *Aquitania* carried many migrants to America during her career, and they made up a large component of the third-class passengers on this voyage. Also aboard were some celebrities, including the mayor of Dublin on a mission for White Cross Relief for Ireland, the singer John McCormack, the pugilist Frank Moran, Major Macklin of the last Shackleton expedition, Colonel D. B. Wentz "who has been shooting tigers in India," and "a prize Sealyham terrier belonging to Mrs. Welch." It is said that Mrs. Welch paid $2,000 extra for her passage in transferring ships to bring the dog two days earlier to Philadelphia.

The following luncheon was served aboard on this final day at sea. The menu does not state which class of passengers enjoyed this meal, but it was not likely to be first class. First class menus had far more extensive choices of more elegant dishes. The food at this luncheon was plain and hearty fare in the English style.

LUNCHEON

Kidney Soup

—

Haddock—Grenobloise

—

Macaroni—Italienne

—

Roast Leg of Mutton—Cumberland Sauce
Pig's Cheek and Cabbage

—

Garden Turnips
Jacket Potatoes

—

Rump Steak and Tomatoes—to order
French Fried Potatoes

—

COLD
Roast Beef   Boiled Ham   Leicester Pie
Pressed Beef   Oxford Brawn
Salad
Rice Pudding   Compote of Fruit and Custard
Cheese   Coffee

Recipes

~~~

Kidney Soup

1 1/2 lbs. ox kidney,	1 small carrot,
1 small turnip,	1 bouquet garni,
3 pints cold water,	1/2 teaspoonful salt,
1/2 lb. shin beef,	1 small onion,
1 1/2 oz. butter or dripping,	1 oz. flour,
1 oz. potato flour,	1/4 teaspoonful pepper,
few drops *browning*.	

Cut the kidney, meat, and vegetables into neat pieces. Toss meat and kidney in flour, pepper, and salt. Melt butter in pan. Brown meat, kidney, and onions, add water, bring to the boil, and remove scum. Add carrot, turnip, and bouquet garni, simmer three to three and a half hours, and strain through a wire sieve. Save some nice pieces of kidney, rub rest of kidney and meat through sieve, but not vegetables; return to pan. Mix potato flour with a little water, add to soup, and stir till boiling. Add pepper, salt, and browning. Pour over pieces of kidney in tureens.

Bouquet Garni

1 blade mace, sprig parsley,
1 bay leaf,
8 or 10 peppercorns.

Tie together in a muslin bag.
Miss H. H. Tuxford, *Miss Tuxford's Cookery for the Middle Classes* (ca. 1920s).

Cumberland Sauce

A sauce made by blanching the shredded zest of oranges and lemons in water, before cooking then in red wine or Port and melted red currant jelly. Served cold to accompany cold meat.

Oxford Brawn

Take the head of a young porker, lay it, after being split, in soak for 24 hours in salt and water; rub it well with common salt and a quarter of an ounce of salt-petre and a quarter of a pound of moist sugar; let it lie in the salting-trough three days; wash it well, and put it on to boil until the meat will come readily from the bones; cut up the meat into small pieces; season to your taste; put it all into a brawn tin, or any earthenware vessel with a flat bottom will answer as well; the tongue should be placed in the middle upright. It is much improved if four or five tongues can be had instead of one. When cold, turn it out.
The Cottage Gardener (London, 1851).

Gravy browning, as its name suggests, was added to gravies, soups, and sauces, to give the desirable rich dark color.

Gravy Browning

1/2 lb. Brown Sugar
1/2 pint Boiling Water

Heat an old iron pan on the fire; rub it with a little dripping. Put the sugar into it, let it melt, stir with an iron spoon till it is dark brown. Draw the pan to the side of the fire, add the water gradually, stirring all the time. Place the pan on the fire again, and stir till all is smooth. Let it cool, and pour it into a bottle, and it will keep for several months.
The Manchester School of Domestic Economy and Cookery, *Middle Class Cookery Book* (1903).

For Brawn, see also September 22.
Pig's cheek: given that this is served with cabbage, it was most likely the cured bacon type (see December 3).
Pressed Beef: see November 18.

April 29

Dinner for Ottoman Visitors
Mayor's Residence, Winchester, England, 1851

The steamer-of-war *Feiza Baari* arrived in England in late April 1851, carrying magnificent examples of Turkish craftsmanship for the Great Exhibition at the Crystal Palace in London. Also aboard, according to the *Daily News*, were a number of "distinguished persons from the Ottoman dominions," including Vice-Admiral Mustapha Pacha and Gemeledin Pacha. The distinguished visitors and ship's officers were invited to lunch by the mayor of Southampton at his country home "beautifully situated on a lofty eminence" outside Winchester.

> The dejeuner consisted of roast beef and chickens, roast lamb, galatine of veal, raised French pies, plover eggs, jellies and creams, ornamental pastry, lobster salads, plain salads, all kinds of cakes and confectionary, and of green and preserved fruits. Amongst the wines and beverages was sherbet.

Not many English cooks of the time would have been familiar with the dietary requirements of Muslim guests, but it appears that the one responsible rose to the culinary challenge and "the utmost care was taken to put nothing on the table forbidden by Mohammedan tastes or prejudices." In other words, the caterers were mindful of Islamic food laws which determine what food is halāl (lawful) and what is harām (unlawful). The determination is made on the basis of the type of food, the method of slaughter, and the handling of the meat after slaughter. The oriental guests' dietary requirements notwithstanding, this was a typical Victorian meal.

Although the sherbet was no doubt specifically chosen to honor the Turkish visitors, since such icy delights were already popular amongst the Victorian elite. A "sherbet," however, was not always a frozen treat. The word derives from the Turkish/Arabic word for "drink" and originally meant a sweetened beverage made from fruit and perfumed with exotic flower essences, musk, and ambergris. Early European travelers spread the good word on their return, and the wealthy who could maintain ice pits or caves were able to chill their sherbets on the hottest days. From this idea, as refrigeration technology made the idea accessible to all, came sherbet, sorbet, granita, and the violently colored "slushies" and "slurpies" sold today.

The plovers' eggs were a real delicacy on Victorian dinner tables. They were prized on account of the beautiful "whiteness" of the white and were usually presented hard boiled, in "nests" of moss or something similar. The season was short and most were imported from Holland—the first to arrive being traditionally reserved for Her Majesty's enjoyment.

Recipes

~~~

Persian and Turkish Sherbet

The method pursued by the Persians, Turks, &c. is to extract the fragrant, rich, and acidulated juices of the finest flowers and fruits, and make them, with the addition of sugar, into what we call fruit jellies or lozenges, which are dissolved in the purest spring water, and thus form the agreeable beverage denominated sherbet. For example, they evaporate the purified juice of citrons in a water bath with a slow fire, till it becomes of nearly the consistence of honey, melting, in the mean time, some finely powdered loaf sugar in a silver dish, and continually stirring it with a flat wooden spoon; when the sugar is very dry, they sprinkle over it, a little at a time, the prepared juice of citron; continuing to stir it till the whole has sufficient moisture to form a paste, which they make into lozenges, and keep in a dry and rather warm situation; in this way they prepare all the acid juices, such as barberries, lemons, gooseberries, &c.: with the less acid and more delicately flavoured fruits they proceed differently, only well heating the sugar in a silver dish, adding to it by degrees the fresh juice and stirring it constantly till a paste is formed. This must not be made into lozenges till perfectly dry, and they must be put into a box lined with paper, and kept in a dry place. They are variously prepared with orange-flowers, roses, &c. The Persians and Turks are said to prepare a favourite sherbet with violet vinegar, pomegranate-juice, and sugar formed into lozenges.

M. E. Rundell, *The New Family Receipt Book* (1837).

American Author Harriet Beecher Stowe
on Plovers' Eggs

At lunch at Stafford House, London, May 8, 1853.

Meanwhile the servants moved noiselessly to and fro, taking up the various articles on the table, and offering them to the guests in a peculiarly quiet manner. One of the dishes brought to me was a plover's nest, precisely as the plover made it, with five little blue speckled eggs in it. This mode of serving plover's eggs, as I understand it, is one of the fashions of the day, and has something quite sylvan and picturesque about it; but it looked so, for all the world, like a robin's nest that I used to watch out in our home orchard, that I had it not in my heart to profane the sanctity of the image by eating one of the eggs.

From *Sunny Memories of Foreign Lands* (1854).

Raised Pies: see October 25.

April 30

Harvard Club of Boston Dinner
Hotel Somerset, Boston, Massachusetts, 1913

The Harvard Club was founded in 1908 in spite of a vote against the idea by the Class Secretaries' Association, who were concerned that the timing was "inopportune" in view of the previous year's financial crash (the "Bankers' Panic"). Twenty-two men were the founders, but nine months later the membership stood at 786, and by the time of this dinner it was 3,500. The aim of the club was "to give effective expression to the Harvard spirit," which appeared to mean serving the university and the Boston community while having fun. Regular dinners were an integral part of the club's life, and until it moved into its own quarters in November 1913, they were usually held at the Hotel Somerset.

The menu for the dinner on April 30, 1913, was sufficiently different from the usual for the club that the newspapers saw fit to comment on the plans in advance.

Corned Beef for Harvard Club

The men of the Harvard Club of Boston are to sit down to corned beef and cabbage at the Hotel Somerset on Wednesday evening. Instead of the usual menu for such occasions, the members are invited to sit down to a New England Boiled Dinner.

The New York Times, April 27, 1913.

The New England boiled dinner is said to be a legacy of the Irish heritage of the region.

Boiled beef and cabbage is certainly associated with St. Patrick's day dinners, but the reality is that many Irish peasants would rarely, if ever, have seen a large piece of meat on their tables. There was a thriving corned meat industry in Ireland (centered around Cork) from the late-seventeenth to early-nineteenth centuries, but most of it was for export. "Corning" means salting—the term comes from the old English use of the word corn to mean "grains" of any type, including grains of salt. Corning was a vitally important way of preserving all types of meat in the days before refrigeration, particularly for long sea voyages.

The newspaper article specified that the dinner was to be "corned beef and cabbage," but as with many other "traditional" dishes of the "one-pot" type (such as the French *pot-au-feu*, see April 7), the exact components are the subject of constant debate. The author of the *White House Cook Book* (1887) wrote that a piece of salt pork was usually included, many recipes include ham instead of or as well as the beef, and the range of vegetables is only limited by their availability.

Recipes

~~~

A New England Boiled Dinner

Select a thick piece of corned beef from the round, weighing about six pounds; wash it in cold water, and put it over the fire in a large pot, with sufficient cold water to cover it three or four inches; set the pot where its contents will slowly reach the boiling-point, and boil very gently for four hours from the time it is first placed on the fire. After the meat is put to cook, wash four large beets very carefully, without breaking the skin or cutting off the stalks or roots, and put them over the fire to boil in another pot, in plenty of actually boiling water. Then peel four large white turnips and one large yellow turnip; cut the latter in four pieces; scrape four carrots and four parsneps; peel a dozen medium-sized pota- toes; trim and wash a firm head of white cabbage, cut its stalk out without breaking the leaves apart, and bind it with broad tape to keep it whole while cooking. As fast as the vegetables are prepared, lay them in plenty of cold water until they are needed for cooking. If onions are used, they should be boiled in a separate saucepan. Some families like a dish of boiled squash mashed with pep- per, salt, and butter, served as part of a boiled dinner; in the fall and winter, pumpkin is often used like the squash.

When the meat begins to boil, the scum which rises to the surface of the pot- liquor should be carefully skimmed off, and a medium-sized red or green pepper put into the pot. As already indicated, the pot must be large enough to hold both meat and vegetables; the vegetables, except the beets and onions, are to be added to the meat in proper succession, allowing sufficient time for each kind to cook. The carrots, parsneps, and turnips will boil in about two hours; the cab- bage and onions, in one hour; the potatoes, squash, and pumpkin, in about half an hour. The beets will boil in from two to four hours, according to their size; they are to be taken up when tender, their skins are to be rubbed off with a wet towel, and then they are to be sliced and covered with vinegar. They are gen- erally served cold; but if they are liked hot, they can be heated at dinner-time, with a little salt, pepper, and butter. When the boiled dinner is cooked, the meat is placed in the middle of a large platter, and the vegetables, with the exception of those specified for separate serving, are arranged around it. A piece of salt pork is sometimes boiled with the beef.

Juliet Corson, *Miss Corson's Practical American Cookery* (1886).

May

May 1

Elvis Aaron Presley (1935–1977), the "King of Rock 'n' Roll," married Priscilla Ann Wagner (b. 1945) on May 1, 1967. Amongst the hundred or so guests at the wedding breakfast at the Aladdin Hotel in Las Vegas was the State Supreme Court Justice David Zenoff, who had performed the ceremony.

Ham
Eggs
Southern Fried chicken
Oysters Rockefeller
Roast Suckling Pig
Poached and Candied Salmon
Lobster
Eggs Minette
Champagne

In addition there was, of course, a wedding cake. It was a white angel food cake decorated with pink hearts.

The menu is a rather strange mix of elegant dishes that would have been at home on any fine dinner table, such as the oysters Rockefeller and poached salmon, and hearty comfort food such as the southern fried chicken—the latter no doubt included because of Elvis's Mississippi origins.

The exact, original recipe for oysters Rockefeller is one of culinary history's best-kept secrets. The dish was invented by Jules Alciatore of the famous New Orleans restaurant *Antoine's* and named for the enormously wealthy John D. Rockefeller. Many attempts at kitchen espionage and laboratory analysis have failed to uncover the secret, and amongst the many supposed "authentic" versions of the dish the only consistent ingredient is the oyster. Alciatore's son Roy did supply a recipe that contained spinach to Life magazine's *The Picture Cookbook*, but there is considerable doubt amongst aficionados of the real thing that spinach is an original ingredient. Craig Claiborne in his *New York Times Cookbook* gave two versions, both containing

Elvis and Priscilla at their wedding. (AP Photo)

watercress, scallions, parsley, chopped fennel, garlic, butter, bread crumbs, and Pernod, one also having lettuce, Worcestershire sauce, Tabasco, and anchovy paste.

As with so many eponymous dishes, there are a variety of stories to explain the name. One story is that it was called "Rockefeller" to indicate the richness of the ingredients, or alternatively that the color of the sauce represents the greenback dollar. Another story says that when Alciatore first prepared it, he said, "That's a dish good enough for Rockefeller." A more cynical (or ironic) tale says that Alciatore created the dish from what was left over in the kitchen at the time—and found he had a winner on his hands.

Recipes
~~~

Oysters Rockefeller

36 fresh oysters on the half shell
6 tablespoons butter
6 tablespoons finely minced raw spinach
3 tablespoons minced onion
3 tablespoons minced parsley
5 tablespoons bread crumbs
Tabasco sauce to taste
1/2 teaspoon Herbsaint, or substitute Pernod
1/2 teaspoon salt

Melt the butter in a saucepan. Add all the ingredients except the oysters. Cook, constantly stirring for 15 minutes. Press the mixture through a sieve or a food mill. Cool. Line six pie tins with rock salt. Set 6 oysters in the rock salt on each pie tin. Divide the topping into 36 equal portions. Place one portion on each oyster. Broil until topping is brown. Serves 6.

Life Magazine, *Picture Cookbook* (1958).

Fried Chicken

Cut the chicken up, separating every joint, and wash clean. Salt and pepper it, and roll into flour well. Have your fat very hot, and drop the pieces into it, and let them cook brown. The chicken is done when the fork passes easily into it. After the chicken is all cooked, leave a little of the hot fat in the skillet; then take a tablespoonful of dry flour and brown it in the fat, stirring it around, then pour water in and stir till the gravy is as thin as soup.

Abby Fisher, *What Mrs. Fisher Knows about Old Southern Cooking* (San Francisco, 1881).

Angel (food) Cake: see September 21.

May 2

Dinner at the Sanitarium
Battle Creek, Michigan, 1900

John Harvey Kellogg (1852–1943) became superintendent of the Seventh Day Adventist Church's Battle Creek Sanitarium in 1876. He was a health and nutrition reformer, and many of his ideas on nutrition are reflected in the following example of the daily offerings in the sanitarium.

MENU	FERMENTE[D] BREADS.
	Coarse Graham Bread Fine Graham Bread
DINNER.	White Bread Zweiback
Tuesday, May 2 1900	UNFERMENTED BREADS.
SOUPS.	Toasted Whole-wheat Wafers
Scotch Pea Fruit	Beaten Biscuits Browned Granose Biscuit
VEGETABLES.	Graham Crackers Passover Bread
Baked Potatoes Mashed Beans	White Bread Graham Bread
Asparagus	
Escalloped Tomatoes	ENTREES.

SALADS.		Boiled Protose　Stewed Nuttolene
		with Potato
Protose		NUT FOODS.
GRAINS.		Nuttose C　Nuttola Nutts
		Nuttolene
Gran Nuts　Granola		Protose
Crystal Wheat　Pearl Barley		COOKED FRUITS.
Wheatose Mould with Grape Sauce		Prune Marmalade　Stewed Apples
Dry Gluten		Strawberries
LIQUID FOODS.		FRESH FRUIT.
Vegetable Broth　Caramel Cereal		Oranges
Boiled Milk　Cream		DESSERT.
Vegetable Cream　Gluten Fruit Gruel		*Coconut Cornstarch Pudding*

ARTICLES PREPARED TO ORDER.

Carbon Crackers　Gluten Biscuit No. 1
Gluten Wafers　Dyspeptic Wafers
Pop Corn　Peas Puree

Junket　Milk Custard　Kumyss
Butter Milk　Milk with Lime Water

Poached Yolks of Eggs　Egg Nogg
Floated Eggs
Tomato Toast
Prune Toast　Grape Toast
Egg Toast　*Snowflake Toast*　Cream Toast

The following will be served by special
order (a moderate charge being made):
Bromose　Malted Nuts　Ambrosia
Maltol　Kumyzoon

Articles, the names of which are printed in italics, contain milk, but will be
served without milk if so ordered. Food, Dishes, Spoons, etc., must not be taken
from the Dining Room. A charge will be made for articles taken in violation of
this rule. Patients ordering meals in rooms should write the name and room
number below.

Mr. . . . . ROOM No. . . . .

Kellogg advocated vegetarianism, fresh air, and exercise as the basis for a
healthy life. It is difficult to argue with these principles today, and they are

Battle Creek Sanitarium. Courtesy of Library of Congress.

increasingly backed up by science. Some of his other ideas, however, seem very outlandish, and a lot less likely to attract modern adherents. He was adamant about the dangers of constipation (which caused "auto-intoxication" he said), and the safest remedy was to start every day with an enema—a practice he apparently followed himself. He also preached the advantages of sexual abstinence, and purportedly his own marriage was celibate.

This menu also demonstrates a nineteenth-century phenomenon—the beginnings of the health food "industry." Kellogg and some of his contemporaries began to develop early meat analogues to encourage adherence to the vegetarian regime in a population reared to believe meat was the basis of every meal. At this time the value of soy beans (see August 17) as a base for meatless meals was not well known, and most of the manufactured substitutes were based on grains and cereals. The Bromose, Protose, Wheatose, and Maltol on this menu are all examples of these "health" foods, as was the "Kumyzoon"—Kellogg's nonalcoholic substitute for kumiss, the supposedly longevity-giving Mongolian drink made from fermented mare's milk.

Recipes

~~~

Ella Eaton Kellogg, the wife of John Harvey Kellogg, assisted him in his health reform work. When it became clear that his patients found his recommended dietary regime most unpalatable, she took it upon herself to learn cookery and find more inviting ways to prepare wholesome food. The recipes below are from her book, *Science in the Kitchen,* published in 1893.

Grape Toast

Stem well-ripened grapes, wash well, and scald without water in a double boiler until broken; rub through a colander to remove sends and skins, and when cool, sweeten to taste. If the toast is desired for breakfast, the grapes should be prepared the day previous. Soften the toast in hot cream, as previously directed, and pack in a tureen. Heat the prepared grapes and serve, pouring a small quantity over each slice of toast. Canned grapes may be used instead of fresh ones, if desired.

Snowflake Toast

Heat to boiling a quart of milk to which a half cup of cream and a little salt have been added. Thicken with a tablespoonful of flour rubbed smooth in a little cold milk. Have ready the whites of two eggs beaten to a stiff froth; and when the sauce is well cooked, turn a cupful of it on the beaten egg, stirring well meanwhile so that it will form a light, frothy mixture, to which add the remainder of the sauce. If the sauce is not sufficiently hot to coagulate the albumen, it may be heated again almost to the boiling point, but should not be allowed to boil. The sauce should be of a light, frothy consistency throughout. Serve as dressing on nicely moistened slices of zwieback.

Graham Bread: see February 5.

May 3

Dilettante Society Dinner
Grand Hotel, Trafalgar Square, London, England, 1891

The Dilettante Society was founded in England in about 1732. It was composed of "noblemen and gentlemen" wealthy enough to have done the Grand Tour of Europe and to have returned with a passion for fine and ancient art. It began as a dining club, with connotations of frivolity and heavy drinking, but however keen the members were to enjoy a good dinner, they were also connoisseurs of fine art, and wealthy enough to indulge their interest. The society ultimately did a great deal to foster the study of ancient art, and many of the classical antiquities stored in the British Museum are there as a result of its work.

MENU DU DINER.

VINS.	HORS D'ŒUVRE.

HORS D'ŒUVRE.

Salade d'Anchois.

POTAGES.

Fine Dry Amontillado.

Tortue Claire.

Crème à l' Ivoire.

POISSONS.

Leibfraumilch.

Turbot, sauce Hollandaise.

Éperlans, sauce Remoulade.

ENTREES.

Pâtés à la Windsor.

Deutz & Geldermann, 1884.

Soufflés de Volaille à la Strasbourgeoise

G. H. Mumm, 1884.

Côtelletes d'Agneau aux Concombres.

GROSSES PIECES.

Filets de Bœuf Garnie.

Jambon au Champagne.

Légumes Divers.

—

Marrow Bones.

ROTI.

Perdreaux Bardés

ENTREMETS.

Asperges en Branches.

Otard's Old Liqueur Brandy.

Abricots en Bellevue.

Gâteaux Napolitains.

Sandemann's Port, 1873.

RELEVE.

Croûtes de Harengs à la Diable.

Château Calon Segur, 1874.

DESSERTS.

Johannis Brunnen Water.

Glace à la Cardinal.

Petits Fours.   Fruits Assortis.

The society had a regular dinner meeting on the first Sunday of the month. The venue changed over the decades and in 1891 was in the elegant Grand Hotel in Trafalgar Square.

It would be expected that the dilettantes would be connoisseurs of fine food, and in the Victorian era this meant a dinner exactly like this. All of the dishes are named in French, even the very English Windsor pies—with the rather odd exception of the marrow bones. Marrow bones were very popular as a small savory dish, and it is said that they were a regular favorite of Queen Victoria. The Victorians had huge empty tables to fill as the old method of *service à la française* (all the dishes on the table at once, see January 17) gave way to *service à la russe* (dishes served sequentially). The Victorians also loved ornate decoration and nicknacks. Both of these conditions contributed to the development of a huge range of tableware that was lined up impressively at place settings. There was a piece of cutlery for everything—asparagus forks, bacon forks, fish knives, and marrow spoons with long handles and slender bowls for retrieving the fatty tasty contents of the hollow bones.

Recipes

~~~

Marrow Bones (to Boil)

2 marrow-bones,
flour and
water paste.

Saw the bones in half, and the ends of the bones even, so that they can stand upright. Put a piece of flour and water paste very carefully over the ends of each, that the marrow may not boil out. Tie each bone up tightly in a very clean cloth, put it (upright if possible) into a saucepan of boiling water, and keep the water boiling until the bones are cooked. Take off the cloths, remove the paste, and serve the bones, standing upright, on a hot napkin, garnished with fresh parsley.

Send some neat pieces of hot toast, 1/2 of an inch in thickness, to table with them.

Ethel S. Meyer, *A Practical Dictionary of Cookery: 1200 Tested Recipes* (London, 1898).

"Pâtés" on an English menu are now "crustless"pies, but the word in French still references pastry. Small mutton pies were a favorite of the royal household in the nineteenth century, and "Windsor Pies" appear on many menus of the time.

Mutton Pies à la Windsor

Cut the lean part of a pound of loin of mutton into very small squares, season this with chopped mushrooms, parsley, and shalot, pepper and salt, and a little brown sauce or gravy, of any kind most convenient; mix altogether in a basin.

Next, line some tartlet or patty-pans with short paste made without sugar; fill these with some of the prepared mince; cover them over with a top, press and pinch them round the edge; egg them over; place a stamped ornament on the top of the patties; make a very small hole in the centre for ventilation, to prevent their bursting while baking; push them in the oven on a baking-sheet for about twenty minutes; and when done, dish them on a napkin and send to table.
Charles Elmé Francatelli, *The Cook's Guide* (London, 1863).

Hollandaise Sauce: see April 14.
Petits Fours: see November 14.

May 4

Kosher Banquet
London, England, 1907

As the twentieth century progressed Britain became increasingly protective of its Empire, and for economic as well as nationalistic reasons, there were many campaigns to promote the produce of its various dominions (see May 24). In May 1907 a Colonial Conference was held in London to discuss those very issues. A great opportunity serendipitously presented itself for a mutual celebration and promotion when the event coincided with the arrival of the first consignment of colonial meat that was approved for sale by the London Jewish Ecclesiastical Board.

Until this time the London Beth Din (the Rabbinical court) had "refused to allow the sale even of those tinned meats which are prepared in Australia under the supervision of the Jewish authorities there" (*Penny Illustrated*, May 4, 1907). The approval, when it came, was greatly welcomed as "London Jews ... have been paying higher prices for meat than their Gentile neighbours." Messrs. F. Barnett and Co. (who had obtained the concession) invited the Colonial premiers to a kosher banquet to demonstrate the newly sanctioned products. The newspapers reported the menu with interest, although the response of the Colonial premiers to the dinner was not noted.

Olives, smoked salmon, anchovies.
"Frimsel" (a kind of vermicelli, home made).
Clear mock turtle (from Australian stock).
Boiled salmon, new potatoes, Indian sauce.
Whitebait.
Quails.
Australian sweetbreads.
Forequarter lamb (Australian).
Australian vegetables.
Surrey fowls.
Sweets.
Dessert (Colonial fruit).
Coffee.
Australian wines.

It is certain that the dishes on this menu were prepared according to the rules of *kashrut* (see July 11). Standard methods of preparation of well-known dishes were adapted by Jewish cooks to ensure that they were kosher. This meant, for example, that at any meal at which meat was to be consumed, no milk products could be used. Oil or chicken fat, not butter, was used for frying, and milk- and cheese-based sauces were avoided.

"Sweetbreads" appeared often on nineteenth- and early-twentieth-century dinner tables. They are not made from sweet yeast bread dough as is commonly believed, but are in fact offal. Sweetbreads consist of the pancreas or the thymus (the more desirable) glands of a young animal and were esteemed a great delicacy. They have gone the way of much offal and are not easy to obtain nowadays, apart from occasionally in restaurants trying to stay ahead of the crowd.

The Australian vegetables are a puzzle. It is difficult to guess what these might have been, given the long sea voyage they undertook. Presumably, like the meat, they had been frozen.

Recipes

~~~

Croquettes are balls or cylinders of finely chopped or minced meat, fish, or vegetables held together with a thickened white sauce, rolled in bread crumbs and deep fried. The basic mixture is essentially the same as for kromeskies (see August 4), which are usually dipped in batter before frying. Like kromeskies, they can be adapted to many ingredients. A kosher version cannot be cooked in butter, as are the croquettes in the recipe given for August 21, as, according to the rules of *kashrut*, dairy products cannot be included at the same meal as meat. Sweetbreads are blanched (briefly pre-boiled) before being prepared in any dish.

This recipe is based on one for chicken croquettes.

Sweetbread Croquettes

Cook one-half tablespoon of flour in one tablespoon chicken-fat, add one-half cup of soup stock gradually, and one-half teaspoon each of onion juice, lemon juice, salt, and one-quarter teaspoon of pepper, one and one-half cups of veal or chicken, chopped very fine, one pair of brains which have been boiled, mix these well, remove from the fire and add one well-beaten egg. Turn this mixture out on a flat dish and place in ice-box to cool. Then roll into small cones, dip in beaten egg, roll again in powdered bread or cracker crumbs and drop them into boiling fat, fry until a delicate brown.

To make the sweetbread version:

Cut the boiled sweetbreads into small dice with a silver knife. Mix with mushrooms, using half the quantity of mushrooms that you have of sweetbreads. Use two eggs in the sauce.

Florence Greenbaum, *International Jewish Cook Book* (New York, 1919).

The instruction to prepare the soup on Friday is in accordance with the Jewish law in relation to ceasing ''work'' on Shabbat (Sabbath), which is Saturday (begins at nightfall on Friday night).

Frimsel Soup

Make this soup on Friday.

Put into a saucepan five pounds of beef brisket, a knuckle of veal, four quarts of water, one root each of parsley and celery, with the leaves attached, one onion, and a teaspoonful of mixed ginger, mace, saffron, and pepper tied in a bit of cloth: boil for three hours slowly, skimming off any scum that may rise: take up the meat, strain the soup, and put it in an earthen pot to stand over night. Just before dinner the next day, take off all the fat, put it in a saucepan over the fire, add four ounces of frimsels or vermicelli, and boil it up; serve as soon as the vermicelli is tender.

New York Times, February 23, 1896.

Whitebait: see August 14.
Mock Turtle: see July 4.

May 5

''May Dinner''
Simpson's on the Strand, London, England, 1932

The 1920s and 1930s were a time of burgeoning interest in food in England. The Wine and Food Society began in 1933, with the aim of raising both awareness and standards in the area of wining and dining (see January 15). The Folk Cookery Association began a few years earlier with a more regional and historic perspective. Its main aim was to ''attempt to capture the charm of England's cookery before it is completely crushed out of existence.''

The association held regular dinners at Simpson's on the Strand, a famous bastion of English cuisine since 1828. On the occasion of their ''May Dinner'' they were brave enough (or confident enough) to invite the French Ambassador Aimé de Fleuriau as guest of honor.

Farmers' soup
Turbot with lobster sauce   Kentish chicken pudding
Cornish cauliflower
New potatoes
Lemon snow and cherry syllabub
Marrow on toast
Potted Stilton cheese and West Riding riddle bread

The ambassador was impressed, or at least gracious. His reply to the inevitable question of how he enjoyed his dinner was most diplomatic. ''An excellent dinner!'' he exclaimed, to great applause. ''In England I prefer to have a typical English dinner rather than an imitation French one. Every country should make the most of its own products.''

The Folk Cookery Association certainly managed a meal representative of English regional food. Every country and county has its own version of ``farmers' soup,'' but in addition to the named dishes from Kent, Cornwall, and the West Riding of Yorkshire, the lemon snow and cherry syllabub were specifically said to be from Sussex and Hampshire. The stilton cheese is an ancient blue cheese which has been made in the Midlands area of England for centuries, although it can only now be legally designated as such if it comes from specially licensed dairies in three counties—Derbyshire, Leicestershire, and Nottinghamshire. Marrow on toast (see May 3) was Queen Victoria's favorite savory, which she had daily.

``Syllabub'' is a frothy wine and milk (or cream) dish, somewhere between a beverage and a sauce, and one of the oldest sweet treats enjoyed by those who had easy access to cows. Originally, the cow was milked directly into the wine—the height and pressure of the jet of milk providing the ``froth.'' Cows were kept in royal parks for this specific purpose, so that one could be brought to the kitchen door, should a royal person call for a syllabub.

Recipes
~~~

Chicken Pudding

A plump chicken or two, as required, a slice of ham, suet crust (see June 3).

Empty the crop, take out the inside, and divide the chickens into neat pieces. Line a pudding basin with suet crust , arrange the pieces of chicken neatly inside, interspersed with the ham, which has also been neatly divided. Season with pepper and salt, and pour over all a little strong gravy, made of the chicken giblets. Cover in the usual way. The addition of one or two sheep's kidneys will greatly improve this dish, as will also a few mushrooms, or, when they are in season, a few oysters. The pudding should be long and gently boiled.

Phillis Brown, *A Year's Cookery* (London, 1879).

Lemon Snow Pudding

(A pretty dish for a juvenile party.)

Pour a pint of cold water over an ounce of isinglass or gelatine. Let it soak for half an hour, then put it into a saucepan over the fire, with three-quarters of a pound of loaf sugar, and the thin rind and strained juice of two fresh lemons. Simmer gently, stirring all the time, until the isinglass is dissolved; then pour it out, and put it aside until it is cold and beginning to set. Stir in the whites of three well-beaten eggs, and whisk all together briskly till it stiffens and assumes the appearance of snow, then pile lightly in a glass dish, and make it look as rocky as possible.

Cassell's Dictionary of Cookery (London, ca. 1870s).

The version of syllabub made by the association was from "cream and sherry flavoured with essence of cherries." This basic version only requires the addition of a little cherry liqueur instead of brandy.

Syllabub

1 pint of sherry or white wine,
1/2 grated nutmeg,
sugar to taste,
1 1/2 pints of milk.

Put the wine into a bowl with the grated nutmeg and plenty of pounded sugar, and milk into it the above proportion of milk frothed up. Clouted cream may be laid on the top, with pounded cinnamon or nutmeg and sugar, and a little brandy may be added to the wine before the milk is put in. In some counties, cider is substituted for the wine; when this is used, brandy must always be added. Warm milk may be poured on from a spouted jug or teapot, but it must be held very high.

Isabella Beeton, *Beeton's Book of Household Management* (1861).

Riddle Bread

The *riddle-bread*, used in Lancashire and Yorkshire, is prepared from oat-meal, leavened by a little sourdough, preserved in the kneading trough from one baking to another. The meal and water are, in this case, mixed thin, and left all night to ferment. Next morning, the dough is poured upon a board, cut by furrows into squares. By a motion similar to riddling corn, the dough is made to expand—hence the name of *riddle-bread*. Bread thus made is spread upon a *cratch*, or a frame of wood, crossed with strings. Here the bread becomes very hard, and will keep almost any length of time. Before eating, it is usually toasted by the fire; and, when well buttered, is remarkably pleasant. A gentleman in Lancashire observes, that the proper quantity of butter, is, the same thickness as the bread.

John Briggs, *The Remains of John Briggs* (1825).

Marrow on Toast: see May 3.

May 6

Breakfast at Sea
SS *Prussian*, 1875

The SS *Prussian* of the Allan Line regularly traveled the Liverpool to Quebec route in the 1870s, carrying migrants to Canada. They came from Europe, Russia, and Great Britain and included many Mennonites looking for a better life free from persecution, and many "child emigrants," who had no choice in the matter.

It was hearty breakfast fare in the days before processed breakfast cereals (see May 2).

BREAKFAST.

Spatchcock & Mushrooms
Fried Ham & Eggs
Fried Potatoes
Mutton Chops
Minced Collops
Dry Hash
Yarmouth Bloaters
Fried Tripe & Onions
Devilled Kidneys
Beef Steak & Onions
Porridge

Porridge and Ham and Eggs are common on modern breakfast menus, but the other dishes are either more familiar at other meals such as the spatchcock dish (now eaten at dinner) or not familiar at all. Tripe is offal, and offal is out of fashion or downright repugnant to many modern tastes. It is one of two cow stomachs: *plain tripe* is from the first stomach, *honeycomb tripe* is from the second. Tripe was one of the staple foods for poor working folk for centuries and used to be sold ready cooked from shops and street sellers—the takeout of the nineteenth century.

Recipes

~~~

Tripe must be thoroughly and meticulously cleaned before use and was often sold partly "dressed," that is, pre-boiled. *Beeton's Household Manual* (1861) gives a general recipe for tripe, with several variations including fried. However it was cooked, tripe was almost always served with plenty of onions. Beeton also gives instructions for preparing bloaters.

To Dress Tripe

Tripe,
onion sauce,
milk
and water.

Ascertain that the tripe is quite fresh, and have it cleaned and dressed. Cut away the coarsest fat, and boil it in equal proportions of milk and water for 3/4 hour. Should the tripe be entirely undressed, more than double that time should be allowed for it. Have ready some onion sauce, dish the tripe, smother it with the sauce, and the remainder send to table in a tureen.

Note—Tripe may be dressed in a variety of ways: it may be cut in pieces and fried in batter, stewed in gravy with mushrooms, or cut into collops, sprinkled with minced onion and savoury herbs, and fried a nice brown in clarified butter.

White Onion Sauce

9 large onions,
or 12 middling-sized ones,
1 pint of melted butter made with milk,
1/2 teaspoonful of salt, or rather more.

Peel the onions and put them into water to which a little salt has been added, to preserve their whiteness, and let them remain for 1/4 hour. Then put them in a stewpan, cover them with water, and let them boil until tender, and, if the onions should be very strong, change the water after they have been boiling for 1/4 hour. Drain them thoroughly, chop them, and rub them through a tammy or sieve. Make 1 pint of melted butter [a sauce, see below] and when that boils, put in the onions, with a seasoning of salt; stir it till it simmers, when it will be ready to serve. If these directions are carefully attended to, this onion sauce will be delicious.

Melted Butter Made with Milk

1 teaspoonful of flour,
2 oz. butter,
1/3 pint of milk,
a few grains of salt.

Mix the butter and flour smoothly together on a plate, put it into a lined saucepan, and pour in the milk. Keep stirring it—one way—over a sharp fire; let it boil quickly for a minute or two, and it is ready to serve. This is a very good foundation for onion, lobster, or oyster sauce: using milk instead of water makes it look so much whiter and more delicate.

Red Herrings,
or Yarmouth Bloaters

The best way to cook these is to make incisions in the skin across the fish, because they do not then require to be so long on the fire, and will be far better than when cut open. The hard roe makes a nice relish by pounding it in a mortar, with a little anchovy, and spreading it on toast. If very dry, soak in warm water 1 hour before dressing.

The Several Types of Herrings

Herring, like cod (see March 11) was a vital commodity in previous times. Both were useful on "fast" days, and as they could be preserved they could be stored against times of need and for long voyages. Unlike cod, herring is too oily to air-dry, so it has to be smoke dried and salted. The various methods produce slightly different products.

Bloater: a whole herring, lightly salted and smoked, must be eaten within a couple of days. Those from Yarmouth, England, were particularly prized.

Kipper: the fish is split, gutted, and smoked.

Buckling: the fish is gutted, beheaded, salted, and hot smoked so that it is also "cooked."

White herring: the fish is salted but not smoked.

Red herring: the fish is heavily salted and smoked for a long period, thus giving it a long shelf life. This process produces a red color and a spectacularly strong smell—enough to put any hunting animal off any scent, giving the metaphorical use of the phrase.

May 7

Officers' Luncheon
HT *Queen Mary*, 1940

The magnificent Cunard ocean liner *Queen Mary* was, like many other luxurious ships, commandeered for war service in 1939. She was sent to Sydney, Australia, to be fitted out as a troopship and sailed out of there on May 4, 1940, as part of Australian Troop Convoy US3. Alongside the *Queen Mary* were other newly converted troopships—the *Aquitania*, *Empress of Japan*, *Empress of Britain*, *Mauretania*, and *Andes*, escorted by the *Canberra*, *Perth*, and *Leander*.

The *Queen Mary*, with 5,000 troops aboard, was still in Australian waters between Sydney and Fremantle, en route to the Clyde (a major shipbuilding center in Scotland) via Cape Town, South Africa, when the officers sat down to the following luncheon on May 7.

Hors d'Œuvre Varies

Consomme Fermiere   Potage Egyptienne

Broiled Whitefish, Claudine
Noodles, Sicilienne
Ox Tail, Saute, Printaniere

Silverside of Corned Beef, Garni
Creamed Spinach   Mashed Turnips
Baked Jacket, Puree and French Fried Potatoes

TO ORDER FROM THE GRILL:
Sirloin Steak and Onions

COLD BUFFET
Sirloin of Beef   Roast Lamb   Leicester Brawn
Bologna Sausage   Ox Tongue
Boiled Ham   Pressed Beef

SALADS
Sliced Tomato   Lettuce   Potato
French Dressing

Compote of Rhubarb and Custard
Ice Cream and Wafers
Cheese   Coffee

Queen Mary leaving New York Harbor, 1940. (AP Photo)

The officers presumably dined in the two-story high first-class dining room (the grand salon), but wherever they ate it was likely a far more luxurious setting than usual for the military men and army cooks. The menu could have been a hotel menu of the time. There is some residual French in the *consommé* and *potage* instead of "soup," and a couple of traditional sauces or garnishes such as the Printanière and Sicilienne, but most of the dishes were recognizable, regular fare.

Recipes

~~~

Australians are the greatest consumers of lamb in the world, and corned beef (i.e. salted or pickled beef) is also popular. Silverside is the cut known in the United States as "bottom round"—so called because of the silvery strip of "skin" along one side.

Boiled Round (or Silverside) of Beef

After taking the meat out of the pickle (in which it should have been lying for about ten days), wash off the salt, skewer it up into a nice round shape, and bind it round firmly with tape, or buy it ready for cooking. As this is not a very fat part of the beef, it is best to skewer a piece of fat in as well.

When the meat is well bound up, put it into a saucepan with cold water to cover, and bring it to the boil. Remove the scum as it rises. The skimming should be carefully attended to, as the appearance of the joint will be much spoiled if it is neglected. When the meat comes to the boil, draw the pan to one side and let it simmer gently for 3 hours. Two hours before it is done, put in the carrots and turnips, previously scraped and peeled and cut into convenient pieces. If the vegetables are young, they will not require so long a time to cook.

When the meat is done, take it up, remove the tape and skewers.

NOTE: if wanted to serve cold, return joint to the pan containing liquor and leave till cold.

Egg Custard

3 yolks of eggs
2 oz. castor sugar
1 pint milk
pinch of salt
1/2 teaspoonful Vanilla Essence

Bring the milk to boiling point in a saucepan or in the top of a double boiler. Beat the egg yolks slightly in a basin. Stir in the sugar and salt, then pour a tablespoon or tow of the milk into the yolks, stirring quickly. Pour the diluted yolks into the milk, stirring constantly, and keep stirring until the mixture thickens and coats the back of a spoon.

New Standard Cookery Illustrated (London, 1933).

Lamb, roast: see April 17.
Pressed Beef: see February 22.
Brawn: see April 28.

May 8

VE Day Dinner
Simpson's-in-the-Strand, London, England, 1945

Victory in Europe Day (VE Day) was declared on May 8, 1945. The war against the Japanese in the Pacific was not to end for several months (see August 16, VJ Day), but the mood in Britain and Europe was euphoric. Many restaurants quickly put together special menus for the day, in spite of the restrictions of rationing. The famous London restaurant Simpson's-in-the-Strand made no obvious patriotic fuss and saw no need to modify the names of its dishes but got quietly on with serving traditional English food.

Authorised House Charge	*Simpson's*	Authorised Charge for
1/6	in-the-Strand	Food 5/-
Empire Port		3/6
per glass		

Muscat Wine 3/6
per glass
Fine Pale Brandy 4/-
per measure

Bill of Fare for the Day
at 5/-

—

Hors d'Œuvre

—

Real Turtle Soup

—

*Roast Loin of Pork and Apple Sauce
*Jugged Hare and Red Wine Sauce
*Cold Roast Turkey with Sausages and Salad
*Stewed Tripe with Peas and Onion Sauce
*Cold Pressed Beef and Salad
Mushroom Omelette and Peas
*Minced Ham with Peas, Mushrooms, and Piquante Sauce
*Salmon Salad and Mayonnaise Sauce

—

Boiled Potatoes   Peas
Roast Potatoes   Cabbage

—

Vanilla Ice   Tipsy Cake
Stewed Apples and Chocolate Sauce
Stewed Damsons and Custard
Stewed Cherries and Custard

—

Welsh Rarebit with Mushrooms on

—

Tea or Coffee 1/-

———

MEALS IN ESTABLISHMENTS ORDER, 1942

By the terms of this Order, it is not permissible to serve or consume more than three
courses at any one meal; nor may any person have at a meal more than one dish marked *
and one marked #, or alternatively, two dishes marked #. Dishes unmarked may
be ordered instead of those marked, or in addition to them, provided that the limit of
three courses is not exceeded, nor the maximum permitted price.

Simpson's-in-the-Strand is an English institution. It has been serving resolutely English food since it opened (as the Grand Cigar Divan) in 1828. After 1848 it was Simpson's Grand Divan Tavern, and it acquired its current name when it reopened in 1904 after extensive renovations. In the mid-nineteenth century Simpson's began the tradition of carving gigantic roasts from trolleys wheeled to tableside. Roasts are still the specialty of Simpson's and they are still served in this way. The chef and management also around this time took a stand against the use of the French language on menus—and specifically against the use of the word "menu" itself. To this day the fare at the restaurant is according to the old English term of "Bill of Fare."

The reminder to patrons of the requirements of the Meals in Establishments Order of 1942 is in reference to the wartime regulations that applied to restaurants and other places serving food. The order was part of the larger picture of rationing, which did not end with the end of the war, but continued in part for another 13 years in Britain (see April 11).

Recipes

~~~

"Jugged" means stewed slowly for a long time in a sealed container—originally an earthenware jug. It is an ancient method of cooking and is the traditional way to prepare hare. Often some of the animal's blood is added, making it a dish that is more properly called a *civet*. Of course, in order to use the blood, the animal must be freshly killed, which is only possible if one can be there at the hunt, or obtain them soon after from the hunter! The first recorded recipe for jugged hare is in Hannah Glasse's *The Art of Cookery*, published in 1747 (see recipe below). Mrs. Glasse does not include the hare's blood, she would no doubt have thought it too Frenchified. In the preface of her book she—like the proprietors of Simpsons-in-the-Strand a century later—took a stand against what she saw as the most undesirable Frenchification of English food. She is quite vehement in her denunciation of the French method of cooking, saying,

> . . . but if gentlemen will have French cooks, they must pay for French tricks.
>
> A Frenchman in his own country will dress a fine dinner of twenty dishes, and all genteel and pretty, for the expence he will put an English lord to for dressing one dish. But then there is the little petty profit. I have heard of a cook that used six pounds of butter to fry twelve eggs; when every body knows (that understands cooking) that half a pound is full enough, or more than need be used: but then it would not be French. So much is the blind folly of this age, that they would rather be imposed on by a French booby, than give encouragement to a good English cook!

Jugged Hare

Cut it into little pieces, lard them here and there with little slips of bacon, season them with Cayenne pepper and salt, put them into an earthen jug, with a blade or two of mace, an onion stuck with cloves, and a bundle of sweet-herbs; cover the jug or jar you do it in so close that nothing can get in, then set it in a pot of boiling water, and three hours will do it; then turn it out into the dish, and take out the onion and sweet-herbs and send it to table hot. If you do not like it larded, leave it out

Tripe with Onion Sauce: see May 6.
Welsh Rarebit: see March 14.
Tipsy Cake: see February 7.

May 9

Dinner at the English Embassy
Aleppo, Syria, 1676

Henry Teonge (1621–1690) was an English parson who became a chaplain in the Royal Navy. He was in his fifties when he went to sea, probably on account of debt—although whether it was to repay these or escape his creditors is unknown. Teonge kept a diary of his adventures, and they are a lively and fascinating insight into the seafaring life in the seventeenth century.

Teonge served aboard his Majesty's ships *Assistance*, *Bristol*, and *Royal Oak*. His first voyage began on June 1, 1675, and one of the early meals he describes aboard ship appears in this book (see July 10). Almost 12 months later the ship was in the harbor at Scanderoon, and Teonge took the opportunity to visit the plains of Antioch and Aleppo. The English consul in Aleppo, Mr. Gamaliell Nightingale, invited "all the nation" to a dinner. Teonge noted in his diary that the "treat of the Consul's providing" is "such a one as I never saw before. The particulars whereof you may see; the dishes being all placed as they stood on the table."

This was a magnificent, and very English, feast. In the seventeenth century all of the dishes for each course were placed on the table simultaneously, in a very regular, ordered arrangement. Balance and symmetry both vertically and horizontally were very important, and the aim was an impressive display of abundance and elegance. The end of Teonge's page is damaged, and it appears that some dishes are "missing." There would probably have been at least two more dishes to "balance" the bottom corners of the table (some dishes were described in cookbooks as being particularly suitable for corners).

A Dish of Turkeys		A Dish of Tarts
	A Plate of Sauceages	
A Dish of Gellys	A Dish of Gammons and Tongs	
	A Bisqué of Eggs	
A Dish of Geese		A Dish of Biscotts
	A Plate of Anchovies	
A Dish of Hens		A Venison Pasty
	A Plate of Anchovies	

A Dish of Biscotts   A Dish of Green Geese
          A Great Dish with a Pyramid of Marchpane
A Dish of Tarts   A Dish of Hens
                    A Dish of Hartichoks
A Pasty   A Dish of Marchpane in Cakes
                    A Dish of Sauceages
A Dish of Gammons   A Dish of Biscotts
                    A Plate of Herrings
A Dish of Geese   A Dish of Turkeys
                    A Plate of Anchovies
A Dish of Marchpane   A Pasty
                        Hartichocks
A Dish of Hens   A Dish of Gellys
                  A Pyramid of Marchpane
A Dish of Biscott   A Dish of Gammons
                        Anchovies

Recipes

~~~

To Stew Hartichokes with Cream

Take the meat of the Hartichokes tenderly boiled, and let them stew softly between two dishes, with cream, sack, sugar and grated nutmegg; so let it stew till it be all alike, then dish it and serve it to the table.

   Hannah Woolley, *The Queen-Like Closet; Or, Rich Cabinet Stored with All Manner of Rare Receipts for Preserving, Candying & Cookery. Very Pleasant and Beneficial to All Ingenious Persons of the Female Sex* (1670).

To Make Polony Sausages to Keep All the Year

You may take a piece of a Gammon of red Bacon, and half boyl it, mince it very small: if your Gammon be not fat, take half as much bacon lard, mince it likewise: mingle them together, and beat them in a Morter: season them with Time and Sage minced very small, and good store of Pepper beaten to dust, with a little Cloves, Mace, and Nutmeg, and a pretty quantity of Salt, for they ought so to be; add to them the yolks of two eggs, and so much Red wine as will bring them up to a stiff body; mingle them well with your hands, fill them into middle skins, as big as four of your ordinary Sassages, so hang them in your Chimney for a time, and when you will use them, they must be cut out very thin round wayes, and put them in your dish with Oyl and Vinegar, and serve them for a Sallet for the second course, or for a Collation before you drink.

> William Rabisha, *The Whole Body of Cookery Dissected, Taught, and Fully Manifested, Methodically, Artificially, and According to the Best Tradition of the English, French, Italian, Dutch, &c.* (1682).

Venison Pasty: see January 2.

May 10

Lewis and Clark Eat with the Nez Perce
Idaho, 1806

The expedition of Meriwether Lewis (1774–1809) and William Clark (1770–1838) during 1804–06 was the first overland crossing of the continent to the Pacific Ocean and back. On March 23, 1806, they began their return trip home. By May 10 they reached the Snake River where they were received with great hospitality—as they had been on the outward journey—by the Nez Perce tribe. The expedition party was in poor condition. They had few remaining supplies, game was still scarce, the salmon were not yet running, and they had been forced to resort to eating some of their horses.

Lewis recorded the generosity of the Indians in his journal entry for May 10.

> The Cheif spoke to his people and they produced us about 2 bushels of the quawmas roots dried, four cakes of the bread of cows and a dryed salmon trout. we thanked them for this store of provision but informed them that our men not being accustomed to live on roots alone we feared it would make them sick, to obviate which we proposed exchangeing a [good] horse in reather low order for a young horse in tolerable order with a view to kill. the hospitality of the cheif revolted at the eydea of an exchange, he told us that his young men had a great abundance of young horses and if we wished to eat them we should by [be] furnished with as many as we wanted. accordingly they soon produced us two fat young horses one of which we killed, the other we informed them we would postpone killing untill we had consumed the one already killed. This is a much greater act of hospitality than we have witnessed from any nation or tribe since we have passed the Rocky mountains. in short be it spoken to their immortal honor it is the only act which deserves the appellation of hospitallity which we have witnessed in this quarter.... our men who have their s[t]omachs once more well filled with horsebeef and mush of the bread of cows.

The *quawmas* (*camas*) and *"bread of cows"* were staple foods of the Nez Perce and were particularly useful because they could be dried and kept for long periods. There was a special danger associated with harvesting the camas (*Camassia quamash*) in that it is almost identical to a similar, but highly poisonous plant (*Zigadenus elegans*) known as the "death camas." The two often grow side by side, and are only harvested safely when the individual plant is flowering—the edible plant having blue flowers and the poisonous one greenish-white. The root can be eaten raw, dried, and pounded to make a starchy powder (its most common use), or boiled down to produce a molasses-like syrup.

The root of the strangely named *bread of cows* (*cous, kouse*) or *Cymopterus bulbosus* could be eaten fresh, when it is said to taste like parsnip, but was most valuable when dried and pounded into meal. This meal was baked into hard cakes that could be kept almost indefinitely, giving it its other names of *Biscuitroot* and *Indian biscuit*.

Recipes

~~~

Recipes for the preparation of "wild food" are not generally found in household cookbooks but rather in the journals of explorers and adventurers. One of the first white women to travel the Oregon Trail and cross the Rocky Mountains was the missionary Narcissa Whitman (1808–1847) and in her journal in February 1836 she described the Indian method of cooking camas.

> We nooned upon Grande Ronde river ... The camas grows here in abundance, and it is the principal resort of the Cayuses and many other tribes, to obtain it, as they are very fond of it. It resembles an onion in shape and color, when cooked is very sweet and tastes like a fig. Their manner of cooking them is very curious: They dig a hole in the ground, throw in a heap of stones, heat them to a red heat, cover them with green grass, upon which they put the camas, and cover the whole with earth. When taken out it is black. This is the chief food of many tribes during winter.

May 11

Eight-Franc Dinner
Grand Hotel, Boulevarde des Capucins, Paris, France, 1887

The *Café de Paris* in the magnificent Grand Hotel was the site of the famous Dinner of the Three Emperors (see June 7) in 1867. Two decades later, less exalted (but still well-to-do) guests could enjoy a fine meal, with wine, for the fixed price of eight francs (the menu does not state for which restaurant or dining room of the hotel).

POTAGE
Pâte Taganrok au Consommé

HORS—D'ŒUVRE
Sardines, Radis, Beurre, Olives

RELEVES
Bar de Seine sauce aux Câpres
Pommes de Terre Nature
CLOS MARATHON

ENTREES
Tournedos Chasseur
Côtelettes d'Agneau à la Printaniere

ROT
Chapon de Mans au Cresson
Salads de Laitue aux Œufs

ENTREMETS
Haricots verts à la Maître d'Hôtel
Crème au Caramel
Bombe Stanislaus

DESSERTS
Oranges, Mendiants, Pommes, Biscuits, Gauffres
Macarons, Fromages
MÉDOC GRAND-HOTEL

Vin de Saint-Raphaël
Goût exquis, tonique et reconstituaunt

Eaux de table
Vals Saint-Jean—Vais cachet vert

Many of these dishes are on the menus of fine French-style restaurants to-day. The *Tournedos Chasseur* and *Crème au Caramel* are instantly recognizable, even for many of those who do not speak French. Fish such as the bar (bass) is still regularly served with caper sauce, lamb cutlets with spring vegetables, and chicken with cress. The *Pâte Taganrok* is unusual. It appears to be a misspelling of Taganrog, the Russian port city on the Sea of Azov. The city has a long association with the Tsars of Russia, so perhaps the dish acknowledges one of the famous guests of the dinner in 1867. The wheat from the region is also famous for its quality and makes particularly fine pasta (pâte means paste, pastry, pasta) so it may be that the chef was simply indicating that he was using the finest variety in his consommé.

There are several versions of the combination of cream with caramel. The earliest is simply cream blended with caramel (i.e. burnt sugar). The French do not have a specific word for the mixture of egg and milk or cream that we call "custard." They simply refer to it as cream, with the addition of a qualifying word. A basic custard sauce for fruit or pie is *Crème Anglais* (English cream.) Today's well-known versions of caramel creams are actually caramel custards. *Crème Brulée* is a baked custard with a layer of sugar on top which is then burnt by holding a hot salamander over it, putting it under a very hot grill, or using a kitchen blowtorch to produce a crisp caramel crust. This is based on a very old idea called "burnt cream," and although the dessert is thought of as French, its origin may well be English. The third version is probably the best known and is a perennial favorite. It is *Crème Caramel*, a version of what the French call a *crème renversé* (a reversed or "turned-out" cream). In this version the burnt sugar is placed in the dish before the custard mixture, so that (after baking then chilling well) when it is turned out for serving the caramel runs down the sides of the custard.

Recipes

~~~

The following recipe is yet another version of a caramel custard or cream. In this recipe the caramel is not separate but is an integral part of the custard, which is not baked but set, like a jelly, with isinglass (or gelatin).

Crème au Caramel

Put four ounces of powdered sugar in a stewpan, which stir over a slow fire till quite melted and beginning to tint, take it off the fire; in another stewpan have three quarters of a pint of milk in which you have boiled an ounce of isinglass, pour it upon the caramel, which stir occasionally until it is quite dissolved, pour into another stewpan with the yolks of five eggs, stir over the fire till it thickens, when pass through a tammie, and finish as before [when cold, set the bowl upon ice . . . keep stirring its contents, and when on the point of setting add three parts of pint of cream well whipped, mix well together and pouring into your mould, keep it on ice until wanted, and when ready to serve dip into warm water, wipe with a cloth, and turn out on your dish].

   Alexis Soyer, *The Gastronomic Regenerator* (London, 1847).

Tournedos

Thick slice of beef taken from the center of the fillet, often tied with string to keep it in a neat round shape. It is usually served on a crouton, and the sauce and garnish determine the name of the dish.

   Béarnaise: With Bearnaise Sauce and a garnish of Chateau Potatoes.
   Bordelaise: No croutons, with Bordelaise Sauce and a garnish of marrow.
   Chasseur: "Hunter-style," with mushrooms and sauce made with the pan juices, herbs and butter.
   Chevreuil: "Venison style," with Sauce Chevreuil and a garnish of chestnuts.
   Choron: With Sauce Choron (a Bearnaise with tomato puree instead of the herbs).
   Paysanne: "Peasant Woman style," no crouton, served on a bed of fresh vegetables braised in butter.
   Rossini: With foie-gras and truffles and rich meat glaze with Madeira.

Macaroons: see February 17.

May 12

Lunch En Route to the Falkland Islands
RMS *Queen Elizabeth 2,* 1982

In early May 1982, with conflict in the Falkland Islands escalating, the most famous cruise ship in the world—the Cunard Line's *Queen Elizabeth 2*—was requisitioned for war service. Her luxury fittings were quickly removed and helicopter pads installed, and she was converted to carry 3,000 troops (a thousand more than the normal number of passengers) and all the other paraphernalia required for fleet headquarters to participate in active service. On Wednesday, May 12, she left Southampton, England, for the Falklands. The following lunch menu was served the same day.

LUNCH

Green Pea Soup
Baked Cheese Macaroni
Breaded Escalope of Veal, Viennaise
Diced White Turnips
Chipped Potatoes
Assorted Cold Cuts
Mixed Salad with Dressings
Apple Pie and Whipped Cream
Cheese and Biscuits
Rolls and Butter
Tea or Coffee

Much of the food on this menu appears to have been "comfort food"—perhaps with 3,000 soldiers to feed the military cooks were simply playing it safe. Scientists say comfort food causes the release of the natural hormones called endorphins that reduce stress levels, and it is possible that, consciously or otherwise, the cooks chose the day's dishes for that reason.

Every nation has its own particular comfort food (or soul food) and it is usually inexpensive, unfussy, plain "home-style" food. It is almost always carbohydrate-heavy and easy to eat, often only requiring a spoon. In most parts of Asia, simple rice would be sufficient, and in the West it is commonly pasta, potatoes, and bread. Many puddings and other sweet dishes are comfort foods, and apple pie would probably make the comfort food list of almost everyone with British or American heritage.

Recipes

~~~

Eliza Acton's *Modern Cookery for Private Families* was published in 1845, and it is still a classic text. Acton was a poet and social reformer who became famous in her own time for her cookbook. She wrote it for the ordinary household cook, all the recipes were tested, and they were all easy to follow. She paved the way for all subsequent cookbooks by being the first writer to list the ingredients separately from the method instructions.

The words "pie" and "tart" are often used interchangeably and there is no consistent usage in relation to the number of crusts (double, top, or bottom) —although many cooks have very strong opinions as to which is "correct." Acton uses "tart," and she has several variations of the apple variety.

A Good Apple Tart

A pound and a quarter of apples, weighed after they are pared and cored, will be sufficient for a small tart, and four ounces more for one of moderate size. Lay a border or English puff-paste or cream-crust round the dish, just dip the apples into water, arrange them very compactly in it, higher in the centre that at the sides, and strew amongst them from three to four ounces of powdered sugar, or more should they be very acid: the grated rind, and the strained juice of half a lemon will much improve their flavour. Lay on the cover rolled thin, and ice it or not at pleasure. Send the tart to a moderately brisk oven for about half an hour. This may be converted into the old-fashioned creamed apple tart, by cutting out the cover while it is still hot, leaving only about an inch-wide border of paste round the edge, and pouring over the apples when they have become quite cold, from half to three quarters of a pint of rich boiled custard. The cover divided into triangular sippets, was formerly stuck round the inside of the tart, but ornamental leaves of puff-paste have a better effect. Well-drained whipped cream may be substituted for the custard, and piled high, and lightly over the fruit.

Cream Crust

(Very good.)
Flour, 1 lb;
Salt, 1 small saltspoonful (more for meat pies);
rich cream, 1/2 to 3/4 pint;
butter, 4 oz., for richest crust, 6 oz.

Stir a little salt into a pound of dry flour, and mix gradually with it sufficient thick, sweet cream to form a smooth paste; it will be found sufficiently good for common family dinners without the addition of butter; but to make an excellent crust, roll in four ounces in the usual way, after having given the paste a couple of *turns*. Handle it as lightly as is possible in making it, and send it to the oven as soon as it is ready; it may be used for fruit tarts, cannelons, puffs, and other varieties of small pastry, or for good meat pies. Six ounces of butter to the pound of flour will give a *very rich* crust.

May 13

Dinner for Nobody's Friends
Hôtel Metropole, London, England, 1891

William Stevens (1732–1807) was an English writer and biographer. He was a deeply religious man who actively supported organizations such as the Society for Promoting Christian Knowledge and for the Propagation of the Gospel. He never married but was a gregarious man and his home was a regular gathering place for his friends, who included many of the prominent clergy of the time. When he became too elderly and frail to host these gatherings, his friends decided to form a dining club in his honor, the meetings to be held at some other venue. Stevens had a keen sense of humor, and one of his favorite jokes was to give nicknames to his friends. The name he gave himself was "Nobody," hence the club was Nobody's Club or The Club of Nobody's Friends. The Hôtel Metropole became a regular venue and did them proud with a menu of classic dishes at their dinner on May 13, 1891.

MENU DU DINER.

HORS D'ŒUVRE.

—

Dry Sherry

Consommé Printanier.

Ox Tail Lié

—

Saumon à la Danoise.

Niersteiner

Whitebait.

—

Soufflées de Vollaile.

G. H. Mumm & Co.,

Noisettes d'Agneau à la Cettoise.

—

Extra Quality,
Extra Dry.

SORBET ÀMÉRICAINE.

—

Filets de Bœuf à la Dauphine.

Jambon Braisé au Madère.

Max Sutaine & Co.,
Extra Quality,
Extra Dry.
1884

—

Petits Pois au Beurre.

Pommes de Terre Parisiennes.

—

Cailles de Vignes Rôties sur Canapés.

Salade.

Fine Champagne
Liqueur Brandy.

—

Asperges, Sauce Mousseline.

—

Macédoine de Fruits au Liqueurs.

Canapés de Caviar.

Bombe Monte Carlo.

Gateaux Savoisiens.

—

DESSERT

Cantenac.

—

Café Noir

—

Cockburn's Old Bottled Port.

—

Johannis Natural Mineral Water.

Recipes

~~~

Canapes, Caviare

4 squares of bread and butter
1 dessert-spoonful caviare
juice of 1/2 lemon
1 small pinch cayenne
4 tiny lettuce leaves about 1 inch long.

Cut 2 or 3 thin slices of white or brown bread, butter them thinly, and cut them into very neat 2-inch squares. The bread should be fresh but not crumbly, and the slices not more than 1/4 of an inch in thickness. Some little practice may be necessary to get the little squares exactly the right size, but as much of the appearance of the canape depends upon the bread and butter being of sufficient substance to hold its dressing neatly without being thick and clumsy, some attention should be given to this point.

Put the caviare on ice for an hour before using; spread the caviare neatly on the squares, squeeze 3 or 4 drops of lemon juice on each canape and add 3 or 4 grains of cayenne, put a tiny little lettuce leaf on each, lay each canape on a plate, and serve.

Allow 1 canape to each person.

Ethel Meyer, *A Practical Dictionary of Cookery (1200 Recipes)* (1898).

A *Macédoine* is a mixture of fruits. When presented on a formal menu it was usually an ornamental dish of jelly, often flavored with liqueur (such as noyeau or maraschino added to the jelly before it sets).

Maçedoine Jelly

Strawberries, raspberries, grapes, currants, and cherries are the only fruit that can be used raw for a macedoine; but it is to be observed, they should be perfectly ripe; peaches, apricots, apples, and pines require to be boiled in syrup before they are put into the jelly: in the first place, have a good clear jelly prepared, rather sweet for a macedoine, because raw fruit takes off the sweetness; put a little jelly into a mould, which you set on the ice, then array the fruit variously, according as your fancy suggests; then pour in some more jelly; when that is firm, lay more fruit and jelly, and continue to do so till you have filled the mould to the top; keep the jelly in the ice till dinner time, then dip the mould into hot water, turning it into the dish you intend to serve: in winter, you may make a handsome macedoine with preserved fruit, such as greengages, peaches, pineapples, plums, and cherries.

I. Roberts, *The Young Cook's Guide* (1836).

Whitebait: see August 14.

May 14

President Franklin D. Roosevelt's Daily Fare
The White House, Washington, DC, 1933

The New York Times published a report of an interview with First Lady Eleanor Roosevelt on May 14, 1933. She was well aware of the public's intense curiosity about the day-to-day life of the president and his family and was most gracious in discussing her philosophy of life and describing her efforts to create in the White House "an atmosphere of simple friendliness." One of her chores was to consider the daily menus suggested by the housekeeper, Mrs. Nesbitt, and as this process was underway when the interview began she kindly handed a copy of the day's menus to the reporter.

BREAKFAST
Cereal   Fruit
Eggs and Bacon   Coffee

LUNCHEON
Tomato Juice Cocktail
Cold Cuts
Creamed Potatoes   Beans
Fruit Salad
Cream Mayonnaise Dressing
Coffee

TEA
Jam and Cream Cheese with
Pineapple Sandwiches
Assorted Cookies   Pastries
Candies   Salted Nuts
Tea

DINNER
Vegetable Soup
Roast Beef   Stuffed Potatoes
Spinach   Creamed Onions
Combination Salad, French Dressing
Strawberry Shortcake
Coffee

The focus of the interview was firmly on Eleanor Roosevelt's domestic role, and to reinforce this *The Times'* single article referred to her as "First Homemaker of the nation," "Hostess for the nation," and "Manager of the national residence." Mrs. Roosevelt gave her opinion on her most important obligation ("social"), on how to decorate a house to make it a home (a reading lamp near a chair, for example), and on the importance of an atmosphere of friendliness (it "may have far-reaching effects"). She was known to be on an economy drive, and in response to the reporter's question about her "economy menus" she responded by saying that they were doing very little formal entertaining, and when they did, the menus were still very simple.

> I am doing away with all the kickshaws—no hothouse grapes—nothing out of season. I plan for good and well-cooked food, properly served, and that must be enough. Our formal dinners now include simply soup, fish, meat, salad, desert [sic].

The return to simple food no doubt pleased the president: the First Lady divulged his favorite dish, scrambled eggs, "And he likes them so well that I believe he would eat them every meal if I would serve them to him." She went on to say,

> I should not presume to dictate to the women of the country what they should do or how they should conduct their homes. They do not need such dictation. They have too much good sense of their own. Rather, I should say, it is for me to follow their standards, to try to bring into this national home of theirs the dignity and simplicity of living of the early republic. They may disagree with me in some of the things I do—because there are a good many different opinions in a country as large as ours—but at least they will know that we are all working together for the same end.

Recipes
~~~

Strawberry Shortcake

(Sufficient to Serve Six)
1 qt. strawberries
1 c. sugar
Biscuit or plain cake dough.

   Mash or chop the berries, add the sugar to them, and let them stand until the sugar has dissolved. Bake the biscuit or plain-cake dough in a single thick layer or, if desired, bake it in individual cakes, cutting the biscuit dough with a cookie cutter and putting the cake mixture in muffin pans. Remove from the pan, cut in two with a sharp knife, and spread half of the berries over the lower piece. Set the upper piece on the berries. In the case of the large cake, sprinkle powdered sugar over the top and then on this arrange a number of the largest and finest of the berries . . . as a garniture. Cut in pieces of the desired size and serve with or without either plain or whipped cream. In preparing the individual cakes, spread a spoonful or two of the crushed berries over the top . . . and serve with whipped cream.
   The Woman's Institute Library of Cookery, Vol. V. (ca. 1922).

Plain Sponge Cake

4 eggs
1 c. sugar
1 c. flour
Juice and rind of 1/2 lemon

Beat the eggs until they are thick and lemon-colored. Add the sugar gradually and continue to beat. Sift the flour several times and fold into the mixture. When the ingredients are thoroughly mixed, add the grated rind and the juice of the lemon, pour into a sponge-cake pan, and bake.
    The Woman's Institute Library of Cookery, Vol. IV. (ca. 1922).

May 15

Coronation Banquet for Nicholas II
Kremlin, Russia, 1896

Nicholas II (1868–1918) was the last Tsar of Russia as well as King of Poland and Grand Duke of Finland. In 1896, a year and a half after his accession, the coronation ceremony was finally held in Moscow on May 14 (according to the Julian or "old-style" calendar). Over the next week there were many banquets, balls, and other celebrations held throughout the city. The menu cards for several of these events were especially commissioned by famous artists and have become collector's items. The beautifully colored lithographed card for the lunch at the Kremlin on May 15 was designed by Alexander Benua (1870–1970), a painter and stage designer who worked for Diaghilev's *Ballets Russes*.

Crab Soup
Meat or Vegetable Pies
Trout from Finland
Spiced Veal
Cold Gellied Partridge
Small Plump Hens and Chickens
Salad of Artichokes with Peas
Hot Sweets
Ice Cream
Dessert

The ordinary citizens of Russia were included in the celebrations, and one of the specially commissioned souvenir items was the indirect cause of a terrible tragedy on May 18. A huge crowd had gathered overnight in the Khodynskoye Pole (field) where food and a commemorative mug were to be distributed. The pressure of the mass of people caused the collapse of some wooden barriers, and in the ensuing chaos over a thousand people were trampled to death. The Tsar was deeply affected by the incident, seeing it as a bad omen as well as a terrible tragedy, and he visited the hospitals where the injured were treated and paid compensation and funeral expenses.

Recipes

~~~

Raised Pie, The Russian Way

Cut in scollops a small slice of salmon; pass it with fine herbs, salt, pepper, and nutmeg. Do the same with a small fat liver. Then chop twelve yolks of eggs, boiled hard; raise the crust about seven inches wide, and four high; line the bottom and sides with rice stewed in consommé of a fowl; the rice must be cold, as well as the rest of the garnish: line the bottom with scollops of salmon, on which strew yolk of egg; place on this half the scollops of fat liver, and cover them with yolk of egg. Repeat this, and on the top put the butter with the fine herbs, in which you have passed the salmon and fat liver; cover the whole with the remainder of the rice; finish as before directed; bake it an hour and a half, and serve.

Joseph Bregion and Anne Miller, *The Practical Cook, English and Foreign* (1845).

May 16

First Academy Awards Banquet
Blossom Room, Roosevelt Hotel, Hollywood, California, 1929

The first "Oscar's Night" was a very different affair from the lavish, highly publicized, grand spectacle it is today. There was no secrecy in 1929 as the winners had been announced three months before, and there was no separate awards-presentation ceremony. The original twelve Academy Awards of Merit (the official name for the Oscars) took only ten minutes to hand out at a banquet at the Hollywood Roosevelt Hotel.

MENU

Terrapin Soup
Jumbo Squab Perigeaux
Lobster Eugénie
L.A. Salad
Fruit Supreme

Within a few years, the Academy Awards presentation had captured the public's imagination, and it seems that the event just keeps on getting bigger and attracting more hype. Only 270 guests (who paid $10 each for the privilege) were present in 1929. The host was Douglas Fairbanks Jr. (1909–2000), first president of the Academy, and his wife, actress Mary Pickford (1892–1979), handed out the awards. Two special awards were made in addition to those for the best in each of the original twelve categories. A special honorary award went to Charlie Chaplin (1889–1977) for producing, directing, writing, and starring in *The Circus*; the other was for the production of *The Jazz Singer*, "the pioneer outstanding talking picture, which has revolutionized the industry".

The first Academy Awards presentation was the last time that a silent movie won the Best Picture award—there would be no looking back for the industry or the public after the first "talkie." Al Jolson (1886–1950), the star of *The Jazz Singer*, was present at the banquet and sang its signature song *Dixie*, but the award was accepted by studio boss Darryl F. Zanuck (1902–1979), who was the only recipient to make a speech.

Enthusiasts of all persuasions often wish to recreate an event that falls within their area of interest. Movie aficionados wishing to recreate this first Academy Awards banquet must be satisfied with using it as inspiration. The Terrapin Soup is certainly politically incorrect today, and may well be illegal, depending on the location and season. The diamondback terrapin (the usual ingredient) was so desirable for the table that concerns about the species were already being aired in the late-nineteenth century. Maryland was the first state to place seasonal restrictions on its harvesting in 1878, and every state in which the turtle is found now applies some level of protection to the species—declaring it either endangered, threatened, or a species of conservation concern.

The names of dishes on a menu—unless they are absolute, long-standing classics—usually do not give enough information to be certain as to how they were prepared. "Squab" means a baby bird, and although it usually refers to a pigeon, young chickens are often called squab, and "jumbo squab" is also used to refer to either. "*Perigeaux*" (*Perigueux*) refers to the Perigord region of France, and dishes styled this way classically include truffles. The name "Eugénie" refers to the wife of Napoleon III, the Spanish princess Eugénie de Montijo, and the most famous interpretation is in a dish of sweetbreads invented by Charles Ranhofer, the chef at Delmonico's. Ranhofer's dish included truffles and fat pork and was served with a cream sauce. Other interpretations have them cooked in sherry and garnished with mushrooms and a cream sauce.

Recipes

~~~

Terrapin Soup, Southern Style

Scald two terrapin [this involved putting the live terrapin into boiling water for two minutes], and remove the shell, skin and intestines. Cut the terrapin in small pieces about one-quarter inch square. Heat four ounces of butter in a casserole, then add the terrapin and fry over a quick fire. Sprinkle with three tablespoonfuls of flour, add three pints of any kind of good broth and one pint of milk, season with salt and pepper, add a glass of good sherry wine, and boil until well done. Bind with the yolks of two eggs mixed with a cup of cream and a glass of dry sherry wine. Set on stove and let it come nearly to a boil, but not quite.

Victor Hirtzler, *The Hotel St. Francis Cookbook* (San Francisco, 1919).

Sauce Perigueux: see April 14.

May 17

English Royals Dine in Canada
Chateau Frontenac, Quebec, 1939

King George VI and Queen Elizabeth of England dined for the first time on Canadian soil on May 17, 1939. They arrived in Quebec aboard the SS *Empress of Australia* and lunch and dinner on their first day were served at the Château Frontenac. Every detail of their visit was reported to a fascinated public by the press in Canada and the United States. *The New York Times* was moved to comment that those charged with the catering clearly thought that "their provincial pride was at stake" and gave the menus of both lunch and dinner to indicate how this laudable national sentiment was expressed—and the disasters that almost sabotaged it.

LUNCH.
Le Melon Canteloupe Frappé
Les Queues de Homards Frontenac
La Poitrine de Poussin Grillée
Le Souffle Glacé Grand Marnier
Les Petits Fours
La Corbeille de Fruits
Le Café

Amontillado
Château Yquem 1928
Veuve Cliquot Gold Label 1928

DINNER.
Les Perles de Sterlet
Le Consommé du Pays
Les Truites des Laurentides au Vin Blanc
La Couronne d'Agneau de Québec aux Primeurs
Le Sorbet au Champagne
Les Petits Oiseaux Blancs de l'Ile
d'Orleans en Aspic
La Salade Gauloise
La Coupe aux Fraises Chantilly
Les Friandises
La Corbeille de Fruits

Amontillado Reina Victoria
Montrachet 1926
Hospice de Beaune Haut-Brion 1928
Irroy 1928
Pommery 1928
Veuve Cliquot 1928

The problems began when "Long ago, those entrusted with the menu which should give the King and queen a good first impression of Canadian culinary capabilities decided that it should combine the exotic with the typical. In the former category come peaches from Southern France grapes from Belgium and melons from California—these gave the least trouble . . . ." The exotic imported fruit was simply expensive, which was of not consequence when royal visitors were to be fed. The melons served at lunch, for example, were flown in at a cost of only $2 each for freight.

The weather did not cooperate with the supply of the local Canadian produce. The winter had been severe. Snowbirds only arrive in the Island of Orleans in the St. Lawrence River when the snow melts, which it had showed no sign of doing. By a "Herculean effort," a thousand of the "tiny toothsome creatures" were eventually procured—barely sufficient when "breasts of six of them served up on toast add up to very few calories." As for the trout, the ice persisted in Quebec's Laurentide Park and the fish could not be caught. Just as a "furtive order" of 600 Adirondack trout was received from New York and placed in the freezers, the Fisheries Department managed to succeed. Luckily the royal arrival by sea was delayed, and freezer space was freed up by feeding the excess imported fish to the waiting newspaper men, security staff, and other officials.

After the great provisioning anxiety was over, the meals themselves went smoothly apart from one brief "protocol moment." Neither the King nor Queen accepted the Grand Marnier soufflé at lunch, leaving the rest of the guests uncertain as to whether they too must also refuse. A signal from the King's footmen (in scarlet) and the Château staff (in blue) indicated that no offense would be incurred, and the guests were free to enjoy the dish. Protocol also constrains royalty, and the King was clearly desperate for a cigarette at lunchtime, but it was not proper for him to smoke until the toast had been made to his royal person. The prime minister must have been made aware of the situation, and the royal couple were toasted in the 1928 champagne—upon which the King immediately lit up before a waiter could provide a light.

Recipes

~~~

Snow Birds

One dozen thoroughly cleaned birds; stuff each with an oyster, put them into a yellow dish, and add two ounces of boiled salt pork and three raw potatoes cut into slices; add a pint of oyster liquor, an ounce of butter; salt and pepper; cover the dish with a crust and bake in a moderate oven.

F. L. Gillett, *White House Cook Book* (Chicago, 1887).

Melon Frappé (melon water ice): see June 20.
Petits Fours: see November 14.
Salade Gauloise: see May 27.

May 18

American Banquet in England
Star and Garter, Richmond, England, 1853

The new American Minister in London, Joseph Reed Ingersoll (1786–1868), was welcomed to his new post in 1853 by his countryman George Peabody (1795–1869) and his niece, Miss Wilcocks.

PREMIER SERVICE

POTAGES.
A la Reine – A la Printaniere – A la Printaniere Clair
Consommé de Vollaile aux Quenelles.
Potage aux Abbatis d'Oie

POISSONS.
Turbot.   Saumon de Gloucester.
Truite à la Genevoise.   Rouges à la Maitre d'Hotel
Perch Suché.   Flounder Suché.   Eels en Matelotte.
Spitched Eels.   Gudgeons Fried.   Flounders Fried.

ENTREES.
Suprême de Volaille à la Royale.
Cailles aux Truffes.
Cotelettes d'Agneau aux Concombres.
Croustades à la Monglas.   Quenelles à la Perigeux.
Filets de Pigeons à la Dauphine.
Filets de Levraut Garni d'Une Escaloppe.
Ris de Veau Pique à la Toulouse.
Epigramme d'Agneau aux Pois d'Asperges.
Filets de Canetons à la Bigarade.
~~~~~~~~~~~~~~
Poulardes au Riz.
Filet de Boeuf à la Jardienere.
Noix de Veau en Bedeau Sauce Tomate
Timbale de Macaroni à la Financière.
Poulets Roti.
Jambon de Westphalie à l'Essence.
Casserole de Riz à la Polonaise.
Chartreuse de Légumes Garni de Pigeon.
Ballotine d'Agneau à la Macedoine.Selle d'Agneau.
Langue de Bœuf aux Epinards.
Poulets à la Godard.
Selle de Mouton.

SECOND SERVICE.
Salade à la Parisienne.
Pommes de Terre Nouvelles à la Maitre d'Hotel.
Haricots Verts à la Poulette.
Salade à la Parisienne.   Canetons.   Levraut.
Oison.

Magnonnaise de Volaille.   Dindonneaux.
Carot Nouvelle Glacé,
~~~~~~~~~~~~~~~
Gelée à la Victoria, – à la Macedoine, – au Marasquin, – d'Anisette.
Compote des Peches en Boidure de Riz.
Suedoise de Raisins.
Crème à la Chantilly, – au Chocolat, – d'Ananas.
Croque en Bouche à la Reine.
Gateaux à la Neapolitaine, – à la Condé.
Flans d'Abricots Verts, – au Cerises.
Patisserie Melée.
Chartreuse des Fraises.   Bavarois des Abricots.

RELEVES.
Baba à la Polonaise.
Pouding Glacé aux Pistaches.   Soufflée à la Vanille.
Beignets de Parmesan.
Pitits Soufflée à la Francaise.
Grapes.   Strawberries.   Pines.   Ices.

Peabody had fulfilled the American dream: he had started out in life "without any advantages of rank, or fortune, or even education," reported *The New York Times*, and had made his fortune in the dry goods trade. He then retired to London where he continued his various commercial and banking interests, and, most importantly "contributed, in an unostentatious but most effective way, to strengthen that feeling of friendship between the people of the two great nations on which so much of their peace and prosperity must always depend." Peabody had his work cut out for him. It might have been 75 years since England lost its former colony, but there was considerable residual resentment and mutual distrust.

Peabody spared no expense for the evening. One hundred fifty guests sat down to this magnificent dinner and musical program. The menu (mangled French, misspellings and all) is a wonderful example of a mid-nineteenth century grand dinner. There is an enormous quantity of food, and a huge number of choices. It is a veritable glossary of classic dishes, with 20 of them styled *"à la"* something or other, and it is full of the ornamental sweet dishes beloved of the Victorians—gateaux, chartreuses, jellies, ices,

AND CAPONS.

Poulet à la Godard.

creams, *bavarois*, and *soufflés*. There was also a *Croque en Bouche*—an elaborate "set piece" designed as much for display as for consumption. The *Croque
en Bouche* is a familiar wedding cake alternative today and is most often
made from small *choux* paste (see November 7) profiteroles covered with
spun sugar, but at this time it was usually constructed of caramelized fruit.

Recipes

~~~

Souffle à la Vanille

Take a pint of milk, quarter of a pound of sugar, and one stick of vanilla, cut in
small pieces; let the milk boil up, then keep it covered by the side of the fire half
an hour.

Take four ounces of flour, mix it with half a pint of cream in a stewpan, then
pass the milk in which the vanilla is boiled into it; add two ounces of butter,
and stir it over the fire till it becomes a thick paste; remove the stewpan, and
immediately mix in ten yolks of eggs, one at a time; the whites are to be put in
a clean basin, and kept in the larder till it is time to put the souffle in the oven;
and whip them strong, and mix lightly with the souffle; it will take from twenty
minutes to half an hour to bake. It is not to be taken out of the oven until the
very moment it is to be served.

N.B. Observe, that all souffles are prepared in the same way, and they vary
only in the flavor given to them. It is of the utmost consequence to the excellency
of the souffle that it is served the moment it is ready. Souffles may be either
steamed or baked.

A *Bavarois* is a custard made with cream, sometimes eggs, and various
flavorings, set with gelatine. It is sometimes called Bavarian Cream,
or Bavarian Cheese (even though there is no cheese in it). Apricots,
stewed and pureed, could be substituted for the strawberries in the following
recipe.

Bavarian Cheese of Strawberries

Take a pottle [half gallon] of strawberries, fresh gathered, and make them into
a purée, by passing them through a tammy with two spoons; afterwards put
a sufficient quantity of pounded sugar to sweeten it; mix melted isinglass with
this purée, beat a pint of cream well, and mix it with the strawberries; put it into
a pewter ice-pot, surrounded with ice, and keep stirring it till it begins to get firm;
immediately put it into the shape [mold], and set it in ice till it is to be served.

I. Roberts, *Young Cook's Guide* (1841).

Macedoine Jelly: see May 13.
Epigrammes of Lamb: see March 26.
Chartreuse de Legumes Garni de Pigeon: see November 9.
Pommes de Terre Nouvelles à la Maitre d'Hotel: see October 21.
Maitre d'Hotel Butter for Fish: see September 3.

May 19

Prison Menu for a Week
Indiana State Prison, 1911

The Indiana authorities reviewed the state prison dietary in 1911 and were pleased with their findings. Not only did the cost compare favorably with the previous year, they determined the food quality to be good:

> The bread is of excellent quality, corn bread being served once each day except Sunday: the meat is sweet and clean; the butterine bears the government inspector's stamp, the vegetables are always fresh, and real coffee is served three times a day.

The prisoners' responses to the food are not noted.

MAY 14.
Breakfast—Stewed figs, butter, bread and coffee.
Dinner—Roast beef, mashed potatoes, gravy, raw onions, bread and coffee.
Supper—Cinnamon rolls and lunch from dinner.

MAY 15.
Breakfast—Steamed potatoes, gravy, bread and coffee.
Dinner—Bean soup, boiled beef, steamed potatoes, crackers, bread and coffee.
Supper—Peach sauce, butter, bread and coffee.

MAY 16.
Breakfast—Hominy and beans, bread and coffee.
Dinner—Boiled pork, boiled beans, pickled beets, bread and coffee.
Supper—Oatmeal, milk, sugar, bread and coffee.

MAY 17.
Breakfast—Pork sausage, steamed potatoes, gravy, bread and coffee.
Dinner—Boiled beef, home stew, potatoes, bread and coffee.
Supper—Prune sauce, butter, bread and coffee.

MAY 18.
Breakfast—Hash beef and pork, bread, and coffee.
Dinner—Boiled beef, mashed potatoes, gravy, bread and coffee.
Supper—Sirup, butter, bread and coffee.

MAY 19.
Breakfast—Hominy, bread and coffee.
Dinner—Boiled beef, New England potatoes, gravy, bread and coffee.
Supper—Boiled rice, milk, sugar, bread and coffee.

MAY 20.
Breakfast—Hash beef and pork, bread and coffee.
Dinner—Boiled beef, stewed onions and potatoes, bread and coffee.
Supper—Raisins stewed, bread and coffee.

Many residential institutions throughout history—prison, asylum, poor house, school—have had a dietary based on watery soup or, if the inmates are lucky—a solid starchy filler such as the hominy on this menu. It is likely that the quantity of food in the prison was sufficient—prison authorities are too well aware that hungry prisoners cause trouble—but this menu is severely deficient in vegetables apart from potatoes and would hardly pass a dietitian's inspection today. The individual dishes are plain and unadorned and could appear on any table today with little need for explanation.

"Lunch from dinner" on May 14 (a Sunday) presumably means leftovers, and *butterine* was an early form of margarine—a cheap butter substitute made from animal fat colored yellow.

Recipes

~~~

Hominy is simply corn without the "germ," boiled and cooked as a cereal. Other variants are samp (coarse hominy) and grits (hominy ground into small grains.) It is therefore essentially the same as the Italian polenta.

Hominy

Wash the hominy very clean through three or four waters. Then put it into a pot (allowing two quarts of water to one quart of hominy) and boil it slowly five hours. When done, take it up, and drain the liquid from it through a cullender. Put the hominy into a deep dish and stir into it a small piece of fresh butter. The small grained hominy is boiled in rather less water, and generally eaten with butter and sugar.

   Eliza Leslie, *Directions for Cookery* (1844).

It is highly unlikely that the prisoners got the cream-enriched version of the following recipe.

Stewed figs

After the thinning out of fresh summer fruits, which occurs in October, the housekeeper who does not approve of canned things begins, to review the winter possibilities. One of these, too often over-looked, is stewed figs, which few women understand how to prepare so as to bring out their full deliciousness. The dried figs which come in strings, whole in form and cheaper in price, are best for stewing. Wash them thoroughly, soak overnight till they swelled to the size of small eggs, then simmer a few minutes until tender. They should be served very cold with an abundance of cream. Thus prepared the wholesome fig becomes practically a new fruit to most household tables. The cream is specially valuable in drawing out the full flavor of the fruit.

   Fort Wayne Sentinel (Indiana), January 16, 1911.

May 20

Banquet of Insects
Explorer's Club, New York, 1992

When the New York Entomological Society decided to celebrate its first 100 years with a feast of insects, the intention was not to cause shock and revulsion but to raise awareness of the worldwide nutritional and economic significance of insects as food. One hundred forty guests enjoyed the following bill of fare on that Wednesday evening:

AT THE BAR
Crudite with Peppery Delight Mealworm Dip
Spiced Crickets and Assorted Worms

BUTLERED HOR D'OEUVRES
Waxworm and Mealworm and Avocado California Roll
with Tamari Dipping Sauce
Wild Mushrooms in Mealworm Flour Pastry
Cricket and Vegetable Tempura
Mealworm Balls in Zesty Tomato Sauce
Mini Bruschetta with Mealworm Ganoush
Worm and Corn Fritters with Plum Dipping Sauce

BUFFET
Chicken Normandy with Calvados Sauce
Rice Pilaf
Roast Beef with Gravy
Roesti Potatoes
Mediterranean Pasta
Melange of Vegetable Ragu
Mesclun Salad with Balsamic Vinaigrette
Assorted Seasoned and Cricket Breads and Butter

DESSERT BUFFET
Lemon Squares
Chocolate Cricket Torte
Mini Cannoli
Peach Clafouti
Cricket and Mealworm Sugar Cookies
Coffee and Tea

Insects belong to the Phyllum Arthropoda—animals characterized by a segmented body, appendages on each segment, and an external skeleton— as do arachnids (spiders) and crustaceans (marine arthropods). Many people gladly eat lobster (sometimes referred to as "the cockroach of the sea" because of it scavenging habit), and most enjoy honey (which has been regurgitated by bees) and figs (which because of the peculiar way in which they are pollinated, inevitably contain the unhatched eggs of fig wasps), yet almost everyone is repelled by the idea of eating insects.

What people eat, and particularly what people refuse to eat, is culturally determined. Eighty percent of the world's population eats insects intentionally, with due regard for their nutritional value and with apparent relish, the rest also eat them but do so inadvertently. Insect fragments (and rodent hairs and excrement) inevitably find their way into food as it moves from farm to factory to dinner plate. The best to hope for is that the acceptable limits set by authorities such as the American Food and Drug Administration (FDA) for these "natural or unavoidable defects in foods that present no health hazards for humans" are not exceeded. Westerners each consume at least a pound (450 gm) of insects in this way over the course of a lifetime.

There are at present nearly 1,500 species on the list of edible insects, and almost certainly many more are waiting to be added, and there is increasing interest in promoting this "microlivestock" in the Western world.

Recipes

~~~

Peppery Delight Mealworm Dip

8 oz cream cheese
1 cup cooked mealworms, minced
3 tablespoon onion, minced
1 tablespoon milk
1 teaspoon horseradish
1/4 teaspoon salt
1 teaspoon pepper
1/3 cup slivered almonds, toasted

Place almonds in a 300°F oven for about 5 minutes or until slightly brown. Combine all ingredients except almonds until well blended. Heat in a baking dish for 15 minutes at 350°F. Place in serving dish and sprinkle with almonds. Serve with vegetables, crackers, breads or chips.

Chocolate Cricket Torte

(Makes 1 8" springform pan)
1 lb butter
4 oz unsweetened chocolate
12 oz semi sweet chocolate
8 eggs, separated
1 cup sugar
1 cup strong liquid coffee
2 cups crickets, toasted and roughly chopped

Butter and flour springform pan. Place chocolates and butter in a bowl over a pot of simmering water to melt. Let cool to room temperature. Whisk together egg yolks, sugar and coffee until well combined. Fold in crickets. Whip egg whites until stiff and fold into chocolate mixture. Bake at 350° F for 30–40

minutes. Center should still be moist. Allow to cool 10 minutes before removing from pan.
    Louis Sorkin, American Museum of Natural History.

Defect Action Levels of Some Foods

Chocolate and chocolate liquor.—Insect filth: Average is 60 or more insect fragments per 100 grams when six 100-gram subsamples are examined *or* any 1 subsample contains 90 or more insect fragments.

Peanut butter.—Insect filth: Average of 30 or more insect fragments per 100 grams. Rodent filth: Average of 1 or more rodent hairs per 100 grams.

Raisins, golden.—Insects and insect eggs: 10 or more whole or equivalent insects and 35 drosophila [fruit fly] eggs per 8 oz.

Tomato paste, pizza and other sauces.—Drosophila fly: Average of 30 or more fly eggs per 100 grams *or* 15 or more fly eggs and 1 or more maggots per 100 grams *or* 2 or more maggots per 100 grams in a minimum of 12 subsamples.

Wheat flour.—Insect filth: Average of 75 or more insect fragments per 50 grams.
    Source: www.cfsan.fda.gov/~dms/dalbook.html#CHPTR.

May 21

A Wedding Feast
Bishopwearmouth, Durham, England 1753

A description of the wedding of a young couple in Bishopwearmouth in the Northeast of England made its way into a newspaper in Boston, America, in 1753.

> May 21: A very particular wedding was solemnized at Bishop-wearmouth between two young persons. All acquaintances and relations on both sides were invited to the nuptials. They set forward to church about half an hour past seven, preceded by three violins and a bagpipe. Seventy couple went hand in hand, all distinguished by blue cockades, besides an innumerable multitude which did not observe such just regularity. The bill of fare for dinner was as follows:—5 bushels of malt brewed for table beer, 10 bushels for ale, 16 quarters of lamb, 8 turkies, 10 green geese, 8 hams, 4 dozen of hens, 12 ducks, 20 quarters of mutton, 10 quarters of veal, 16 neat's tongues, a quarter of beef roasted whole, 20 stones of beef boiled, 6 bushels of white peas, 80 pounds of butter, 16 pies ; the bride's pie was carried between two persons, on a hand-barrow to the bake-house; 20 gallons of brandy, 8 dozen of lemons, 7 stones of double refined sugar, 10 bushels of wheat, a hundred weight of tobacco, 6 gross of pipes, tarts, whip-possets, cheese-cakes, and jellies innumerable. All things were carried on with the strictest order and decorum till near eleven o'clock at night, when the young couple were put to bed, with all the formalities of singing, throwing the stocking, and sack posset.

Why was this called a "particular" wedding? The *Oxford English Diction-ary* gives a number of meanings of the word "particular," and the one that seems to be suggested by the tone of this report is that it is something "so unusual as to excite attention, peculiar, odd, strange." There is no hint in the report, however, as to just what exactly it was about this ceremony that made it so unusual as to have that effect on the other side of the world.

Perhaps it had something to do with the spectacle of 70 pairs of blue-cockaded guests walking hand in hand to the church? A cockade is a knot or rosette of ribbons worn to demonstrate a particular allegiance. A few decades later a blue cockade in England became symbolic of "true Protestantism"—that is, of virulent anti-Catholicism; a hundred years later in the United States it came to represent the Confederate Secession movement; amongst some German Freemasons it was worn as a symbol of freedom and equality. There are no clues in the report as to their significance at this wedding, so it must remain conjecture.

The version of the report that appeared in the *The Boston Weekly News-Letter*, which was identical in all other respects, specifically mentioned that this couple were "Salters." There was a salt industry in this part of England from medieval times, and this in turn drove the development of the coal and shipping industries, so that by the time of this event the area was thriving, but this wedding hardly seems noteworthy on account of its size and extrava-gance alone.

The bill-of-fare for the wedding feast was standard for the time, although in an era noted for its huge pies, perhaps one requiring two persons and a handbarrow to take it to the bakehouse was a little unusual. A bride pye was the high point of the wedding feast at this time. It was eventually super-seded by the bride cake, which became the modern wedding cake. The shell of these large pies was of the coffin type—that is, it was made from very thick, hard pastry, usually of rye flour, and was not meant to be eaten. The lid was removed and the contents scooped out, in exactly the same way as we would use a casserole dish today. It was the norm for these pies to be taken to the local baker for cooking; for a fee they would be placed in the still-hot bread oven after the bread was removed and cooked in the residual heat.

Recipes

~~~

There were no specific ingredients to a bride pie, it contained whatever deli-cacies could be procured at the time. Pies of this nature were often called "battalia" pies, from the Latin beatilles, meaning small precious things. This recipe, from a cookbook of the era, demonstrates the concept very well:

Batalia Pye, or Bride Pye

Take young Chickens as big as black Birds, Quails, young Partridges, and Larks, and squab Pigeons; truss them, and put them in your Pye; then have Ox-palates boiled, blanched, and cut in pieces, Lamb-stones, Sweet-breads, cut in halves or quarters, Coxcombs blanched, a quart of Oysters dipped in Eggs, and dredged over with grated Bread, Marrow. Having so done, Sheep's Tongues boiled, peeled, and cut in slices; season all with Salt, Pepper, Cloves, Mace, and Nutmegs, beaten and mixed together; put Butter at the bottom of the Pye, and place the rest in with yolks of hard Eggs, Knots of Eggs, Cocks-stones and Treads, Forc'd-meat Balls; cover all with Butter, and cover up the Pye; put in five or six spoonfuls of Water when it goes into the Oven, and when 'tis drawn, pour it out and put in Gravy.

Eliza Smith, *The Compleat Housewife . . . The Second Edition* (London, 1728).

"A Receipt for All Young Ladies That Are Going To Be Married"

To Make a Sack-Posset.

From famed Barbadoes on the Western Main
Fetch sugar half a pound; fetch sack from Spain
A pint; and from the Eastern Indian Coast
Nutmeg, the glory of our Northern toast.
O'er flaming coals together let them heat
Till the all-conquering sack dissolves the sweet.
O'er such another fire set eggs, twice ten,
New born from crowing cock and speckled hen;
Stir them with steady hand, and conscience pricking
To see the untimely fate of twenty chicken.
From shining shelf take down your brazen skillet,
A quart of milk from gentle cow will fill it.
When boiled and cooked, put milk and sack to egg,
Unite them firmly like the triple League.
Then covered close, together let them dwell
Till Miss twice sings: You must not kiss and tell.

From, *The New York Gazette*, February 13, 1744.

May 22

Seafood Feast
Squantum Club, East Providence, Rhode Island, 1901

The Squantum Club was "Rhode Island's most famous social organization" around the turn of the century. The name of the club is derived ultimately from that of the Indian Squantum or Squanto, who is said to have helped the Pilgrims in 1621. He is a shadowy, controversial figure, but nevertheless his name is firmly embedded in the history of the area. In the first few decades of the nineteenth century a tradition of "Squantum Festivals" developed in New England at which white Americans had a fine time "playing Indian." A focus of these festivals was a seafood feast or clambake, apparently in recognition of the importance of fish to the Indians in the area and the Indians' role in assisting the new settlers to acquire a taste for it. Only the most delicate types of fish made it to elegant tables at that time. Shellfish was the food of the poor in England for centuries, obtained by scavenging from the seashore, and fish for most ordinary folk meant the hard dry salted variety which was for "fast" days, was cheap and kept well, but was often not particularly palatable.

By the end of the nineteenth century the seafood bounty of the East was thoroughly appreciated, and the Squantum Club revived and refined the idea of Squantum feasts. On May 22, 1901, the Squantum Club held one of its regular seafood feasts but was unable to resist "playing Indian" completely, and the menu was written in an Indian dialect as well as English. The menu cover read:

SQUANTUMET
At Squantum

Sequanakeeswush=neesneechick=nab=neese
May (or Spring month)   twenty-second

Nquittemittànnug paskugit tashepawsuck nquit
One thousand   nine   hundred   one

And the food for lunch and dinner was as follows:

NOMPAEMETSUONK	POHSHEQUAEMETSUONK
Lunch (or Breakfast)	Dinner
Ashaūnt-kenugkiyeuonk	Nippi sickisuog-nootattamwaetchuash
Lobster salad (or mixture)	Clam broth (or water) in cups
Pease-sitchipuck-sickissuog	Sickissuog-kengkiyeuonk
Little neck clams	Clam chowder (or mixture)
Petukqui namaig	Abbamochashaūntabawsuck
Balls of fish	Deviled lobster in shells
Issattonaneise-aunachimonash	Apwosu-missuckequocke
Doughnuts (or bread nuts)	Broiled Bluefish
Puttuckqunnegonash	Neahketeamuk-acawmé

Crackers (or cakes)

French-fried potatoes (or plant from the
other side)

Munnunnug-machipoquat
Cheese (or milk soured)

APWOSU
Baked, or roasted

Sickissuog   Tautog
Ashaūnteaug   Clams   Blackfish
Lobsters

Quahocke
Quahogs

Neahketeamuk-weekonash
Sweet Potatoes

Wuttattash
Punch (or drink)

Uhpuonkash
Cigarettes (or pipe and tobacco)

Miscuppauog
Sickissu-puttockquinege
Soup   Clam fritters (or cakes)

Kenugkiyeuonk
Salad

Nasaump
Indian Pudding

Munnunnug-machiopoquat
Puttuckqunnegonash
Cheese   Crackers

Wunnemechimmuonk-wenomeneash
Fruit (or "rare apples" and "grapes")

Acawmé manusqussedash
Coffee (or "across the water beans")

Recipes

~~~

Soft Clam Bisque

Separate the soft from the hard portions, cut the latter small and cook them with an equal bulk of water for fifteen minutes to extract the flavor. Strain and discard the tough portions. Blend together 2 level tablespoonfuls of butter and flour without allowing them to boil; when smooth, add gradually 3 cups of milk and stir until boiling. Add the soft parts of the clams and simmer for five minutes. Pour in the strained liquor, season to taste and sprinkle a little finely chopped parsley over the top before serving.

The Atlanta Constitution, August 11, 1912.

Deviled Lobster

Boil and pick a lobster. Boil one pint of cream with one quarter of a pound of butter, one teaspoonful of flour, a little mustard, one small saltspoonful of cayenne, half a teaspoonful of salt. After it has boiled, mix in the yolks of two eggs and stir well. If not sufficiently thick, add a little more flour.

Let the lobster be well picked, warm all together and put in the shell. Cover with bread or cracker crumbs and butter and put in the oven and brown. Before putting in the mustard to boil mix it with a little cream.

Trenton Evening Times, January 2, 1907.

Baked Indian Pudding

Boil one pint of milk; stir in four tablespoons yellow Indian meal and cook ten minutes. Cool it and add one pint of cold milk, half a cup New Orleans molasses, half a teaspoon each of salt and cinnamon, and two eggs well beaten with half a cup of sugar. Bake in a hot oven two hours; when it has baked half an hour add one cup of cold milk. Do not stir it in. Eat with cream or butter. This is a genuine New England Indian pudding.

Los Angeles Times Cook Book (1905).

May 23

Harriman Expedition Dinner
En Route to Seattle, Washington, 1899

The American Railroad executive E. H. Harriman (1848–1909) was ordered by his doctor to take a vacation early in 1899. Harriman threw himself into the idea with as much vigor and attention to detail as he had the work which had exhausted him and came up with a magnificent plan. His vacation was to be a scientific expedition to explore the coast of Alaska, to study and photograph its wild beauty, and catalog its flora and fauna. The expedition covered 9,000 miles in two months and was an amazing achievement all round, although it did have its darker side. Harriman was later accused of looting and stealing Alaskan artifacts and treasures and relics, but the matter, in the way of such accusations against rich men, never really came to anything.

On May 23, Harriman's party left New York aboard a private luxury train for Seattle, where the expedition was to start. The group of experts, guests, and family members sat down to a fine dinner on their first night together.

Neck clams, green turtle consomme, cucumbers.
Baked blue fish with fine herbs, potato Saratoga.
Prime roast beef, roast Philadelphia capon, potatoes, spinach, peas.
Peach fritters, tomato salad.
Apple tapioca pudding, hard and brandy sauce, ice cream, assorted cake.
Preserved fruit marmalade, dried Canton ginger.
English and graham wafers, strawberries and cream.
Roquefort, Canadian Camembert and Edam Cheese, Danish water crackers.
Café noir.

Recipes

~~~

Saratoga Potatoes

Pare potatoes, and slice thin as wafers, either with a potato-slicer or a thin-bladed, very sharp knife. Lay in very cold water at least an hour before using. If for breakfast, over-night is better. Have boiling lard at least three inches deep in a frying kettle or pan. Dry the potatoes thoroughly in a towel, and drop in a few slices at a time, frying to golden brown. Take out with a skimmer, and lay on double brown paper in the oven to dry, salting them lightly. They may be eaten either hot or cold. Three medium-sized potatoes will make a large dishful; or, as they keep perfectly well, enough may be done for several meals, heating them a few minutes in the oven before using.

Helen Campbell, *The Easiest Way in Housekeeping and Cooking* (1903).

Peach Fritters

Peel the peaches, split each in two and take out the stones; dust a little powdered sugar over them; dip each piece in the batter, and fry in hot fat. A sauce to be served with them may be made as follows: Put an ounce of butter in a sauce-pan, and whisk it to a cream; add four ounces of sugar gradually. Beat the yolks of two eggs; add to them a dash of nutmeg and a gill each of cold water and rum; stir this into the luke-warm batter, and allow it to heat gradually. Stir constantly until of a smooth, creamy consistency, and serve. The batter is made as follows: Beat the yolks of three eggs; add to them a gill of milk, or half of a

cupful, a saltspoonful of salt, four ounces of flour; mix. If old flour is used, a little more milk may be found necessary.
White House Cook Book (Chicago, 1887).

Brandy Sauce, Cold

Two cupfuls of powdered sugar,
half a cupful of butter,
one wine-glassful of brandy,
cinnamon and nutmeg, a teaspoonful of each.
Warm the butter slightly, and work it to a light cream with the sugar, then add the brandy and spices; beat it hard and set aside until wanted. Should be put into a mold to look nicely, and serve on a flat dish.
White House Cook Book (Chicago, 1887).

Plain Cold, Hard Sauce

Stir together one cupful of white sugar, and half a cupful of butter, until it is creamy and light; add flavoring to taste. This is very nice, flavored with the juice of raspberries or strawberries, or beat into it a cupful of ripe strawberries or raspberries and the white of an egg, beaten stiff.
White House Cook Book (Chicago, 1887).

May 24

Empire Day Luncheon
Junior Carlton Club, London, England, 1933

Empire Day was a Canadian idea, first put forth in 1898 "to advance the cause of unity within the Empire." The birthday of Queen Victoria (1819–1901) was, according to *The Times*, chosen "so that ultimately the anniversary of her Majesty's birthday throughout the length and breadth of her dominions might be associated in the minds of her subjects (especially of the young) with that vast Empire which has in so large a measure been the product of her long and glorious reign." One of the major aims was to remind the subjects of the Empire of the "duties and responsibilities attaching to British citizenship."

A national duty is to keep as much of the profit at home as possible. As a promotional exercise for Empire products a special luncheon was held on Pall Mall in London by the Empire Marketing Board on Empire Day in 1933. The 187 major ingredients were sourced (many of them as gifts) from 45 of the Dominions and Colonies of the British Empire. *The Times* newspaper report gave the details:

> The soups will include North Borneo bird's nest, Straits Settlements shark's fin, Fiji cucumber, and Ascension Islands green turtle; and among the fish dishes will be Irish salmon, Dover sole, grilled mackerel with Uganda chilly sauce,

whitebait with Kelantan Malayan pepper, Halibut with Bombay chutney sauce, and fried whiting with New Zealand melted butter. Roast Welsh milk lamb, Surrey fowl and Ulster bacon, braised sweetbread and Jersey peas, liver and Canadian bacon, and Indian mutton curry will be among the hot dishes, while the cold side-table will include a baron of Scotch beef, New Zealand lamb, Gambia ground-nut rissoles, English veal, and wild duck and Windward Islands Guava jelly. Among the sweets will be Malta figs and cream, Turk's Island tamarinds, Rhodesian buckwheat cakes and maple syrup, Mauritius pineapple, Canadian apple pie, Kenya coffee mould, and Banbury pancakes.

Britain's industrial growth and international trade were begun slowing as the twentieth century advanced, and it became increasingly necessary for her to look to her own lands for necessary goods. The campaign began in earnest in 1923 with a series of events designed to educate the public as to the necessity to make the Empire self-supporting. In October the British housewife was encouraged to participate in an "Empire shopping week," and in the following month a series of exhibitions arranged by the British Empire Producers' Organization, the Army and Navy Cooperative Society, the Dominion Governments, the Governments of India, and the Colonial Agencies began around the country. The British housewife was encouraged to buy Empire goods, by which she would save not just the Empire, but indeed the whole world.

> If every housewife would prefer Empire goods to the extent of half-a-crown, it would mean about one and a half million pounds per week to the Empire. It was necessary for the future of the world that there should be a strong British Empire, and we could only be strong if we were self-supporting.

The Empire Marketing Board had been established in 1926 to continue this "practical propaganda" by way of a variety of promotional and educational activities. A series of formal Empire dinners was held, and a small booklet of Empire menus was published to help the average Briton to follow suit. There was no earthly reason not to participate, for as well as cost-saving, "we have every clime and every season within our borders, and cold storage has annihilated distance, we may dine as elegantly, as exotically, as we choose. . . . and *gigot de pré-salé* is only leg of mutton after all."

The board also commissioned a series of advertisements in the *Radio Times* in 1929 to promote specific "Empire-quality" goods such as East African coffee, Canadian apples, South African oranges, Indian rice from Bengal and Burma, and Irish free state butter, eggs and bacon (and Southern Rhodesian tobacco and cigarettes). Buying from the colonies was all very well of course, but Empire begins at home, and the public were particularly exhorted to buy British when possible, and especially to "Eat more fish. Caught by British Fishermen."

Recipes

~~~

The guava is a tropical fruit native to the Americas, Caribbean, and parts of North Africa. The jelly made from the fruit was highly prized and became an important industry in the West Indies. Large quantities were exported to Britain, where it was considered a great delicacy. The basic method of making it is the same as for any other fruit jelly.

Guava Jelly

8 lbs. ripe guavas.
1 lb. sugar-candy.
10 limes.

Peel and cut the guavas in four, boil in a little water, and press out the juice through a cloth; add the juice of the limes and the sugar; boil and skim very carefully till it will jelly. Guava cheese is made in the same way, only the fruit must be rubbed through a coarse sieve.

The Englishwoman in India: Information for Ladies . . . By a Lady Resident (1864).

Coffee Mould

| 1/4 pint milk | 2 tablespoons coffee essence |
| 1/2 oz. gelatine | 2 tablespoonfuls sugar. |

Soak the gelatine in a little cold milk; when dissolved add to it the remainder of the milk and coffee essence and boil; add the sugar, pour into a wet mould, turn out when set. Strong coffee can be used instead of essence, but must be very carefully strained.

Laurie's Household Encyclopaedia (London, 1931).

Birds' Nest: see March 8.
Sharks' Fin: see March 8.
Buckwheat Cakes: see March 24.

May 25

Parliamentary Dinner
Carlton House, London, England, 1816

It is not unusual for individual dishes at a banquet to be named after famous people, and a dinner served by the English clergyman Thomas Ackland (1791–1844) in 1816 was unusually replete with such dishes. A writer for the radical newspaper *The Morning Chronicle* took great delight in reporting that

Sir Thomas Ackland gave a splendid dinner to the Prince Regent's Ministers, and a large party of Parliamentary Friends. With that good taste which is so eminently his character, he lost no opportunity of delicately complimenting his Ministerial friends ; and even his Bill of Fare, furnished by the Carlton House Cook, breathed the language of Saintly flattery—as it was received with great applause by the company, we have obtained a copy, and present it to our readers.

POISSONS.
Harent laité, sauce moutarde à la Pole;
Turbot, sauce à la bonhommie de Curtis;
Ecrevisses, sauce avare à la Rose;
Morue à la Provençale de Lascelles.

ROTS.
Dindon, garni d'effronterie au galimatias
de Castlereagh
Dindonneau nouveau, sauce Binning;
Oison au Wood;
Perdreau Rouge à la Peel;
Bécasse au Vyse;
Canard sauvage au Joseph Yorke.

ENTREES.
Cotelettes d'agneau à la veille financière au Vansittart;
Tête de veau au naturel de Bragge;
Poulet gros à la Tartare au Vesey;
Palais de Bœuf, à l'Allemande au Bloomfield;
Chou-croute garnie des petites platitudes de Robinson;

HORS D'ŒUVRES.
Boudin noir à la Comptou;
Cotelettes de porc frais, sauce Lopez;
Pieds de chochon au Hiley;
Saucisson au Sturges.

PATISSERIES.
Vol-au-vents de cervelle de veau à la Gower;
Deux petits patés aux Cranbourne et Valletort, &c. &c. &c.

DESSERT.
Gelée de groseilles au Warrender;
Petit pot de rhum à la Kirkwall;
Quatre mendian[t]s aux Marryatt, Leslie Foster,
Holmes, et Wallhouse Littleton, &c.

This menu is a veritable catalogue of the MPs and other politicians of the day, with many of their foibles exposed. It is hard to say whether it is gently mocking or savagely satirical, and it is likely that some of its targets would have been insulted by the dishes named for them.

The "turkey garnished with effrontery and gibberish" was assigned to Robert Stewart Castlereagh (1769–1822), an Anglo-Irish Whig politician who crossed the floor (meaning he changed his Parliamentary allegiance and left the Whigs to join the Tories) in 1795 and was involved in several controversial events—namely, the passing of the Irish Act of Union in 1800 and a duel against the Foreign Secretary George Canning (1770–1827). The *Poulet Gros* (fat chicken) represents William Vesey-Fitzgerald (1783–1843), an Irish statesman who managed to obtain significant political advancement in spite of his dubious behavior. The *Quatre Mendiants* (literally, four beggars, see January 17) are John Leslie Foster (1781–1842), William ("Billy") Holmes (1779–1851), Edward Wallhouse Littleton (1791–1863), and Joseph Marryat (1790–1876), brother of Frederick Marryat (1792–1848) the author of *Mr Midshipman Easy*.

The correspondent who submitted the article considered the possibility that the *Gelée de groseilles* (literally, jelly of gooseberries) was in fact what would be called in English a gooseberry fool. A "fool" (culinarily speaking) is "a dish composed of fruit stewed, crushed, and mixed with milk, cream, or custard" and is commonly made from gooseberries. In this menu the "fool" is George Warrender (1782–1849), a Scottish MP and First Lord of the Admiralty who was known as a *bon vivant*, hence his nickname of "Sir Gorge Provender."

Recipes

~~~

</div>

To Make a Gooseberry Fool

Take two quarts of gooseberries, set them on the fire in about a quart of water. When they begin to simmer, turn yellow, and begin to plump, throw them into a cullender to drain the water out; then with the back of a spoon carefully squeeze the pulp, throw the sieve into a dish, make them pretty sweet, and let them stand until they are cold. In the meantime take two quarts of new milk, and the yolks of four eggs beat up with a little grated nutmeg; stir it softly over a slow fire; when it begins to simmer, take it off, and by degrees stir it into the gooseberries. Let it stand till it is cold, and serve it up. If you make it with cream you need not put any eggs in: and if it is not thick enough, it is only boiling more gooseberries. But that you must do as you think proper.

Hannah Glasse, *The Art of Cookery Made Plain and Easy* (1947).

Glasse's book also includes recipes for other "fools," including a "Westminster fool," which, on the basis of its name alone, would have suited the theme of this menu even more perfectly. It is a sort of trifle, with custard poured over a base of sherry-soaked bread.

May 26

<div align="center">

Royal and Plebeian Supper
Madison Square Garden, New York, 1893

</div>

When their Royal Highnesses Infanta Doña Eulalie (1864–1958) and Infante Don Antonio (1866–1930) of Spain visited New York in 1893, there was more agonizing over the rules of protocol than there was over the catering arrangements. The political and civic dignitaries were apparently relieved when the Infanta let it be known that "she would be guided entirely by American etiquette during her stay here, and that she did not desire any of the ceremony which attaches to Courts."

On the evening of May 26, there was a gala ball tendered by "the Circulo Colon-Cervantes of the City of New York under the auspices of their Excellencies the Ministers Plenipotentiary and Envoys Extraordinary of Spain, Mexico, Peru, and Brazil to the United States" (*The New York Times*). The ball was "of the most exclusive character," and the ball supper was spectacular. All guests were seated in the same room, but the royal visitors and the other particularly honored guests sat at an elevated table as they would have in medieval times, and there were two separate menus. Many of the dishes were named in honor of Spain, its royal family, and the mutual history of the two countries.

MENU AT THE TABLE OF THE INFANTA.

Little Neck Clams.

POTAGE.
Consommé de Volaille.   *Chablis*.

HORS D'ŒUVRES.
Timbale Pinta.   *Amontillado*.
Olives Espagnole.   Amandes Salé

POISSON.
Escaloppe de Bass, à la Barcelona.   Pomme Gastronomme.

RELEVÉ.
Chablis.
Filet de Bœuf Mignon, Sauce Madere.
Tomate, à la Reine.

ENTRÉE.
Amontillado.
Terrapine à l'Americain.

PUNCH.
Colombo.

RÔTI.
Chapon Farcie, aux Truffe et Marron.

SALADE.
Château Latour.
Salade de Lartno.

PIÈCE FROID.
Pâtés de Foie Gras.
Pâtés de Gibier.
Gallantine de Chapon, aux Truffe.

GLACÉ.
Santa Maria Champagne.
Biscuit Diplomatique.

DESSERT.
Gateaux Assortis.
Fruit Glacés.
Coraquet.
Fruits de Saison.

PIÈCE MONTÉE.
Café.

MENU AT THE OTHER TABLES.

POTAGE.
Consommé en Tasse.

HORS D'ŒUVRES.
Chablis.
Olives.   Radis.   Amandes Salé

POISSON.
Saumon, Sauce Tartar.

RELEVÉ.
Chablis.
Filet de Bœuf, à la Barcelonnaise.
Pommes Parisienne.

ENTRÉE.
Pâtés de Ris de Veau.
Légumes.   Petits Pois.   *St. Julien.*

PUNCH.
Espagnole.

RÔTI.
Pigeons sur Canape, aux Cresson.

SALADE.
Champagne.
Salade de Volaille.   Mayonnaise d'Homard.

GLACÉ.
Santa Maria.   Columbus.   Biscuit Madrid.

DESSERT.
Gateaux Assortis.   Bonbons.   Cosaques.
Café.

In spite of the relaxation of the rules of etiquette, there were some embarrassingly uncertain moments as guests were presented to the royal couple, with several whom were overanxious overdoing the bowing (one also genuflecting), walking backward (it is improper to turn one's back on a royal person; one must take several steps backward before turning away), and getting entangled in others' gowns. The excitement of being presented first to the Infanta caused several guest to completely overlook the fact that Don Antonio also had to be acknowledged.

The hierarchy in the two menus is quite clear. The menu for the lesser guests (the newspapers referred to it as the Plebian version) did not include the terrapin, the truffled dishes, or the *foie gras*, for example, and their wine selection was less fine.

Recipes

~~~

Foie gras ("fat liver") has been a favorite delicacy for millennia: the ancient Egyptians and Romans are known to have enjoyed it. It has recently been the subject of some controversy based on the alleged treatment of geese and ducks, and for some it is considered an unethical product. It was originally served in a pastry shell (the legacy remaining in the name *pâté*, meaning pastry), although today only the filling is served. Charles Ranhofer, the chef to Delmonico's of New York, gave a long recipe for pâté de foie gras in his book *The Epicurean* (1894). It is summarized here.

Pâté de Foie Gras

Ranhofer wrote, "This cold pie is intended for very large suppers." The construction is complex and requires several steps. A Foie Gras terrine is made, which becomes the filling. A raised pie shell is baked "blind," then filled with chopped savory jelly and slices of foie gras, "finish filling with the prettiest slices, dressing them in a compact circle, and filling the inside of this with fine chopped jelly. Fasten the pie on a cold dish, surround the base with croutons of jelly, and on top of the chopped jelly lay a fine truffle, peeled and cooked in wine."

Terrine of Foies Gras

Put two and a half pounds of fat ducks' liver in a terrine, after removing the gall, seasoned with foies gras spices and larded with large fillets of raw truffles. Pound the truffle parings with five ounces of fresh chopped fat pork and six ounces of very white lean veal or pork meat, free from sinews, also chopped up finely, and four ounces of raw lean ham, adding the liver parings, salt and spices. Infuse a piece of cinnamon stick in a little Madeira wine, pass it through a sieve and mix it with the forcemeat, also six spoonfuls of cooked fine herbs; season the whole to perfection.

Spices for Pâtés de Foie Gras

Four ounces of nutmeg, four ounces of cloves, four ounces of basil, four of marjoram, four ounces of thyme, two and a half ounces of black pepper, three ounces of white pepper, two and one-third ounces of bay leaf, two and a half ounces of mace, two and a half ounces of ginger, two and a third of coriander seeds, one and two-thirds ounce of sweet pepper. One ounce of these mixed spices to every two pounds of salt.

Potatoes Gastronome

From some raw potatoes trim cylindrical one inch in diameter by an inch and a quarter long; blanch them for ten minutes, then drain off and finish cooking in clarified butter; when done pour this butter off and add salt, lemon juice, a small quantity of meat glaze, chopped truffles and a little Madeira wine. Range and serve in a vegetable dish.
    Charles Ranhofer, *The Epicurean* (1894).

Pommes Parisienne: see June 23.
Sauce Madere : see February 28.

May 27

Dinner for the Norwegian Royals
Elysée Palace, Paris, France, 1908

When King Haakon VII (1872–1957) and Queen Maud (1869–1938) of Norway visited France in 1908 they were subject to the usual round of official banquets and receptions. The man in charge of the dinner held at the Elysée Palace on May 27 was Auguste Escoffier (1846–1935), one of the most famous chefs of all time. Escoffier is considered the father of *haute cuisine*. He took the ornate dishes and complex methods of Antonine Carême (see January 18) and simplified and codified them, and he promoted and popularized the modern *service à la Russe* (see January 17). His book *Le Guide Culinaire*, published in 1903, is still required reading today for serious chefs and culinary students.

MENU DU DINER

Offert par M. le President Fallieres
a LL. MM le Roi et la Reine de Norvege
27 Mai 1908

Melon frappé
Consommé Théodora
Crème de Volaille à l'ancienne
Truites Saumonée u vin du Rhin
Poulets de grain à la Parisienne
Selle de Pré-salé Forestière

Foies gras frais glacés au Xérès
Granité à l'orange
Sorbets au kummel
Dindonneaux au truffés
Jambons d'York au Champagne
Salade Gauloises
Asperges d'Argenteuil sauce Crème
Poires Crassanes
Friandises
Dessert

A feature of this menu is that the provenance and exact type of many of the main ingredients is specified. To the best chefs, this is extremely important. The asparagus was from Argenteuil, a few miles northwest of Paris. Argenteuil asparagus has white stalks grading to purplish below the green tips and has been famous since the seventeenth century. The "pears" are specifically Crassanes, or *Passé-Crassanes*, which are grown from pears grafted onto quince stock and are a superb cooking variety. The *Selle de Pré-salé Forestière* is lamb with particularly delicate slightly salted flesh due its being raised on the salt marshes of Normandy and the Atlantic coast.

Dinners such as this always included a frozen punch, sorbet, or granita part way through the meal to "cleanse the palate" for what was to follow. For some reason Escoffier chose to present two variations at this dinner. *Kummel* is a liqueur flavored with caraway seed, which has been considered a good digestive aid for many centuries. The original "comfits" served at the end of a meal from ancient times were usually made from caraway seeds coated in sugar and are much like the multicolored fennel seeds that are commonly given in Indian restaurants.

Recipes

~~~

A consommé is a clear soup (broth, *bouilli*) with a base of meat, fish, or occasionally vegetable stock. The various garnishes determine the name of the soup. Many examples appear on the menus in this book.

Consommé Théodora

Put in the consommé, equal parts of small chicken dumplings, royal, and boiled asparagus tips. Before serving add some chopped chervil.
  The Hotel St. Francis Cook Book (1919).

Champagne Sauce (for ham)

3/4 pint Espagnole Sauce
1 glass of champagne

2 cloves
6 peppercorns
1 bay leaf

Put the cloves, peppercorns, bay leaf, and espagnole sauce into a stewpan on the fire; let it reduce a little, add the champagne, and the essence remaining from the braised ham. Reduce the whole for ten minutes, or longer if found too thin. Strain through a pointed strainer and serve with braised ham.
Charles Herman Senn, *The Book of Sauces* (1915).

Salad Gauloise

This is a "compound salad." It usually consists of a mixture of mushrooms, truffles, asparagus tips, globe artichokes and celery, with a mayonnaise dressing.
Some recipes include potato.

Melon Frappé (melon water ice): see June 20.

May 28

Wedding Feast
Milan, Italy, 1368

When Lionel, the Duke of Clarence (1338–1368) and second son of King Edward III of England was to be married to Violante of the enormously powerful Visconti family of Milan in 1368, he traveled from London with a retinue that included 2,000 English horsemen. At that time, London was a medieval city of wooden buildings and unpaved streets, but in northern Italy the Renaissance had already begun, and there was a great flowering of all the arts—architectural, artistic—and culinary.

Dynastic marriages were about power and politics, and the wedding that Galeazzo Visconti gave for his daughter left no doubt as to who had the edge on sophistication.

After the ceremony in the Basilica of Santa Maria Maggiore, a spectacular banquet was held in the open courtyard in front of his palace in the Piazza dell'Arenga. The illustrious guests were seated according to rank at two huge tables, and amongst them were the French chronicler Jean Froissart (ca. 1337–ca.1405), the Italian poet and humanist Petrarch (1301–1374), and possibly also the author of the *Canterbury Tales*, Geoffrey Chaucer (1343–1400.)

It was said that the banquet was so sumptuous that the leftovers would have fed 10,000 men. There were 18 courses of fabulous food, much of which was gilded with real gold. With each course, Gian Galeazzo, the bride's brother and other well-born young men brought fantastic and extravagant gifts to the table, as recorded in Bernadino Corio's *Storia di Milano*, published in 1503 (translated by Marisa Raniolo Wilkins):

In the first spread was a double offering [i.e. it was served in duplicate, as a mark of special honor], that is meat and fish for the Duke's table; presented were two gilded piglets with fire coming from their mouths: some fish called golden piglets [*porcellete*—perhaps porcelain crabs]; and accompanying these were two grey-hounds with velvet collars and silk cords, and twelve pairs of bloodhounds with golden chains: leather collars and silk cords, that is every pair of bloodhound tied on to one strand, then joined into fours.

The second spread consisted of gilded hares and gilded pikes, with twelve pairs of greyhounds with silk collars and golden clasps, and cords, six made of silk, one per pair, and six gos-hawks with buttons and with tags, six made of silver and with the enamelled coat of arms of Signor Galeazzo and Signor Conte.

The third spread was an entire calf all gilded, and gilded trout, and twelve hunting dogs with velvet collars, and clasps and golden studs; with silk cords, that is one per pair.

The fourth spread consisted of golden quails and partridges, with roasted gilded trout, twelve sparrow hawks with pressed harnesses, silk hoods, and silver buttons, accompanied by twelve hunting dogs with gilded chains, twelve of imitation gold with ties, six in all, that is one per pair.

The fifth spread consisted of gilded ducks, gilded herons, gilded carp, falcons, six with little caps made of velvet with pearls and buttons on top, and with silver tags with their emblems on top.

The sixth spread consisted of beef, fat capons with garlic sauce and sturgeon in water and twelve metal cuirasses with silver clasps with the insignias of the favourite signori.

The seventh spread consisted of capons and meat in lemon sauce with fish in the same sauce with twelve suits of [tournament] armour, twelve saddles, and an equal number of lances, all with the corresponding insignias, and golden shields, two for each armoured man, two saddles decorated with silver and enamel for the bridegroom and the others made of imitation gold.

The eighth spread consisted of beef pies also some made with fat eels, and twelve suits of war amour, two decorated with silver for the bridegroom.

The ninth spread consisted of meat moulded in jelly [aspic] and fish, with twelve pieces of gold brocade and twelve of silk.

The tenth spread consisted of meat moulded in jelly and fish, chiefly lampreys, and two silver and enamelled flasks; six basins made of silver, gold and enamel, one flask filled with Malvesia and the other with Vernaccia wine.

The eleventh spread consisted of roasted kid, and roasted shad, with six pairs of horses and saddles decorated with gilded silver, six lances, six golden targets, six metal helmets two made of gilded silver for the Count and one other of imitation gold.

The twelfth spread consisted of hare and venison on golden trays, with many other different fish on silver trays, and six great coursers with saddles decorated with gold and each with the emblem of the squad to which they belonged. There were two decorated especially for the bridegroom.

The thirteenth spread consisted of beef and venison moulds and six steeds with gilded bridles and green velvet cloaks with a button and a red bow at the edge of the cloak and with silk fringes.

The fourteenth spread consisted of capons and poultry in red sauce and the green [sauce] of citrons and tench reversed [turned inside-out], six steeds with gilded bridles, red velvet cloaks with buttons and with gold bows and crimson velvet halters.

The fifteenth spread consisted of peacocks, salted [pickled] tongue, carp, with vegetables, and a heavy mantle and hood covered with pearls and lined with ermine.

The sixteenth spread consisted of rabbits, peacocks, roasted swans and ducks, with a great silver basin: a clasp, a ruby, a diamond, a pearl, and [other valuable jewels].

The seventeenth spread consisted of junket and cheese with twelve fat oxen.

The eighteenth spread consisted of fruit and sweetmeats, and two coursers for the bridegroom, called the Lion and the Abbott.

Recipes

~~~

The following recipes are taken from the Italian work *Epulario*, first published in 1516 but based on earlier works. The following recipes are from the English translation, published in 1598.

To Dresse Capon, Peacocke, Feisant, and Other Foule

Shoveler, Puet, Ducke, Crane, wild Goose, Heron and Storke, are all good and would be stuffed with Garlike, onions, or such like things. Peacocke, Feisant, Partrich, wild Henne, Quailes, Thrush, blacke Bird, and all other good Birds are to be rosted. Pigeons are good both rosted and sodden [boiled], yet best rosted. King Doves and wild Pigeons are good rosted, but better boiled with Pepper, Sage, Parsely, and Margerum. Capon is good both boiled and rosted, and likewise the Henne.

To Make Good Garlike Sauce

Take blanched Almonds well stamped [crushed, or ground], and being halfe beaten, put as much Garlike to them as you think good, and stampe them together, tempering them with water least it be oiley, then take crummes of white bread what quantity you will, and soke it either in leane broth, of flesh or fish as time serveth; this sauce you may keepe and use with all meats, fat or leane as you thinke good.

May 29

Sunday Dinner
Hotel Emery, Cincinnati, Ohio, 1892

When the Hotel Emery opened its doors in Cincinnati in 1877 it was well ahead of its time. The site incorporated an arcade of shops, a restaurant, and offices all under the same roof as the hotel. Guests at the hotel could choose to stay on the "American Plan" (meals included) or the "European

Plan'' (meals not included). The Hotel Emery's charges at this time started at $1 a day which presumably applied to the European plan, so that guests wishing to enjoy the Sunday dinner on May 29 would have had to pay extra.

SOUP

Cream of Asparagus.   Consomme Royal.

—

Sliced Tomatoes.   Cucumbers.   Olives.
Young Onions.

FISH

Filet of Sole, au Vin Blang.
Potatoes Quartier.

BOILED

Boiled Chicken, Parsley Sauce.

ROAST

Roast Beef,   Spring Lamb, Mint Sauce.

ENTREES

Mountain Oysters, Fried, Villeroy.
Larded Sweetbreads, Braised French Peas.
Queen Fritters, a la Vanilla.

—

Wine Sherbet.

SALADS

Chicken Mayonnaise.   Lettuce French Dressing.

VEGETABLES

Mashed Potatoes.   Asparagus.
String Beans.   Egg Plant.

DESSERT

Fruit Pudding, Brandy Sauce.
Strawberry Ice Cream.
Pear Pie.   Blance Mange, Vanilla Sauce.   Apple Pie.
Strawberries.   Charlotte Russe.   Assorted Cakes.
Apples.   Oranges.   Bananas.

—

Water Crackers and Cheese.   Coffee.

It was of course traditional at this time for a hotel menu to appear to be written at least partly in French, even if the actual knowledge of the language was rudimentary and resulted in such phrases as *Vin blang* (presumably *vin blanc* or white wine) and *Blance mange* (*blanc-mange*, see January

7). The choice of French (or approximately French-sounding) words was intended to give an air of sophistication to an establishment, and the habit persisted well into the twentieth century. Sometimes, however, the choice of words is not to add refinement but to avoid vulgarity, as with the "mountain oysters" on this menu.

Mountain oysters are steer testicles. They are known by a variety of coy or coarse names such as cowboy caviar, swinging beef, barnyard jewels, Mississippi Valley scallops, farm oysters, and calf fries. In France they are sold as *animelles* ("little animals", see September 29) or *rognons blancs* ("white kidneys"). In old English cookbooks they are referred to rather prosaically as "stones"—and even those of the cockerel were considered delicacies.

Recipes

~~~

Mountain Oysters

These are usually served breaded and deep fried. The Emery Hotel took this dish well away from the ranch and made it very high class by serving it with a classic *Sauce Villeroi* (albeit misspelled). As with most classic sauces, the "correct" way is long and involved, requiring several preliminary steps, and they were rarely prepared this way in the domestic kitchen. Simpler versions appear in many books, such as the very comprehensive *The Book of Sauces*, (1915) by Charles Herman Senn. The book also described the four basic "grand sauces" of the classic French repertoire which are the foundation of many of the dishes in this book. The recipes below are taken from this book.

Villeroi Sauce

Prepare a Bechamel or other rich white sauce, and mix it with finely chopped cooked ham or tongue or both, and finish with a liaison of yolks of eggs and fresh butter or cream.

Parsley Sauce

Prepare half a pint of Bechamel or other white sauce, to this add 1 dessertspoonful of finely chopped and washed parsley and a few drops of lemon-juice.

Vanilla Sauce

Boil 1 gill of milk with 1/2 a vanilla pod; cream 3 egg yolks with 1 oz. of castor sugar, and pour over, whilst stirring, the milk.

Return all into the stewpan and stir over the fire till it thickens, but must not boil. Strain and serve as required (hot or cold).

Brandy Sauce

4 oz. loaf sugar
1/2 oz. cornflour
1/2 gill brandy
1/2 pint water.

Put the sugar and rather more than a gill and a half of water in a copper stew-pan, boil a few minutes, take off the scum, and reduce to a thin syrup. Mix the cornflour with a little cold water, stir into the boiling syrup, and whisk over the fire for about five minutes. Add the brandy, strain, and serve hot with the pudding.

Blancmange: see January 7.
Charlotte Russe: see September 4.
Queen Fritters: see June 1.

May 30

State Dinner
Hall of Facets, the Kremlin, Soviet Union, 1988

In 1988 the general secretary of the Soviet Union, Mikhail S. Gorbachev (b. 1931) and U.S. President Ronald Reagan (1911–2004) met for their fourth scheduled summit. The previous conferences had been held in Geneva, Rejkjavik, and Washington, and the negotiations were ultimately to assist the end of the Cold War. The fourth and final meeting was in Moscow. As is usual for such diplomatic occasions, official dinners were part of the proceedings. On the night of May 30, about a hundred guests attended the state dinner at the Kremlin in honor of President and Mrs. Reagan. The Soviet news agency Tass released details of the menu.

Fresh Caviar
Puff Rasstegay
Assorted Fish with Lemon
Stuffed Turkey Fillet with Fruits
Fish Soup a la Suzdal
Asparagus Cream
Pike-Perch Baked with Crabmeat
Loin of Veal Stewed with Vegetables

Fruit Cream Parfait with Nuts
Fruit Tea
Coffee Pastries
Cakes

The Wines
Manavi Georgian White Wine, 1985
Mukuzani Georgian Red Wine, 1985
Sovetskoye Sparkling Brut
Yubileiny Armenian Brandy, 1977

The evening was described in the usual glowing terms by the newspapers the next day. The dining room was opulent, and the first ladies elegant (Nancy Reagan in red chiffon, Raisa Gorbachev in blue and lavender), but no comment was made about the food itself. The menu was typical for a diplomatic dinner, centered around internationally recognized classical dishes, with a few concessions to "Russian" cuisine. The caviar of course was virtually obligatory as it is a rare and famous product of the region. The only other local dishes were the rasstegay (or *rastegaïs*—see January 8) and the fish sourced from one of the waterways of the Suzdal region northeast of Moscow.

The only surprise at the dinner was President Reagan's speech, in which he appeared to illustrate his theme of "not just the tragedy of war, but the problems of pacifism, the nobility of patriotism, as well as the love of peace" with a lengthy description of the plot of *Friendly Persuasion*, a 1956 film starring Gary Cooper. The newspapers the next day also did not fail to point out that the president at one point appeared to doze off during Gorbachev's speech.

Recipes

~~~

The following recipe comes from *La Cuisine Française. French Cooking for Every Home. Adapted to American Requirements* (Chicago, 1893), but the author, François Tanty, was an expert in Russian cuisine. He served as chef to the tsar of Russia and was also proprietor of the Grand Hotel and the Restaurant Dussaux at St. Petersburg and purveyor to the French and Russian Armies.

Russian Fish Soup

For five persons:

Fresh perch, 4 lbs.
Vegetables,
2 onions,
4 carrots,
4 stalks of celery,
some parsley, thyme and laurel

1st. Clean and wash carefully about 4 lbs. very fresh perch. Take the fillets off and put them apart. 2d. Put the heads and the back bones in a kettle with two onions, 2 carrots, 2 celery stalks, some parsley, thyme and laurel, 2 quarts of water, a little salt, let boil for 1 hour. 3d. Slice in "julienne" (See No. 8), 2 celery stalks and 2 carrots, let them cook in some water until quite tender, then let them drip. 4th. Put the dripped vegetables in a sauce pan with the fillets, pour over the fish "stock" and let cook again for 1/4 hour.

This soup, which may be made with quite every kind of fish, provided it is very fresh, can be served advantageously with lean [i.e. fast-day] dinners and is matchless for camping parties.

Rastegay (rastegais): see January 8.

May 31

French President Lunches aboard a Luxury Train
France, 1925

In May 1925 French President Gaston Doumergue (1863–1937) visited the Bas-Rhin (Lower Rhine) *département* of France—an area that has at several times in its history belonged to Germany. He traveled in a train run by the *Compagnie Internationale des Wagons-Lits* (International Sleeping-Car Company), which had been formed in 1872 by the Belgian businessman George Nagelmackers and was modeled on the American Pullman design.

The menu was classic and elegant, as guests aboard a luxury train would have expected.

DÉJEUNER

Oeufs Frits Catalane
Tournedos Béarnaise
Pommes Noisette
Asperges Sauce Gribich
Terrine de Canard Truffée
Glace Plombière
Dessert

George Pullman (and his followers) designed their trains to be hotels (or palaces) on wheels, and passengers expected elegant multi-course meals. Kitchens took up part of the dining car, and some trains had dedicated kitchen cars but space was still very restricted compared with that in a normal restaurant—or even an ordinary home. A great deal of care went into equipment, storage, and provisioning arrangements to maximize efficiency. Dishes needed to be either capable of being prepared ahead of time (such as the ice cream and the sauces) or quickly cooked with minimum equipment (such as the eggs, the tournedos, and the *pommes noisette*). Railroad chefs aboard luxury trains also had to be able to whip up at short notice special dishes to accommodate the dietary requirements or whims of their wealthy passengers.

Recipes
~~~

Bearnaise Sauce

1/2 gill tarragon vinegar	3 shallots finely chopped
6 peppercorns, crushed	4 yolks of eggs
1 tablespoonful of white sauce	1 sprig thyme
4 oz. butter	lemon- juice
meat glaze	

Put the shallots, peppercorns and thyme with the vinegar in a stewpan, cover and boil until well reduced, remove the thyme, add the sauce and a little dissolved meat glaze. Whisk in the yolks of eggs, taking care not to let the sauce boil, remove the stewpan from the fire, and work in by degrees the butter. Only a little butter must be added at a time, otherwise the sauce will get oily. Strain through a pointed strainer or tammy. A little finely chopped fresh tarragon and chervil, and a few drops of lemon-juice may be added after the sauce is strained.

Bearnaise Sauce (Brune): Prepare an ordinary Bearnaise as above, with the addition of meat glaze to give it a brown color.

Gribiche Sauce

Take half a pint of Mayonnaise sauce, and add sufficient mixed mustard to flavor, then stir in some finely chopped fresh savory herbs (fines herbes) and serve.

Pommes Noisette

Noisette is French for hazelnut, and the dish consists of potato cut into small balls the size of the nuts, and gently fried in butter until lightly brown (nut-brown).

Charles Herman Senn, *The Book of Sauces* (1915).

Tournedos: see May 11.

Glacé Plombière: see November 21.

Oeufs Frits Catalane: Dishes styled ''Catalane'' often have a garnish of eggplant (aubergine) and rice but in the case of eggs sometimes refers to an accompaniment of tomatoes and peppers.

June

Author Nathaniel Hawthorne (1804–1864) said of Willard's Hotel "This hotel, in fact, may be much more justly called the center of Washington and the Union than either the Capitol, the White House or the State Department. You exchange nods with governors of sovereign States; you elbow illustrious men, and tread on the toes of generals." He was speaking during the Civil War, which had officially gotten underway a few weeks before the hotel offered this menu to its guests on June 1.

SOUP.
Clamb a la Royal.

FISH.
Striped Bass, barbacued.

BOILED.
Corned Beef.   Ham and Cabbage.   Leg of Mutton, Caper Sauce.
Smoked Tongue.   Chicken, Cream Sauce.   Jowl and Greens.
Roulade of Beef, braized, with Onions.

COLD DISHES.
Pressed Brisket of Corned Beef.   Ham.   Mutton.   Roast Beef.
Fowl.   Smoked Tongue.

SIDE DISHES.
Small Tenderloin of Beefsteak, broiled and glace, with rich Gravy.
Lamb Cotelettes, saute and glace, on Croutons, Fine Herb sauce.
Vol-au-Vent furnished with Snipe, in Comporte, a la Rine.
Broiled Young Spring Chicken, on Toast, Butter and Parsley Sauce.
Stuffed Shoulder of Lamb, braized, Tomato sauce.
Baked Cod-fish and Potatoes, Normand fashion.
Calf's Head and Feet, braized, Piquante Sauce.
Broiled Squabs, on Croutons, fresh Butter Sauce.
Chicken Pot-pie, sauce, in Fine Herbs, Virginia style.

Stewed Mutton, with Vegetables, Spanish sauce.
Baked Macaroni and Cheese, Italian style.
Stewed White Beans, a la Maitre d'Hotel.
Queen Fritters, with Sugar.
Baked Shad Roe, au Gratin.

ROAST.

Beef.   Lamb, Mint sauce.   Tame Duck.   Ham, Sweet sauce.
Chicken.   Pork.

VEGETABLES.

Green Peas.   Mashed Potatoes.   Plain Potatoes.   Homony.   Rice.
Fried Parsnips.   Asparagus.   Onions.

RELISHES.

Cucumbers.   Cranberry Sauce.   Pickled Beets.

PASTRY AND DESSERT.

Gooseberry Pie.   Rice Pudding.
Vanilla Ice-cream.   Sponge Cake.

FRUITS.

Oranges.   Pecan Nuts.   Raisins.   Almonds.

NOTICE:—Gentlemen having friends to dine will please give notice at the
office.
Meals, Lunches, or Fruit, sent to room, or carried from the table by guests, will
be Charged extra.
Waiters are furnished with wine cards and pencils.

THE GONG will be rung for the early dinner only.

No Seats will be Reserved at the Breakfast Table.

President Abraham Lincoln was a frequent guest at the Willard and had stayed there between February 23 and March 4, 1860, when the discovery of an assassination plot in Baltimore caused a sudden change in his plans.

The notes at the bottom of the menu advising guests about the gong and the extra charge for fruit carried away from the table (and the lack of individual prices for items) suggest that this was a *"Table d'Hote"* type (see October 10) meal. There is a huge range of food here, solidly meat-based as was the norm, with a standard selection of sweet items at the end.

Recipes

~~~

Queen Fritters are made from choux paste (the same as is used to make profiteroles [see November 11]).

Queen Fritters

1 cup water—1/2 pint full measure.
2 ounces butter or lard—large egg size.
1 round cup flour—4 ounces.
5 eggs.

Set the water on to boil in a saucepan and the butter (or lard) in it. Stir in the flour all at once and work the paste thus made with a spoon till smooth and well cooked. Take it from the fire and work in the eggs one at a time, beating in one well before adding another, and when all are in beat the mixture thoroughly against the side of the saucepan. Make some lard hot. It will take half a saucepanful. Drop pieces of the batter about as large as eggs and watch them swell and expand in the hot lard and become hollow and light. Only four or five at a time can be fried because they need plenty of room.

If dropped small, say, not much larger than a walnut, the above will make 25 fritters. They show their remarkable lightness better, however, when made larger.

Jessup Whitehead, *Cooking for Profit* (Chicago, 1882).

To Cook a Shad Roe

Drop into boiling water, and cook gently for twenty minutes; then take from the fire, and drain. Butter a tin plate, and lay the drained roe upon it. Dredge well with salt and pepper, and spread soft butter over it; then dredge thickly with flour. Cook in the oven for half an hour, basting frequently with salt, pepper, flour, butter and water.

F. L. Gillette, *The White House Cook Book* (1887).

Macaroni, Italian style: see March 26.
Rice Pudding: see January 12.
Sponge Cake: see May 14.
Maitre d'Hotel Butter/Sauce: see September 3.

June 2

Coronation Dinner
Westminster Abbey, London, England, 1953

The coronation of Her Majesty Queen Elizabeth II was just the tonic Britain needed in the drab post–World War II years. The immediate postwar optimism and excitement had long since given way to the dreary reality of everyday life. Eight years later, the British were still struggling with rationing, and it was not to end for thirteen more months.

The royal family were not exempt from the restrictions, and the royal kitchens would have been expected to cater for the various coronation functions with rationing firmly in mind.

Immediately after the ceremony, the Queen and her family had luncheon in the Earl Marshal's room at the Abbey. The Earl Marshal is an ancient

Coronation of Queen Elizabeth II. (AP Photo)

hereditary office of state held by the Duke of Norfolk, and it brings with it the responsibility of arranging important functions such as coronations. It was a modest lunch for such a significant occasion, but grand state banquets were to follow on the next two days.

Consommé Royale.

Filet de Boeuf Mascotte.

Salade.

Glacé à la Mangue.

The event was celebrated all over the country with breakfasts, lunches, dinners, and banquets in every hotel, restaurant, and pub. A great number of Her Majesty's subjects, however, dined in a very novel situation—in front of the newfangled household gadget called a television. Newspapers and magazines kindly published recipes that could be prepared in advance, so that mother too could escape from the kitchen and watch the spectacle on the tiny black and white screen.

Some of Her Majesty's subjects were specially catered for on the day. Fourteen hundred of the well-to-do who could afford the 12 guineas a head dined at the Savoy. The faithful who lined up for hours in the rain along the procession route were well served with refreshment stalls, and "hot dogs" and tea were the most popular snacks. Forty-three thousand troops from home and abroad, on duty in various roles, were issued with special "Haversack rations" that contained "one cheese roll, one Spam roll, one bar of chocolate, one portion fruit slab cake, one apple, 2 oz barley sugar, with modifications where necessary for overseas detachments." Meat was still rationed, but the Ministry of Food gave concessions to towns and villages who applied in advance to hold a traditional coronation ox-roasting, provided they undertook to give the meat away for free and that there was a tradition of such an event at coronations in the community.

Recipes
~~~

Consommé Royale

2 pints beef consommé
Egg royal garnish
2 whole eggs
3 yolks
1/2 pint single cream
salt, pinch of sugar, pinch of nutmeg

Vegetable garnish: 2 tablespoons pimento cut in pieces, 2 tomatoes peeled, seeded and cut in strips.
Heat beef consommé, reduce to appropriate strength and season to taste.

To Make the Egg Royal:
Whisk the eggs and egg yolks together with the cream, add the seasoning. Grease a souffle dish with butter and pour in the mixture. Poach in a tin of hot water in the oven for about twenty minutes or until set. When cold turn out and cut in small diamond shapes.
Garnish the hot soup with egg royal and thin strips of pimento and tomato.
Mrs. McKee's Royal Cookery Book (1964). Mrs. McKee was cook to Her Majesty The Queen and Her Majesty The Queen Mother.

Filet de Boeuf Mascotte

600g Mid-cut Beef Fillet
24g Salted Butter
1/5 Bunch Watercress
0.4pt Madeira Sauce
Mascotte Garnish
Salt and Pepper for seasoning

Roast the fillet of beef and slice, placing the pieces on a serving plate. Add on one side the Mascotte garnish then nape the sauce over the meat. Add the watercress to decorate.

For the Madeira Sauce add 1fl. oz. of Madeira to 0.4 pt. of Half Glaze Sauce. For the Mascotte Garnish quarter one and a half globe artichokes. Add cocotte potatoes and whole peeled truffles. Season and add a small amount of parsley then combine.

The Official website of The British Monarchy, http:/www.royal.gov.uk/output/page2227.asp.

Pommes Cocotte

As for Pommes Château, but cut much smaller.

Pommes Château.

Take twenty potatoes, turn them with a knife into olive shape, boil them in salted water for five minutes; drain them and put them on a baking-tin with salt and butter or dripping. Cook them in a very hot oven for thirty minutes, moving them about from time to time. Sprinkle on a little chopped parsley before serving.

Mrs. Brian Luck, *The Belgian Cook Book* (1915).

The most famous dish associated with the festivities was "coronation chicken." It was invented by Constance Spry and Rosemary Hume of the Cordon Bleu Cookery School for an informal luncheon for the foreign visitors in London to attend the coronation. It instantly became a popular classic.

One would not venture to serve, to a large number of guests of varying and unknown tastes, a curry dish in the generally accepted sense of this term. . . . I doubt whether many of the three hundred odd guests at the coronation luncheon detected this ingredient in a chicken dish which was distinguished mainly by a delicate and nut-like flavour in the sauce. For convenience in serving on the occasion mentioned, the chicken was arranged at one end of an oblong dish, and a rice salad as given below was arranged at the other.

Coronation Chicken (Cold) (For 6–8)

2 young roasting chickens;
water and a little wine to cover;
carrot;
a bouquet garni;
salt;
3–4 peppercorns;
cream of curry sauce (recipe follows).

Poach the chickens, with carrot, bouquet, salt, and peppercorns, in water and a little wine, enough barely to cover, for about 40 minutes or until tender. Allow to cool in the liquid. Joint the birds, remove the bones with care. Prepare the sauce given below. Mix the chicken and the sauce together, arrange on a dish, cover with the extra sauce.

Cream of Curry Sauce

1 tablespoon oil
2 oz onion finely chopped
1 dessertspoon curry powder
1 good teaspoon tomato purée
1 wine-glass each of red wine and water
bay leaf, salt and pepper, sugar
slice or two of lemon and a squeeze of juice , possibly more
1–2 tablespoons apricot purée
3/4 pint mayonnaise
2–3 tablespoons lightly whipped cream a little extra whipped cream

Heat the oil, add onion and cook gently 3–4 minutes, add curry powder. Cook again 1–2 minutes. Add purée, wine, water, and bay-leaf. Bring to boil, add salt, sugar to taste, pepper and the lemon and lemon juice. Simmer with the pan uncovered 5–10 minutes. Strain and cool. Add by degrees to the mayonnaise, with the apricot purée to taste. Adjust seasoning, adding a little more lemon juice if necessary. Finish with the whipped cream. Take a small amount of sauce (enough to coat the chicken) and mix with a little extra cream and seasoning.

The Constance Spry Cookbook (1956).

June 3

Meal aboard a Clipper Ship
En Route to Melbourne, Australia, 1856

The discovery of gold in the colonies of New South Wales and Victoria, Australia, in 1851 set off a great wave of migration. The discovery also proved a gold mine to those companies and individuals who could provide transport or services to emigrants willing to spend every penny they had to make their fortune. The shipbuilding industry was given a great spur, with fierce competition to build bigger and faster ships for the lucrative trade. When it was first built, the *Champion of the Seas* of the Black Ball Line was the second largest clipper ship plying the Liverpool-to-Melbourne route.

The passengers aboard the ship on June 3, 1856, were within a few days of arriving in Australia, after leaving England on March 9. There were no doubt the full complement of 500 passengers aboard, spread over first, second, and steerage classes. Some of them, probably the second-class passengers, sat down to this bill of fare on the day.

Salmon
Roast Beef
Mutton Puddings
Roast Shd^r Mutton
Beef Steaks
Cold Ham

Boil'd Leg Mutton
Stew'd Kidneys
Roast Loin Mutton
Roast Beef
Mutton Chops
Gooseberry Tart
Rhubarb— "
Plum— "
Jam Roll Pudding
Tapioca – "
Marmalade Tartlets
Currant Fritters

This was a solid, sustaining meal of plain British fare, made up of large joints of meat and plenty of puddings. To the British, "pudding" today usually means dessert, but until recently it was equally likely to be a savory item. The word derives from the French *boudin*, meaning sausage, which originally meant entrails stuffed with meat. Eventually the word came to apply to the stuffing itself, so a fish or rabbit could be cooked "with a pudding in its belly." Eventually the starchy mass itself, however cooked, became the pudding, even when the arrangement was reversed, and the starch became the casing or base for some other sort of filling, including the sweet.

Every regional cuisine has its starchy filler—whether it is frumenty (see September 23), hominy (see May 19) or hasty pudding, polenta, Yorkshire pudding (see December 24), or in Asian countries—rice. The principle is the same—to fill the stomach and reduce the appetite for the more expensive protein. The classic pudding dough is made from suet and flour and could be boiled, steamed, or baked. It lent itself to an almost infinite number of variations—although if one was very poor, an unfilled lump of plain dough boiled as a dumpling might be dinner.

Recipes

~~~

Eliza Acton (1799–1859) was the first cookbook writer to list ingredients separately, and her book *Modern Cookery for Private Families* (1845) became a classic in its own time. She gave a basic recipe that can be filled or cooked as required.

Suet-Crust, For Meat or Fruit Puddings

Clear off the skin from some fresh beef kidney-suet, and with a sharp knife slice it thin, free it entirely from fibre, and mince it very fine: six ounces thus prepared will be found quite sufficient for a pound of flour. Mix them well together, add half a teaspoonful of salt for meat puddings, and a third as much for fruit ones, and sufficient cold water to make the whole into a very firm paste; work it smooth, and roll it out of equal thickness when it is used. The weight of suet should be taken after it is minced. This crust is so much lighter, and more wholesome than that which is made with butter, that we cannot refrain from recommending it in preference to our readers. Some cooks merely slice the suet in thin shavings, mix it with the flour, and beat the crust with a paste roller, until the flour and suet are perfectly incorporated. Flour, 2 lbs.; suet, 12 ozs.; salt, 1 teaspoonful; water, 1 pint.

Mutton Pudding

Mutton freed perfectly from fat, and mixed with two or three sliced kidneys, makes an excellent pudding. The meat may be sprinkled with fine herbs as it is laid into the crust. This will require rather less boiling than the preceding puddings, but it is made in precisely the same way. [In summary, she says to line a buttered basin with dough, fill it, cover with the remaining dough, tie it all in a floured cloth, and boil for several hours.]

Jam Roll Pudding

The same dough, flattened out, spread with jam, rolled, wrapped in a cloth and boiled gives the Jam Roll Pudding on this menu.

Tapioca Pudding: see September 26.

June 4

Medici Wedding Feast
Palazzo Medici, Florence, Italy, 1469

When Lorenzo de' Medici, known as Lorenzo the Magnificent (1449–1492), married Clarice Orsini (ca. 1453–1487), a young woman from a noble Roman family, the Medici family orchestrated a celebration that simultaneously demonstrated both modest humility and abundant generosity.

The couple had been married by proxy in February, in an arrangement that united the wealth of the Medicis to the nobility of the Orsinis in a way entirely satisfactory to both families. In early June, Clarice and her retinue arrived in Florence for the religious ceremony in the Church of San Lorenzo, which took place on Sunday, June 4, and was followed by the nuptial feast.

The feasting went on for days. The whole population participated as vast quantities of food and wine began to be distributed throughout the city before the wedding day. The 200 or so special guests were banqueted at the Medici Palace for three days. One guest was Piero de Marco Parenti (1450–1519), and he wrote a long account of the events in a letter to a friend. Tables were set up in the palace and courtyards, the men and women strictly segregated as was the custom. In the garden under a loggia sat the bride and 50 young women, inside the palace were the groom's mother and the older women, in the entrance hall were the groom and his brother with the young men, and the elders of the city were at other tables. The tables in the courtyard were set around Donatello's famous bronze statue of David, which had been commissioned by the groom's grandfather Cosimo de' Medici (1389–1465). Music and dancing continued throughout the whole event.

Parenti discussed the table settings, the manner of serving, and the food itself. There were five banquets each day for three days (Sunday, Monday, and Tuesday), "the order of which was alike." Each course was announced by trumpeters and carried in on great silver platters by a procession of bearers. The serving was orchestrated with great precision so that the food was laid on each table at exactly the same time and cleared at the same time. Parenti also gave a summary of the food "particularly the Sweetmeats and Sugar-Plums," of which over 5,000 pounds were consumed.

> On Monday morning to all who had received veal, jelly was given, and then about 1500 trenchers full were presented to others. Many religious [monks and nuns] also received gifts of fowls, fish, sweetmeats, wine, and similar things.
>
> After the guests at the first tables had finished many hundreds ate. They say that between the house here and that of Messer Carlo. more than a thousand people ate, and at Messer Carlo's every day one hundred barrels of wine were drunk.
>
> The banquets [for the special guests] were prepared for a marriage rather than for a magnificent feast, and I think this was done *de industria* as an example to others not to exceed the modesty and simplicity suitable to marriages, so there was never more than one roast. In the morning a small dish, then some boiled meat, then a roast, after that wafers, marzipan and sugared almonds and pine-seeds, then jars of *pinocchiati* [sugared pine-nuts] and sweetmeats. In the evening jelly, a roast, fritters, wafers, almonds, and jars of sweetmeats. On Tuesday morning, instead of the roast were sweet pies of succulent vegetables on trenchers; the wines were excellent malvasy, trebbiano, and red wine.

Recipes

~~~

The Italians at this time were the masters of pastry work and confectionary. The *pinocchiati* mentioned in the account were a particular favorite. They are essentially pine nut pralines.

On Pine Nuts

Pine kernels are drawn from pine nuts, which hold resin when they are separated, and when eaten in food generate the best of humors, settle thirst, take away the imbalance of humors of the stomach and purge the urine. Pine kernels are eaten rather frequently with raisins and are even believed to incite latent passion. They also have the same force seasoned with sugar. The nobler and rich eat these often in Lent at the first and last course. Sugar is melted, and pine nuts are rolled in it with a scoop and made into the shape of a pastille. Gold leaf is added to these, for magnificence, I believe, and for pleasure.

De Honesta Voluptate et Valetudine (Platina, 1475), trans. Mary Ella Milham, 1998.

June 5

Journalists' Dinner
Bohemian Club, San Francisco, California, 1889

The Bohemian Club was founded in San Francisco in 1872, initially as a journalists' club. It fairly quickly accepted other (wealthier) members and has developed a reputation in more recent times as an all-male "secret society" of the rich and powerful.

In 1889 a young English journalist who had only been in America for a couple of weeks attended a banquet at the club. His name was called Rudyard Kipling (1865–1936), and he was to become famous as the author of many books such as *The Jungle Book* and the *Just So Stories*. The guest of honor at the dinner was Lieutenant James W. Carlin, of the U.S. Navy. A few months previously Carlin had acted with great heroism during a typhoon in Samoa, when his captain was swept overboard and his ship sunk. Kipling had mixed feelings about the speeches but was impressed with the food. He wrote "Devoured a dinner, the memory of which will descend with me into the hungry grave."

Huitres.

Potage à la Reine.

POISSON
Truite à la Hollandaise

ENTREES
Terrapin à la Maryland
Filet de Bœuf,
Perigueux Ris de Veau, en caisse

PONCHE A LA CARLIN

LEGUMES
Asperges froid   Petits Pois vert

ROTI
Poularde des Maus

DESSERT
Tutti Frutti Fruits Divers
Pièces Montés Café

This was a fine dinner of elegant, classic dishes without the overwhelming quantities and huge number of choices so common on late-nineteenth-century menus. The caterer could not quite relinquish the *Pièces Montés*—the highly decorative show-off pieces of the pastry cook-confectioner that had been enormously important earlier in the century. He could certainly not ignore the expectation of ice cream and presented it in the form of *tutti-frutti* (Italian, meaning "all fruit").

Recipes

~~~

Terrapin à la Maryland was said to be the finest of the classic ways of preparing turtle.

Terrapin à la Maryland

Carefully cut up two terrapins as described [below]; place them in a saucepan with half a wine-glass of good Madeira wine, half a pinch of salt, and a very little cayenne pepper, also an ounce of good butter. Mix well a cupful of good, sweet cream with the yolks of three boiled eggs, and add it to the terrapin, briskly shuffling constantly, while thoroughly heating, but without letting it come to a boil. Pour into a hot tureen, and serve very hot.

Terrapin: How to Prepare It

Take live terrapin, and blanch them in boiling water for two minutes. Remove the skin from the feet, and put them back to cook with some salt in the saucepan until they feel soft to the touch; then put them aside to cool. Remove the carcass, cut it in medium-sized pieces, removing the entrails, being careful not to break the gall-bag. Put the pieces in a smaller saucepan, adding two teaspoonfuls of pepper, a little nutmeg, according to the quantity, a tablespoonful of salt, and a glassful of Madeira wine. Cook for five minutes, and put it away in the ice-box for further use.

Tutti-Frutti

Prepare a pint of vanilla ice-cream, half a pint of strawberry ice-cream, and half a pint of lemon water-ice; let them remain in the freezers. Put four ounces of candied cherries onto a plate, cut them in halves, and add two candied apricots cut into small pieces. Take six tutti-frutti molds, open one of them, and lay on the cover a spoonful of strawberry ice-cream, with a spoonful of the lemon water-ice, one beside the other, press the sixth part of the candied fruits onto the ice-cream in the cover of the mold, filling the bottom with vanilla ice-cream, and close together firmly. Lay it immediately into a pail with broken ice and rock-salt at the bottom, cover the mold slightly with more ice and salt, then proceed to prepare the other five molds exactly the same. When they are all in the pail and covered as the first one, fill it up entirely with broken ice and salt, and let it freeze for one hour. Have a vessel containing warm water ready at hand, and prepare six small dessert-plates with a small fancy paper on each, lift up the molds, one after the other, wash them off quickly with the warm water, and unmold the tutti-fruttis onto the cold plates, and serve.

Alexander Filippini, *The Table: How to Buy Food, How to Cook It and How to Serve It* (1889).

Potage à la Reine: see February 17.
Sauce Perigueux: see April 14.

June 6

Wedding Supper
England, 1699

When Lady Arran, widow of the Irish peer Lord Richard Butler, wished to arrange the wedding supper for their only child Charlotte to Charles Cornwallis, 4th Baron Corwallis of Eye in June 1699, she called on one of the most famous cooks of the time.

Patrick Lamb was for "near fifty years Master-Cook to their late Majesties King Charles II, King James II. King William and Queen Mary, and to her present Majesty Queen Anne." He was clearly a man of great stamina to have spent five decades in the extraordinarily demanding job of master cook, particularly in a place such as St. James' palace. He also found time to write a cookbook, and in it he included the bill of fare for Lady Arran's daughter's wedding.

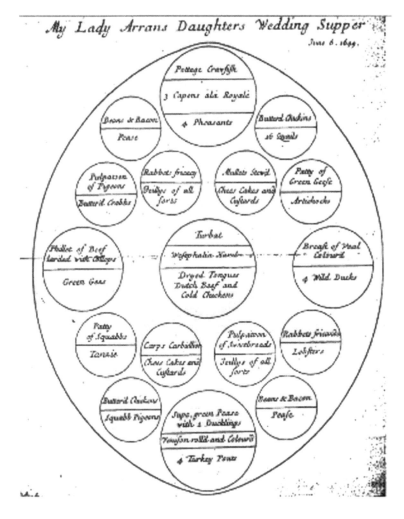

Placement of dishes at wedding supper.

Lamb's bill of fare for this single course *ambigu* (see September 5) was not simply a list of dishes. The method of service at the end of the seventeenth century was as it had been since the Middle Ages (see May 9)—all dishes for each course (with no separation of "sweet" and "savory") were placed on the table before the guests entered the dining room, with geometrical precision and absolute regard for symmetry both horizontally and vertically. The spectacle was all-important—and much of the food must have been cold before the guests managed to eat it.

Recipes

~~~

To Stew Pease the French Way

Take Lettice, and cut them in little Bits, and three or four Onions, Slices of Bacon, a little Butter, Pepper, and Salt, and toss them over a Stove till the Lettice is hot; then add your Pease, and hold them stewing until they are tender; then add to them a little Boiling Water or good Broth; So let them stew softly, and serve them with a Piece of Bacon in the Middle of the Dish, broil'd with Parsley and grated Bread. So serve it to the first Course.

To Make Fine Custards

Take a Quart of Cream, and boil with whole Spice, then put Rosewater, with the Yolks of ten Eggs, and five Whites, and when the Cream is almost cold, put the Eggs into it, and stir it very well; then fill up your Custards [i.e. the pastry shells] and bake them. Serve them with French Confits to them.

Patrick Lamb *Royal Cookery; or, The Complete Court-Cook. Containing the Choicest Receipts in All the Particular Branches of Cookery, Now in Use in the Queen's Palaces* (London, 1701).

From the Preface of His Book:
Patrick Lamb Explains His Mission

... the Author has not here undertaken to cook out an Art of Gluttony, or to teach the Rich and Lazy, how to grow fatter, by ranging Epicurism under the several headings of Jellies, Soupes, and Pottages; but his chief Aim was to represent the Grandeur of the English Court and Nation, by an Instance which lay most within his View and Province: the Magnificence, I mean, of those publick Regales made on the more solemn Occasions of admitting Princes to their Thrones, Peers to their Honours, Ambassadors to their Audience, and Persons of Figure to the Nuptial-Bed. Now, these are Solemnities which call for good Looks and better Chear than ordinary; what in other Cases might be justly term'd Profuseness, does, in this, change its Name, and become a Debt, both to Custom and Decency ...

Sorbet au Champagne: see November 13.

June 7

Dinner of the Three Emperors
Café Anglais, Paris, France, 1867

Paris was "bloated with Majesties and Highnesses" from April to October 1867, thanks to the success of the city's first Universal Exposition. Over 100 members of royalty from all over the world visited the city during that time, and three of the most powerful got together one evening over dinner.

SOUPS.
Impératrice
Fontanges

RELEVES.
Souffle à la Reine
Filets de Sole a la Venitienne
Escalope de Turbot au Gratin
Selle de Mouton Purée Bretonne

ENTREES.
Poulet à la Portugaise
Pâté Chaud de Cailles
Homards à la Parisienne
Sorbets au Champagne

RÔTS.
Canetons a la Rouennaise
Ortolans sur Canape

ENTREMETS.
Aubergines à l'Espagnole
Asperges en Branches
Cassolette Princesse
Bombe Glacée

VINS.
Madere Retour de l'Inde 1810
Xeres Retour de l'Inde 1821
Châteaux d'Yquem 1847
Chambertin 1846
Châteaux Margaux 1847
Châteaux Lafite 1848

The venue for the exposition was a building erected on the Champ de Mars, the same site where the Eiffel Tower would be constructed two expositions and 22 years later. The dinner was held across the city on the other side of the Seine, at one of the most famous restaurants in Europe— the *Café Anglais* (which no longer exists), and the famous guests were Tsar

Alexander II (1818–1881), his son the Tsarevich (1845–1894) who became Alexander III, and Wilhelm I (1797–1888) of Prussia, who was accompanied by Prince Otto von Bismarck (1815–1898).

The chef was Adolphe Duglére who had trained under the legendary Antonin Carême (see January 18) and was a celebrity in his own right. Duglére was no doubt given *carte blanche* to produce this dinner for the illustrious guests, and he created a meal of pure, classic French dishes, served in the customary manner of the time. In spite of the luxury and range of dishes, it is said that the Tsar complained (or perhaps merely commented) on the lack of the traditional French delicacy, *foie gras*. The proprietor instantly replied "Sire, in *Gastronomie Française* it is not the custom to eat foie gras in the month of June. If you will but wait until October, you will have no cause for regret." Naturally, he made sure to send the Tsar a good supply of foie gras (see May 26) when October came around.

Recipes

~~~

As with so many of the classic dishes of the time, each recipe is based on a subset of previously prepared components.

Braized Leg of Mutton, à la Bretonne

Prepare and braize a leg of mutton as directed ... [The leg is boned, larded, stuffed with forcemeat, and braised with the usual vegetables for about four hours.]; when done, glaze and dish it up on a bed of white haricot beans dressed *à la Bretonne*; garnish it round with a border of potatoes cut in the shape of large olives, and fried in butter, of a light colour; ornament the bone with a paper ruffle, and send it to table.

White Haricot Beans, à la Bretonne

Boil the haricot beans as directed above, and when done, drain them in a colander, put them in a stewpan with some Bretonne sauce (see next recipe) and set them to simmer over the stove-fire for five minutes; toss them together, and dish them up.

Bretonne Sauce

Cut two large onions into thin slices; fry them of a light brown colour, in a little butter; then add sufficient brown sauce, according to the quantity required, a little *consommé*, and a pinch of pepper; boil the sauce gently for quarter of an hour, then pass it as you would a *purée*, through the tammy, and put it into a *bain-marie* for use.

Charles Elmé Francatelli, *The Modern Cook* (1860).

June 8

Women's Institute Luncheon
Hotel Windsor, Alliston, Ontario, Canada, 1923

The Alliston Women's Institute gave a luncheon during the visit of the lieutenant governor of Ontario, Henry Cockshutt (1868–1944) in 1923. Canada belongs to the Commonwealth of Nations, an association of independent sovereign states that represents about a third of the world's population. The Commonwealth is a legacy of the British Empire, and most of its members are former colonies of Britain. In Canada, the official representative of the English monarch is the lieutenant governor who plays various constitutional and community roles.

The Alliston women presented a simple menu of everyday food, made more homely by its accompanying quotations.

Eat, drink, and be merry, for tomorrow
you may go hungry.

MENU

Olives   Radishes   Celery
Clear Tomato Soup

"The onion is a homely plant,
And rank as most that grows,
And yet it beats to mix with soup,
The lily of the rose."

ROASTS
Roast Lamb with Mint Sauce
Roast Pork with Apple Sauce

VEGETABLES
New Potatoes   Green Peas

The turnpike road to a man's heart lies
through his stomach.

SALADS
Lettuce and Tomato Salad

The daintiest last
to make the end most sweet.

DESSERT
Strawberry Short Cake and Cream
Apple Pie   Lemon Pie
Ice Cream

Tea   Ice Drink   Coffee

Never speak ill o'them wha's bread ye eat.

Many of the traditional accompaniments to roast meat—such as the lamb with mint, and pork with apple—have been served for centuries, and the reason lies in old agricultural practices. It is often said that the flesh of pigs has a natural taste affinity with apples. More likely it is simply pragmatic—wherever the country was suitable for apple orchards, pigs were often kept and allowed to forage for the dropped fruit which would otherwise have been wasted—so whenever there was pork there were apples available to cook with it. Turkey, a bird from the Americas, was paired with cranberries, also from the Americas. The lamb and mint combination may go back to ancient mountain sheep grazing on wild mint, and there may be an association too with the traditional "bitter herbs" eaten with lamb at Easter in the Middle East.

Recipes

~~~

</div>

<div align="center">

Tomato Soup

</div>

One pint of stewed tomatoes, add a pinch of soda, stir till it ceases foaming, then add one pint boiling water and one pint milk, strain and put on the stove, and when near boiling, add a tablespoonful of cornstarch, wet it with a little cold milk, one tablespoon butter, a little pepper and salt to taste.

<div align="center">

Lemon Pie

</div>

Take two lemons, three eggs, two tablespoonfuls melted butter, eight tablespoonfuls white sugar; squeeze the juice of the lemons and grate the rind of one, stir together the yolks of three eggs and white of one with sugar, butter, juice and rind, then one (coffee) cup of sweet cream or milk, beat all for a minute or two; have ready a plate lined with paste, into which pour the mixture which will be sufficient for two pies of the ordinary size. Bake till the pastry is done. Meanwhile beat the remaining whites to a stiff froth and stir in four spoonfuls of white sugar. Take the pies from the oven and return them quickly to the oven and bake a delicate brown. Take care that the oven be not too hot, or they will brown too quickly and cause the pie to fall when taken out.
    My Pet Recipes, Tried and True, Contributed by The Ladies and Friends of St. Andrew's Church (Quebec, 1900).

Strawberry Shortcake: see May 14.

<div align="center">

June 9

Banquet for Henry Morton Stanley
Waterloo Rooms, Edinburgh, Scotland, 1890

</div>

Henry Morton Stanley (1841–1904), the man commissioned by *The New York Herald* to seek the missing African explorer David Livingstone (1813–1873), visited Scotland in 1890, and a dinner was given in his honor by the Royal Scottish Geographical Society. Stanley did find Livingstone (who had been out of contact with the outside world for six years) on November 10, 1871, near Lake Tanganyika, and according to popular but unsubstantiated history greeted him with the famous words, "Dr. Livingstone, I presume?" Morton had a mixed reception on his return to England. There was controversy over the accuracy of the accounts of his experiences, some of his methods were criticized and his behavior considered ungentlemanly—and worse, he had chosen to take up American citizenship. He was, however, keenly sought as a dinner speaker and attracted hero-worshipping crowds wherever he went. On the occasion of this dinner, the planners had gone to a deal of trouble to feature his African experiences. In addition to "the usual dishes," the menu included the following:

> White Nile soup,
> Salmon with Red Sea sauce,
> Pigeon cutlets à la Congo,
> Zanzibar curry and rice,
> Egyptian quails and cresses,
> Ivory jelly, Niam-Niam cream,
> Bananas à la Ruwenzori.

The African theme continued to the decorations, but no apparent cultural dissonance was caused by the procession into the dinner being preceded by three Scottish pipers playing a lively quickstep. Behind the chairman was "a miniature African forest, formed of tall palms and grasses, which had a fine appearance," and there were representations of a paddle steamer *The Stanley*, and one of the jungle with the relief party emerging from it. One hundred twenty "influential gentlemen" attended the dinner, the ladies being allowed to occupy the balconies after dinner, to listen to the speeches.

The exact recipes for the dishes were invented or adapted for the day. The "Niam-Niam cream" is particularly intriguing. There is a group of people in Central Africa, in the area now called the eastern Sudan, who are called *Niam-Niam*. The name apparently means "great eaters" and may refer to their reputation for cannibalism. It is apparently pronounced something like "Yum-Yum," and "yum" according to the *Oxford English Dictionary* is an "echoic" word—that is, it is "an exclamation of pleasurable anticipation, with implication of sensual or gustatory satisfaction; frequently reduplicated as *yum-yum*." "Creams" were popular dishes from the seventeenth through the nineteenth centuries—and still are. They are essentially flavored and chilled cream or custard, and the basic idea is almost infinitely variable (see July 3, September 29).

The islands of the Zanzibar archipelago (now part of Tanzania) used to be called the Spice Islands (as did some of the Indonesian Islands). Zanzibar was on the major trading route for spices and at one time grew 90 percent of the world's cloves, as well as significant amounts of nutmeg, cinnamon, and pepper. It is not surprising that "curry" (i.e. spicy) dishes are common in East Africa.

Stanley meets Livingston. Courtesy of Library of Congress.

Recipes

~~~

Ivory jelly actually used to be made from the dust produced during the manufacture of the handles of knives and forks from real elephants' tusks. Frank
Buckland (1826–1880), the naturalist famous for eating anything that came
his way (see January 23, December 19), wrote *Curiosities of Natural History*
in 1859. He included a recipe for the jelly, first saying of the dust that it

> is sold at the rate of sixpence a pound; and when properly boiled, and otherwise
> treated, makes the finest, purest, and most nutritious animal jelly that we know
> of. I lately recommended this ivory jelly to a patient who required some form of
> food highly nutritious, but yet not bulky, and my prescription answered admi-
> rably. The ivory-dust can be procured at most of the large ivory-turners in Lon-
> don. Years ago ivory jelly used to be a fashionable remedy, and much sought
> after, and it only now requires to be known to be appreciated.

Receipt to Make Ivory-Dust Jelly

In a brown stewing-pan with a cover, put 1 Ib. of ivory-dust, and three quarts
of water; let it gently simmer for twelve hours, or until it is reduced to one

quart; then put it away to cool, and take the clear jelly off. Add wine and sugar ad libitum.

Quail with Cresses

This is a variation of the age-old chicken (or other bird) with cress (see February 21).

June 10

Luncheon at Sea
SS *Lurline*, 1939

The SS *Lurline* was built for the Matson Line and launched in 1932. For most of her working life she traveled between San Francisco and Honolulu and was, like other luxury cruise ships, pressed into service as a military transport ship during World War II. The outbreak of the war was still a few months away when the *Lurline*'s passengers sat down to the following delightful set of luncheon choices.

Spring Onions   Garden Radishes

APPETIZERS

Filet of Marinated Herring in Cream
Chilled Tomato Juice

Iced Hawaiian Pineapple   Poi Cocktail
Smoked Salmon

French Sardines in Oil   American Meat Salad

Cantaloupe

SOUP

Potage Parmentier (Potato and Leek Soup)
Consomme Palestro

FISH

Boiled Rock Cod, Parsley Butter, New Potatoes

EGGS

Shirred Eggs, Cubanaise

==================================
SPECIAL: BOILED SHORT RIBS OF BEEF, TURNIPS
HORSERADISH SAUCE, BOILED POTATOES, CELERY.
==================================

ENTREES

Stuffed Breast of Veal with Creamed Carrots and New Peas
Curry of Chicken with Rice, Madras Condiment Platter
Assorted Fresh Vegetable Platter with Ravioli

VEGETABLES

Creamed Carrots and Peas   Baked Hubbard Squash

Steamed Rice

POTATOES

Mashed in Cream   Saratoga Chips

COLD BUFFET

Homemade Head Cheese, Vinaigrette

Smoked Breast of Gosling

Assorted Cold Cuts with Matson Fresh and
Smoked Sausages

Prime Ribs of Beef, Vegetable Salad   Boiled Polish Ham

SALADS

Fruit   Hearts of Lettuce

Spanish

DRESSINGS

French   Russian   Paprika

DESSERTS

Pineapple Sherbet   Diplomate Pudding, Lemon Sauce

CHEESE

Brie   Liederkranz

BEVERAGES

Ceylon, Oolong, Green, Lipton or Orange Pekoe Teas

Coffee   Iced Tea   Iced Coffee   Milk

Almost every long menu has its little quirks and mysteries, and it is odd that the composer of this menu felt the need to explain the *Potage Parmentier* but not the *Consommé Palsetro* and chose to mention one tea by brand name (Lipton). As with most luxury cruise ships, the menu offers a range of international choices in the hope and expectation that every passenger would find something appealing. It is surprising that there are only two concessions to Hawaiian cuisine—the *poi* cocktail and the pineapple dishes. Although the pineapple originated in South America, thanks to the Dole company in the early 1900s Hawaii became its adopted home, and within half a century it was producing over eighty percent of the world's crop.

Almost every country has its starchy staple, and in Hawaii it was the taro (*Colocasia esculenta*), and the usual way of preparing it was as *poi*. Poi is made by baking the roots, then pounding them to a thick paste which can be stored for long periods to be retrieved and mixed with water to the desired consistency when wanted. It is eaten from a communal bowl, for *poi* in more ways than one is the center of family and community life. It seems that sometime around the time of this menu, the poi cocktail was developed, apparently as a concession to non-Hawaiians.

Recipes

~~~

Before it was a frozen concoction, "sherbet" was a simple fruit drink (see April 29). The type of frozen sherbet that included beaten egg whites is a later development.

Pineapple Sherbet

1 quart water
2 cups crushed pineapple,
2 cups sugar fresh or canned
1 lemon
2 egg-whites

Boil water and sugar together for five minutes. Scald the pineapple in the boiling sirup, and rub through a sieve. Cool, add lemon-juice and freeze to a mush. Add the beaten whites of the eggs and continue freezing.
Ruth Berolzheimer, *The American Woman's Cook Book* (1939).

"Shirred" eggs, have nothing to do with the decorative needlework technique. The name may be related to "shard" referring to a broken piece of pottery, perhaps because eggs were often cooked on pottery plates.

Shirred Eggs

Cover the bottoms of individual dishes with a little butter and a few fresh bread-crumbs; drop into each dish two fresh eggs; stand this dish in a pan of hot water and cook in the oven until the whites are "set." Put a tiny bit of butter in the middle of each, and a dusting of salt and pepper.
Sarah Tyson Rorer, *Many Ways for Cooking Eggs* (1903).

Poi, According to Mark Twain

Poi is the chief article of food among the natives, and is prepared from the *taro* plant. The taro root looks like a thick, or if you please, corpulent, sweet potato in shape, but is of a light purple color when boiled. When boiled it substitutes as passable substitute for bread. The buck Kanakas bake it underground, then mash it up well with a lava pestle, mix water with it until it becomes a paste, set it aside and let it ferment, and then it is poi—an unseductive mixture it is, almost tasteless before it ferments and too sour for a luxury afterward. But nothing is more nutritious. When solely used, however, it produces acrid humors, a fact which sufficiently accounts for the humorous character of the Kanakas. I think there must be as much of a knack in handling poi as there is in eating with chopsticks. The forefinger is thrust into the mess and stirred quickly round several times and drawn as quickly out, thickly coated, just as if it were poulticed; the head is thrown back, the finger inserted in the mouth and the delicacy stripped off and swallowed—the eye closing gently, meanwhile,

in a languid sort of ecstacy. Many a different finger goes into the same bowl and many a different kind of dirt and shade and quality of flavor is added to the virtue of its contents.
  Roughing It (1872).

Poi Cocktail

The "poi" cocktail is prepared by diluting the paste with milk, then adding sugar or salt, and serving ice cold. The drink is found to be very beneficial to dyspeptics and those recovering from fever.
  The New York Times, December 4, 1898.

Potage Parmentier: see January 12
Saratoga Chips: see May 23.

June 11

Picnic for the English Royals
"Springwood," Hyde Park, New York, 1939

No reigning British monarch had ever set foot on American soil when President Franklin Delano Roosevelt (1882–1945) invited the King and Queen of England to visit in 1939. One hundred sixty-three years after independence there were still scattered spots of ill-feeling and mistrust on both sides, and with war in Europe seeming inevitable and imminent, Roosevelt was determined to forge a new alliance. The visit was a resounding success on all fronts, and Roosevelt's intention of greater political alliance between the two countries was realized. It was not all business, however, and a great deal of effort went into ensuring that the social side of the visit was also a success. This was the province of Eleanor Roosevelt (1884–1962), the enormously popular first lady. When the planned menus for the visit were made public, one in particular caused a great deal of uneasiness and debate, but Eleanor trusted her instincts, stuck to her guns, and refused to change the plans.

Beer and soft drinks.
Hot dogs (if weather permits).
Cold Ham from various States.
Turkey, smoked and plain.
Various salads.
Baked beans and brown bread.
Doughnuts and ginger bread.
Cookies.
Coffee.

This was to be a picnic lunch at "Top Cottage," the hilltop retreat on the Springwood estate. Many thought that a picnic was undignified and a picnic featuring hot dogs was beyond the pale. One of the anxious critics was Eleanor's mother-in-law, Sara Roosevelt, and Eleanor wrote about the decision in her newspaper column "My Day."

May 25, 1939.

Oh dear, oh dear, so many people are worried that the "dignity" of our country will be imperiled by inviting Royalty to a picnic, particularly a hot dog picnic! My mother-in-law has sent me a letter which begs that she control me in some way. In order to spare my feelings, she has written on the back a little message: "Only one of many such." She did not know, poor darling, that I have "many such" right here in Washington. Let me assure you, dear readers, that if it is hot there will be no hot dogs, and even if it is cool there will be plenty of other food, and the elder members of the family and the more important guests will be served with due formality.

Some concessions have to be made for royalty, however, and although the day was informal (guests were advised not to extend their hands in meeting the King and Queen), the picnic was no rough outdoor experience, nor was

From left, First Lady Eleanor Roosevelt; King George; Sarah Delano Roosevelt, the president's mother; Queen Elizabeth; and President Franklin D. Roosevelt on the front porch of the Roosevelt family home at Hyde Park, New York, June 11, 1939. (AP Photo)

it a small family get-together. A select number of the 150 guests sat with the royals on the front porch of the cottage, at proper tables, with proper plates and cutlery. There was picnic entertainment too, in the form of a presentation of Indian folklore by two "royal" American Indians (dressed of course, in full regalia), Princess Te-Ata and the baritone Ish-Ti-Opi.

The concerned citizens and diplomats need not have worried. King George VI (1895–1952) and Queen Elizabeth (1900–2002) had a fine old time, and to the delight of all involved in the preparations, the King asked for a second hot dog.

Recipes
~~~

Boston Baked Beans

1 pint pea beans
1/8 pound salt pork, part fat
1 small onion
1/2 teaspoon dry mustard
1 1/2 teaspoons salt
2 tablespoons molasses

Soak beans in cold water overnight. In the morning drain and turn into a bean-pot; or simmer until skins begin to burst, but not long enough to be mushy, then turn into the bean-pot. Pour boiling water over salt pork. Scrape the rind until white, score in half-inch strips, and bury meat in beans, leaving only the rind exposed. Mix salt, mustard and molasses in a cup, fill with hot water, stir until well mixed, and pour over the pork and beans. Add water to cover, and bake in a 250–350 F. oven six to eight hours, adding more water to cover until the last hour, when pot cover is removed and pork raised to the surface to crisp.

Boston Brown Bread

1 cup corn-meal
1 cup rye flour
1 cup graham flour
1 teaspoon salt
1/4 molasses
2 cups sour milk or 1 3/4 cups sweet milk.
3/4 tablespoon soda

Mix and sift the dry ingredients. Mix the molasses and milk and add to the dry ingredients. Beat thoroughly and turn into well-greased molds, filling each mold about two-thirds full. Cover and steam three hours. Remove the covers and bake the bread (375 F.) long enough to dry it off.

Sweet Milk Doughnuts

2 tablespoons shortening
1 cup sugar
3 eggs
1 cup milk
3 teaspoons baking-powder
1 teaspoon salt
1/2 teaspoon nutmeg
1/2 teaspoon lemon extract
Flour

Beat the eggs till very light, add the sugar and when foamy add the melted shortening. Sift the baking-powder, salt and nutmeg with one cup of flour and stir into first mixture, alternating with the milk. Add the lemon flavoring and just enough flour to make a soft dough which can be handled. Roll out three-fourths inch thick on a lightly floured board. A soft dough makes light, tender doughnuts when cooked. Fry in deep fat (360–370 F.) and drain on unglazed paper.

Ruth Berolzheimer. *The American Woman's Cook Book* (sometimes called the *Delineator Cook Book*) (1939).

June 12

After-Concert Dinner
King's College, Cambridge University, Cambridge, England, 1893

The Cambridge University Musical Society (CUMS) celebrated its 50th anniversary in 1893 with a weekend of festivities that was astonishing in its scope. The highlight of the celebrations was a performance of contemporary music by six eminent living composers, each of whom agreed to attend and conduct his own piece. At the last minute Edvard Greig was prevented from attending due to illness, but the other five—Max Bruch, Saint-Saens, Boito, Tchaikovsky, and the society's own conductor C. V. Stanford performed as planned. So astonishingly impressive was the musical program that it precipitated another unprecedented event—the cooperation of the organizers of the college boat races, who, in "a touching act of homage" delayed the start by half an hour so as not to affect the afternoon concert.

Naturally, an edible bill of fare followed the musical one. One hundred guests attended a dinner after the concert, for which they had paid one guinea per head. The meal was fine and classical, as would be expected, although entirely without the historic significance of the musical event that preceded it.

POTAGES.
Consommé Sévigné.
Purée d'Asperges.

POISSONS.
Saumon, sauce capres.
Blanchailles frites au Naturel et Diable.

ENTRÉES.
Corbeilles à la Financière.
Timbales de Volaille à l'Essence.

RELEVÉ.
Selle de Mouton.
Fonds d'artichaut à l'Italienne. Haricots verts.

RÔTI.
Canetons et Petits Pois.

ENTREMÊTS.
Soufflée à la Vanille.
Gelée à Champagne aux Fruit.
Bombe glacée aux almondes pralinée.

SAVOURIE.
C[r]oûtes à la Darmstadt.

There were no women present at this dinner. Women were not eligible for full membership of the CUMS; they were merely allowed to be associates. They were, however, allowed to attend the "Conversazione" at the Fitzwilliam Museum, which followed the dinner. About a thousand people filled the museum to enjoy more music—this time performed by the Blue Hungarian Band—and to be suitably awestruck by the wonderful electric lighting, specially installed in time for the occasion.

Recipes
~~~

Consommé Sevigné is a classic clear soup served with quenelles of chicken and usually garnished with asparagus tips and a julienne of lettuce. It was named (almost two centuries later) in honor of the aristocratic French woman Marie de Rabutin-Chantal, Marquise de Sevigné (1626–1696). She is famous on account of the detailed and witty correspondence with her daughter which is a marvellous source of information and gossip about the seventeenth-century French court.

Consommé Sevigné

One quart of consommé.
2 ounces of cooked chicken.
Two Eggs.
Three tablespoons of Milk.

Twelve drops of Almond Essence.
Salt, Cayenne, and Nutmeg.

Pound the chicken and pass it through a hair sieve. Then mix with it the eggs, milk, salt, cayenne, nutmeg, and almond essence. When thoroughly blended, turn the mixture into three of four small dariole moulds well greased, and steam slowly for twenty minutes, or until set. Turn out very carefully, cut into fancy shapes, and serve in the consommé. A few asparagus points and chervil leaves may also be served in this soup.

Timbales de Volaille

Half a pound of quenelle meat.
Six ounces of the breast of a cooked Chicken.
Two ounces of lean cooked Ham.
Six Mushrooms.
One Truffle
One gill of White Sauce.

Cut the chicken into very small pieces. Chop up the mushrooms, truffles, and ham, and stir into the white sauce. Butter well nine small timbale moulds; line them neatly with the quenelle meat, not leaving a particle uncoated; fill in with the minced chicken; coat them neatly over the top with the quenelle meat. Steam them for twenty minutes; dish in a circle on spinach or mashed potatoes; pour good white sauce over and round, and serve peas or mixed vegetables in the centre.

Mrs. Charles Clarke (of the National Training School for Cookery in London), *High Class Cookery Recipes* (1893).

Quenelles, Quenelle Meat: see October 15.
Blanchailles Frites au Naturel et Diable (Whitebait, natural and devilled): see August 14.
Caper Sauce: see December 8.

June 13

King Ludwig's Dinner
Hunting Lodge, the Tirol, 1885

Ludwig II (1845–1886) was king of Bavaria from 1864 until shortly before his death. He was called the Swan King, for his love of the bird, and the Fairy Tale King for the fantastic castles he built. He was also called "Mad King" Ludwig. Certainly his behavior was eccentric and embarrassing at times, which might have been explained by some of the strange aspects of his upbringing. It was also feared that he was homosexual and would therefore not do his kingly duty and produce an heir. In June 1889 he was declared insane by a psychiatrist who did not examine him, and three days later he drowned in a lake. The official verdict was that his death was accidental.

Ludwig was certainly passionate about many artistic endeavours such as architecture and music. He also loved food, although his dental problems meant that it had to be soft. Some of his odd (or perhaps simply lonely) behavior related to his meals. He ate at odd hours, with imaginary guests, and on one occasion invited his favorite horse to the dinner table to eat from the fine china. The staff at his various castles had to be ready to present him with a meal at any time as he would turn up without warning. He took imaginary journeys around the riding pavilion, his staff waiting with a picnic basket for when he dismounted at his imaginary location.

He was in a real location, at his hunting lodge in the Tirol, when he enjoyed the following dinner on June 13, 1885.

Consomme with liver dumplings.
Hechtenkraut (Fish Pudding with Sauerkraut).
Trout with Hollandaise sauce.
Lemon sorbet.
Chicken fricassee.
Paté made from wild venison and peas.
Fruits in wine jelly, vanilla ice cream, and orange sauce.

These dishes fulfilled Ludwig's need for soft food, and they were clearly "German." Perhaps they were comfort food for the troubled king.

Recipes
~~~

Calf's Liver Dumplings

Mince half a pound of cooked calf's liver; take out all the veins, skin, etc., and then mix well with two tablespoons of beef marrow or butter; add a pinch of marjoram, grated lemon rind, a clove of garlic mixed to a paste with salt, a pinch of mace, and pepper; add enough bread crumbs to make the mixture neither stiff nor thin. Bread crumbs swell in boiling, and if too many are used the dumplings will be hard. Form in balls and cook in boiling soup ten minutes.

Bertha M. Wood, *Foods of the Foreign-Born in Relation to Health* (Boston, 1922).

Fish Pudding

Take cold boiled fish, the part that is white, and mashed potatoes, an equal quantity; mix well together, breaking the fish very fine; add two ounces of melted butter, or cream instead of the butter; season with salt and pepper. Butter a pudding dish, put the mixture in, keeping the top rough, and put it in the oven till heated through, and the top nicely browned.

Jennie June, *American Cookery Book* (New York, 1870).

Hollandaise Sauce: see April 14.
Sauerkraut: see July 8.

June 14

Telephone Banquet
Symphony Hall, Boston, Massachusetts, 1916

The Golden Jubilee of the Massachusetts Institute of Technology in 1916 was celebrated with a whole week of events and demonstrations. The culmination of the celebration was a banquet held by the MIT Alumni Association in Symphony Hall, Boston, on the night of June 14. For the 1,500 guests (and the similar number observing the proceedings from the balconies) it was, by all accounts, a singularly exciting evening. The food itself bore no responsibility for the excitement—although doubtless it was very fine, it was stock standard banquet fare.

Clear Green Turtle
—
Medaillon of Penobscot Salmon, Hollandaise Sauce
New Peas
—
Filet of Beef, Larded, Fresh Mushroom Sauce
Potatoes, Fines Herbes
String Beans
—
Sweetbreads Glace with Asparagus Tips   Cigarettes
—
Roast Jumbo Quail, Farcies
Lettuce and Tomato Salad
—
Fancy Frozen Puddings and Ices
Assorted Cakes   Cigars
—
Coffee   Clysmic Water

According to the American Telephone Company, it was "the most elaborate trans-continental telephone stunt ever staged" that absorbed the attention of the "Techys" present not just in Boston, but at locations in 34 other cities across the country where simultaneous alumni banquets were held. Beginning at 9 P.M., there was a spectacular demonstration of "transcontinental telephony." A telephone rollcall was made from Boston to each of the participating cities, and greetings were exchanged between the notable men present. Each guest was provided with an individual receiver—and it was gratifying for the engineers and scientists that the clarity of the communication exceeded all expectations.

Among the guests who exchanged greetings at the banquet were Alexander Graham Bell (1847–1922), the man credited with the invention of the telephone, Orville Wright (1871–1948)—along with his brother Wilbur, a pioneer of "the flying machine," and Thomas Edison (1847–1931) the inventor of (among many other things) the electric light bulb (see April 24).

During the evening, the president of MIT, Richard C. Maclaurin (1870–1920) announced that $3.5 million had been pledged for "new technology" during the course of the evening—the massive total thanks to a mysterious benefactor known only as "Mr. Smith" who had pledged $5 for every $3 donated by others. The evening ended with a rendition of the "Star Spangled Banner" sung in unison by all of the alumni clubs.

The vogue for bottled water is often assumed to be a modern one, and it attracts a fair amount of controversy on a number of counts. The plastic bottles are shaping up to be an environmental disaster, and in countries such as the United States where the water supply is clean, they represent a lucrative marketing triumph. The ground was prepared for the modern popularity of bottled mineral waters by the health reform and temperance movements of the nineteenth century. As happens today, the supposed unique qualities of water from various sources was extolled with the help of testimonials from professionals (especially medical) and consumers. The "Clysmic Water" on this menu came from the Clysmic Mineral Spring in Waukesha, Wisconsin, and was marketed commercially as early as 1878. In 1907 a vigorous new marketing program—what would now be called a "branding" exercise—was commenced with the slogan "The King of Table Waters."

Recipes

~~~

Mushroom Sauce

Place one and one-half cups of milk in a saucepan and add four tablespoons of flour. Stir until dissolved and then bring to a boil. Cook for five minutes and then add

One cup of diced and par-boiled mushrooms
One well-beaten egg
One teaspoon of salt
One teaspoon of paprika
Three tablespoons of finely chopped parsley

Beat to mix then cook for two minutes and use.
Mary A. Wilson, *Mrs. Wilson's Cook Book* (Philadelphia, 1920).

Hollandaise Sauce: see, April 14.

June 15

Royal Luncheon
Ascot Racecourse, Ascot, Berkshire, England, 1933

The English have been passionately fond of horse racing for centuries—and none are more fond than the English royal family. One of the most famous racecourses in the country was founded in 1711 by Queen Anne

(1665–1714) at Ascot, a convenient six miles from the royal residence at Windsor Castle. In June a special race meeting called Royal Ascot Week is the high point of the social season, and, as the name suggests, the royal family always attends.

June 15, 1933, was the second day of Ascot week, and it dawned brilliantly sunny. King George V (1865–1936) and Queen Mary (1867–1953) drove up in semi-state to the Royal Enclosure and watched the races and enjoyed lunch from the Royal Box.

MENU

Mayonnaise de Homard
—
Selles d'Agneau Printanière
Poulets Devonshire
Cailles Malmaison en Aspic
Petites Pâtés de Mouton à la Windsor
—
Petits pois à la Française
Pommes nouvelles persillées
—
BUFFET
Derby Beef, Jambon, Langue, Agneau,
Roast Beef, Poulet, Pigeon Pie.
—
Asperges Vinaigrette
Salade de Tomate
—
Eton Mess
Petits Gateau

Even at a race meeting, this royal menu was formal, as was (and still is) the dress code in the Royal Enclosure. Men must wear morning coats and top hats at all times (and be ready to doff them as the monarch drives by in the traditional open carriage), and women must wear a proper hat (that is, one that covers the crown of the head). The menu is in French, as royal menus still are—although a little English sneaks in occasionally in a very inconsistent way. There is no logical or historic reason why beef on this menu is not *bœuf*, but lamb is *agneau*.

Recipes

~~~

Eton Mess

This is traditionally served at Eton College at the annual prize-giving day picnic. According to Rene Roussin, the royal chef of the 1930s, it is a mixture of chopped up strawberries mixed with plenty of thick cream. It now usually contains pieces of meringue.

"Mess" may refer to the appearance of the dish, or to a specific quantity of food—as the military uses the word (see January 6).

Ox Tongue

An Ox Tongue for a cold table should be soaked in a preparation known as a *saumure*, which is made as follows:

2 quarts water
2 1/2 lb. coarse salt
5 oz. moist brown sugar
6 juniper berries
1 small sprig of thyme
1 small bay leaf

Put all the above ingredients into a large saucepan and boil, stirring occasionally, for one hour. Let the liquid cool.

Prick a raw, fresh tongue all over with a large needle or a very thin-tined fork and rub it energetically with 1 oz. of coarse salt to which a generous pinch of saltpetre has been added.

Put the tongue in a deep, narrow basin and pour the cold *saumure* over it so that it is completely bathed in the liquid.

Leave for 6 days in summer, 8 in winter.

Before cooking the tongue should be placed for 3 to 4 hours in plain cold water. Then put it in a saucepan with ample fresh cold water, bring it to the boil and cook it till it is done, allowing about 2 hours for a medium to small tongue, 3 for a large one.

As soon as the tongue has been taken from the water, remove the skin—it will come away easily—and at once wrap the tongue in buttered paper. Contact with the air will quickly dry and discolour it. Put it in a cool place to chill.

Prepare a dressing of 1/2 lb. of gelatine dissolved in 3 1/2 gills of water and stain it a dark scarlet-brown with 2 or 3 drops of cochineal and a little browning. When the tongue is really cold, coat it with a thin layer of this quick-setting dressing so that it presents a shiny, dark red appearance.

Rene Roussin, *Royal Menus* (1960).

Mayonnaise de Homard (lobster mayonnaise): see March 31.
Petites Pâtés de Mouton à la Windsor: see May 3.
Petits Pois à la Française: see July 11.
Pommes Nouvelles Persillées: see December 6.

June 16

A Banquet to Nelson Mandela
Pretoria, South Africa, 1999

A lavish banquet was held in honor of Nelson Mandela when he retired as president of South Africa in 1999. The advance publicity about the banquet advised that "food indigenous to South Africa" would be served.

Smoked Chicken Timbales on a bed of Salad with edible flowers,
and Morogo Mayo.

Medallions of Beef Fillet on a Leek Rosti in a Pastry Cage, served with tied
bundles of vegetables.

African Chocolate next to Chocolate Pots filled with Marbled Chocolate Mousse
and Berry Coulis.
Individual loaves of Health Bread.

South African wine.

Coffee and Inauguration Chocolates.

It is difficult if not impossible to justify the publicists' claims about the local origin of the ingredients on this menu. The only real claimant is the *morogo*—"the South African National Dish" which is a staple food in many rural areas. The word comes from the Tswana (a Bantu) language and is a generic word for vegetables, although it is most commonly used to mean wild spinach (of which there are several species). It is useful because it can be dried and is highly nutritious because it is contains 36 percent protein—higher than many varieties of soybean. The only other contender is the coffee, which certainly originated in the African continent—but it is indigenous to Ethiopia, not South Africa.

As for the other dishes, their origins are distant indeed. Chicken and cattle of one species or another have been domesticated and eaten for millennia all over the world; there is no evidence that they are "indigenous" to South Africa, or anywhere in Africa for that matter.

The leek probably originated around the Mediterranean and was popularized and spread around Europe by the Romans. To further the divide, at this dinner the leeks were cooked in a Swiss style as *rösti*, a word related to *roasted* and referring to "cakes" fried crisp and golden.

The chocolate used at the dinner may technically have been grown locally —both Cadbury and Nestlé have factories in South Africa where it has become an important crop. It is, however, unequivocally a New World food, having originated in Central South America.

The statement about the banquet brings up the whole question of authenticity in cuisine. The reality is that cooking, like other cultural practices, is in a constant state of adaptation and blending. It seems impossible to imagine Italian food without the tomato, or Indian without the potato or chilli, but these are both also New World foods, not known outside the South African continent until the last decade of the fifteenth century.

Recipes

~~~

Preparing a Dish of Morogo

Cook the leaves in boiling water. Add tomatoes and onions or potatoes and onions. Flavour the dish with salt and pepper.

Chocolate Mousse

Put a three-quart mould in a wooden pail, first lining the bottom with fine ice and a thin layer of coarse salt. Pack the space between the mould and the pail solidly with fine ice and coarse salt, using two quarts of salt and ice enough to fill the space. Whip one quart of cream, and drain it in a sieve. Whip again all the cream that drains through. Put in a small pan one ounce of Walter Baker & Co.'s Premium No. 1 Chocolate, three tablespoonfuls of sugar and one of boiling water, and stir over a hot fire until smooth and glossy. Add three tablespoonfuls of cream. Sprinkle a cupful of powdered sugar over the whipped cream. Pour the chocolate in a thin stream into the cream, and stir gently until well mixed. Wipe out the chilled mould, and turn the cream into it. Cover, and then place a little ice lightly on top. Wet a piece of carpet in water, and cover the top of the pail. Set away for three or four hours; then take the mould from the ice, dip it in cold water, wipe, and then turn the mousse out on a flat dish.

Maria Parloa, *Chocolate and Cocoa Recipes and Home Made Candy Recipes* (1909).

An African Explorer's
View of Wild Spinach

Samuel White Baker, who traveled to Africa in 1861 hoping to discover the source of the Nile, had this to say about one evening's dinner in his book *The Albert N'yanza, The Great Basin of the Nile* (1868):

Fortunately there were three varieties of plants growing wild in great profusion, that, when boiled, were a good substitute for spinach; thus we were rich in vegetables, although without a morsel of fat or animal food. Our dinner consisted daily of a mess of black porridge of bitter mouldy flour that no English pig would condescend to notice, and a large dish of spinach. "Better a dinner of herbs where love is," etc. often occurred to me; but I am not sure that I was quite of that opinion after a fortnight's grazing upon spinach.

June 17

Lunch with the Emperor of Ethiopia
Ambassador Hotel, Los Angeles, California, 1954

His Imperial Majesty Haile Selassie of Ethiopia (1892–1965) visited the United States for the first time in 1954, at the invitation of President Dwight D. Eisenhower (1890–1969). The purpose of his visit was to stimulate interest in his country and the intended modernization and to raise capital for the necessary developments in agriculture and industry.

Selassie, who traced his ancestry back to the biblical King Solomon and Queen of Sheba, was accompanied on his royal visit by his youngest son and one granddaughter. While they were in California the royal family visited

Yosemite and attended a variety of official functions. On June 17 they were welcomed by the City of Los Angeles (represented by Mayor Norris Poulson) at a luncheon. Musical entertainment was provided by the City of Los Angeles Symphonic Chorus and Manny Harmon and his orchestra, and the bill of fare was by the Ambassador Hotel.

Melon Balls Orientale
Stuffed Boneless Squab Chicken, Narcisse
Parisienne Rissole Potato
Asparagus Polonaise
Beaudry Salad
French Dressing
Orange Fantaisie
Petit Fours Glace.

As the second half of the twentieth century progressed there was a gradual move away from classically prepared and classically named dishes, which means that it can be difficult or impossible to know exactly what was served. Simultaneously, French was also losing its monopoly as the universal culinary language, which in theory should have made menus more easily understood. Sophisticated diners, however—even those who spoke not a word of French—knew what they would get when they ordered classic dishes such as *Sole Colbert* or *Consommé à la Reine*. Customers and guests do want to know what to expect, and eventually the trend away from classic cuisine and French menus caused the evolution of the modern menu, in which detailed descriptions (almost like recipes) substitute for short, well-known phrases.

The menu for this luncheon is on the cusp of those changes. Ostensibly it is in English, so that there are squab chickens and potatoes but the word order and qualifying words are French, so that these are styled *Narcisse* and *Parisienne*, respectively. Some of these qualifying words are from the classic repertoire, and assuming that the chef did not take too many liberties, the asparagus dish in the *Polonaise* (Polish) style would have had browned breadcrumbs and hard boiled egg (see here and October 20) and the potatoes would have been cut into small balls and sautéed. The Beaudry salad was presumably a local or hotel specialty named in honor of Prudent Beaudry (1818–1893), the mayor of Los Angeles from 1874–76. As for the chicken *Narcisse*—there is no common classic chicken dish by this name, although there was an Edwardian era dish called *Crème a la Narcisse*, which was a rich almond ice cream.

Recipes

~~~

French Dressing is the English name for what the French call *vinaigrette*. Purists say it should consist only of the best-quality olive oil and lemon juice or wine vinegar, in proportion of 3:1, plus salt and pepper, but there are as many variations and additions as there are cooks.

French Dressing

Two teaspoonfuls of salt, one teaspoonful of mustard, one-quarter teaspoonful of black pepper, one-half teaspoonful of paprika, the juice of one lemon, and the same amount of vinegar. Put in a quart bottle, fill with olive oil, and shake thoroughly.

Asparagus Polonaise

Put four pounds of boiled fresh, or two cans, of asparagus on a platter. Have the asparagus very hot. Sprinkle the tips with salt and pepper, one chopped boiled egg, and some chopped parsley. Melt in a pan, three ounces of sweet butter, add two tablespoonsful of bread crumbs, fry until brown, and pour over the tips of the asparagus.
  Victor Hirzler, *The Hotel St. Francis Cook Book* (1919).

June 18

''Uncooked Banquet''
Hotel Hygeia, New York, 1903

An enthusiastic group of vegetarians, physical culturists, Christian Scientists, members of the One Hundred Year Club, and various other ''food reformers'' met on this date in New York to partake of a ''new and infallible nature cure.'' They were in the experienced hands of the one and only ''elementary cook'' in the entire region, who prepared for them a banquet of ''marvelous dishes'' without the aid of heat in any form. Such ''relics of barbarism'' as cooking ranges were eschewed by these food reformers, as were animal flesh and intoxicating liquors and the use of condiments such as vinegar.

The *New York Times* reported the bill of fare with some amusement the next day.

The first course was soup natural, ripe olives and almonds. . . . The soup was made of milk, ground grain and celery. . . . the next dish was brought in. It was a salad called Brassica-Lactula . . . consisted of a piece of lettuce, sliced tomatoes, cucumbers, and some pignolias. Nuts, it may be said here, formed the better half of nearly every dish . . . the third course. This consisted of oatflakes and cream, pecans and brazil nuts, bread, sweet butter, fruit-oryza, and raisistata. What the two latter dishes were was a secret which was not divulged. The bread, however, also called crackers-avena, resembled a small yellow brick. It was made by grinding the grain, soaking it in water, and then letting it dry in a form. The next course was called Fructo-Salata. It was another salad, the ingredients this time being sliced oranges, bananas, strawberries, figs, dates and other fruits.

Then came Persian prunes, dried fruit, cream cheese, and finally some canta-loupes filled with ice cream. The whole dinner was washed down with fruit punch, which was very refreshing, but its only resemblance to any more stimu-lating beverage was that there was a cherry stuck in it.

Humans started to use fire for cooking at least 350,000 years ago, perhaps a great deal earlier, and evolutionary biologists believe that the human jaw shows evidence of adaptation away from eating very tough, uncooked food. It is probably fair to say that most people, most of the time, like most of their food to be cooked. This certainly applies to meat; the occasional gourmet choice of *steak tartare* being the exception that proves the rule. Fruit and salad vegetables are obvious options, although they were once viewed with some suspicion. The seventeenth-century diarist Samuel Pepys (1633–1703) was sure that one of his neighbors had died from eating ``cowcumbers,'' for example. This belief in the health risks of eating raw food was probably dis-tantly due to the old humoral theory (see February 23) that determined many of them to be undesirably ``cold'' in their effects, but it is possible that there was an awareness that they might be associated with disease—an event that would now be attributed to contact with contaminated water.

The intentional following of an uncooked diet would be an incomprehen-sible choice to our ancestors, but such a movement began towards the end of the nineteenth century in the wake of the vegetarian movement (although not all raw foodists were vegetarian). Adherents of the raw food diet have been almost evangelical about the health benefits of the regime, as well as its ethical correctness.

Recipes

~~~

The following recipes are taken from *Uncooked Foods & How to Use Them*, a book published in 1924 by the organizers of the uncooked banquet—Eugene Christian and his wife Molly Griswold Christian.

Cream Cheese

Take thick cream and tie it in a wet cloth. Stir a teaspoonful of salt into every pint of cream. Hang it in a cool airy place for three or four days to drain. Then turn it into a clean cloth, which must be put into a mold and under a weight for about twenty-four hours longer, when it will be fit for use.

Cream of Celery

Oat Flakes,
Cream,
Celery,
Celery Salt,
Flaked Wheat.

Make same as tomato, only add tender celery chopped fine, instead of tomato, and a dash of celery salt.

Cream of Tomato Soup

Oat Flakes,
Milk or Cream,
Fresh Tomatoes,
Salt.

Take one pound of oat flakes, cover well with warm milk and let stand three or four hours, or until very soft. Then mash through a coarse strainer, which will produce a very thick cream, which forms the body of the soup. Add to this sufficient milk or cream (cream preferred) to make quantity desired, and the juice of half a dozen ripe tomatoes. Any cream soup can be made in the same way, using different articles.

Much care should be exercised in adding the milk, so as not to destroy the thick, creamy consistency of the soup.

Why This Book Was Written

The following text is from the preface to *Uncooked Foods* written by Eugene Christian in 1924.

SOME years ago we, the authors of this work, both became so impaired in health as to almost totally disqualify us for the performance of our daily work. A very exhaustive study of our condition convinced us that it was caused mainly, if not wholly, by incorrect habits in eating. This brought forth a very careful and studied series of experiments in diet which was confined entirely to cooked foods, because we at that time accepted implicitly the common theory that foods could be predigested and improved by heat.

Failing utterly in this, our attention was turned toward what have been called natural foods, but what in reality mean food in its elementary or unchanged state. Less than a year of study and experimenting with this system of feeding resulted in the total elimination of all stomach disorders and our complete restoration to perfect health. From scientific research, in addition to these failures and successes, we have studied out a system of both eating and drinking, which has been tried by many others under our direction, and in every instance health, strength and vitality have come to those who have obeyed our instructions.

In order to bring this theory more conspicuously before the public we gave a seven course dinner or banquet of uncooked foods, which was attended by many distinguished New York people. It received much attention by the New York press, and was widely commented on all over this and foreign countries through the press exchanges. A flood of inquiries concerning the use of uncooked food, especially referring to their remedial values, followed this publicity. This gave the first hint of the great interest that the public is now taking in this method of living.

June 19

Banquet for Queen Catherine
Bishop's Palace, Paris, France, 1549

Henry II (1519–1559) became King on March 31, 1547, on the death of his father Francis I (1494–1547). The traditional site for the coronation of French kings was the cathedral at Rheims, and Henry was crowned there on July 25, 1547. It was believed at the time that kings and queens should be seen, and to do that they undertook royal progresses (tours) across the country, making triumphal entries into the cities and towns. The "entry" of a king or queen into a city was an occasion of great celebration with processions, banquets, tournaments, and all sorts of other festivities. In the two years after his coronation Henry made nearly 30 entries—and finally, it was Paris's turn.

Henry entered Paris on June 16, and Queen Catherine (1519–1589), who had been Catherine de' Medici, entered on June 18. The splendor of their entries surpassed all previous in scale and originality. Planning had begun months before, with not just the arrangement for the various festivities to be made, but many issues of protocol had to be solved such as the order of precedence for presentation to the monarchs and who could and could not wear scarlet.

On the day after her entry the king and queen attended mass at Notre Dame, and in the evening the City of Paris gave a great banquet in her honor. It was not held in the Hotel de Ville as originally planned, but the palace of the bishop of Paris. It is not known how many guests were at the banquet, but the list of food is impressive.

30 peacocks,
33 pheasants,
21 swans,
9 cranes,
33 ducks,
33 ibises,
33 egrets,
33 young herons,
30 young goats,
99 young pigeons,
99 turtle doves,
13 partridges,
33 goslings

3 young bustards,
13 young capons,
90 quails,
66 boiling chickens,
66 Indian chickens,
30 capons,
90 spring chicken in vinegar,

> 66 chickens "cooked as grouse,"
> 66 rabbits,
> 30 goats.
>
> 144 artichokes
> 500 asparagus and
> 4 bushels of beans.
>
> There were also pastries and sweetmeats of great variety.

Most of the meat consisted of birds, which were considered fine food suitable for royalty, their intrinsic value being greater because they were harder to catch, and because being creatures of the air they were closer to God. There was no beef (although it may have been used in broths, and the fatty marrow was always prized) because the meat itself was considered coarse and ordinary, and fit for the lower classes. The "Indian chickens" are interesting. They are turkeys—and this dinner represents one of the earliest recorded use of the New World bird.

The events of the entries of Henry and Catherine were not all feasting and merriment, however, and one particular spectacle was symbolic of the rest of Henry's reign. One of the entertainments at the conclusion of the queen's coronation was an *auto-da-fe*, or burning of heretics (that is, Protestants) in the *Place de Grève*. Four men convicted of Lutheranism were chained to huge beams attached to pulleys and were burned slowly by being raised and lowered into a huge fire. It is said that Henry was greatly upset by the spectacle, but this did not prevent his reign being marked and marred by savage persecution of the Protestant Huguenots.

Recipes

~~~

Before the technological developments of the Industrial Revolution enabled the manufacture of shaped metal baking dishes, meat was cooked either by roasting on a spit in front of a fire or in an oven after being encased in a pastry shell or "coffin" which functioned like a modern casserole dish. The pastry of these "pies" or *bake-metes* was very thick and very hard, and was not necessarily meant to be eaten. Small birds such as pigeons were often cooked this way as it prevented them from drying out and allowed them to be served in a gravy or sauce.

To Bake Pygeons in Short Paest as You Make to Your Baken Apples

Season youre pigeons with peper saffron cloues and mace, with vergis [verjuice] and salte, then putte them into youre paeste, and so close them up, and bake them, they wyl bake in halfe an houre, then take them forthe, and yf ye thinke theym drye, take a lyttle vergis and butter and put to theim and serve theym.
A Proper Newe Booke of Cokerye (ca. 1545).

Each dish would have been accompanied by the appropriate sauce. It would not have been considered necessary to list them—this was often simply assumed. A common sauce for fish and small birds was a *galantine* (the word now means a sort of jellied dish), and the following one shows the heritage of bread stuffing for turkey.

**Galandine for a Crane or Hearne (Heron)
or Any Other Foule That Is Black Meat**

Toste Bread and lay it in soke in vinagre, and straine it with Vinagre and a little Claret wine, boile it on a chafing dish of coles and put in it sugar, Cinnamon, and Ginger.
  A. W., *A Boke of Cookrye* (1591).

June 20

Dinner for the Transatlantic Air-Race Winners
Savoy Hotel, London, England, 1919

In 1913, the *Daily Mail*, a British newspaper, offered a prize of £10,000 for the first aviator to cross the North Atlantic. The competition was put on hold almost immediately when the First World War broke out but was resumed again at the war's end in 1918. Aviation technology and aviator skills were inevitably accelerated by the war, and there was a great deal of interest in the revived competition. The war also resulted in a change of the rules—the British newspaper now determined that the race was open to any nationality except those of "enemy origin."

The eventual winners of the competition—Captain John Alcock (1892–1919) of the Royal Air Force and Lieutenant Arthur Whitten-Brown (1886–1948) of the Royal Flying Service began their attempt on the afternoon of June 14, 1919, from St. John's, Newfoundland, in a Vickers Vimy bomber. They arrived in Clifden, Ireland, 16 hours 27 minutes later after a flight of 1890 nautical miles. The event was simultaneously a great adventure, a superb engineering feat, and an example of great personal heroism.

The Directors of the Associated Newspapers (Limited) gave a luncheon to honor the aviators, and the Secretary of State for War, Winston Churchill (1874–1965), presented the cheque—and announced the extra honor of a knighthood to the winners. Even the menu was a celebration of their achievement.

Melon Frappé au Maraschino.
Oeufs Pochés Alcock.
Suprême de Sôle à la Brown.
Poulet de Printemps à la Vickers Vimy. Salade Clifden
Surprise Britannia
Gateau Grand Succès
Café

The décor too, was in theme. The top table
was covered with linen fabric used in making the wings of an aeroplane, with, at
intervals, red, white, and blue centre-pieces similar to those used to identify
British machines. In the middle of these circles were clusters of red roses. Suspended in the ceiling in front of the airmen was a model of an aeroplane filled
with pink and mauve sweet peas. Two smaller models, similarly loaded, hung
from candelabra in the centre of the room, which was also draped with the flags
of Newfoundland, Ireland, and the Allies.

The flight itself was not without its food story. Not only did the men nearly
freeze due to the heating problems, they were also very hungry as all they
had to sustain themselves during the long flight—the weight of every article
aboard being critical—were some sandwiches. As very hungry people do, they
fantasized about the meal they would have when (and if) they arrived—
deciding on a dish of duck and green peas.

Recipes

~~~

Poached Eggs

Unless an egg-poacher is used, eggs are best poached in a large frying-pan nearly
filled with water. A little vinegar and salt should be added to the water, as the
eggs will set more quickly. Each egg should first be broken into a separate cup,
and then slipped into the rapidly boiling water; cover them up and allow them
to boil only just long enough to have the whites set, which will take about 2
minutes. Quite newly laid eggs take a little longer. Have ready hot buttered
toast, remove the eggs from the water with an egg-slice, and slip them on the
toast. Always have plates and dishes very hot for all kinds of egg dishes.
   Dr. Allinson's Cook Book (1915).

Melon is often paired with a cherry liqueur such as maraschino (made from
maraschino cherries) or kirsch (made from morello cherries). In both these
liqueurs, the cherry pits add an almond-like flavor. A little maraschino
liqueur can be added to the following recipe, to create a version of the dish
in the menu. It can be served "slushy" if wished.

Melon Water Ice

To make a quart of melon-water ice, skin and pound the whole of a ripe melon,
and pass it through a sieve. Mix with a pint of juice a syrup made of a quart of
water and a pound and a half of sugar and the juice of a lemon. Freeze in the
usual manner.
   Cassell's New Dictionary of Cookery (1910).

June 21

Dinner with Amelia Earhart
Hotel Grand Preanger,
Bandung (Bandoeng), Batavia
(Indonesia), 1937

Amelia Earhart (1897–1937) was an American aviatrix and author who set many aviation records. Among many other feats she was the first woman to fly solo across the Atlantic and Pacific Oceans and nonstop across the continental United States. She was only the 16th woman to be awarded a pilot's licence, and her fame did much to advance the acceptance of female pilots. She was attempting an equatorial around-the-world flight when she disappeared in 1937.

Amelia Earhart in the cockpit of a plane. (AP Photo)

Earhart and her navigator, Fred Noonan, had set off from Florida on June 1 in their Lockheed Electra. They arrived in Bandoeng, Indonesia, on June 21 and stayed in the Grand Hotel Preagar where they had dinner.

Mock Turtle lié.

Medaillons de Merluza pôché, Sce. Caviar
Pommes Vapeur.

Beefsteak au beurre noir.
Choux de Bruxelles frais.
Pommes Anna.

Pièce de Langue à la Strassbourgeoise.

Pêches Siberienne.

Fruits.

Café.

The progress of the flight was delayed in Bandoeng by the weather, and Earhart and Noonan did not set off again until June 27. They left Lae in Papua New Guinea on July 2 and were planning to stop at Howland Island in the central Pacific Ocean. They never arrived. The mystery has

never been solved, although it has fueled many theories and many archeo-
logical expeditions.

Recipes

~~~

"Black butter" sometimes refers to a fruit preserve (usually an apple puree)
cooked with spices, but in this context it means a savory sauce made by heating butter until it is dark brown (not actually black). Sometimes vinegar and
capers or parsley are added. It is a classic sauce with a history dating back to
medieval times. It is also called brown butter and burnt butter sauce. It is a
classic accompaniment to fish and sometimes steak.

Black Butter Sauce

1 1/2 oz. butter,
1 teaspoonful finely chopped parsley,
1/2 teaspoonful vinegar.

Put the butter in an omelette pan, fry over a quick fire until it becomes a nut-
brown color, then add the vinegar and parsley. Pour over the article to be
served.
  Charles Herman Senn, *The Book of Sauces* (1915).

Pommes (de terre) Anna is a classic French dish. Occasionally (but not classically) cheese is included. There are various theories as to whom it is named
after. The favorite theory is that it was Anna Deslions, a famous and very
beautiful nineteenth -century French courtesan who never charged her clients, but was happy to accept gifts such as homes in the country and fabulous
jewels.

Pommes de Terre Anna

Peel and cut raw potatoes into thin slices—all of the same thinness otherwise
they will not cook evenly. Put them into cold water for about quarter of an hour.
Butter the dish they are to be cooked in, and then arrange in it the slices of potatoes (which must be dried when they come out of the cold water). The slices of
potatoes must be arranged in layers and tightly packed, and melted butter or little pieces of butter put generously over each layer. The dish must be entirely
filled with potato slices, and butter spread over the top. The lid must be made
airtight with a paste made of flour and water. Bake it in a slow oven for forty-
five minutes. Then take out the dish, cut the potato cake in it across in four
pieces, turn them upside down, put the cover on again and bake for another
ten minutes. Serve on a very hot plate, pouring the melted butter in the dish
over the cake.
  C. F. Leyel and O. Hartley. *The Gentle Art of Cookery* (1925).

Mock Turtle lié (soup): see July 4.

June 22

Midwinter Dinner
Winter Quarters, Commonwealth Bay, Adelie Land, Antarctica, 1912

The mid-winter equinox is always celebrated with great enthusiasm in Antarctica. As with the Christmas celebration in the northern hemisphere, it marks the welcome return of the sun and the lengthening days—an event that is even more significant after months of almost complete darkness and great boredom. The members of the Australasian Antarctic Expedition of 1922 threw themselves into the occasion with the usual great enthusiasm. The cooks for the day were Walter Hannam (1885–1964) and Francis Bickerton (1889–1954), and their efforts were recorded by the expedition leader, Douglas Mawson (1882–1958.)

Their menu de dinner to us was a marvel of gorgeous delicacies. After the toasts and speeches came a musical and dramatic programme, punctuated by choice choruses. The washing up was completed by all hands at midnight. Outside, the wind was not to be undone; it surpassed itself with an unusual burst of ninety-five miles per hour.

Menu du Diner

Escoffier Potage à la Reine

Noisettes de Phoque
Haricots Verts
Champignons en Sauce Antarctique   Claret Tintara

Pingouin à la Terre Adélie
Petits Pois à la Menthe
Pommes Nouvelles   Burgundy Chauvenet 1898

Asperges au Beurre Fondu

Plum Pudding Union Jack
Pâté de Groseilles   Port Köpke

Desserts

Café

During dinner the Blizzard will render the usual accompaniments ... The Tempest, for Ever and Ever, etc.

Of course, any fine menu of the time was in French, even when the party guests were Australian, and the location was Lat. 67° 00&amp; amp;amp;quot; S. Long. 142° 36" E. Food has a social, cultural, and symbolic value beyond its

simple caloric and nutritional requirement, and this is never more so than when people are far from home, in inhospitable and dangerous surroundings. Explorers in all times and continents have noted the importance of maintaining the traditional celebrations of their homeland (and mid-winter in the Antarctic clearly substituted for Christmas), and the great morale-boosting effect of good food. Giving grand names to the dishes clearly enhanced the fun—canned or dried asparagus and mushrooms do not sound nearly so elegant as *Asperges au Beurre Fondu* and *Champignons en Sauce Antarctique*.

No doubt many of the ingredients—such as the dried fruit for the obligatory plum pudding had been hoarded for the day—but the main dishes were definitely local in spite of their French names: *pingouin* is obviously penguin, and *phoque* is seal.

Recipes

~~~

The Antarctic Treaty's Protocol on Environmental Protection, signed in 1991, makes recreation of this menu impossible. It prohibits even the "disturbing" of any wildlife on the frozen continent.

Antarctic Food:
Through the Eyes of Explorers

During the early Antarctic expeditions, explorers were very reliant on local species to supply their food needs—and to give variety to their provisions. Antarctic cooks simply adapted standard recipes, and named their dishes accordingly, so that there are records of dishes such as the noisettes of seal in the menu above, penguin ragout, and seal liver maitre d'hotel. The situation was different during an off-base expedition when ingredients, equipment, and time were at a premium, and conditions severe. At these times a generic one-pot hot dish called "hooch" was often made, using whatever meat and whatever flavorings were available.

> The penguin, as an animal, seems to be made up of an equal proportion of mammal, fish, and fowl. If it is possible to imagine a piece of beef, an odoriferous codfish, and a canvas-back duck, roasted in a pot, with blood and cod-liver oil for sauce, the illustration will be complete.

> Frederick Cook, *Through the First Antarctic Night* (1900).

> We were on tinned food. It was supplemented by penguin meat and Kerguelen cabbage when available. The former was black meat. We ate the breasts of the penguins grilled or fried in butter. It was just like steak. We did not bother with the rest of the birds, only the breasts.

Arthur Scholes, *Fourteen Men: Story of the Australian Antarctic Expedition to Heard Island* (1949).

...breakfast...usually consisted of a plate of porridge followed by seal or penguin steak, and a better breakfast it would be hard to obtain. Appetites in the Antarctic are seldom, or never, small, and penguin breast cooked as Dickason or Browning could cook it was a delicacy worth travelling some way to taste.

Raymond Priestley, *Antarctic Adventure: Scott's Northern Party* (1914).

I tasted penguin steak the other day and found the meat excellent, almost like ptarmigan.

Tryggve Gran's Antarctic Diary 1910–1913.

We got six adelie and 1 Emperor penguins & a seal. So we have as much blubber as keep the pot boiling for a month at least. We had for supper... stewed penguin heart liver eyes tongues toes & God knows what else with a cup of water.

Harry McNeish, in *Quest for a Continent* by Walter Sullivan (1914).

Different hooches were made by adding new ingredients—like seal, horse, curry powder, salt, sugar, oatmeal, or chocolate—to the mixture. Hoosh is the hot meal that used to be eaten on a sled journey.

Meredith Hooper, *A for Antarctica* (1991).

Potage a la Reine: see February 17.

June 23

Yale Reunion Dinner
Bishop's Colonnade, Savin Rock, West Haven, Connecticut, 1908

Bishop's Colonnade Restaurant became the regular venue for Yale reunions as soon as it opened in 1904. It was a spectacular venue built on pilings right out over the Long Island Sound, and it was *the* fashionable place to be and be seen until it was destroyed by fire in 1921. The restaurant could accommodate almost a thousand guests at one time, and in addition to the live music there was much to entertain the guests while they were waiting for their meals. There were fine views across the water, of the ferries and other boats, and the activities in the adjacent park, but there was also—most unusually for the time—a gleaming, pure white open kitchen, so that diners could observe the food preparation.

The restaurant was famous for its fine menu, and it is likely that the "Class of '88" would have been pleased by their meal.

Lobster Cocktail

—

Canape, Bove

—

Olives   Radishes   Salted Almonds

—

Consomme Pierre le Grand

—

Paupiette of Sea Trout, Venetienne
Cucumbers   Creamed Celery with Mushrooms

—

Roman Punch

—

Filet of Beef, a la Richelieu
June Peas, Anglais   Fresh Tomatoes, Boera

—

Squab Guinea Hen au Cresson
Potatoes Parisienne

—

Salad Colonnade

—

Nesselrode Surprise

—

Café Demi Tasse   Roquefort Cheese
Guava Jelly

A fine dining restaurant of the time would have been expected to serve all the classic dishes, plus one or two of its own signature dishes. The best known of the Colonnade's signature dishes was not given to the Yale men, although it did appear on the regular menu for the same day. It was crab meat Tokyo—a dish that gives new meaning to the modern idea of fusion cuisine. The crab meat was served in brown bean pots with "Mongol sauce" made from a mixture of tomato and pea soups. Perhaps the Yale guests were fortunate to receive the salad colonnade, although there does not appear to be any surviving recipe.

Of the classic dishes, the *paupiettes* are interesting because the idea incorporates so much culinary history. A *paupiette* (or *poupiette, polpet, poupet* etc) is a thin slice of meat or fish rolled around some sort of filling, so it is similar to a *turban* (see April 24). The French word is related to the Italian word *polpetta* referring to a type of meatball (polpa means flesh), and in one form or another they have been popular since at least the sixteenth century. The name is an example of a French modification of an old concept, to make it sound fashionable. In English, the same dish (when made with beef or veal) is called an *olive*. The word *olive* in this context is an example of folk etymology—the process by which an unfamiliar word is changed to match a more familiar word with similar pronunciation, often due to a mistaken belief about its meaning. In very old English manuscripts, they are called *alowes* (*aloes*, etc.), which originally referred to small birds (an *alouette* is a lark), which in a convoluted way explains why they are also called "beef birds."

Recipes
~~~

Venitienne Sauce

1/2 pint Allemande or Bechamel sauce,
1 oz. lobster butter,
1 dessertspoonful meat glaze,
the juice of half a lemon,
pepper,
nutmeg,
and salt,
1 teaspoonful finely chopped tarragon leaves.

Heat up the sauce, stir in the lobster butter and meat glaze when required for serving, add lemon juice, sufficient pepper, grated nutmeg, and salt to taste, and, last of all, the chopped tarragon.
Charles Herman Senn, *The Book of Sauces* (1915).

Filet of Beef, a la Richelieu

Trim the fillet as for larding, but instead of larding the smooth surface ... it is to be neatly covered with a thin layer of beef-suet, about a quarter of an inch thick, fastened on with string tied all along the fillet at distances of an inch from each other. The fillet is to be braized in all respects as in the foregoing cases, excepting that a glass of wine or brandy should be added. When done, clarify, reduce, and incorporate the stock with some Richelieu sauce [see below]; garnish round the base with quenelles, truffles, mushrooms; pour the sauce over all, and serve quite hot.
Charles Elmé Francatelli, *The Cook's Guide & Butler's Assistant* (1867).

Richelieu Sauce

Peel, slice, and fry four onions, add a few roast game bones chopped fine, and an ounce of flour; mix well together, moisten with a glass of sherry, and half a pint of good stock, a little pepper and salt, and a bit of glaze; stir over the fire for a quarter of an hour, then rub through a tammy or hair sieve, and keep hot in a small stewpan for use.
Charles Elmé Francatelli, *The Cook's Guide & Butler's Assistant* (1867).

Potatoes Parisienne

Parisienne potatoes are cut into small balls from raw potatoes with a French vegetable cutter or a round spoon. They may be either fried, or boiled and served with maitre d'hotel sauce [see September 3].
  Marion Harland, *Marion Harland's Complete Cook Book* (Indianapolis, 1903).

Squab Guinea Hen au Cresson: this is a variation of the classic Poulet au Cresson. See February 21.
  Punch à la Romaine (Roman punch): see July 1.
  Salted Almonds: see April 3.

June 24

Dinner for Ulysses S. Grant
Nagasaki, Japan, 1879

Ulysses S. Grant (1822–1885) and his family set off on a two-year around-the-world tour when he completed his term as the eighteenth president of the United States. On June 24 he and his party were entertained at a civic dinner in Nagasaki, Japan. The English language newspaper, the *Japan Weekly Mail*, reported the bill of fare of the "native dinner."

Menu of Native Dinner
Given in Honour of General U. S. Grant
By the Citizens of Nagasaki on June 24, 1879

First Course.
  Naga-noshi.—On white wooden stand and mounted with "hosho" paper and gold and silver cords.
  Matsu-no-dai.—On white wooden stand and mounted with isinglass, dried cuttle fish, and edible sea-weed.
  A set of three unglazed porcelain wine cups, on white wooden stand.
  A bowl of water for washing wine cups, on white wooden tray.
  A long-handled wine holder—decorated with red "hosho" paper, gold and silver cords, and paper flower at mouthpiece.
  A hoop-handled wine holder—decorated in the same way as above.
  A pile of dried sardine.
  Zauni.—Composed of crane, pauyu, biche-de-mer, seaweed, potatoes, rice, bread, and cabbage.
  A pile of pickled gilum.
  A pile of sea moon.
  Soup.—Prepared of red snappers.
  A pile of black and white bean.

Main Course.
  Namasu.—Composed of snappers, clam, chestnut rock, mushroom, and ginger.

Soup.—Composed of dock, truffle, round turnips, and dried bonito.

Pickled vegetables.—Composed of melon, long turnips, "shiso," pressed salt, and aromatic shrub.

Tsubo.—Snipe, egg plant, and bean jelly.

Takamori.—Boiled rice.

Hira-sara.—Red snapper, shrimp, potatoes, mushroom, and cabbage.

Soup.—Bass and orange flower.

Choku. Powdered bonito flavoured with plum juice and walnut.

Sashimi.—Sliced raw carp.

Dai-hiki.—Mashed fish.

Yakimono.—Baked red snapper in bamboo basket.

Soup.—Isinglass and "jimmaso."

Nakazara.—Fish broiled with pickled beans, wine, rice, hot and cold water.

Powdered tea and sweetmeat composed of white and red bean jelly, cake, and boiled black mushroom.

Interval: tea and sweetmeats.

Interval Course.

Shimadai.—Decorated with plum trees; bamboos, and tortoise, and composed of varieties of fish.

Shimadai.—Decorated with peony and shackio (a doll with long-red hair), and composed of mashed fish, kisu (kind of fish), shrimps, potatoes, rabbits, golden fish, and ginger in shape of flower.

Dish of Sashimi (sliced raw. fish).—Decorated with cherry tree and sea gull, and composed of live carp, black "Kuwai," muscles of whale, "shiso" and horse radish.

Dish of Sashimi.—Decorated. with chrysanthemum and birds, and composed of live snapper, long turnips, sea moss, cabbage, and horse radish.

Dish of Sashimi.—Decorated with "Yebisu" (an idol), and composed of live sole, zingeber mioga, rock mushroom, modsuku (kind of sea moss), and horse radish.

Dish of Sashimi.—Decorated with scenery of carp climbing up a waterfall, and composed of live bass, lettuce, sea moss, and branches of "shiso."

Final Count.

Pears prepared with horse radish.

Wheat flour cake.

Powdered ice.

Fruits.

And

Soup.—Carp, mushroom, and aromatic shrub.

Sara-hiki.—Red snappers prepared into alternate squares of red and white and "matsuna."

Oh-tsubo.—Skylark, wheat flour cake, and gourd.

Soup.—Stoke, buckwheat, and egg-plant.

Oh-hira.—Mashed pauyu, fungus, lily roots, and stem of pumpkins, all prepared with arrowroots and horseradish.

Oh-choku.—Vermicelli of arrowroots and powdered ice.

Soup.—Shell fish and sea moss.

Suzuributa.—Mashed fish, eggs, "sushi" of shrimps, plum cake, black mushroom, plum, and finely cut orange.

Hachi.—Quail and loquat cake.

Hachi-zakana.—Three different preparations of red snappers (Ikada, Koganemushi, and Midoriyaki), long roots dressed with "Uni," aralia, and pickled ginger.

Oh-ju. Fried snappers, shrimps, eggs, egg-plants, and mashed long turnips.

Shimadai.—Decorated with scenery of Futamiga-ura, and composed of mashed fish, pauyu, bolone, jelly, and chestnut

Shimadai. Decorated with the old couple of Takasago under pine, bamboo and plum trees in snow, and composed of shrimps in shape of ship, Ai fish, potato, black and common Kuwai (kind of water potato), eggs, and Arame (kind of sea-weed).

Shimadia. Decorated with pine trees and cranes, and composed of varieties of fish.

And

Sweetmeats and variety of fishes in box.

The occasion was described as "regal in its quality." Entertainment was provided by 36 Geishas dressed in costumes which incorporated Japanese and American flags "arranged as the customary crest on the back," who danced and sang specially arranged pieces. There were over 50 "courses" of food, most of which would have been very unfamiliar to the members of Grant's party. Japan had been opened up to the West for only a little over two decades, and very few Europeans and Americans had any experience with Japanese cuisine.

Fish (salt and fresh-water, some of it raw) and other produce of the sea—including whale and seaweed—dominated this meal. The *biche (beche) de mer (Holothuria species)* is a creature of the deep sea floor. Westerners find the animal ugly and its flesh tasteless, but it has been an enormously important food in Asia since ancient times. The name comes from the Portuguese *bicho de mar* (vermin of the sea)—the Portuguese being early traders in the Indonesian waters where it is harvested. It is also known as trepang, sea-cucumber, and sea-slug. Traditional processing involves throwing it into boiling water, splitting and gutting it, then drying (and sometimes smoking) the flesh, whereupon it can be kept for long periods of time.

Recipes

~~~

Peony Eggs

Boil five eggs hard. Place in cold water. Remove shells carefully, so as not to blemish whites. Carefully cut off top with thread, one end between teeth, the other between fingers, drawing thread through egg. Remove the yolks. Boil a small pink snapper (fish) in hot water for ten minutes, or steam for thirty. Remove all bones and fins, and chop together until fine. Mix with finely mashed miso, pepper, and salt. Chop yolks daintily and fluffily, and mix with fish meat. Fill the whites with this mixture. Now place the filled whites in center of a lettuce head and arrange fine strips of udo shoots round it. To fix lettuce head properly, all the leaves should be carefully adjusted and separated, washed, and then put back into shape again. It looks now like a bouquet, and is held together with toothpicks.

Boiled Whale or Bass

Two pounds of fish; one half teacupful of syou; orange and lemon skin; two long, large radishes; two tablespoonfuls of vinegar; salt, and dash of cayenne pepper.

Take off all bones and slice the fish daintily in long slices, and then in half-inch dice. Sprinkle with salt, and leave for about fifteen minutes. Cut radishes in long, even, delicate strips. Boil for a few minutes, strain, then add half a cupful of syou sauce and two tablespoonfuls of a fine vinegar. When it boils, drop in the fish slices. Boil up, then push to back of range, and, covered tight, let it simmer for half an hour. Grate the peels of half a lemon and half an orange, and sprinkle over the fish, after having removed it to a hot platter. Serve with boiled rice.

Sara Bosse and Onoto Watanna [pseud.], *Chinese-Japanese Cook Book* (Chicago, 1914).

June 25

Dinner on the Eve of the Korean War
Blair House, Washington, DC, 1950

The North Korean Army (armed and equipped by the Soviet Union) crossed the 38th parallel into South Korea (armed and equipped by the United States) early in the morning of June 25, 1950, leaving their individual allies no choice but to enter the conflict. President Harry S. Truman (1884–1971) and his chief military and foreign affairs advisors met that evening at Blair House, the temporary home of the president while the White House was undergoing extensive repairs. After preliminary cocktails, the 14 most powerful men in the nation continued their discussions over dinner.

Fruit Cup

Fried Breast of Chicken
Current Jelly
Cream Gravy

Shoestring Potatoes
Buttered Asparagus
Scalloped Tomatoes
Hot Biscuits

> Hearts of Lettuce
> Russian Dressing
>
> Vanilla Ice Cream
> Chocolate Sauce
> Cup Cakes

The meeting was clearly convened at very short notice, and in view of the political agenda it is highly unlikely that the menu items came up for discussion, if they were noticed at all. It seems ironic, more than half a century later, that the lettuce salad was served with Russian Dressing. During the first world war "sauerkraut" had been renamed "liberty cabbage" as a demonstration of anti-German sentiment, and a similar nationalistic fervor resulted in Bismarck herrings becoming Eisenhower herrings in World War II, and french fries briefly becoming freedom fries during the Gulf War. Perhaps, had the chef anticipated the intensity of feeling about "traitorous" culinary language, he might have poured something like "MacArthur dressing" over the lettuce.

In view of the gravity of the situation, the dessert selection seems a little incongruous. Some of the most powerful men in the world, on the eve of a major international conflict, regaled themselves with treats regularly found at children's birthday parties. Or perhaps they were a conscious decision on the part of the chef—intended as comfort food for this enormously stressful evening.

Recipes

~~~

The name Russian dressing comes from the earliest versions that included a distinctly Russian ingredient, caviar.

Russian Dressing

Make one-half pint of mayonnaise dressing and add to it the following: Two hard-boiled eggs chopped fine, two to four tablespoons of tomato catsup, one tablespoon of finely chopped parsley, one teaspoon of finely chopped or grated white onion or shallot, after these ingredients are mixed, fold them into one cup of mayonnaise and serve. Enough for ten people.
   Florence Kreisler Greenbaum, *The International Jewish Cookbook* (1919).

Cup cakes are so called because originally they were actually baked in small tea-cups.

Cup Cakes

Take four well-beaten eggs, mix with them four ounces of powdered loaf-sugar and four ounces of fine dry flour. Rub the insides of ten or twelve small cups with butter, sift sugar into them, strew in a few currants well cleaned and dried, and half fill the cups with the mixture. Bake until they are well browned, and when cold turn them into a dish.

Richard Bentley, *Everybody's Pudding Book. Foreign Desserts for English Tables* (1862).

Baking Powder Biscuits

3 cups flour.   1 1/2 tablespoons shortening.
1 teaspoon salt.   1 teaspoon soda.
2 teaspoons cream of tartar.   1 cup milk.

Sift flour, baking powder, and salt together. Rub shortening in with finger tips. Add milk slowly and mix to a soft dough. Roll out on a lightly floured board to 1/2 inch thickness. Cut with a biscuit cutter. Bake in a quick oven (450°F.) 10 to 15 minutes.

Yield: 12 biscuits.
The Lily Wallace New American Cookbook (New York, 1946).

June 26

British Empire Breakfast
North Pole, Dartford, London, England, 1902

All of Britain was feverish with excitement as the coronation day of King Edward VII approached in 1902. The ceremony was to be on June 26, and hotels, restaurants, and public houses around the country expected a very profitable few days as a by-product of the great wave of patriotic sentiment. It turned out to be an expensive exercise for caterers and restaurateurs, however, as the King developed acute appendicitis and coronation festivities were postponed at the last minute, to be finally held on August 9.

The intriguingly named North Pole restaurant close to the old Naval yards of Deptford had planned an Empire-themed breakfast for the day. The chef would have had an overflowing larder full of supplies in preparation. Did the meal go ahead as planned, with presumably fewer guests? Was much food thrown out? It was certainly a fine breakfast selection that was offered.

Scotch Oatmeal Porridge.

Newfoundland Cod Fish Cakes.
British Columbian Salmon.
Filleted Sole.

Welsh Rarebit.
Omelette.   Tomato Egg.
Cream of Ham.

Roast Beef of Old England.
New Zealand Lamb.

Australian Ox Tongue.
York Ham.   Roast Chicken.

Indian Curry.
Irish Butter.   Canadian Honey.
Natal Jams   Marmalade made from Orange Colony P.
Indian Tea.   Ceylon Coffee.
Trinidad Cocoa.   Demarara Sugar.

Tasmanian Apples.   Jamaica Bananas.
Malta Oranges.   Singapore Pineapples.

North Pole Ices.

Borneo Cigars.   Egyptian Cigarettes.

The meal offered on this day was certainly hearty, but it was not what is thought of today as a "traditional English breakfast." There is surprisingly little agreement as to the essential components of this type of breakfast. Most would consider bacon and eggs to be the foundation, but some would add sausages, or black pudding, or "bubble and squeak." Others would insist on baked beans (from a can), or mushrooms, or fried tomatoes, or fried bread. Many would vigorously debate the inclusion of tomato ketchup or "brown sauce," or any sauce at all. The fact is, the concept of a "traditional" British breakfast is very recent. In the Victorian era, a middle-class household would have expected at breakfast a number of savory choices (often based on leftovers from the previous night's dinner), including a variety of egg dishes, and such things as kippers, liver and bacon, potted shrimps, and the Anglo-Indian favorite of "kedgeree" (see June 27), along with copious amounts of toast, butter, and marmalade or jam. The number of choices has dribbled away over the century, and the remaining quickly cooked dishes that do not require an army of servants are the ones that remain.

Recipes

~~~

Orange Marmalade

Wash and dry well 6 Seville Oranges, also 1 lemon, squeeze the juice out of these, saving the pips, and put the rinds through a mincer or cut into slices; then weight the juice and rind, and allow 3 pints cold water to the 1 lb. fruit, pour a little of this water over the pips, allow to stand until the following day, boil the mixture, putting the pips into a piece of muslin and boiling with the oranges for one hour; then weight this again and allow 1 lb. sugar to 1 lb. fruit and water, boil altogether for 1 hour or until the orange chips are transparent. Put into jars and keep airtight.
    Miss Tuxford, *Cookery for the Middle Classes* (ca. 1925).

Welsh Rarebit (rabbit): see March 14.
Porridge, Oatmeal: see June 27.

June 27

Breakfast at Central Station Hotel
Glasgow, Scotland, 1908

There was intense competition between railway companies in the late nineteenth century in Great Britain. Successful railways were enormously lucrative businesses, and although most of the emphasis was on speed, companies tied up the peripheral profits by running their own hotels at major train intersections. Caledonian Railway Company passengers in Glasgow in 1908 could stay at the Central Station Hotel, which had a great range of breakfast choices, Scottish and otherwise.

Porridge and Cream.

Tea.   Coffee.   Chocolate.   Cocoa.

—

Fresh Herrings.   Fried Whitings.
Kedgeree of Salmon.   Findon Haddock.

—

Mutton Chops and Tomatoes.
Saute Kidneys.   Minced Collops.
Grilled Ham.   Bacon.   Boiled Eggs.
Poached Eggs.   Scrambled Eggs.   Savoury Omelette.
Lyonnaise Potatoes.

—

Cold Roast Beef.   Chicken.   York Ham.
Spiced Beef.   Ox-Tongue.   Galantine.

—

Raspberry Jam.   Marmalade.   Black Currant Jam.

—

Apples.   Bananas.   Stewed Prunes.   Figs.

FRUIT CHARGED EXTRA.

For those guests who wanted to "eat local" as one would say now, there was the quintessential Scottish dish of porridge. There was also Findon haddock (or "Finnan Haddie")—a regional variation of the great British breakfast and supper favorite of cured and smoked fish from the town of Findon, south of Aberdeen.

Another popular British breakfast (or supper) dish is the kedgeree. Like "curry" (see January 1) and mulligatawny soup (see September 15) it is a peculiarly Anglo-English dish and a legacy of the Empire. The name comes from the Hindi *khichr* or Sanskrit *k'rsara* which means "a dish of rice and *sesamum.*" In India it refers to a dish of rice cooked with pulses and sometimes eggs. In Britain it is almost always made from rice and precooked (often leftover) fish and hard boiled eggs.

Recipes

~~~

Porridge, Oatmeal

Oatmeal porridge is a leading article of food with the Scottish peasantry. It is generally accompanied with milk, when milk is to be had; when milk is very scarce butter is sometimes used, and sometimes sugar.

Put a pint and a half of water, or milk and water, into the saucepan, and add a pinch of salt. When the liquid fully boils, as it is rising in the pan, sprinkle gradually two ounces of oatmeal into it with the left hand, and at the same time stir briskly with a fork held in the right hand. Keep stirring until the lumps are beaten out. Boil the mixture for quarter of an hour, pour it on a plate, and eat it with milk and sugar or treacle.

Kedgeree

Kegeree, or kidgeree, is an Indian dish, generally used for breakfast: it may be made of the cooked remnants of such fish as salmon, brill, soles, John Dory, whiting, and shrimps. Boil three quarters of a pound of rice in the same way as for curry. When soft and dry, put it into a saucepan, first with two ounces of butter, and afterwards with a quarter of a pound of the flesh of the fish, freed from skin and bone, and divided into small pieces. Season with cayenne, salt, and pepper—as much as may be required. Salt the kegeree over the fire until quite hot, then add two well-beaten eggs, mix thoroughly, and serve at once.

Findon or ``Finnan'' Haddocks

These haddocks are held in great esteem for their peculiar and delicate flavour. The genuine Finnan may be known by its odour and creamy yellow colour. Strip off the skin, and broil before the fire or over a quick, clear one. Rub the fish over with butter, and serve hot. Some persons prefer to cut them in pieces and steam them in a basin of boiling water or milk. Heat the basin first, pour boiling water or milk on them, and cover closely with a plate; if kept on a hot stove, they will require from ten to fifteen minutes, and when drained, should be placed on a hot dish and rubbed over with butter. Serve hot. Excellent as a breakfast dish.

Cassell's New Dictionary of Cookery (1910).

Poached Eggs: see June 20.
Lyonnaise Potatoes: see October 17.

June 28

Coronation Dinner for the Poor
St. Martin-in-the-Fields, London, England, 1838

The approach to the poor was, in Victorian England, punitive, because the underlying philosophy was that many of them were deserving of their state by virtue of their laziness or prodigality. Consequently, living conditions in the workhouses were deliberately set to act as disincentives, and many were worse than prisons (see August 12). The public face of the institutions, however, was one of great Christian charity towards the inmates, and a great deal of publicity was generated by the authorities of workhouses at Christmas when details of the dinners generously provided to inmates took up several columns of the newspaper each year. In 1838 there was a second marvelous opportunity to demonstrate this generosity when Queen Victoria was crowned, as this letter to *The Times* shows.

> Sir, I beg leave to hand you the bill of fare provided for every inmate of our workhouse, upon the occasion of Her Majesty's coronation;—viz. six ounces of roast beef free from bone, half a pound of potatoes, three-quarters of a pound of plum pudding, and one pint of porter. I regret your reporter did not receive this information, but I suppose our porter had the fear of the Poor Law Commissioners before his eyes.
>
> Robert Cuff, Chairman of the Board of Guardians,
> St. Martin-in-the-Fields, Pall Mall East, June 29, 1838.

Similar treats were extended to inmates of other institutions such as orphanages and schools, and "the food, generally speaking, was of an excellent description, and the greatest attention was paid to the poor by the various parochial authorities." Over 600 children were given a "substantial dinner of roast beef and plum pudding" as their coronation treat, in a tent set up on Palace Green opposite Kensington Palace. The dinner at Christmas and on these rare special occasions did not vary throughout the entire era. It was always beef and plum pudding. The inmates of the workhouse at St. Martin-in-the-Fields a mere six months before ("paupers 440, mostly infirm and superannuated") had, for their Christmas dinner allowance "one pound of roast beef, half a pound of potatoes, 12 ounces of plum pudding, and one pint of porter."

Some workhouse inmates were very lucky, being allowed beef and pudding "ad libitum," and some even got tobacco and tea. At the Dover Union warehouse the expenses of the coronation dinner caused some discussion, and *The Times* reported the less than charitable action of the reverend gentleman who chaired the meeting to settle the dispute.

> Meeting on the previous day: some discussion whether the pint of beer should be paid by a subscription, not out of the rates. In relation to the Dover Union workhouse, only 6 guardians were present, 3 for and 3 against: the rev. chairman, having the casting vote, gave the same against the poor people. It was hoped that a more kindly feeling might have influenced the breast of this worthy gentleman in holy orders. If no kindness is permitted, it is no wonder that the unions get into disrepute among the rate-payers of the respective parishes.

Recipes

~~~

The attitude to the poor was quite different at a community level. It was the Christian duty of every household (or housewife) to provide for the poor in their own neighborhood—where one would presumably be personally aware of those that had fallen on hard times in spite of themselves and were therefore deserving of charity. Many nineteenth-century cookbooks had chapters on cooking for the poor, and the recipes often served the double purpose of using up scraps and leftovers, thus avoiding wicked waste.

Cheap Plum Pudding without Eggs or Milk

Eight ounces beef-suet, minced; ten ounces of flour; eight ounces currants or raisins; two tablespoonsful of sugar; one tea-spoonful of salt; the zest of two carrots grated, and one glass of sweet wine.

Tie up tight in a cloth, boil three hours, and serve with sweet sauce.

"Cheap Dishes and Cookery for the Poor," in *The Cook and Housewife's Manual* by Christian Isobel Johnstone (1856).

June 29

Cornell Students Dine aboard
RMS *Saxonia*, 1924

The European summer tour became a traditional rite of passage for young college men in the late-nineteenth and early-twentieth centuries, and in 1924 the Cornell men of the Class of '24 thought of a novel way to attend the Olympic games in Paris and "the usual Continental attractions." They chartered the entire third cabin (class) of the newly refurbished RMS *Saxonia*. The "College Third Cabin" arrangement was both "unique and truly an innovation in shipping circles" and exclusive, for "immigrants and outsiders have been definitely excluded from both sailings" (*Capital Times* [Wisconsin], March 14, 1924). The Cornell men were on the last night of their outward journey when they enjoyed the traditional *Diner d'Adieu* (farewell dinner) with the Captain.

CUNARD COLLEGE SPECIAL.

CAPTAIN'S DINNER.   THIRD CABIN.

DINER D'ADIEU.
Portugaise au Cornell.
Boiled Salmon—Williams.
Escaloppe de Veau, Harvard.
Spaghetti, Amherst.
Roast Turkey—Northwestern.
Green Corn, Yale.   Colgate and Michigan Potatoes.
Plum Pudding—Dartmouth.
Canteloupe—Princeton.
Glaces—Oberlin.
Dessert, Rice.   Coffee, Ohio.

The *Saxonia* chefs had clearly created a special college-themed menu for the night. It is likely that the dishes were classics slightly varied or simply renamed for the occasion as to create ten new dishes for one dinner would be an enormous undertaking for any kitchen. It is not known for certain what was in the dishes at this dinner, especially considering that even basic cooking terms were used quite loosely.

An *escaloppe*, for example, is traditionally taken to mean a thin slice of boneless meat which is fried. It takes its name from the shape of the piece that is rounded like a scallop shell and hence is also called a *collop* or *scollop*. Escaloppes are usually made from veal, but the term is interpreted very broadly, and in some recipe books can refer to fish or even vegetables and fruit. An escaloppe is also sometimes made with minced meat, sometimes filled and rolled like a *paupiette* or *olive* (see June 23) and occasionally the nomenclature gets very confused and it is a piece of meat with a bone—a dish more usually called a chop, or a cutlet (which can also be boneless).

The "College Third Cabin" idea captured the imagination so well and was so successful that the *Cornell Alumni News* of August 1925 announced that "The College Third Cabin movement may now almost be classed as a species of emigration, and one liner sailed for Europe this summer carrying only girls in its third cabin." Presumably the parents of these young women were more likely to agree to their daughters traveling to Europe for the summer on an all-girls tour.

Recipes

~~~

Veal Collops, Braised

Cut about a pound of fillet of veal into neat rounds half an inch thick and about the size of a crown piece. Pick the leaves from a handful of parsley, wash them and chop them small, then mix with them a minced shallot and a small bunch of chives. Butter a stewpan thickly, sprinkle some of the herbs into it, and place in it alternate layers of veal and herbs until all the ingredients are used. Season each layer of veal with salt and pepper, and add a small slice of butter or a teaspoonful of olive oil occasionally. Cover the whole with slices of bacon, and lay a round of oiled paper on the top. Put the lid on the stewpan, put a few red-hot cinders upon it (if this can be done) and stew the veal as gently as possible over a slow fire until it is tender. Arrange the pieces of veal in a dish. Half a glassful of light wine should be poured in when the meat is half-dressed. Put a little brown sauce into the stewpan, let it boil, and pour it over the collops.
Cassell's New Dictionary of Cookery (1910).

The following recipe is minimalist. Some versions include bacon and garlic.

Potage Portugaise

Mix one quart of tomato sauce with one quart of consommé and bring to a boil. Season with salt and pepper, and add a cup of boiled rice before serving.
Victor Hirtzler, *Hotel St. Francis Cook Book* (1919).

June 30

Her Majesty's Dinner
Buckingham Palace, London, England, 1841

The young Queen Victoria (1819–1901) entertained the King and Queen of the Belgians on a number of occasions in the summer of 1841. She was not merely doing her duty in receiving other royals, it was a family event too, as King Leopold I (1790–1865) was uncle to both herself and Albert. With the Coldstream Guards playing in the background, about 40 aristocratic and important persons sat down to the following repast on June 30.

4 Potages:
Printannier.   A la Reine.
2 à la Tortuë.

4 Poissons:
Les Truites à la sauce Génévoise.
Le Turbot à la sauce homard
Les Filets de merlans frits.   Les white-bait frits.

4 Hors d'œvres:
Les Petites pàtés de homards.

4 Relevés:
Les Poulardes trûffés à la sauce Périgeuex.
Le Jambon glacé de fêves de marais.
La Selle d'agneau farcie à la Royale.
Le Filet de Bœuf piqué à la Napolitaine.

16 Entreés:
2 Les Nageoires de Tortuë sauce au vin de Madère.
2 Les Filets de poulets à l'écarlate aux concombres.
2 Les Côtelettes de mouton braisées à la purée d'artichauds.
2 Les Aiguillettes de canetons aux pois verts.
2 Les Riz de veaux piqués glacés à la Toulouse.
2 Les Côtelettes de pigeons panées à l'Allemande.
2 Les Chartreuse de tendons d'agneau à l'essence.
2 Les Timbales de macaroni à la Mazarine.

Side Board:
Haunch of Venison.
Roast Beef.   Roast Mutton.
Vegetables.

SECOND SERVICE

6 Rôts:
2 de Cailles.   2 Lévrauts.   2 de Poulets.
6 Relevés

2 Les puddings à la Nesselrode.   2 Les souffles à la fécule de pommes de terre.
2 Les puddings de Cabinet.

2 Flancs:
Le Pavillon Mauresque   La Tente Militaire.

4 Contre-Flancs:
Le Nougat aux amandes.   Le Biscuit de Savoie à la vanille.
La Sultane Parisiènne.   Le Croque-en-bouche historié.

16 Entremêts:
Les trûffes au vin de Champagne.   Les petits pois à la Française.
Les artichauts à la Lyonnaise.   Les haricôts verts à la poulette.
Le Buisson de prawns sur socle.   L'aspic de blancs de volaille à la Belle-vue.
L'anguilles en bolute au beurre de Montpellier.   La salade de légumes
à la Italiènne.
La gelée de groseilles garnie de pêches.   La Macédoine de fruits.
Les tartelettes de framboises.   Le Bavaroix de chocolat panaché.
Les Génoises aux fruites transparents.   La crême aux amandes prâlinées.
Les petites pains à la Parisiènne.   Les gâteaux de Péthiviers.

Victoria was suffering for the second time with what she referred to as the "unavoidable inconvenience" of the married state—that is, she was pregnant (with the future Edward VII). It would have been most improper to mention this directly in the newspaper reports of course, but it was noted in *The Times* that the Queen of the Belgians brought with her "a series of beautiful robes, (commonly called baby linen) principally composed of Valenciennes and Brussels lace, and a great proportion of them ornamented with elaborate embroidery, the work of her own hands, as a present to Her Majesty Queen Victoria."

There would have been no strange "English" dishes on this menu for the Belgian guests. The aristocrats of Europe were essentially a huge single family, intermarried for reasons of politics and power, who enjoyed a generic upper-class cuisine. Menus were always in French and rarely made a feature of national specialties. The exceptions on this menu are the various plain roasts displayed on the sideboard, which are listed in plain English (and which the French, ironically, would have listed as *rosbif*) and are unequivocally considered to be English specialties.

There certainly appears to be an intention to be fashionable, however, as two of the puddings appeared to have come on the scene in the early part of the nineteenth century. Cabinet pudding is a steamed pudding made with custard and cake (or bread, for the economical version), in a shaped mold. Its heritage is mysterious, although it does appear to have a political connection as it is sometimes called Chancellor's pudding or Diplomat pudding. Nesselrode pudding is an iced pudding made from chestnuts. It is named for the Russian diplomat Count Karl Nesselrode (1780–1862) and was said to have been invented for him by his own chef. It became enormously popular and almost obligatory at fine dinner parties over the next century.

Recipes

~~~

Charles Elmé Francatelli (1805–1876) was chef to Queen Victoria at the time of this dinner. He included the menu in one of his cookbooks—*The Modern Cook* (1860). The following recipes for two enormously popular Victorian puddings are taken from this.

Cabinet Pudding

Spread the inside of a plain mould with butter, and ornament the sides with dried cherries and candied citron; fill the mould with alternate layers of sponge-cakes and ratafias or macaroons; then fill up the mould with a lemon custard made with eight yolks of eggs, a pint of milk or cream, six ounces of sugar, a glass of brandy, and the grated rind of a lemon. This custard must not be set, but merely mixed up. Steam the pudding in the usual way, for about an hour and a half, and when done, dish it up with either arrowroot sauce, or a custard.

Nesselrode Pudding

Boil three dozen chestnuts in water, and when done, peel, pound, and rub them through a sieve; put this pulp into a stewpan with eight yolks of eggs, a pint of cream, two sticks of vanilla, previously pounded, half a pint of pine-apple syrup, and very little salt; stir these ingredients over a stove-fire until the eggs are sufficiently set in the custard, then rub the whole through a tammy, and put the cream into a basin. Cut four ounces of green citron, six ounces of pine-apple (previously simmered in the syrup above alluded to), and place these in a basin with six ounces of dried cherries, and four ounces of Smyrna raisins; to these add two wine-glasses of maraschino, and allow the fruit to steep for several hours. Place the chestnut cream in a freezing-pot immersed in rough ice, and freeze it in the usual manner; then add half a pint of whipped cream and the fruit. Mix the pudding, and continue working the freezing-pot for a few minutes longer; when the pudding is thoroughly set firm, put it in the mould, cover it down, and immerse it in ice until it is required to be sent to table.

Potage Printanier: see February 28.
Potage a la Reine: see February 17.
Sauce Perigeuex: see April 14.
Petit Pois a la Francaise: see July 11.